A Call for Judgment

AMAR BHIDÉ

A Call for Judgment

Sensible Finance for a Dynamic Economy

UNIVERSITY PRESS

2010

OXFORD
UNIVERSITY PRESS

Oxford University Press, Inc., publishes works that further
Oxford University's objective of excellence
in research, scholarship, and education.

Oxford   New York
Auckland   Cape Town   Dar es Salaam   Hong Kong   Karachi
Kuala Lumpur   Madrid   Melbourne   Mexico City   Nairobi
New Delhi   Shanghai   Taipei   Toronto

With offices in
Argentina   Austria   Brazil   Chile   Czech Republic   France   Greece
Guatemala   Hungary   Italy   Japan   Poland   Portugal   Singapore
South Korea   Switzerland   Thailand   Turkey   Ukraine   Vietnam

Copyright © 2010 by Oxford University Press, Inc.

Published by Oxford University Press, Inc.
198 Madison Avenue, New York, NY 10016

www.oup.com

Oxford is a registered trademark of Oxford University Press.

Library of Congress Cataloging-in-Publication Data
Bhidé, Amar, 1955–
A call for judgment : sensible finance for a dynamic economy / Amar Bhidé.
    p. cm.
Includes bibliographical references and index.
ISBN 978-0-19-975607-0
1. Finance—United States.   2. Capitalism—United States.
3. United States—Economic policy.
I. Title.
HG181.B42 2010
332.0973—dc22   2010011238

9 8 7 6 5 4 3 2 1

Printed in the United States of America
on acid-free paper

For Lila,
Question, but deeply.

CONTENTS

This book reflects a long-standing skepticism about modern finance born out of two sides of my professional experiences. For more than thirty years I have studied innovation and entrepreneurs in the real economy, and I have had some involvement in starting new ventures. I have also written papers in finance (my doctoral dissertation was on hostile takeovers), consulted for financial institutions, served on the staff of the commission investigating the crash of 1987, worked for an investment bank, managed a hedge fund, and traded on my own account.

The world of innovation and entrepreneurship has been uplifting. The optimism of the entrepreneurs I have studied has rubbed off. Innovation has generated unimaginable advances in our standard of living; given the right incentives and rules, I believe it can take us a long way toward solving problems ranging from the overconsumption of fossil fuels to a health care system that gobbles up vast resources without providing commensurate improvements in our well-being.

The world of finance, in contrast, has been a downer (although not as personally unrewarding as my entrepreneurial ventures, which were complete failures). Perhaps because my worldview was shaped by observations of real-world innovation, I questioned the common belief that developments in modern financial theory and practice were good for society. Rather, I believed there was something pathological about a financial system completely at odds with the dynamism of the real world. The real world is entrepreneurial and interconnected. Finance is monolithic, almost Soviet-like in its conformity and far removed from its users. Forward-looking innovators expect and envision change. Finance relies on mechanistic, backward-looking models that assume an unchanging world.

In the early 1990s, I wrote several articles arguing that the much-vaunted breadth and liquidity of U.S. equity markets had serious hidden costs, and took issue with the passive, judgment-free style of investing. In March 2002, I emailed Matthew Bishop who was writing a survey on the future of capitalism for the *Economist* that capitalism was in great shape—except in the financial sector. "The financial system," I wrote, "faces a much sharper change in the trajectory it's been on since the early 1980s—much more so than the other elements of the modern capitalist system that I think are here to stay. Of course if the financial sub-system starts unraveling, the other elements may also be affected."

But what now? In 2007, about a year before the Lehman bankruptcy created a global panic, I offered[1] what then seemed like far-fetched proposals for financial reforms, on which I have elaborated in the concluding chapter of this book. Similar proposals are now being advanced by more distinguished advocates, although they remain far from the establishment view and the Dodd-Frank financial reform bill of 2010 that has just been signed into law by President Obama.

The case I make here is based on history, logic, and circumstantial evidence. I cannot provide incontrovertible proof. Nor do I claim to offer a totally objective, unbiased account (if such a thing is possible). My hope is that after taking into account the perspective it reflects, readers will find the argument persuasive.

Cambridge, Massachusetts

A Call for Judgment

Introduction

The economic crisis that began when the housing bubble peaked in 2006, that spread through virtually the entire financial sector, and that, in less than two years, brought the world's economy to a near standstill, has engendered two unwarranted interpretations: one too broad and the other too narrow.

The excessively expansive view sees the financial crisis as the consequence of basic flaws in capitalism as a whole. Few people, businesses, industries, or countries have been sheltered from the crisis, and the wide spread of its woes has rejuvenated anticapitalist critiques. Denunciations of globalization, supranational corporations, the unfettered pursuit of self-interest, the eroding power of unions, and the unjust accumulation of wealth that rang hollow in good times now resonate. And the agenda of many critics extends far beyond banking and finance. It includes higher and more steeply progressive taxes, rollbacks of Reagan-era deregulation, managed instead of free trade, the assertion of state control over large corporations (starting with General Motors, now nationalized in all but name), and stronger trade unions.

And why not, if you believe that all of capitalism is broken—or if you didn't like it in the first place? Opportunities to revamp the existing order don't come by often. The time for a new New Deal may be now.

As Rahm Emanuel, President Obama's chief of staff, said in November 2008, "You never want to waste a good crisis." In fields as diverse as energy, health, education, tax policy, and regulatory reforms, the crisis provided an opportunity to "do things that you could not do before."[1]

The too narrow view focuses on finance and is usually offered by those who have been involved as researchers, regulators, and, practitioners. This inside view sees little wrong with the structure and evolution of financial institutions, markets, and practices—except to the degree that the regulatory apparatus has fallen behind and some incentives are misaligned. A smorgasbord of technical fixes, accessible mainly to those in the know, follows from this diagnosis. It includes the trading of instruments such as credit default swaps (CDSs) on an exchange; improved transparency through more stringent disclosure requirements; countercyclical capital requirements; changes in the models used by rating agencies and how those agencies get paid; and teaching MBA students about developments in behavioral finance.

Insiders reject radical measures that some outsiders have proposed, such as prohibiting CDSs. Only troglodytes, they claim, fail to see the huge value that modern financial technologies would provide if only they were a little better regulated. Some go further, arguing for an even wider range of risk-management products so that we can hedge away all serious risks.

This book challenges both views. It rejects the proposition that capitalism as a whole has failed and requires comprehensive reform, and it rejects the view that the financial system just needs technical tweaks.

Commerce and markets are ancient but modern, and what Marx called "technologically progressive" capitalism started only with the First Industrial Revolution, around the time of the American War of Independence. In short order, capitalism helped unleash extraordinary economic growth. Before the Industrial Revolution, wealth was largely taken, that is, transferred from somewhere else, not created. Individuals and nations prospered at the expense of others, and until the eighteenth century, world GDP growth per capita was virtually zero. As capitalism gathered traction in the nineteenth century, however, per capita incomes more than doubled, and then, in the twentieth century, increased more than eightfold. Growth was especially robust in the industrial nations of the West.[2]

Its capacity to deliver the goods allowed capitalism to prevail over socialism and communism. And although it didn't abolish misery, it produced considerably less of it than its rival systems.

But the dynamism of modern capitalism may not survive assaults from its reenergized critics if the financial sector continues to do business more or less as usual. Finance has acquired features that are sharply at odds with a system built to support a dynamic, capitalist economy. And this is not a recent problem. Finance has been on the wrong trajectory for more than a half a century: Its defects derive from academic theories and regulatory structures whose origins date back to the 1930s.

Because my diagnosis differs from the two views I have outlined, my prescriptions are different too. They urge vigilance against opportunistic assaults on the vital elements of capitalism—a system that has delivered unprecedented and widespread prosperity. And they go beyond tinkering with the financial system to urge bold changes in the rules.

The centerpiece of my proposals entails tough, straightforward limits on the activities of commercial banks and other entities, such as money market funds, which now total more than $8 trillion in deposits that are for all practical purposes guaranteed by taxpayers. I see no reason to ban CDSs or impose further restrictions on hedge funds. Nor do my proposals require commercial banks to stop taking risks. They would merely stop banks from abusing protections provided to them by taxpayers to enable the pathologies of modern finance that have almost wrecked capitalism. Although the scope of the rules I propose is narrow, they would profoundly change the nature of the financial game.

Crucial Features of Modern Capitalism

Critics attribute many unsavory features to capitalism: Cold-blooded, profit-maximizing calculation rules. Personal relationships don't matter: It's all a trade in which price is everything and there is a price for everything. The fewer the rules the better—they only get in the way of profit maximization. And a few winners of this ruthless free-for-all capture most of the spoils. Even mainstream economic theories, which don't intend to criticize capitalism, incorporate some of these disparaging views. In the typical college economic text, the idealized economy features nerveless automatons that maximize profits (or utility) by buying and selling in anonymous markets.

These are mischaracterizations—far removed from the realities of a well-functioning capitalist system—but understandable ones. The nature of capitalism is difficult to grasp. One reason is its relatively short, two-and-a-half-century history. Adam Smith's *Wealth of Nations*, now regarded as a capitalist bible, was published before capitalism came into its own. Another is its dynamic, evolving character. Capitalism in the twentieth century wasn't what it was in the nineteenth century; and, by virtually all measures, the change was for the better. So it's not surprising that misconceptions abound and that any sketch of capitalism's essence—including the one that follows—will have subjective elements.

My list of key elements of a contemporary, well-functioning system of capitalism draws heavily on, and extends, Friedrich Hayek's pioneering characterization.

Let's start with some well-known basics: The continued prosperity of modern societies, it is now widely recognized, requires *constant innovation*—the development and use of new products and processes. How capital is mobilized to expand the output of tried and tested technologies, or how the supply of existing goods is matched with demand ("static efficiency"), is an important but secondary factor.

Extensive decentralization, which allows many individuals an opportunity to undertake initiatives of their choosing, gives "Hayekian" economies an outstanding capacity to innovate because they harness the energy, talent, and know-how of many individuals that would be wasted if people were told what to do. The democratization of innovation—the development of new goods by the many for the many—is one of the great strengths of the modern economy. Steve Jobs may orchestrate the development of iPods and iPhones, but the success of these products requires the contribution of thousands of engineers, designers, marketers, and even copyright lawyers—employed by Apple and its wide network of suppliers and providers of applications and add-ons—as well as the venturesomeness of millions of consumers of Apple's products.

In a dynamic economy, it isn't just the so-called knowledge workers who innovate. In industry after industry, assembly-line and piece-workers are also innovators. As Japanese automobile companies have shown through the success of quality circle programs, top managers and time-and-motion experts don't always know best.

Decentralization of initiative isn't simply a matter of dispersing robotic calculations—replacing a giant mainframe at headquarters with smaller personal computers in local offices so they can calculate utility-maximizing levels of output and consumption. Rather, it involves giving many individuals *the autonomy to make subjective judgments* in which emotions and feelings inevitably play a role (see box).

Subjective Judgments

Whether and how to try something new cannot be simply a matter of objective calculation. No one can predict whether a new initiative will succeed, or even calculate the right probability of various outcomes. How much happiness will follow success also is unknowable; sometimes the realization of long-standing dreams can lead to letdowns. Unfathomable emotions and subconscious drives, not just the pursuit of wealth (or the possibility of pleasurable consumption that wealth provides), play a crucial role in determining whether someone makes a "leap in the dark."[3]

The importance of primal passions was well recognized by economists of a prior era. Joseph Schumpeter's *Theory of Economic Development* credited innovation to entrepreneurs with the "dream and will to found a private kingdom" and the "will to conquer." In his *Principles of Economics,* published in 1890, Alfred Marshall wrote that just as a racehorse or athlete "delights" in "strain[ing] every nerve" to get ahead of competitors, a "manufacturer or trader is often stimulated much more by the hope of victory over his rivals than by the desire to add something to his fortune."*

Nor do individuals rely on mechanistic calculations alone in figuring out how to pursue their objectives. In undertaking something new, we cannot reliably extrapolate from the past—even with the fanciest of econometric tools. Historical patterns and models serve as valuable starting points, but they must be adapted to novel present circumstances. For this sort of assessment of prospects, individuals draw heavily on their imagination and what we call hunches, gut feel, or intuition. And because of differences in innate temperaments, upbringing, or life experiences, different individuals make different choices. Reasonable people, in other words, can disagree.

Economies characterized by widespread decentralized innovation force everyone, even those who are happy with the status quo, to make subjective judgments. In a static society, or one tightly controlled by a central authority, bakers can use the same kinds of ovens to bake the same kinds of loaves day after day, secure in the knowledge that nothing will upset their bread pile. In a dynamic economy, bakers must respond to the introduction of high-end croissants or cheap, mass-produced sliced bread by competitors and to their clientele's craving for something new. Here, too, the past provides limited guidance—bakers must somehow guess what to bake next.

*Marshall urged his fellow economists to study such motives carefully, because in some cases they could "alter perceptibly the general character of their reasonings" (cited by Robb 2009). As it happens, the force of the will to win has been taken more seriously by novelists than in the economic literature.

Decentralized responsibility goes hand in hand with the decentralization of judgment. *Well-functioning capitalism requires individuals to bear at least some of the consequences, good and bad, of their choices* (see box).

Responsibility, for Better and for Worse

Even those who play the game mainly for the rush they get from competition are rarely indifferent to the material rewards. As Frank Knight, often considered to be the founder of the Chicago school of economics,[4] wrote, the "motivation of competitive sport" and the "pursuit of the gratification of consumption" go hand in hand. Economic activity is a game in which "the most vital substantive goods [and] comfort" are "stakes, inseparably combined with victory and defeat and their bauble-symbols." A game that offered only bauble-symbols might turn off some outstanding players who value real prize money, thus eroding even some of the intrinsic thrill of top-flight competition.

Conversely, requiring individuals to bear some of the downside helps discourage them from pursuing whimsical or ill-considered initiatives. Having skin in the game concentrates the mind. It also discourages sticking with ventures that happen to turn out badly for reasons that cannot be foreseen in a world of autonomous choice. Entrepreneurs may diligently investigate their markets and competitors, but they cannot force customers to switch to their offering, though it may be objectively superior, or always avoid being trumped by another entrant who appears out of nowhere.

That harsh consequence of unlucky ventures may seem unfair, just as it may seem unfair to provide large rewards to individuals who get lucky, but it does no one any good to keep throwing good money after bad. In a world with unpredictable outcomes, decentralized responsibility works pretty well in balancing "Nothing ventured, nothing gained' and "Fortune favors the brave" with "Look before you leap" and "Don't buy a pig in a poke." And in judging the fairness of capitalism's rewards, we should remember that modern societies moderate the effects of good and bad luck through such mechanisms as progressive taxes, limited liability, liberal bankruptcy codes, and unemployment benefits, while keeping most of the benefits of individual responsibility, although the balance isn't easy to strike.

The advantages of decentralized initiative tied to individual responsibility isn't news to those predisposed to believe in capitalism. The territory has been well trodden by the followers of Hayek. But now we examine features that may give more readers pause.

Prices, especially those set in an anonymous market, play a role in modern capitalism that, while important, is limited. For some economists, the price system is the sine qua non—the very essence—of capitalism. They dream of complete markets that match supply and demand for all goods, services, and contingencies, as a Promised Land to be reached through diligent pursuit of capitalist ideals.

Well-functioning price mechanisms are usually an excellent way of allocating resources—labor, capital, real estate, and consumers' purchasing power—across the myriad activities that individuals and businesses undertake in a decentralized economy. In Hayek's terms, they aggregate information that individuals generate. Interfering with prices is usually a bad thing, but when a society tries to promote certain behavior, working through prices is usually best—raising prices of fossil fuels through a carbon tax is a more sensible way to stimulate the development of renewable energy than subsidizing ethanol.

But prices aren't a be-all and end-all. Competition is rarely just about price, and most decisions—about buying houses, securing employment, seeking medical treatment, or going to the movies—involve considerations far beyond how much money will change hands. Prices do facilitate decentralized innovation by helping coordinate independent initiatives, but they are not the only mechanism that does so.

Dialogue—between two individuals or among large groups, and in person, over the phone, or via the Internet—plays at least as important a role in coordinating actions and aggregating information. Extensive dialogue with suppliers is particularly crucial for innovators who integrate cutting-edge technologies and components from many suppliers. Smartphones can't be designed by examining the prices listed in vendors' catalogs.

Anonymous or arm's-length markets play an even less important role in the modern world than do prices. Markets in metals and in produce (which are arm's-length and practically anonymous) have existed since antiquity, but such markets' share of commercial activity has decreased since the advent of modern capitalism. In contrast to traditional commodities—such as fish, vegetables, gold and silver—few modern goods are traded in an anonymous market. A significant proportion of transactions now take place within firms (or "hierarchies," to use the term favored by some institutional economists). The rest (unfortunately, in my view) are labeled market transactions, but few are, in fact, arm's-length auctions in substance or form. Yes, businesses like eBay or Priceline conduct Internet auctions for products and services ranging from broken laser pointers (the first item ever sold on eBay) to hotel rooms, but their share of overall commerce is small.

Many transactions in modern industrial societies remain "closely embedded" in ongoing relations (or "networks" of such relations),[5] as sociologist Mark Granovetter wrote in 1985 in a seminal article. We consult the same physician, have our hair cut by the same barber or hairdresser, and report to work every day to the same boss—unless we have compelling reasons to switch. These ongoing relations not only help protect against malfeasance and fraud, as Granovetter emphasized, but also coordinate decentralized initiatives. Relationships between engineers at Apple and engineers at its suppliers of hard drives, for example, help both sides align their plans for new products.

Now we come to two observations that are more controversial. The first is about the role of governmental laws and regulation, and the second about the division of the fruits of progress in a capitalist economy.

Advocates of free enterprise often take a dim view of government intervention in the economy. Many believe that governments should protect citizens from physical harm and enforce property rights, but that doing much more is futile or, worse, harmful. Enterprising individuals will flout the rules—ignoring speed limits and using radar detectors to thwart the highway patrol's efforts to catch violators. Rent-seekers go further, manipulating the state's coercive power for their private gain: A small number of sugar growers, for instance, can raise the price everyone pays for sugar by lobbying for tariffs on imports.

This hostility toward more rules probably helps nurture the belief that capitalism is an anything-goes, practically lawless system. I argue, however, that in a dynamic, decentralized economy, an expansion of the role of government is inevitable and two-sided: Technological advances often require an expansion of the government's role; they also create opportunities for injurious rent-seeking (see box). To figure out whether a particular expansion is desirable or not requires a judgment that takes specific circumstances into account.

An Inevitable Expansion

Arguments about the extent of the powers of the state predate modern capitalism. *Leviathan*, written by Thomas Hobbes during the English Civil War, which broke out in 1642 and presumably framed Hobbes's book, makes the case for a strong central authority: In a "state of nature" without government or other social restraints, everyone can rightfully claim everything. Inevitably, conflict—a "war of all against all"—ensues, making life "solitary, poor, nasty, brutish and short." Individuals, therefore, enter into a social contract, surrendering their natural rights to an authoritarian sovereign in exchange for protection against disorder, and even accepting some abuse of power by this authority as the price of peace.

Classic liberalism, as exemplified by Adam Smith, took the opposing view: "Repressive political structures" in Granovetter's characterization of the liberal view, "are rendered unnecessary by competitive markets that make force or fraud unavailing."[6] Even informal social associations can do more harm than good by facilitating collusion ("conspiracies against the public or in some contrivance to raise prices," as Smith put it) that weakens the discipline of competitive markets. To the extent competition doesn't fully do the job, innate sentiments such as empathy step in.

The U.S. Constitution and other governmental arrangements established after Independence followed the principles of classic liberalism rather than Hobbes. But then, especially in the twentieth century, the role of government and the resources it controls increased to an extent that would have astounded the Founding Fathers. Many public choice theorists suggest that such expansion is the inevitable and unfortunate consequence of lobbying by special interests.

Does this mean, then, that the Founding Fathers made a mistake in their initial design, or does democracy inevitably lead to overbearing government? And why, if the expansion of the government is so bad, was economic growth in the twentieth century higher than in the nineteenth century, when government expenditures and taxes were extremely low—there was no income tax, except during the Civil War—and no federal bureaucracy to impose minimum-wage laws, regulate health and safety standards, or resist monopolies and trusts?

At least some of the expansion in government, I suggest, has occurred because technological advances increased what most people would consider its minimal roles on a variety of fronts.

The transformation of U.S. society from agrarian to industrial created the need to define and enforce new kinds of intellectual property, for instance. Initially, this regulation consisted of patents on "inventions"; then, as economic activity became more specialized and diverse, the scope of what was regarded as intellectual property expanded to include brand names, logos, designs, software code, and even customer lists. Legal protections had to be defined and enforced for such property through new state interventions such as broader copyright rules,[7] the policing of counterfeiting, and the expansion of common laws governing trade secrets.

New technologies created the need for rules to coordinate interactions between individuals or groups. The invention of the automobile, for example, necessitated the formulation and enforcement of driving rules and a system of vehicle inspections. The growth of air travel required a system to control traffic and certify the airworthiness of aircraft. Similarly, radio and television required a system to regulate the use of the airwaves in order to avoid the collision of signals by competing broadcasters.

Modern technology created new forms of pollution that didn't exist in agrarian economies. Governments had to step in to make it unrewarding to pollute. Likewise, antitrust laws to control commercial interactions and conduct emerged after new technologies created opportunities to realize economies of scale and scope—and realize oligopoly or monopoly profits. These opportunities were largely absent in preindustrial economies.

But even if what governments should do increases with technological progress, this does not mean we should embrace the opposite principle that that government governs best which governs most. New technologies not only create real needs for new rules, they also generate more opportunities for unwarranted meddling and a cover for rent-seeking. It's one thing for the Federal Aviation Administration to manage the air traffic control system, quite another for the Civil Aeronautics Board (b. 1938, d. 1985) to regulate airfares, routes, and schedules. The construction of the Interstate Highway System may have been a great boon to the U.S. economy, for example, but it did not take long for Congress to start appropriating funds for bridges to nowhere.

In other words, government matters a lot in advancing or sabotaging progress. The right question to ask isn't whether there is too much or too little intervention in the abstract, but whether a specific policy or law is of the right kind.

The inevitable efforts to game the rules aren't an argument against introducing new rules when changes in technologies or social arrangements so require. An assessment of how much gaming—or outright cheating—is likely, and what would be required to control it, should, however, be an important consideration.

Interested parties will lobby to shape new rules to their advantage; in an open, democratic society that protects freedom of expression, there is no way to stop this effort. In fact, lobbying by competing interests can help shape rules that are, on balance, good, or lead to the discarding of bad rules. That said, people are no more prescient about rules than they are the about their customers or competitors, so the canniest businesspeople or lobbying groups can mistakenly resist rules that are in their best long-term interest and ignore ones that pose mortal threats.

These mistakes will play an important role in the story I tell in this book.

The technological advances that dynamic capitalism unleashes help make some people richer than others and may allow a few to lead exceptionally opulent lives. Many new technologies amplify differences in material rewards that arise from differences in individual talent, temperament, and luck. When agricultural technology was relatively primitive, a settler who received title to 160 acres under the Homestead Act could expect to make roughly the same living from farming as his neighbor. With modern technology, however, farmers who have the ability to use tractors, harvesters, hybrid seeds, crop rotation techniques, and futures markets to hedge their output—or have good fortune in their choices—can earn significantly higher returns than those who don't. Similarly, businesses that realize economies of scale in producing tractors can be much more profitable than the craftsmen who made plows or the blacksmiths who shod horses.*

This does not mean, however, that developers or users of innovations secure great wealth at someone else's expense. "Behind every great fortune lies a great crime," the old saying goes,[8] but it is rarely true in capitalist life today, especially on the innovative trails. Rather, entrepreneurs who make large fortunes through technological advances create much larger benefits for users of their innovations (see box). The rising tide of capitalism raises a great many boats, and some happen to be yachts.

Who Benefits? (and Contributes?)

New products and services usually generate value to users considerably in excess of the price. If they didn't, why would customers take a chance on a new product or service? The threat of competition also encourages innovators to cede much of the value to their customers.[9]

Of course, the large users' total shares may be obscured by the relatively small individual amounts: Successful innovators, such as the founders of Google, can secure extraordinary wealth, whereas the dollar value that goes to a single user is often quite small; therefore, it is tempting to think that innovators are the main beneficiaries. But users outnumber innovators by a wide margin—tens of millions of individuals and businesses benefit from Google searches—so small amounts add up to a lion's share of the total. For instance, Yale economist

---

*Chicago's Frank Knight apparently had similar and firmly held beliefs: George Stigler (1985, 6) has written that Knight tenaciously stuck to the view that a "competitive enterprise system inherently leads to a cumulative increase in the inequality of the distribution of income... [A]t countless lunches this was challenged on both analytical and empirical grounds by Milton Friedman, each time leading Knight to make temporary concessions only to return to his standard position by the next lunch."

William Nordhaus analyzed data for the nonfarm business economy and for major industries in the United States. He found that producers captured a "minuscule" fraction of returns (on the order of 3 percent) from technological advances over the period from 1948 to 2000, "indicating that most of the benefits of technological change are passed on to consumers."[10]

But consumers aren't just passive beneficiaries. Their venturesomeness—manifested, for instance, in their willingness to take a chance on unproven products and their resourcefulness in using them—plays a crucial role in realizing the value of innovations. Indeed, a great strength of our widely diffused and decentralized system of innovation lies in harnessing the talents of a large number of individuals and rewarding them for their contributions. In the nineteenth century, new products were developed by a few individuals. Edison brought forth a remarkable cornucopia—incandescent bulbs, motion pictures, and gramophones—from a small facility in Menlo Park (New Jersey, not California) with fewer employees than the typical Silicon Valley start-up. Alexander Graham Bell had one assistant. Such small organizations couldn't quickly develop good products at affordable prices, so many inventions were, at the outset, playthings for the rich. Now, because of a widely inclusive system of innovation, products like iPods and netbooks hit mass markets from the get-go.

A Dangerous Divergence

Doesn't the unsparing global economic crisis we have witnessed shred this cheerful sketch of modern capitalism? I argue that it does not. Modern financiers often regard themselves as über-capitalists, but, in reality, finance has drifted well away from the practices that make capitalism successful, and toward the caricature drawn by its critics. Consider just a few of these vanishing features.

The financial system has been giving up, albeit unwittingly, on the decentralization of judgment and responsibility. Case-by-case judgments by many, widely dispersed financiers with the necessary "local knowledge" have been banished to the edges, to activities such as venture capital (VC), which accounts for a useful, but tiny proportion of financing activity. The core is now dominated by a small number of very large firms that have little direct contact with the ultimate real users or providers of finance.

Case-by-case judgment has also retreated. Instead, financiers rely on centrally designed, mechanistic models that cannot take local variations into account. The use of blind diversification has also grown, not merely as a complement to case-by-case analysis and judgment, but as a substitute. Blind diversification implicitly outsources decisions to a few specialized research and rating outfits or a centralized anonymous market. But employees of the organizations that produce research and ratings—and the traders whose aggregated opinions constitute the wisdom of crowds—usually don't have much case-by-case local knowledge. They, too, often rely on statistical models, or just take their cues from each other.

The growth of tradable instruments has expanded the role of anonymous markets. Such markets include the listing of equity interests in companies once considered unsuitable for public ownership, such as unproved technology companies, professional service firms, and investment banks; "securitized" interests in bundles of what used to be illiquid loans; and a vast range of derivative or "contingent" claims on other securities or slices thereof. This increase in what is known as market breadth has not only allowed financiers to outsource more judgment, but has also changed the basic nature of many financing relationships.

Credit and equity investments once embedded in ongoing relationships have become arm's-length and impersonal. There may be some discussion of terms up-front between issuers of stocks and bonds before a security gets traded (although even that contact is often indirect: The issuer and investors communicate through the investment bank charged with underwriting the security). Afterward, however, even that communication tails off. As a practical matter, issuers cannot have a meaningful dialogue with a large number of diffused security-holders, many of whom aren't in it for the long haul. And they cannot provide confidential information: Saying anything to stock- or bondholders is tantamount to making a public announcement. Bond- and stockholders can only know what the world knows; and, given easy opportunities to exit in a liquid market, continuation of the "relationship" does come down just to price—and whatever terms may have been established at the outset.

Finally, the principle of giving top decision-makers chances to profit if things go well, but also requiring them to bear the consequences if they don't, has been sacrificed as the financial industry has become more centralized and concentrated. When investment banks were partnerships, for instance, partners made handsome livings, but they also had to risk their personal wealth. Top executives of commercial banks didn't do quite as well as partners in investment banks and, symmetrically, didn't have as much to lose, although their well-paid and prestigious jobs were on the line. Now, with a large proportion of financial activity shoehorned into a few publicly listed and highly leveraged megafirms, the rewards for presiding over, if not actually running, the behemoths have entered the stratosphere. Yet the downside hasn't increased much, and (compared to the risks borne by the partners in investment banks) may even have declined.

Little good has come of these changes. Reduced case-by-case scrutiny has led to the misallocation of resources in the real economy. In the recent housing bubble, for instance, lenders who, without much due diligence, extended mortgages to reckless borrowers helped make prices unaffordable for more prudent home-buyers. Similarly, during the Internet boom, public markets made indiscriminate investments in freshly minted dot-coms, making it hard for worthy start-ups to make a go of it because they had to compete with businesses that shouldn't have been funded.

The replacement of ongoing relationships with securitized arm's-length contracting has impaired the adaptability of financing terms. No contract can anticipate all contingencies in a dynamic economy. But securitized financings make ongoing adaptations infeasible; the providers and users of finance must adhere to the deal that was struck at the outset because of the great difficulty of renegotiating terms. Recontracting only occurs in extremis—as when bond committees are formed to renegotiate terms after a bankruptcy filing.

Centralization has increased systemic risks. To err is human, and when decision making is in the hands of a small number of bankers, financial institutions, or quantitative models, their mistakes imperil the well-being of individuals and businesses throughout the real economy. Decentralized finance isn't immune to systemic mistakes; for example, individual financiers may follow the crowd in lowering down-payments for home loans. But this behavior involves a social pathology, a mania and a suspension of independent judgment. With a centralized authority, the process requires no widespread mania—just a few errant lending models. Moreover, the absence of personal responsibility induces a calculated carelessness, making the centralized system especially vulnerable.

Finally, more centralization has allowed a small number of financiers to accumulate wealth on the scale of the titans of the Gilded Age—though without emulating their contributions to progress—and political clout that nineteenth-century railroad barons might have envied.

All this has been nourished by an unwholesome goulash of rules: Finance as a whole hasn't been underregulated or overregulated, although that is the case with some of its parts. The main problem has been one of *mis*-regulation.

Deconstructing the Housing Bubble

The recent housing bubble highlights the havoc that overcentralized, robotic, arm's-length finance can wreak, even if the bald facts sketched below might suggest a one-of-a-kind episode.

"The upward turn in housing prices that began in 1997," write Steven Gjerstad and Vernon Smith (a Nobel laureate in economics), "was sparked by rising incomes and the 1997 Taxpayer Relief Act which, for the first time exempted residential homes (of up to half a million dollars) from capital gains taxes. And, rising prices became 'self-nourishing' by drawing the attention of investors."[11]

The recession of 2001 might have popped the housing bubble early on, but prices continued to rise thanks to the Federal Reserve's decision "to pursue an exceptionally expansionary monetary policy in order to counteract the recession." Gjerstad and Smith observe that when the Fed opened its liquidity valve, money "naturally" flowed into housing because prices were already rising and because both public policy and private incentives "combined to erode mortgage-underwriting standards. Mortgage lenders, the government-sponsored enterprises (Fannie Mae and Freddie Mac), and investment banks that securitized mortgages, used rising home prices to justify loans to buyers with limited assets and income. Rating agencies also accepted the notion of ever-rising home values, so they gave large portions of each securitized package of mortgages an investment-grade rating, and investors gobbled them up." Mortgage-loan originations grew at an annual rate of 56 percent from 2000 to 2003, increasing from $1.05 trillion to $3.95 trillion.[12]

In June 2004, the Fed started raising interest rates, and in the following twelve months, prime mortgage lending (made to creditworthy borrowers) fell by half, but subprime* lending skyrocketed. In 2003,

---

*A loan may be classified as "subprime" for several reasons. The most common is that the borrower has a low credit score because of a limited credit history or a record with past delinquencies, judgments, or bankruptcy filings. A mortgage may also be considered subprime because of a large loan amount compared to the borrower's income or down payment or if the borrower does not document income or assets.

subprime loans amounted to a few tens of billions of dollars. However, in just three years after June 2004, $1.6 trillion of subprime loans were issued. According to Gjerstad and Smith, "The relaxation of lending standards"—through the now notorious subprime loans—"provided a flood of new buyers.... When even subprime lending couldn't keep new buyers arriving fast enough, the financial wizards turned to the interest-only adjustable rate mortgage (ARM)" and finally to the "magic potion" of the "negative-equity option ARM."[13]

But then the decline of housing prices, which started in the second half of 2006, turned the policies designed to realize the American dream into an unintended nightmare. Trillions of dollars were loaned to buyers whose risk was limited to their small down-payment. When housing prices fell, many homeowners with low income and few assets defaulted because they had little equity to lose. Consequently, the majority of the delinquencies were "transmitted directly into the financial system." Uncertainty about which banks were vulnerable—a large proportion of the subprime mortgages had circled back into lenders' balance sheets in the form of securities[14]—then hobbled the entire financial system. Its "subsequent collapse abruptly ended the fine performance of the broader economy."[15]

Gjerstad and Smith also note that credit-default swaps (CDSs) "were the linchpin of the housing-finance market."[16] How was this?

Simply put, CDSs provide insurance against the default of debt securities or bundles of securities. They played a vital role in the explosion of dicey subprime mortgages that more than offset the decline in prime mortgages after 2004. Thanks to CDS insurance, securities constructed from subprime mortgages received an imprimatur of safety from rating agencies and thus were sold by the truckload to investors. The money realized from the sale could then be used to make more mortgage loans—mortgage lenders only needed enough funds to finance their warehouse of loans waiting to be packaged into securities and sold. Without insurance, there would have been much less selling, fewer subprime loans for homebuyers, and less upward pressure on prices.

But the CDS market didn't grow from covering $631.5 billion of securities in the first half of 2001 to over $62.1 trillion in the second half of 2007 just by providing insurance to the owners of securities. Speculators, to a much larger degree, used CDSs to bet on defaults—you didn't need to own a security to "insure" it. They were great way to gamble: In contrast to stocks, where short sellers (who bet that prices will fall) usually have to post margin amounting to half the stock sold, CDS bets on defaults could be placed for small insurance premiums. The price of the insurance was naturally sensitive to the market's expectations of the likelihood of defaults, allowing speculators to make very high rates of return—or lose their entire initial outlay. For instance, the cost of insuring a $10 million basket of mortgage-backed securities jumped from $472,000 on December 4, 2006, to $3.842 million on February 27, 2007.[17] This more than eightfold increase in just three months was a great trade for those who bought in December, but gut-wrenching for the sellers.

Traders at Goldman Sachs, who played a leading role in creating and selling subprime-based securities, became concerned about large-scale defaults in the underlying mortgages when housing prices started to decline in 2006. But rather than withdraw from a still-profitable business, Goldman began using the CDS market to bet against the very securities it was selling customers in December 2006.[18] Then, as housing prices continued to fall and in spite of CDS insurance rates that had already jumped, Goldman bought more insurance on mortgage-backed securities. This ploy, write Gjerstad and Smith, hastened "the trouble that Goldman anticipated."[19] Goldman's purchases drove up insurance rates, making it prohibitive to issue more subprime-based securities and thus sharply reducing the funds available to make more loans. Without new buyers, overheated housing prices went into free fall, encouraging more "underwater" borrowers with little equity to default. In other words, CDSs were both pump and pin for the housing bubble.

Financial firms that had large exposures to mortgages—in warehouses awaiting packaging and sale, through their holdings of securities or CDS insurance—were "drawn into the undertow from the collapsing housing market. Bear Stearns, Lehman Brothers, Merrill Lynch, A.I.G., Citigroup, Washington Mutual, and Wachovia all collapsed, in one way or another, as a result of their exposure to the mortgage crisis."[20]

The collapse of AIG, once an AAA-rated insurance giant, through its role in the CDS debacle is especially noteworthy. A team at the banking behemoth, J.P. Morgan, had invented CDSs in 1997 as part of a plan to create and sell securities based on loans the bank had made to large corporations: The team figured that if an insurer assumed some of the risk, J.P. Morgan would have to set aside less capital as reserves against the defaults of the loans. Less capital would mean higher profits for the bank, and, for reasons that we will see later, minimizing the use of capital (aka taking on huge leverage) had become central to the extraordinary profitability of the financial sector. AIG's Financial Products unit (AIGFP) provided the insurance for J.P. Morgan's securities.

Normally, transferring risk ought not to reduce significantly the amount of capital reserved against future losses. If AIG were taking on some of J.P. Morgan's risks, then AIG should have set aside the capital that J.P. Morgan wasn't. But, in fact, no one—insurance regulators who supervised AIG, rating agencies, or purchasers of the J.P. Morgan securities—required AIG to set aside more reserves. And AIG's managers didn't have the incentive. Although the premium AIG received from insuring the securities was small in amount, with no additional capital set aside, the nearly infinite leverage made the profitability wondrous—as long as the underlying loans didn't go bad.

For AIG and the Wall Street firms that purchased insurance, writes Michael Lewis, this was just the start. "The banks that used A.I.G. F.P. to insure piles of loans to IBM and G.E. now came to it to insure much messier piles that included credit-card debt, student loans, auto loans, prime mortgages, and just about anything else that generated a cash flow." The assumption was that the piles were so diverse—and the deductible so high—that AIG would never have to pay anything out. Then, in 2004, the "amorphous, unexamined piles" of consumer loans that AIG was insuring zoomed from 2 percent subprime mortgages to 95 percent subprime mortgages. But "no one at A.I.G. said anything about it." They were rubber-stamped by Joe Cassano, who ran the FP unit, and then again by AIG brass. And very likely, writes Lewis, "Neither Cassano nor the four or five people overseen directly by him, who worked in the unit that made the trades, realized how completely these piles of consumer loans had become, almost exclusively, composed of subprime mortgages."[21]

A few traders ended up selling trillions of dollars of credit default swaps on a mountain of U.S. subprime mortgages. "We were doing every single deal with every single Wall Street firm, except Citigroup," a trader told Lewis. "Citigroup decided it liked the risk and kept it on their books. We took all the rest."

Cassano did come to realize the problem, and AIGFP stopped writing insurance on subprime securities before the slide in housing prices started in 2006. But, by then, the "people inside the big Wall Street firms who ran the machine had made so much money for their firms that they were now, in effect, in charge. And they had no interest in anything but keeping it running." So they themselves took on the risks—otherwise the game would have ended. "The hundreds of billions of dollars in subprime losses [later] suffered by Merrill Lynch, Morgan Stanley, Lehman Brothers, Bear Stearns, and the others," according to Lewis, "were hundreds of billions in losses that might otherwise have been suffered by A.I.G. F.P."[22]

Although AIGFP escaped losses from the 2006 and 2007 securities, the insurance it had written on the relatively higher quality 2005 pools proved its undoing. As I have mentioned, AIG didn't have to set aside a capital reserve to cover losses on the securities it insured. But at least some of the buyers of insurance had secured contractual protections against the possibility that when the time came, AIG might not have the funds to pay out claims. One provision required AIG to post collateral if the securities it had insured fell in value. On the surface, this was eminently reasonable: A fall in the value of the securities indicated an increased likelihood of default. Surprisingly, however, because the securities weren't liquid and there were no reliable market prices, the contracts allowed the insurance buyer to determine their value and thus the amount of cash that AIG had to fork over.

In the summer of 2007, the prices of all subprime securities—including the 2005 vintages—fell. The big Wall Street banks raced to obtain billions of dollars of collateral from AIG. Goldman Sachs was first in line, asserting "shockingly low prices" for the securities AIG had insured. Cassano wanted to dispute Goldman's valuations in court, but, before he could do so, he was fired. By March 2008, AIG didn't have the cash to meet Goldman's collateral demands, "but that was O.K. The U.S. Treasury, led by the former head of Goldman Sachs, Hank Paulson, agreed to make good on A.I.G.'s gambling debts. One hundred cents on the dollar."[23]

The sorry, dramatic tale of the housing bubble exemplifies the multifaceted pathologies of modern finance and their toll on the real economy, although many other lessons can also be drawn.

Borrowing large sums to purchase expensive homes in the hope that future incomes will justify the price has been a widespread and long-standing practice in the United States. Accounts of middle-class families living on the financial edge because of housing debts go back a century. In fact, venturesome consumption—of housing and a wide range of other goods—has been a distinctive and valuable feature of American life. Immigrants cheerfully left behind the practice of thrift when they arrived in the United States and, in so doing, helped transform by 1914 an agrarian society into the world's leading industrial economy.

But consuming and borrowing without limit isn't a sustainable strategy for individuals or countries, and one of the tasks of the financial system has been to provide the credit that people want to buy their dream home, car, or appliance without allowing debts to balloon to a point that later trigger widespread defaults. In the past, a credit system based on decentralized judgment helped achieve this balance. Under the classic banking model, borrowers would apply for a mortgage from their local bank, with which they often had an existing relationship. A banker would review the application, perhaps interview the borrower, and make a judgment that took into account what the banker knew about the applicant, the applicant's employer, and the property and conditions in the local market. Loans stayed on the bank's books, so bankers had an incentive to balance prudence with their need to lend. The decentralization of judgment—individual banks made independent lending decisions—was tied to accountability.

Banks or bankers could make mistakes or act recklessly, but their lending was limited by the deposits they took in, generally from long-term customers, and by their capital. Mistakes or recklessness did not endanger the economy as a whole unless a large number of banks made bad decisions at once.

The new lending machine has a fundamentally different character. On the front lines, loan officers have made way for mortgage brokers. In 2004, approximately 53,000 mortgage brokerage companies employed an estimated 418,700 employees and originated 68 percent of all residential loans in the United States, according to a study by Wholesale Access Mortgage Research & Consulting. In other words, less than a third of all loans were originated by the lenders' own employees.[24] The mortgage broker's judgments and relationships are used for marketing, not evaluating loan applications. The brokers' role in the credit process lies mainly in helping or coaching applicants in filling out forms. In fact, no one now makes subjective case-by-case credit judgments. Mortgages are made (and new mortgage products like option ARMs are designed) using statistical models that take little heed of the specific facts on the ground and are conjured up by a small number of faraway wizards.

The securitization and sale of mortgages has eliminated long-term borrower relationships—and the lenders' accountability for long-run outcomes. It has also promoted centralization, by allowing some institutions to capture a large share of the market. Thanks to securitization, the mortgages that a financial company can originate aren't limited by its deposit base or capital. As long as mortgage securities can be sold, the sky is the limit. Countrywide Financial, for instance, which was started in 1969, grew from a two-man operation to a mortgage behemoth with approximately five hundred branches. Before it imploded in 2007, it had issued nearly a fifth of all mortgages in the United States.[25] The Federal National Mortgage Association (Fannie Mae) and Federal Home Loan Mortgage Corporation (Freddie Mac) made Countrywide's role in the mortgage market seem small. By the time they collapsed in 2008, the two government-sponsored enterprises owned or had guaranteed about half of the country's $12 trillion worth of outstanding mortgages.[26]

The buyers of securitized mortgages also don't make case-by-case credit decisions. Buyers of Fannie Mae or Freddie Mac paper weren't taking on any risk that homeowners would default on their mortgages. Rather, they believed they were buying the debt of the U.S. government—while earning a higher return than they would in buying treasury bonds. Even when securities weren't guaranteed, buyers didn't analyze the creditworthiness of individual mortgages. Instead, they relied on the soundness of the models of the wizards who developed the underwriting standards, the dozen or so banks (the likes of Lehman, Goldman, and Citicorp) that securitized the mortgages, three rating agencies that vouched for the soundness of the securities, and AIGFP and other insurers that wrote credit default swaps.

This highly centralized system bestowed enormous wealth on some individuals in controlling positions. Franklin Raines, the CEO of Fannie Mae, earned more than $90 million from 1998 to 2003.[27] Angelo Mozillo, the cofounder and CEO of Countrywide, received more than $470 million in the five years preceding the collapse of his company in 2008.[28] Joe Cassano of AIGFP made $280 million—but because he was a true believer, he apparently kept much of his wealth in AIG's stock, which became nearly worthless after the insurer imploded. The influence of a small group of individuals who often shared the same worldview was also remarkable. Cassano and his traders, for instance, may have facilitated a trillion dollars of mortgages and triggered a substantial portion of the increase in housing prices in the United States in 2004 and 2005. Great malfeasance was unnecessary to topple this system—although malfeasance and self-dealing were hardly scarce. The mistakes and calculated carelessness of the few who mattered was enough.

Out of the Blue?

An investigation that intends to forestall future disasters rather than merely assess culpability for a specific calamity will look into more than just the immediate causes. For instance, even with seemingly freak accidents—an airplane downed by a flock of birds sucked into its engines or a New Orleans leveled by Hurricane Katarina—the question of whether the pilot or the Federal Emergency Management Agency responded competently invites scrutiny. It is also important, however, to ask whether the engine or flood control system had design flaws that would lead to a crash or disastrous deluge. A broad inquiry can also reveal defects that impair everyday performance, even if they may not lead to catastrophic failures.

Yet much of the discourse and analysis of the recent financial crisis—including the thumbnail sketch provided in this introduction—focuses on the relatively recent missteps that triggered the debacle. The easy-money policy of the Greenspan Federal Reserve after 2000, misaligned exchange rates that sustained large global financial imbalances, a housing bubble inflated by Fannie, Freddie, and subprime lenders, forays by insurance companies such as AIG into activities outside the purview of insurance regulators, AAA ratings bestowed on dodgy securities, and the recklessness of the large banking houses have received their due reproach.

It's possible that these one-time events are all there is to the crisis. It could have been a bolt from the blue, triggered by events and mistakes that had no common antecedents but unhappily converged. A well-maintained car traveling at a safe speed may hit a pothole, spin out of control, and cause a multivehicle crash. If such were the case with this financial crisis, there would be no deep cause to identify or structural defect to cure. Some rejiggering of the machinery would suffice. This was likely the case with the Crash of 1987, officially deemed a "market break" (see box).

Sound and Fury, Signifying Nothing

On October 19, 1987 ("Black Monday"), the Dow Jones Average fell by 508 points, a decline of 22.6 percent—the largest one-day drop ever.[29] The crash was global in its effects, hammering markets in Hong Kong, Australia, New Zealand, Spain, Britain, Canada, and the United States. Thirty-three eminent economists from around the world issued a joint statement in December of that year warning, "Unless…decisive action is taken to correct existing imbalances at their roots, the next few years could be the most troubled since the 1930s."[30] Nothing of the sort occurred. The Federal Reserve and other central banks did what they always do in such situations—they lowered

---

rates and added liquidity. A presidential commission's recommendations for technical stock market changes (such as "time-outs" or "circuit breakers") were implemented. A popular "portfolio insurance" strategy that many blamed for the crash quietly went out of existence on its own. Yet, without any "decisive action" the crisis passed. The Dow Jones finished 1987 with a small gain for the year. The real economy didn't miss a beat.

The speed with which the crisis unfolded in 2008—with little prior warning from the brightest and best—seems to support out-of-the-blue explanations. As I have mentioned, until 2004 the amount of subprime mortgages was small, and CDSs based on such mortgages did not exist. Until recently, few lawmakers, regulators, or economists raised alarms about the structural defects in the financial system. In fact, many believed that the U.S. financial system was a jewel rather than a time bomb and celebrated the wonders that financial innovations did for controlling risk.

Standing against the possibility that the crisis was sudden and unforeseeable is the fact that, while its consequences were exceptionally fearsome and broad, it wasn't the first financial crisis in recent times. Financial wizardry may, or may not, have contributed to the Great Moderation of inflation and fluctuations in economic growth after the mid-1980s (although some of us think productivity-enhancing innovations in the real economy deserve most of the credit). But financial innovators did not bring much peace and quiet to their own neighborhood. The financial system has been rocked by a series of crises, some regional, some national, and, in an increasingly interconnected world, many with global ramifications. By the IMF's count, there were more than 300 serious banking, currency or sovereign debt crises after 1980, and the IMF's list does not include events such as the bursting of the Internet bubble in 2000 or the emergency rescue of Long-Term Capital Management (LTCM) orchestrated by the Federal Reserve in 1998.

Each crisis had its own idiosyncrasies and dramatis personae. The savings and loan crisis of the late 1980s featured cowboy bankers in the hinterlands; LTCM starred Connecticut-based wunderkinds and the Wall Street firms who traded with them; and the Internet bubble was inflated by shills masquerading as stock analysts. But could it be that all instances were out-of-the-blue mishaps that had nothing to do with each other and with the big one that hit in 2008?

The frequency of crises suggests otherwise. Greed, herding behavior, and decaying memories—in conjunction with the ingenuity of sharp operators on the prowl to take advantage of the enduring foibles of human nature—ensure that manias stoked by cunning practice will always be with us. But typically they are well separated by time and space. The British Railway mania of the 1840s came more than a century after the South Sea Bubble of 1720. Nearly four decades elapsed between the Great Crash that ended the Roaring Twenties and the Nifty Fifty nuttiness of the late 1960s and early 1970s. The current debacles have been much more closely spaced. Less than two years separated the LTCM and Internet blowups.

This isn't just an unlucky streak of unrelated mishaps. Each ailment may have been triggered by different microbes, but ready susceptibility resulted from a chronic constitutional weakness. An excessive focus on specific proximate causes and symptoms has allowed this overall weakness to escape proper scrutiny and treatment (see box).

A Low, Common Denominator

The collapse of the Internet bubble, which erased $5 trillion in the value of high-tech companies from March 2000 to October 2002, found an obvious culprit in the conflicts and carelessness of analysts who had issued strong buy ratings on stocks that turned out to be worthless. Eliot Spitzer, then New York State attorney general, published damning emails that revealed analysts' more candid evaluations. "I can't believe what a POS [piece of shit] that thing is," Merrill Lynch's Henry Blodget wrote just weeks before issuing a research report calling Lifeminders "an attractive investment." Under threat of prosecution, Merrill agreed to pay $100 million in fines and to change the way its analysts did business.[31] The SEC charged Blodget with securities fraud. He paid a $2 million fine and $2 million disgorgement and was disbarred from the securities industry for life.[32]

Now it's the turn of the "big three" credit-rating agencies, Moody's, Standard & Poor's, and Fitch, which certificated the soundness of subprime securities and AIG. In July 2008, the SEC reported, after a year-long enquiry, that it had uncovered "significant weaknesses" in the agencies' ratings practices: The agencies suffered from conflicts of interest because issuers, rather than investors, paid for ratings. They had failed to disclose "significant aspects of their ratings process" and to cope with the complexity of the securities issued after 2002. In addition, the rating agencies had overworked their analysts and lacked the capacity to verify whether their models were accurate. The SEC reported an internal communication in which an analyst "expressed concern that her firm's model did not capture 'half' of the deal's risk," but stated that "it could be structured by cows and we would rate it."[33]

As it happens, overworked analysts at the rating agencies didn't receive the multi-million-dollar compensation that the Internet bubble's luminaries such as Henry Blodget and Morgan Stanley investment banker Mary Meeker earned. Their models—although apparently deeply flawed—were mathematically more sophisticated. They used binomial expansion techniques[34] to predict defaults, whereas Internet analysts had valued dot-coms by applying an arbitrary multiple to the number of—usually nonpaying—visitors to the dot-coms' web sites ("eyeballs"). Both cases, however, are manifestations of the problem of mechanistic centralization without accountability: Enormous amounts were invested on the say-so of a small number of individuals who simply couldn't make case-by-case judgments and didn't have much responsibility for their mistakes.

What Lies Ahead

In Part I (chapters 1–4) we will look more closely at why decentralized subjective judgment and responsibility, dialogue, and ongoing relationships play an important role in the real economy—and ought to in the financial sector as well. This introduction has relied on the reader's everyday experience; the four chapters to follow will examine the underlying reasons and interrelationships.

The second part of the book (chapters 5–13) provides a historical analysis of how we got here. I argue that the dysfunctions of modern finance have evolved over many decades. Finally, chapter 14 proposes a bold but simple strategy for getting out of this mess that does not rely on complicated new rules.

The proposals I offer seek to *realign the interests of the real economy and the financial sector*. The realignment requires a financial sector with more decentralized judgment, responsibility, and ongoing relationships and thus the *reform of rules that have promoted mechanistic, centralized, arm's-length finance in which financiers bear little responsibility for their mistakes*. The realignment would transform finance in a way that is completely at odds with the views of many in the Federal Reserve and Obama administration, and economists such as Yale's Gary Gorton, who predicts that "if we don't resuscitate securitization…we won't be able to resuscitate the economy."[35] I argue that we should not restore securitization of credit to it pre-2008 level.

Mine isn't an absolutist argument, however. The popular dichotomy between the arm's-length, securitized "Anglo-American" model of finance and the relationship-based Continental European model is false. There is nothing un-American about venture capital, angel investing, or bank loans; half of U.S. businesses rely mainly on such relationship-based finance. Conversely, there is nothing un-German about bonds issued by Deutsche Telecom and other utilities. The question is how much and of what kind: My argument is that for the last two decades, arm's-length financing has displaced relationship-based finance to an excessive degree and there is now no good reason to revive the sort of securitization that proliferated well before subprime fiasco.

My description of how innovation works in the real economy is also not new. It follows the line that evolutionary economists have been taking for more than thirty years,* although their views have received short shrift in mainstream economics. The more novel feature of my analysis lies in tying ideas about innovation in the real world to the effective functioning of the financial system.

---

*Readers who are interested in learning about evolutionary economics could start with a 2008 essay by Richard Nelson (whose 1982 book with Sidney Winter is considered a landmark in the field) and *Inside the Black Box: Technology and Economics,* by Nathan Rosenberg (1982).

PART I

ORDERING THE INNOVATION GAME: BEYOND DECENTRALI-ZATION AND PRICES

The measure of a financial system ought to be the service it provides the economy as a whole, not the employment or bounties it bestows on finan-ciers. Understanding how the real economy embeds the widespread inno-vations that sustain broad-based prosperity must therefore precede any sensible discussion of how the financial system should be organized. To reverse the proverb: We need to specify what kind of cart needs pulling before we figure out what financial horse we need in harness.

Understanding innovation is not easy, however. Modern capitalism nourishes an unruly innovation game. A large and diverse set of players par-ticipates and in quite different ways. Some play on their own, while oth-ers join teams, large and small. Rivals can become allies, and confederates can compete. Rules evolve and referees are added as the players innovate. There is no overall coach or captain who tells the players what to do, though individual teams may have leaders who exercise some control. And there is no final whistle: The game never ends.

In the next three chapters, we will look past the superficial unruliness and fluidity in order to focus on the underlying and relatively stable features of the game that have made it so rewarding for most players and for soci-ety as a whole. The survey covers the decentralization of initiative and its coupling to responsibility for outcomes, subjective judgment, dialogue, and ongoing relationships. It highlights the advantages and some limitations of these features—why, for instance, the decentralization of responsibility and judgment is a good general principle, but also why ceding some authority to centrally controlled organizations helps innovation and growth.[1] In chapter 4, we will see what this means for a well-ordered financial system.

I will not, however, provide a complete, in-depth analysis of innovation or capitalism. Rather I will focus on those features that a financial system should mirror and support. I will also have nothing more to say in the next four chapters about the "rules" governing the innovation game that are laid down and enforced by legislators, courts, and regulators. The discussion of their contribution in the introduction provides an adequate basis for an extensive analysis of financial rules in later chapters of this book.

Chapter I

The Decentralization of Judgment

The classic economic case for decentralized decision-making—letting individuals be "free to choose"—will be familiar to many readers. The benefits of a price system in coordinating individual choices and providing the incentive to make good ones are also well known. The standard arguments, however, focus on rapid adjustment to economic fluctuations, rather than long-run progress; they don't explicitly address how decentralization facilitates the development and use of new technologies. In addition, the question of what kinds of decisions an individual is free to make in a decentralized system is glossed over. In fact, standard economic theories accord no more freedom to decentralized decision-makers than belongs to robots or software programs that process whatever data they are given in a completely mechanistic way.

I argue that what matters for innovation is the decentralization of subjective *judgment*. The great strength of modern capitalism lies in the freedom it gives many individuals to make choices based, not just on the objective facts they observe, but also on their unique imagination, temperament, and perspective. We will also see why robotic, centralized decision-making cannot replace decentralized, subjective judgments—no matter how much effort is put into developing econometric models.

▮▮▮▮ Why Decentralize? The Classic View

Friedrich Hayek's essay "The Use of Knowledge in Society" makes an eloquent argument for decentralized choice. It was published in 1945 when central planning seemed to offer an attractive solution to the economic and political problems capitalist societies faced during the Great Depression and the Second World War. By now the sledgehammer style of central planning—the target of Hayek's critique—has fallen out of favor; nevertheless, the argument for decentralization he made more than sixty years ago is worth recalling.

Planning, in its broadest sense of thinking about what to do before doing it, is essential, Hayek wrote. But, plans are best made by individuals rather than a central planner because the necessary knowledge is "not given to anyone in its totality." Rather, it exists as dispersed and frequently contradictory bits possessed by separate individuals. In principle, some kinds of knowledge—which Hayek called scientific—can be speedily communicated to "an authority made up of suitably chosen experts." But, argued Hayek, this is not the only kind of knowledge needed to make good choices. Knowledge of the particular circumstances of time and place that cannot be easily communicated is also vital, although it is "generally regarded with a kind of contempt" as compared to "theoretical or technical knowledge":

> We need to remember only how much we have to learn in any
> occupation after we have completed our theoretical training,
> how big a part of our working life we spend learning particular
> jobs, and how valuable an asset in all walks of life is knowledge
> of people, of local conditions, and of special circumstances.
> To know of and put to use a machine not fully employed,
> or somebody's skill which could be better utilized, or to be
> aware of a surplus stock which can be drawn upon during
> an interruption of supplies, is socially quite as useful as the
> knowledge of better alternative techniques. And the shipper
> who earns his living from using otherwise empty or half-filled
> journeys of tramp-steamers, or the estate agent whose whole
> knowledge is almost exclusively one of temporary opportunities,
> or the arbitrageur who gains from local differences of
> commodity prices, are all performing eminently useful functions
> based on special knowledge of circumstances of the fleeting
> moment not known to others.

The need to adapt to "constant small changes" makes knowledge of the fleeting moment crucial. Hayek rejected the belief that "with the elaborate apparatus of modern production, economic decisions are required only at long intervals, as when a new factory is to be erected." Practical experience shows that "the task of keeping cost from rising requires constant struggle." Furthermore, the law of large numbers, or the "mutual compensation of random changes," cannot account for the relative stability of the total output of the economy. Rather, Hayek says, "Stability and the continuous flow of goods and services is maintained by constant deliberate adjustments, by new dispositions made every day in the light of circumstances not known the day before, by B stepping in at once when A fails to deliver. Even the large and highly mechanized plant keeps going largely because of an environment upon which it can draw for all sorts of unexpected needs; tiles for its roof, stationery for its forms, and all the thousand and one kinds of equipment in which it cannot be self-contained and which the plans for the operation of the plant require to be readily available in the market."

A central authority cannot make these adjustments because the necessary data cannot be reduced to inputs for an all-encompassing statistical model: In some way or other, decisions requiring such knowledge must be "left to the 'man on the spot.'"

The Marvel of Prices

Although decentralization—leaving decisions to people familiar with specific circumstances who know directly the changes and the resources immediately available to meet them—enables "rapid adaptation," it isn't enough. According to Hayek, "The 'man on the spot' cannot decide solely on the basis of his limited but intimate knowledge of the facts of his immediate surroundings. There still remains the problem of communicating to him such further information as he needs to fit his decisions into the whole pattern of changes of the larger economic system."

This, in turn, raises the question: "Which of the events which happen beyond the horizon of his immediate knowledge are of relevance to his immediate decision, and how much of them need he know?"

Like the central planner, the autonomous individual cannot know everything. But although "there is hardly anything that happens anywhere in the world that might not have an effect" on his decision, complete knowledge of these events is unnecessary. It doesn't matter why "at the particular moment more screws of one size than of another are wanted, why paper bags are more readily available than canvas bags, or why skilled labor, or particular machine tools, have for the moment become more difficult to obtain. All that is significant for him is how much more or less difficult to procure they have become compared with other things with which he is also concerned, or how much more or less urgently wanted are the alternative things he produces or uses."

This information is provided by the "marvel" of the price system.

Suppose, writes Hayek, that somewhere in the world a new use for tin is discovered or a tin mine is closed, making the commodity scarcer. Users don't need to know why the scarcity has arisen. Rising prices are an adequate signal for individual users to reduce consumption. Higher prices also encourage the deepest cuts in uses where tin is the most dispensable, so the overall supply goes customers where it is most valued. Prices, in Hayek's words, "act to coordinate the separate actions of different people."

The price system, in conjunction with property rights,[1] also ties the individual's freedom to make choices to responsibility for the consequences. In fact, we can say that such a tie is necessary for the price system to serve as an effective coordination mechanism. A user who fails to respond to rising prices faces greater losses than the user who does respond, and in some cases may go out of business altogether. This is not to say that businesspeople are motivated just by profit, but rather that without such a motivation, changes in prices would not have much of an effect. In a decentralized, price-based economic system, autonomy and responsibility—that has real financial consequences and isn't just cosmetic—go hand in hand.

The Role of Judgment

Hayek's essay argued that "the economic problem of society is mainly one of rapid adaptation to changes" and this idea was a sufficient basis for his argument about the value of decision making by the "man on the spot." Yet the success of the modern economy turns at least as much on proactive initiatives to change the status quo as it does on adaptation to changes (a point which Hayek himself made in his other work). As it happens, decentralization is superior to central planning for both innovation and adaptation; but the reasons are not exactly the same.[2]

As with adaptation, the difficulty of communicating information to a central planner favors decentralized innovation. New initiatives also usually require man-on-the-spot knowledge of, for instance, a place, customer segment, or technology. A few innovators may come out of nowhere and revolutionize an industry—Jeff Bezos, who worked at a hedge fund before launching Amazon, had no prior experience of selling books. But such dramatic transformations by outsiders are rare. Technology usually progresses through the accretion of incremental advances rather than discontinuous breakthroughs, although the steps may follow in such rapid succession as to create the illusion of a single great leap.* And unlike Jeff Bezos, most innovators have on the spot knowledge that gives them the detailed insights that outsiders don't have. Bill Gates and Paul Allen were attuned to the opportunity presented by the launch of personal computers in 1975 because they had been computer hackers through high school. Sam Walton did not open his first Wal-Mart until 1962; he started in retailing by buying what he called a "real dog" of a franchised store in a small town in Arkansas in 1945 and added more franchised stores through the 1950s. Google grew out of search algorithms that Larry Page and Sergey Brin developed as PhD students at Stanford.

The other advantage of decentralization that applies more to innovations than to simple adaptation lies in their development by competing innovators and selection by independent users. In principle we could think of a centralized process controlled by organizations like the National Science Foundation (NSF) and Food and Drug Organization (FDA) that would convene panels of experts to screen innovation proposals and then decide which new products merited sale to consumers. As we will see next, however, such centralization would be incongruent with the mental processes of innovation and the impossibility of knowing whether a new product or service is better than all possible alternatives.

Effective adaptation to unpredictable but repeated patterns of changes does not require much creativity of imagination. "On the spot" knowledge in conjunction with skill in detecting patterns (filtering the

---

*As shown by Nathan Rosenberg and other evolutionary economists and discussed extensively in my own previous work. Schumpeter's theories, which involve great breakthroughs by larger-than-life entrepreneurs, are catchy but, I believe, a poor representation of reality.

signal from the noise) and familiarity with responses that have worked well in the past may suffice. This is not the case with innovation, however. Deep local knowledge alone rarely leads innovators to surefire schemes or pure arbitrage opportunities.[3] Nor is the innovator's conception of an opportunity simply the recognition of historical pattern (or what Herbert Simon called "intuition")[4] that a physician might rely on to diagnose an obscure ailment.

Historical patterns and local knowledge are but starting points; to innovate, to go someplace new or along a path that hasn't been traveled before, requires imagination. New products like the spreadsheet require the *creative* defining and solving of problems, and not just knowledge of the situation at hand or of historical precedents (see box). Imaginative leaps may be shorter in incremental advances; nonetheless, all innovations require at least some creative insight.

Birth of the Spreadsheet

Dan Bricklin's conception of the spreadsheet—the "killer app" that turned the personal computer from a curiosity to ubiquitous modern artifact—was partly the result of his deep knowledge of computers and software, and his prior experience in developing word-processing software for Digital Equipment Corporation in the mid-1970s. But it also required imagination. If software could be used to insert changes in a text document without having to retype everything else, Bricklin asked himself, why couldn't the same be done with numbers in a spreadsheet? Bricklin recalls:

> The idea for the electronic spreadsheet came to me while I was a student at the Harvard Business School, working on my MBA degree, in the spring of 1978. Sitting in Aldrich Hall, room 108, I would daydream. "Imagine if my calculator had a ball in its back, like a mouse..." (I had seen a mouse previously, I think in a demonstration at a conference by Doug Engelbart, and maybe the Alto). And "...imagine if I had a heads-up display, like in a fighter plane, where I could see the virtual image hanging in the air in front of me. I could just move my mouse/keyboard calculator around on the table, punch in a few numbers, circle them to get a sum, do some calculations, and answer '10% will be fine!'" (10% was always the answer in those days when we couldn't do very complicated calculations...)
>
> The summer of 1978, between first and second year of the MBA program, while riding a bike along a path on Martha's Vineyard, I decided that I wanted to pursue this idea and create a real product to sell after I graduated.

Bricklin then refined the idea, again *creatively* incorporating his knowledge of what was then technically feasible:

> Eventually, my vision became more realistic, and the heads-up display gave way to a normal screen. I tried prototyping the product's display screen in Basic on a video terminal connected to the Business School's timesharing system in the spring of 1978. (Prototyping is a great way to force you to work out design problems.) That's when the desire for general placement of numbers, formula results, and text turned into rows and columns to give them human-friendly names. It also was when I decided upon the status line for displaying the formula and formatting behind the values being displayed.
>
> The hope for using a mouse was replaced in the first personal computer prototype in the early fall of 1978 by the game paddle of the Apple II. (This was a dial you could turn to move game objects back and forth, for example in "Pong.") You could move the cursor left or right, and then push the "fire" button, and then turning the paddle would move the cursor up and down. The R-C circuit or whatever in the Apple II was too sluggish and my pointing too imprecise to accurately position the cursor that way, so I switched to the two arrow keys of the Apple II keyboard (it only had 2) and used the space bar instead of the button to switch from horizontal movement to vertical.[5]

The imagination inherent in an innovative concept obviously compounds the communication problems that arise in a centralized system: Innovators would not only face great difficulty documenting all the relevant facts, but reducing their creative hunches—many of which are developed on the fly as unexpected problems arise—to writing in a comprehensive proposal to a central authority would be virtually impossible.

Spawning and Selecting

Decentralized systems have another crucial advantage beyond bypassing the problem of communication, owing to the *kind* of imagination and judgment that an innovation requires.

Contrast an innovator's creativity with that of a natural scientist: Scientists use their imagination to infer, from specific observations, general causal relationships (such as the laws of gravity) that already exist in nature, but innovators imagine goods and services that have never existed. And whereas scientists believe that there is just one causal pattern or law awaiting discovery, innovators can conceive of a vast array of possibilities both in how problems are defined and their feasible solution. From this vast set, innovators make subjective judgments about the "best feasible" possibility. This judgment, too, is based on imagination—not just logic and knowledge of the facts.

But how can we test such a judgment? Natural scientists run experiments to test whether a causal principle is generally true by trying to falsify it under a broad variety of circumstances. Similarly a test of a commercial innovation may show that it just doesn't work because of some physical defect or because no one wants to use it. Yet even if something "works," it doesn't prove the innovator's judgment that it's the best feasible option.

A decentralized capitalist economy does not rely on the track record or qualifications of the innovator[6] or expert panels to say yea or nay. Rather, all are free to act on their judgments, if they can muster the necessary resources. As a result, the system summons forth a considerable variety of innovations: Many individuals confronted with the same situation perceive problems and formulate solutions in different ways because of differences in their past experiences or in the way their brains are wired. The process does involve duplication of innovative effort. But it eliminates the favoritism and aversion to far-out ideas that a centralized system would entail. Would a panel of experts have given the green light to Bricklin's personal-computer-based spreadsheet in an era of mainframes?

Symmetrically, a decentralized system relies on the independent choices of users to select from the many innovations that are offered: Innovations that are more highly valued by customers—the "fittest" available candidates rather than some hypothetical best—flourish, while the less valued ones fall by the wayside. And because a nearly continuous stream of innovations is often offered, a rapid sequence of small advances can turn out to be revolutionary.

Inevitably, users make subjective judgments rather than robotic choices about which innovations to adopt. Innovators therefore rarely face an objective test. Like movie producers, developers of high-tech products face buyers who must take shots in the dark (see box). Decentralization of consumer choice does, however, protect innovators against sheer bad luck by giving many buyers the right to make their own judgments. Industry experts can have disproportionate influence, but no veto. Movies panned by critics, and products deemed technically inferior by industry gurus, nonetheless do well. Granted, the negative opinion of

FDA panels can block the sale of a new drug, but such instances are not the norm in a capitalist economy. Furthermore, an innovation doesn't have to win over all consumers, or even a majority of them, from the get-go. If it brings in enough revenue over costs, an innovation that falters at first can survive and change to shine later.

Why Users of Innovations Must Take Shots in the Dark

Like developers of innovations, consumers face risks they cannot objectively evaluate. Innovations may not actually do what they are supposed to, for instance. A product that works in the lab or in a few beta sites may not work for all users because of differences in the conditions of its implementation; a product that works fine at the outset may fail later. Repeated use of a product may bring to the surface hidden defects that cause serious harm. Defects in a word-processing or email package that costs just a few hundred dollars may wipe out many years of invaluable files and correspondence. Tires that wear badly can have fatal consequences. And the belated discovery of the hazards of asbestos can lead to tens of billions of dollars in removal costs.

Consumers face risk if they invest in new products that work perfectly well for them but fail to attract a critical mass of other users. If that happens, vendors (and providers of complementary add-ons) often abandon the product and stop providing critical maintenance, upgrades, and spare parts. Or vendors may go out of business entirely—a common occurrence in IT.

Whether an innovation will deliver more value than its price is also uncertain. In the schema of neoclassical economics, consumers have a gigantic, well-specified utility function for all goods, those extant as well as those not yet invented: When an innovation appears, consumers consult their utility functions, as they might a tax table, and know exactly its worth to them.

This assumption seems farfetched. It is improbable, for instance, that anyone who wears glasses or contact lenses has a firm grasp of the economic value of corrective laser surgery, or that someone who has a conventional TV can gauge the value of switching to a higher definition digital product. Indeed, I doubt that people who have laser surgery or buy a digital TV can ever quantify its value. Before or after a purchase, the enhanced utility—like the risk—is a matter of subjective opinion.[7]

In an economy characterized by a high level of innovation, producers and purchasers of mature, "low tech" goods also have to make subjective judgments that can be affected by advances originating in seemingly remote high-tech industries, or simply in the desire of consumers to try new things of every sort. Return to Hayek's example of a user of tin adapting to rising prices: Suppose a manufacturer tries to cope by switching to alloys with more copper or by altering the product mix. In a constantly advancing economy, where the past isn't prologue for anyone, the manufacturer cannot rely on repeating what worked the last time the prices were high. The manufacturer has to guess how customers and competitors will respond given changes in technologies or tastes that have occurred since the last spike in prices. Sophisticated cost-accounting systems and optimization software can help, but they can't replace judgments that take into account the specific conditions of the here and now.

▨▨▨▨ The Challenge of Codification

The ubiquity of subjective judgment in a decentralized economy, however, does not mean that there is nothing to be gained from objective methods of decision making. Using objective models tends to be faster and less labor intensive because the models generally use fewer variables as inputs. Properly constructed, they are also less susceptible to unwarranted biases and stereotyping, cognitive defects (of the sort studied by behavioral economists), and mood swings. Wherever possible, therefore, people have tried to codify subjective procedures, often by studying experts to capture the essence of what they do. The information technology revolution has provided a strong economic and psychological boost—if IBM's Big Blue computer can be programmed to beat the world chess champion, what else couldn't it do?

Nonetheless, the use of mechanistic decision-making models in the business world remains limited in spite of extensive and long-standing efforts to promote a more "scientific" approach to management (see box).

A Difficult Cause

In 1959, both the Ford Foundation and the Carnegie Foundation published critiques of business education arguing that there now finally existed a "management science" that combined decision-making tools developed in the Second World War with the theoretical insights of economics and other behavioral sciences. This new science "would allow mangers to make decisions solely on analytical and rational grounds without recourse to fuzzy notions such as intuition or judgment." Both foundation reports also argued that teaching

---

and researching this "new science of administration" required business school faculty who were "focused more on fundamental research than on descriptive analysis and deriving decision making principles more from theory than from existing practice."[8]

The recommendations, backed up with the funding of more scientific research and the reform of business school curricula, "led to dramatic changes," including "a sharp rise in analytical courses," a "tighter alignment with traditional academic disciplines" such as applied mathematics, economics, and statistics and a "greater commitment to rigorous, theory-based scholarship."[9] But all this scientific training and research in objective decision-making has been put to remarkably little use outside business school classes. According to a recent study, business executives are "virtually unanimous in their lack of interest in business school research."[10] In my experience, business school graduates rarely use quantitative tools, even basic ones such as regression analyses, in their working lives. Social scientists themselves, I should note, almost never use statistical models to manage their departments and schools.

Why do executives—who do rely heavily on "hard" data to makes choices about specific cases—use econometric techniques in exceptional circumstances, rather than as a matter of routine, even after being trained at business schools deeply committed to the statistical methods of the modern social sciences? I don't think it's because they are less sophisticated or capable than social scientists. These are not innumerate individuals to start with—the proportion of MBAs at top schools with undergraduate degrees in engineering or the natural sciences exceeds the proportion in the college-educated population as a whole. It tells us something when regressions and other advanced statistical methods are rarely used by individuals who will look for any edge to get ahead.

In reality, statistical models of human behavior are ultimately a form of history, a simplified numerical narrative of what happened in the past. They may reveal broad tendencies and suggest causal relationships, but as a rule they cannot provide accurate predictions (see box).

Pitfalls of Predictive Models

Scientists and mathematicians have developed many models to reliably predict outcomes in the natural world. As we learn in high school, a body accelerates at rate equal to the force applied to the body divided by its mass. When the ends of a wire of length *l* and radius *r* made of a metal of conductivity σ is connected across a battery of voltage V, the current that flows through the wire equals $V/(s\pi r^2 l)$. The surface area of a closed cylinder of radius r and height h equals $2(\pi r^2 + \pi rh)$, and that of a right circular cone equals $\pi r(r + \sqrt{r^2 + h^2})$ The differences between the predicted and observed outcomes (for mass, currents or surface) areas are small and derive almost entirely from random measurement errors.

Such exact models are unknown in the world of human behavior. Differences between predicted and observed outcome are invariably large and "randomly" distributed (on a bell curve) mainly by assumption. The complexity and fluidity of human behavior and interactions makes it impossible to formulate reliable, accurate models of the sort found in the physical world.

A large number of variables affect outcomes and to quite a significant degree. Modelers can try to make guesses about the important ones but cannot know what they miss. Instead they follow the convention of attributing the effects of the omitted variables to random noise.

Interdependencies between the causal factors are complex, but the modeler has no way of knowing what they might be. Standard practice assumes linear relationships. For instance, to predict how a college education affects wages, the traditional econometric procedure would start with a linear "model" of the form

$$Y = a + b_1 x_1 + b_2 x_2 + \dots + b_n x_n + \varepsilon.$$

In this equation, Y would the wages of an individual, x_1 would be the independent variable of interest—whether the individual went to college—and the remaining x's control variables such as gender and years of experience. A standard statistical package would then provide the value of b_1—how wages vary with going to college. For instance, according to a recent study, adjusting for work experience and gender, employers now pay college graduates 75 percent more than they pay high school graduates, while 25 years ago they paid 40 percent more.

The procedure can yield the right value, however, only under the arbitrary assumption that wages are the result of a linear combination of the x's. But why should the equation be linear? Nature, after all, is replete with instances—acceleration, the surface areas of cones and cylinders, and electrical current passing through a wire—whose values depend on nonlinear combinations of their independent variables. Arbitrarily using a linear specification when the true relationships are nonlinear will produce errors.

Unfortunately, there is no way to know what the right model really is. In the natural sciences, researchers can posit a relationship and test it through controlled experiments. In social phenomena, proper controlled experiments are virtually impossible.

Instead, researchers will sometimes "try out" relationships to see which one best fits the data. But the problem with this method is that relationships discovered through such fishing expeditions ("data mining") can throw up spurious relationships. With sufficient effort one can always find equations that happen to fit historic data but have little predictive value.

Another problem is that there isn't just one pattern to be discovered, one model that drives all outcomes. Think of the problem of controlling for years of work experience to predict incomes. For different occupations we'd expect quite different relationships between incomes and years of work experience: We would expect a consistently positive relationship between incomes and experience for lawyers and surgeons; for assembly line workers, we might expect incomes to flatten after a few years; and for fashion models and professional athletes we would expect an inverted U-shaped relationship between incomes and experience. In other words, it's not merely that the slopes (or other such parameters) are different, but that the basic equations most likely are not the same for different occupations.[11] The usual procedure of using a single linear model is akin to using a ruler to measure the lengths of rods twisted in quite different shapes.

Using historical data to make predictions is also problematic when it comes to human affairs, where many individuals are looking for opportunities to change the status quo. And even individuals who don't change their behavior are affected by others who do. Mechanistic extrapolations from past events therefore tend to yield erroneous predictions. For instance, a model may tell us that in a particular year, college graduates earned 75 percent more than high-school graduates. But we can't use this result to make accurate predictions if high payoffs (net of the costs) increase college enrollments and the share of college graduates in the workforce, or conversely if low payoffs reduce enrollments and share. In a dynamic, innovative economy, the predictions of quantitative models will be accurate only in exceptional circumstances.[12]

Mechanized predictions are particularly ill suited (as argued in the box) to the dynamism of a capitalist economy. Models that must treat unique events as a draw from uniform, stable distribution, abstracting away from their specific character, are fundamentally incongruent with what makes decentralization effective. As Hayek pointed out in 1945, the inability of central planners to cope with granular, context-specific information makes them inflexible. They cannot easily adapt to (and we might add, initiate) localized changes because

> the statistics which such a central authority would have to use would have to be arrived at precisely by abstracting from minor differences between the things, by lumping together, as resources of one kind, items which differ as regards location, quality, and other particulars, in a way which may be very significant for the specific decision. It follows from this that central planning based on statistical information by its nature cannot take direct account of these circumstances of time and place.

But that's just what statistical models do. In other words, if the problem with subjectivity is unwarranted bias, then the problem with objective methods is the failure to discriminate between situations that are materially different—inadvertently using programs optimized for chess to play checkers. Such misapplications are the result the very parsimony that gives objective methods their speed and cost advantages; and are especially likely to occur if objective methods are applied to innovative activities, which inherently involve novel circumstances.

Even procedures that work well at the outset can become victims of their success because individuals and businesses are quick to imitate successful innovations. A yield management program used by an airline to fill airplanes, or a "by the numbers" sabermetric method to manage a baseball team (as described in Michael Lewis's *Moneyball*) can work wonderfully for the first airlines and baseball teams that use them, but tend to lose their potency with their widespread adoption. Then it's back to relying on subjective judgment. The half-life of effective mechanistic models is quite short in a dynamic decentralized economy.

Furthermore, reducing subjective decisions to a codified model itself implicitly requires subjective judgments about, for example, the scope or category of events the model will cover, and what variables to include or exclude, that modelers may not be aware they are making. Like all judgments, a choice about the scope and structure of a codified model is prone to error. Worse, the codification can create a false sense of security, making users of the procedure oblivious to deeply embedded mistakes in the design.

There are, however, circumstances under which largely mechanized decision-making beats the man-on-the-spot judgments. These instances are also worth noting. One involves the optimization of complex networks such as an airline or trucking fleet connecting many locations, or the national electricity grid. This just cannot be done by the seat of the pants. The operation of high-volume manufacturing plants, particularly in the chemical and other such process industries, is another example of effective, mechanized decision-making complemented by a relatively small amount of human judgment.

Several special factors are at play here, however, as Richard Nelson's work suggests.[13] The inputs and outputs are passive or inanimate entities that obey the laws of nature (or mathematical rules) and do not deliberately or subconsciously resist efforts to control them. The process to be controlled is highly automated, and most of the kinks were previously ironed out. Outcomes can be precisely measured, making it feasible to use automated feedback and adjustments. And the environment is highly controlled: Plants are physically shielded from the elements and isolated from the far more turbulent commercial parts of the enterprise. Efforts to mechanize innovation and creative thinking in general, which date back at least to J. S. Mill's methods for induction, have repeatedly failed to live up to expectations (see box). This isn't to suggest that broad frameworks, systematic routines for sifting through ideas, or brainstorming techniques have no value: They can lead innovators to think more broadly or to anticipate problems. But they are helpmates for imagination and subjective judgment, not replacements.

How Automated Innovation Fizzled

Early in the twenty-first century, reports Reena Jana, "auto-innovation was trumpeted as the Next Big Thing." Computers were expected to "create goods on their own by exhaustively combining bits and pieces of previously successful products." Hewlett-Packard set up GP (Genetic Programming) Lab to develop "computer code that could analyze the 'genes' of earlier inventions and point to evolutionary advances." The pharmaceutical company Pfizer gave some 1,500 scientists "software that could identify chemicals that might turn into drugs." In 2005, California programmer John Koza's "auto-innovation" software "earned the first U.S. patent ever awarded to a nonhuman."

But "as quickly as auto-innovation swept through research and development departments, it was gone." HP shut down GP Lab in 2004, four years after it had opened. It had "suggested some dazzling new designs for data-storage products" but "failed to turn up any that customers were likely to buy." HP's Jaap Suermondt, who oversaw the project, said that it had "worked to make theoretically good designs" but then became "a hammer in search of a nail." Pfizer's auto-innovation "was blamed for leading researchers down dead ends and bloating the budget." The patent secured by Koza's software, "a microchip that controls a machine's operations, never turned into a commercial product."[14]

Concluding Comments

The United States didn't choose to decentralize innovation for economic reasons. Rather, decentralization was adopted in preindustrial America mainly because of hostility to centralized political control. "An emphasis on individuals," Kindleberger notes, goes back to the Constitution, "the preamble of which starts 'We, the people,' not 'We, the states.' "[15]

Decentralization turned out to be a great boon for the transformation of the economy by stimulating and harnessing the imaginations and enterprise of innumerable developers and users of innovations. Many could contribute and benefit—both the producers and purchasers of potato chips and the producers and purchasers of computer chips. In fact many people had to participate; opting out became less and less feasible. By accident rather than by design,* decentralization became the organizing principle of a massively multiplayer innovation game.

What the game decentralizes also is crucial. Individuals don't merely respond to changes in the manner of a robot. Rather, decentralization gives individuals the opportunity to initiate the development of new products and technologies. This, in turn, requires the exercise of subjective judgments that incorporate the individual's imagination and background, not just the objective facts the individual observes. And because of differences in imaginations and backgrounds, decentralization spawns many competing initiatives. Similarly, the system relies on the independent judgments of many users to select from these competing initiatives.

Relying on case-by-case judgment does have drawbacks: It is labor intensive and slow. But mechanized decision-making is rarely a good alternative when the choices involve willful humans.

The decentralization of judgment in the real economy also has important implications for finance that we will discuss in chapter 4. Financiers bear a considerable share of the downside of the misjudgments of the individuals and businesses they provide funds to. Making a loan or an equity investment therefore requires second-guessing someone else's judgment. This second-guessing also requires proximity (or on-the-spot knowledge of the specific circumstances) *and* subjective judgment. Simply put, financiers cannot easily make sensible choices from afar using mechanistic models.

Furthermore, the judgments that financiers must second-guess are widely diffused through capitalist economies. For instance, a large number of users, many from "old economy" industries, exercise judgment in buying or using high-tech products to which financiers are

---

*My point echoes Hayek's argument that a price system didn't emerge because it "happens to be best suited to modern civilization." Rather the price system came first. Man was then "able to develop that division of labor on which our civilization is based because he happened to stumble upon a method which made it possible" (Hayek 1945, p. 528).

directly or indirectly exposed: Several high-profile manufacturing and retail companies—and their creditors—have been seriously harmed by failed attempts to install Enterprise Resource Planning (ERP) systems. The knock-on effects of innovation make even the judgments of home-buyers a matter of concern to financiers. Even changes that have no obvious technological basis matter. The creditworthiness of an elegant, old-fashioned restaurant can be impaired if the neighborhood is repopulated by residents with edgy, modern tastes. Because forward-looking, case-by-case choices in the real world aren't restricted to elite scientists, engineers, or founders of software or biotech companies, the exercise of judgment by on-the-spot financiers is important throughout the economy, not just in isolated, high-tech pockets.

Chapter 2

The Halfway House: Coordination through Organizational Authority

In the last chapter we stayed with the comparison in Hayek's essay of 1945, "The Use of Knowledge in Society," between complete decentralization and central planning. In that essay, Hayek raised and quickly dismissed any middle ground: "The halfway house...about which many people talk but which few like when they see it, is the delegation of planning to organized industries, or, in other words, monopoly." In fact the halfway house of modern capitalism has an oligopolistic structure—many industries are dominated by a few large players, but they aren't monopolized by one (or controlled by a cartel for that matter). I argue in this chapter that partial centralization through large organizations, on balance, plays an important role in the innovation game. Most notably, it helps coordinate the initiatives of individual players, thus complementing the "marvel" of the price system. Realizing these benefits, however, requires well-designed organizations that maintain the right balance of autonomy and control and do not overextend the managerial capacities of their leaders.

▆▆▆▆ Pulling to the Center

The U.S. economy today is more centralized than it was in an agrarian, preindustrial society. Individual autonomy has been circumscribed by a great expansion of rules imposed by the government, as discussed in the introduction. But it isn't just the scope of the coercive power of the state that has grown. Individuals also now voluntarily subject themselves to the authority and rules of private organizations. These organizations proactively and consciously coordinate the activities and initiatives of individuals, whereas the price system does so in an indirect way.

The most obvious case is that of employees of large corporations whose choices are circumscribed by many policies and procedural rules and who are subject to the authority of bosses. But there are many other cases of voluntarily surrendered autonomy. Small subcontractors and suppliers are also subject to the authority of large corporations, sometimes to a greater degree than the people who work there: Outside lawyers and consultants are often more responsive to the wishes of corporate executives than are their subordinates.

Why is organizational control so pervasive? The origins of many of today's controls date back to efforts to solve the coordination problems necessary to realize economies of scale and scope in the nineteenth and early twentieth centuries (see box).

How Control Systems Helped Realize Economies of Scale and Scope

According to the business historian Alfred Chandler, firms initially grew by increasing the volume of their outputs using innovative, labor-saving technologies. These technologies stimulated the development of mechanisms to control and coordinate employees. In the prior "putting out" system of production, workers were paid according to a piece rate;[1] assembly line manufacturing required the control of effort through time and motion studies and the employment of foremen and supervisors. The greater complexity of the new technologies also increased the problem of coordinating the actions of individual employees. In the railroads, coordination failures sometimes had fatal consequences, as in the collision of two passenger trains in 1841. "The resulting outcry," according to Chandler, "helped bring into being the first modern, carefully defined, internal organization structure used by an American business enterprise."[2]

High-volume production encouraged firms to grow through vertical integration. General Motors (GM), for instance, acquired some of its upstream suppliers, such as the Fisher Body Company.[3] The benefits of vertical integration[4] could not be realized, however, without solving the coordination problems it created. For example, an upstream unit might build excess capacity because it overestimated the requirements of the downstream unit. By the 1920s, most large U.S. companies adopted "functional" organizational structures to control such problems.[5]

Growth through diversification followed growth through vertical integration. Diversification further increased the problems of information aggregation and placed an "intolerable strain on existing administrative structures." The problems of manufacturing and marketing a number of product lines "made the tasks of departmental headquarters exceedingly difficult to administer.... The coordination of product flow through several departments proved even more formidable."[6] These problems led large diversified companies to establish "divisions" with dedicated resources. For instance, after a financial crisis in 1920–21, General Motors formed the Cadillac, Buick, Oakland, Olds, and Chevrolet divisions. Between 1921 and 1925 GM created divisional offices, considerably expanded its central office staff, formed interdepartmental committees, and "worked out highly rational and systematic procedures" to coordinate the operating divisions and plan policy for the organization as a whole. By 1925, the divisional and general office staffs "were drawing up comprehensive over-all plans for all operating units" based on "carefully thought-out, long term forecasts."[7]

In the first half of the twentieth century, the scope of professional management grew to encompass the control of innovation. As Chandler's research shows, top managers of large companies such as General Motors evolved a systematic approach in deciding what innovations to undertake, taking into account factors such as market opportunities, the firm's capabilities, expected capital requirements, and returns. Managers also developed techniques to control how the innovations were undertaken: Large companies transformed innovation into a "routine and predictable process."[8] When the digital revolution unfolded, IT producers followed in the footsteps of their "old economy" predecessors in adopting a disciplined approach to the development of new products (see box).

Controlling Digital Development

The high-tech industry has a reputation for developing new products through spontaneous individualism. In reality, high-tech companies make an extensive effort to coordinate and control development. For instance, according to cofounder Gordon Moore, Intel's process for R & D budgeting required each product group to "submit a project list ordered in decreasing priority, explain in sometimes excruciating detail why the list is ordered as it is, and indicate where the line ought to be drawn between projects to work on and projects to put off."[9]

Along the same lines, Cypress Semiconductor, according to CEO T. J. Rodgers, developed a "goal system" to monitor development projects. For example, designing and shipping the company's third generation of PROM chips was accomplished by completing 3,278 goals over roughly two years.[10] Cypress management reviewed project goals more or less continuously. After project teams met on Monday, goals were fed into a central computer. On Tuesday mornings, functional managers received printouts on the status of their direct reports' new goals. On Wednesday mornings, the vice presidents of the company received goal printouts for the people below them. On Wednesday afternoons, the CEO reviewed reports with the vice presidents.[11]

Critics of this managerial approach claim that it is bureaucratic and stifling; but unlike the inventions of solo inventors, complex development projects that use large teams simply cannot be undertaken without rules and organization. To play in the big leagues, even companies that start off with no management to speak of, such as Microsoft, have to routinize their approach to development—and sometimes hire managers from large companies to oversee the new routines. Companies backed by venture capital hire executives from large companies to implement (albeit with suitable adaptation) systematic managerial processes from the get-go.

The Evolution of Power Sharing

The emergence of the giant business enterprise and other large organizations such as multinational professional service firms and global standard-setting bodies created a halfway house between complete decentralization and central planning in more ways than one: Large organizations learned to give many employees some opportunity to take initiative and exercise judgment.

At the outset, in the late nineteenth and early twentieth centuries, popular theories of scientific management and Taylorism sought to reduce rank-and-file employees to automatons or clerks. At the Ford Motor Company, assembly-line workers were well paid, but they were also worked hard and told what to do by a small cadre of industrial engineers. Henry Ford relied on his personal judgment to make bold decisions. ("If I had asked my customers what they wanted," he once said, "they would have said a faster horse."[12] He also decreed that customers could have a car in any color as long it was black.) Some of Ford's judgments succeeded spectacularly. Others would ultimately cause his company to lose its lead and allow General Motors to dominate the industry.

The sociologist Max Weber provided intellectual legitimacy in celebrating the bureaucratic model of organization. Weber's idealized bureaucracy comprised experts who had duties and rights within a "specified sphere of competence" and made decisions "according to calculable rules."[13] Although its procedures could impede "the discharge of business in a manner best adapted to the individuality of each case," Weber argued that bureaucratization offers "the optimum possibility for carrying through the principle of specializing administrative functions according to purely objective considerations." In its perfectly developed form, bureaucracy eliminates "love, hatred, and all purely personal, irrational and emotional elements which escape calculation."[14]

Eventually, however, big business gave up on extreme forms of centralization. It was demotivating to tell workers exactly what to do—paying high wages did not buy Ford great loyalty. And, as Hayek would have predicted, it was wasteful: Workers on the spot who had knowledge of specific circumstances weren't empowered to make adjustments or undertake new initiatives. Organizations therefore adopted what Peters and Waterman call "loose-tight" controls, with structures that centralize some activities and decentralize others. Instead of fully centralized planning, where all important projects are conceived, debated, and refined by a single authority at the top, many individuals at lower levels in the organization were given the authority to "initiate" subject to "ratification" or refinement by their bosses.*

The role of top executives also evolved from a focus on projects to a focus on managing people. Frank Knight observed in 1921 (when large, multibusiness corporations were starting to emerge) that except

---

*Fama and Jensen (1983) argue that the separation of the initiation and implementation of decisions from their ratification and monitoring (or "decision management" from "decision control") is an essential feature of organizations, such as publicly traded companies, in which "decision agents do not bear a major share of the wealth effects of their decisions" (p. 301).

in very small businesses, bosses controlled organizations mainly by exercising judgment over people, leaving choices about production and other such matters to their subordinates. Today, with the development of new organizational techniques and practices, the top executive's job entails a wide range of judgments. But many still involve managing subordinates: For instance, top executives review and ratify the budgets and projects proposed by subordinates, adjudicate disputes and turf battles, and make decisions about the reporting relationships, control systems, and compensation. A CEO such as Steve Jobs who micromanages product development is rare. In the normal case the CEO's influence on projects is indirect and typically derives from setting the overall strategy of the enterprise.

The development of management techniques that help top executives to delegate many business and technological decisions has also encouraged them to control a broader range of activities. The improved ability to decentralize *within* organizations, in other words, has fostered centralization *across* organizations. Nonetheless, there are cognitive and other limits to what top executives can control. Bosses don't need to be able to do their subordinates jobs, but some familiarity with their tasks is necessary. And there is only so much a human can learn; therefore, when too much is put in the same organizational package, the package may be less than the sum of the parts.

The Dilution of Responsibility

Deviating from fully decentralized decision-making also dilutes individual responsibility for outcomes and requires the construction of alternatives to the principle "Eat what you kill and starve if you don't." Why should subordinates who make decisions within constraints established by a boss agree to take full financial responsibility for what happens? In Frank Knight's theory, they don't: The boss (or "entrepreneur" in Knight's terminology) gives subordinates a fixed wage (determined by a competitive labor market) and takes full financial responsibility for outcomes good or bad. But why should the subordinates put in their utmost effort if they are going to be paid a fixed wage regardless of what happens?

No simple solution to the problem of providing the right incentives for subordinates has been discovered. Instead we find pragmatic and somewhat messy arrangements that require the exercise of subjective, case-by-case judgment. For instance, a subordinate may be paid an above-market salary (an "incentive wage") so that concern about being fired provides an incentive to do a good job. But now the boss has to monitor and second-guess the decisions of the subordinate to determine if a good job is in fact being done. This takes up the boss's time, and the boss may not have the knowledge to assess performance properly. Alternatively, the subordinate may be put on a pay-for-performance bonus plan. But such plans can encourage subordinates to roll the dice (since they get a bonus if their gamble pays off but don't lose if it doesn't) or to compromise the long-term interests of the organization. To guard against these possibilities, the boss must again monitor and second-guess whether subordinates are taking reckless chances.

Delegation to a subordinate, in other words, inevitably involves an "agency cost" that an astute boss who has the judgment to design and implement a good incentive plan can minimize but cannot eliminate.

Similar issues arise in the relationship between bosses and financiers. According to Knight's theory, the entrepreneur-boss bears all the risk, giving financiers a market-determined rate of return (just as entrepreneurs give subordinates a fixed wage). That's fine if the enterprise does well, but what if it fails? Bosses presumably don't have the personal wealth to bear the full loss—otherwise, why would they raise outside capital? The bosses' high upside and limited downside now requires financiers to monitor and second-guess to keep the bosses from reckless gambles. Here, too, some case-by-case judgment is necessary: Prohibiting the boss from pursuing all risky ventures isn't in the financiers' interest.

This "agency" problem is severe in large organizations because the bosses' share of the downside is usually small and their judgments are difficult for financiers to monitor and second-guess. The challenge faced by investors in controlling bosses, like the bosses' own capacity to manage subordinates, therefore limits the extent to which businesses can expand in an economically effective manner.

Concluding Comments

As Alfred Chandler has shown, the large, professionally managed corporations that appeared in the last half of the nineteenth century become a major force for developing and deploying innovative products in the twentieth century. Companies such as DuPont, for instance, developed new materials, like nylon, in their research labs, produced them on a mass scale at low cost, and created large markets for their use. By the 1960s, this organizational form became ubiquitous. In 1967, J. K. Galbraith observed that the 500 largest corporations produced nearly half the goods and services annually available in the United States.

Contrary to predictions, however, large corporations did not wipe out smaller, more "entrepreneurial" organizations. In fact, shortly after Galbraith's book was published, their share of economic activity stabilized. By the early 1980s, professionally managed venture-capital funds began to see explosive growth, and the firms they invested in came to be regarded as the new standard-bearers of innovative enterprise. The once-hot large corporation was regarded as passé and on the path to eventual extinction.

As it happened, just as large corporations did not make the classic self-financed entrepreneur obsolete, VC-backed businesses did not knock out large corporations. Rather, large organizations now undertake innovative activities that are different from and complementary to those undertaken by smaller organizations. I have discussed their comparative advantages and limitations extensively in earlier work.[15] Here it is sufficient to note that large organizations are, and will likely remain, important players in the innovation game, especially in those arenas where coordination through the price system doesn't get the job fully done.

Paradoxically, these large organizations, whose value in coordinating innovative activities requires that many individuals submit to some form of centralized authority, are in many ways *less* centralized than small businesses, whose owners often exercise tighter control over employees (and bear more of the consequences for the performance of the enterprise). Thus, designing and constructing an organization that delegates the right responsibilities to individuals and provides them with the proper incentives becomes an important task for top executives. This task also requires judgments that incorporate the specific circumstances (of traditions and personalities, for instance) rather than mechanistic decision-making.

Looking ahead to the implications for finance: The partially centralized decision-making structures, the diluted consequential accountability of the top executives for results, and the scale of the projects undertaken all affect the relationships that large companies have with financiers. Investing in a large company, for example, entails different challenges than does providing venture capital to a start-up. But, as we will see in chapter 8, the U.S. financial system is now much better equipped to make venture capital investments than it is to invest in the stocks of large publicly held companies.

Another implication that we can carry forward from this chapter has to do with the limits to the size and scope of large companies. Even with the great advances that have been made in organizational technology, companies can become too large or too diversified to be managed effectively. In chapter 4, I will argue that such limits are even tighter for financial firms.

Chapter 3

Dialogue and Relationships

Hayek's assertion that prices "act to coordinate the separate actions of different people" is indisputable. However, as I argued in the last chapter, when innovations involve economies of scale and scope, indirect, adaptive coordination through prices may not be enough. More direct coordination by a centralized organizational authority is often a valuable complement. This chapter looks at the role of dialogue and relationships in this direct (and directed!) coordination of innovative activity—not just within large hierarchical organizations, but also of independent individuals and small businesses.

Dialogue

The role of prices in efficiently coordinating individual actions has been highlighted not just in Hayek's essay, which appeared in the *American Economic Review*, but also in publications intended for the wider public, such as Milton and Rose Friedman's *Free to Choose* (see box).

Transmitting Information: The Role of Prices

Suppose, write the Friedmans, a baby boom increases the demand for lead pencils:

> Retail stores…will order more pencils from their wholesalers. The wholesalers will order more pencils from the manufacturers. The manufacturers will order more wood, more brass, more graphite—all the varied products used to make a pencil. In order to induce their suppliers to produce more of these items, they will have to offer higher prices for them. The higher prices will induce the suppliers to increase their work force to be able to meet the higher demand. To get more workers they will have to offer higher wages or better working conditions. In this way ripples spread out over ever widening circles, transmitting the information to people all over the world that there is a greater demand for pencils—or, to be more precise, for some product they are engaged in producing, for reasons they may not and need not know.
>
> The price system transmits only the important information and only to the people who need to know. The producers of wood, for example, do not have to know why the demand for pencils has gone up, or even that the demand for pencils has gone up. They need to know only that someone is willing to pay more for wood and that the higher price is likely to last long enough to make it worthwhile to satisfy the demand. Both items of information are provided by market prices—the first by the current price, the second by the price offered for future delivery.
>
> A major problem in transmitting information efficiently is to make sure that everyone who can use the information gets it without clogging the in-baskets of those who have no use for it. The price system automatically solves this problem. The people who transmit the information have an incentive to search out those who can use it, and they are in a position to do so. Those who can use the information have an incentive to get it, and they are in a position to do so. The pencil manufacturer is in touch with people selling the necessary wood. The manufacturer is always trying to find additional suppliers who can offer a better product or a lower price. Similarly, the producer of wood is in touch with customers and is always trying to find new ones. Meanwhile, people who are not engaged in production that uses wood, and don't expect to be in the future, have no interest in its price and will ignore it.[1]

Explaining the value of a flexible price system is a worthy enterprise, given a common propensity to regard price fluctuations with suspicion and sometimes to see price increases as evidence of gouging. But emphasizing the virtues of flexible prices—and the benefits of price increases—can lead economists to downplay the role that direct communication plays in coordinating decentralized initiatives. The Friedmans, for example, comment that the price system enables "people living all over the world to cooperate" without requiring them to "to speak to one another."[2]

But cooperation and coordination, especially in a technologically advanced economy, often requires extended mutual reliance and thus the exchange of promises of future performance through written or oral contracts. Sometimes the contracts are highly standardized, take-it-or-leave-it documents, such as an automobile lease that can be completed without much conversation. In other cases, however, extensive dialogue is necessary. When an automobile company places an order for a part that requires the supplier invest in special tooling, extensive negotiations may be necessary to assuage the buyers' concerns about delays in production.

Similarly, innovation requires a great deal of communication between the creators and the users of innovations. New products are often developed through an interactive dialogue with leading-edge users that goes far beyond, say, commissioning a structured consumer survey (see box).

Interactive Development

The dialogue between innovators and potential customers starts early in the development process, as I found in my previous research. One high-tech CEO I interviewed, Netuitive's Nick Sanna, said the company started with "very sophisticated algorithms. But turning breakthrough algorithms into a commercial product required a true partnership with customers.... They tested the product; they suggested extensions and validated the concepts. Step by step and incremental improvement after incremental improvement, we got to a solution that most of the market would want."

Aaref Hilaly of Clearwell Systems also described interaction with customers: "After we shipped the first version, we immediately got feedback on what was missing. We scrambled to put out a second version that included two key missing features. That was a very difficult release. But you only get your comments after someone has used a product, and by that time you are almost to the point where you need to be doing the release. It's a moving target for the engineering team."[3]

Dialogue with users usually doesn't stop even after a product is fully developed. As I have mentioned, all buyers, including those who aren't leading edge, face uncertainty about the value and risk of their purchases. And, although their "venturesomeness" plays an important role, buyers generally don't resolve uncertainty about a new product on their own. The seller has to help them along, not only by providing objective information, but also by clarifying inchoate anxieties, providing reassurance, and framing the product's benefits in an attractive way (see box).

More Than Puffery and Happy Talk

Bruce Singer, founder of RPM Rent-A-Car, who started selling used cars to pay for a JD/MBA program, describes how he learned about the value of persuasive conversations:

> When I started in the used car business, the Federal Trade Commission wanted to standardize used car dealers. I thought it was a neat idea—I would be the most honest used car dealer in the world. I would have an accurate description of each car in the windshield, and run a silent auction. It failed miserably! You need someone to make the sale. Cold facts by themselves are frightening if you just read them. Say you read on a form, "XYZ part may need to be replaced." You are scared away. But, if there is a salesman who points out that if you are a student who is only going to drive around campus for six months, and therefore you are unlikely to have to replace the part, you are going to feel more secure. Customers need a human being to decipher how certain facts fit their needs.[4]

With sophisticated products and customers, the process of reassurance can be much more protracted and labor intensive, not less. Sales and marketing is sometimes regarded almost as a parasitical function, but its professionalization has played a crucial role in the effective deployment of advanced technologies, without which these technologies would not have any economic value.[5] The sales process that was pioneered by IBM in the 1930s (when the company sold punch card–based tabulating equipment, not computers) could require salesmen to spend a year with customers before asking for an order. An IBM salesman was expected to learn "as much about the customer's business as the customer himself," according to historian Richard Tedlow. And because IBM relied heavily on testimonials, the sales staff not only had to sell equipment, but ensure it was effectively used. Salesmen couldn't be "knockers-on-doors"; they were "efficiency engineers."[6] The IBM process has evolved, but its core principle of deep engagement with customers remains, and has become a model for many high-tech companies.

Innovators also need to communicate with suppliers and producers of complementary goods to coordinate development plans. Apple's iPods and iPhones, for instance, combine hardware and software developed by many other technology companies: the CPU (the "brains") from ARM, hard drives from Hitachi and Seagate, flash memories from Toshiba and Samsung, and audio-codecs from Wolfson Electronics. In planning new versions of its product, Apple has to communicate with these suppliers to figure out what developments they have in the pipeline. As suppliers figure out new features for their products, they benefit from knowing Apple's wish list. Similarly, when Microsoft develops a new version of its Windows operating system, it consults closely with developers of applications software and keeps them apprised of its features and progress, so when it is released, improved and compatible applications are available right away.

Communication within organizations is notoriously unrelenting. Employees of organizations large and small complain about constantly attending meetings and answering the phone or emails instead of doing "real work." But contrary to appearances, this communication isn't all a waste of time. Meetings, memos, and emails exchange information and opinions, and coordinate the actions of different functions and individuals. Even gossiping in the corridors can serve a purpose. The value of such conversations is one reason that organizations are reluctant to outsource product development tasks and prefer to have teams—designers, engineers, marketers, and product managers—work in the same location.[7]

Persuasive dialogue is necessary not just for a salesperson trying to secure an order, or a subordinate selling an idea to a boss, but also for the effective exercise of authority by top management. Just issuing orders rarely works: Executives have to explain the reasons and address concerns to secure the commitment of subordinates. Alfred Sloan Jr., who created the modern General Motors after taking over the deeply troubled, debt-laden, and disorganized company in 1920, was "patient, persuasive and systematic."[8] Sloan wrote in his memoir that "an industrial organization is not the mildest form of organization in society" and that "there is a strong temptation for the leading officers to make decisions themselves without the sometimes onerous process of discussion, which involves selling your ideas to others." Sloan did not, in principle, discount his power as CEO, but he did exercise his power with discretion because he "got better results by selling my ideas than by telling people what to do."[9]

The costly and time-consuming nature of dialogue does encourage individuals and companies to cut it back. They may try to reduce the costs of labor-intensive, interactive sales by using one-way persuasion through advertizing in the mass media. New technologies—high-speed printing and radio and television in the twentieth century, and now Internet search engines—have facilitated the substitution. The need for extensive two-way communication naturally declines as products mature or activities become routinized. Buyers of personal computers, for example, are now comfortable making selections from a catalog or a website where they once would have required a conversation with a salesperson in a retail store.

But there is no evidence of an overall downward trend—the number of professional salespeople at work hasn't declined, for instance. One-way advertizing turns out to be well suited for a small number of goods, such as soap, cereal, and toothpaste. Even automobile companies that use advertizing to draw buyers into showrooms rely on salespeople to close the sale.[10] As some products get commoditized, new ones are introduced that require face-to-face selling: Many personal computer retailers have gone out of business, while Apple's retail stores do a brisk business selling iPods and iPhones. Nor has technology been a one-way street, as it were. Radio, TV, and cable are used mainly for one-way broadcasts but many technologies—telephones (first landlines, then cellular, and now peer-to-peer, such as Skype), faxes, email, video conferencing, and instant messaging—have created an explosion in two-way communication that is deeply woven into commercial and everyday life.

Relationships

A frequently cited advantage of a pithy price system is impersonality and anonymity. "When you buy your pencil or your daily bread," write the Friedmans, "you don't know whether the pencil was made or the wheat was grown by a white man or a black man, by a Chinese or an Indian." The thousands of people who cooperate to produce the pencil you buy "live in many lands, speak different languages, practice different religions [and] may even hate one another."[11] How can such ignorance in people, even animosity, deliver a pencil to a customer? Because "the *impersonal operation* of prices" brings their contributions together."[12]

In the real world, where commerce is hardly laconic, ongoing relationships complement extensive dialogue. An important benefit of continuing to do business with the same party is that it creates reusable knowledge that reduces the need to repeat conversations—talk isn't always cheap! Someone with allergies or finicky tastes may have to explain what food he wants at a restaurant, but by becoming a regular patron he saves himself that trouble—and the restaurant can count on a reliable customer to fill tables. Similarly, when a new employee joins an organization, she needs time to learn the ropes, through a formal training program, from colleagues as the occasion arises, or perhaps through trial and error. But once she has figured out how things work, she can reuse this knowledge—as long as she doesn't switch employers.

Knowledge accumulated through continued relationships can reduce misunderstandings and ambiguities that exist even in carefully negotiated contracts. No matter how much discussion takes place, gaps in agreements cannot be eliminated because words are never precise. What is a "best effort"? Diligence in the eyes of one party may be seen as sloppiness by another. Likewise, the same medium rare steak can be just right for one patron and overcooked for another. Learning by doing through repeated transactions helps the parties anticipate what each one means and expects.

Learning also helps make the adjustments necessary when things go wrong. A vendor may fail to make timely delivery, triggering the buyer's contractual right to cancel the purchase. Cancellation might be sensible if the delay is due to a design flaw that will take a long time to fix. But an extension would be in order if, as the seller claims, the problem lies in a temporary problem in the production line. The seller is likely to have more credibility if the buyer has found the seller reliable and truthful in the past. An ongoing relationship also smoothes over problems of recontracting because accounts can be left temporarily unbalanced: One party can make a concession under the understanding that it will be compensated for the next time around.

Ongoing relationships can help ameliorate problems of opportunism and fraud that cannot be fully covered by contract. If both parties are invested in a long-term relationship, they will avoid actions that end it. An employer will be reluctant to break an oral promise to pay a bonus to an employee if she pulls off a challenging project: The savings from that unpaid bonus could be wiped out by the costs of having to train a new employee. Moreover, the bad publicity and ill will generated by one opportunistic act can spill over into other relationships. An employer who reneges on a promised bonus not only risks losing that employee's services, but also the loss of other employees who fear they could be next. Ongoing relationships can create empathy and solidarity: We are likely to be kinder to people whom we know than to strangers.* (Regular patrons will give more generous tips to their regular waiters, because it is the human thing to do.)

Commercial relationships aren't permanent, however—they aren't like staying married, according to the old vow, "till death do us part." Rather, modern business ties, like modern marriages, have the presumption of continuity and a willingness to invest in the relationship, but not an absolute commitment to staying together. For instance, Apple's first Macintosh ("Mac") computer, launched in 1984, used microprocessors (the 68000 line) from Motorola, a company headquartered in Schaumburg, Illinois, rather than those developed by Intel, Apple's neighbor in Silicon Valley. The Apple-Motorola relationship continued for many years afterward. In 1994, Apple introduced Macs that used PowerPC microprocessors endorsed by the AIM alliance (Apple, IBM, and Motorola) formed to challenge the dominant "Wintel" (Windows + Intel) platform. The challenge ultimately failed, and in 2006 Apple switched to Intel microprocessors, ending a twenty-two-year relationship.[13] Similarly, although most labor isn't traded in a spot market (except for some kinds of manual services), ongoing employment isn't expected to be forever.

Nor does the value of ongoing relationships preclude forming new ones; if it did, start-ups could never get going. Indeed, the willingness to take a chance on a new business that offers an exciting new technology, based on a weak personal tie, or sometimes none at all, is a hallmark of business practice in an innovative economy. The feudalistic norm of excluding newcomers and sticking with existing relationships discourages enterprise. The preference for continuity merely means that parties who start as strangers often invest in building a relationship.

Finally, ongoing relationships aren't all sweetness and light. Unforeseen asymmetries in dependencies can develop that allow one party to dictate onerous terms—the "holdup" problem, as it is called in economics. In addition, the complacency that develops through a long relationship and the knowledge gained about vulnerabilities can be abused. Ongoing relations can lead to both "enormous trust and enormous

---

*In *The Theory of Moral Sentiments* Adam Smith (1808; first ed. 1759) argued, for instance, that "habitual sympathy" from constant contact creates strong family ties (cited by Kindleberger 1996, 15).

malfeasance," as Granovetter has pointed out. Infidelity and discord are as old as the institution of marriage. And there is no simple or mechanistic way to forestall holdups or malfeasance, just as there is no formula to prevent unhappy marriages. As in most aspects of business—and life— realizing the benefits of a long-term relationship while minimizing the risks and costs requires skill, good judgment, and some luck.

Concluding Comments

We started chapter 2 by recapitulating Hayek's argument that the price system and the decentralization of decision making enable rapid adaptation. The argument is quite general, applying to all nonstatic economies (i.e., ones subject to change), and does not focus on nurturing innovation. Such nurturing requires, I have argued, not just adaptation (which can be mechanistic) but also judgments that incorporate an individual's imagination and on-the-spot knowledge. In chapter 2 and this chapter, we considered whether prices alone are sufficient to coordinate individual judgments about innovative activities (as distinguished from adaptive responses to repeated patterns). In chapter 2, I argued that partial centralization, through organizations that delegate some but not all decisions to individuals, plays a valuable role—provided good judgment is exercised in the construction of the organizations. In this chapter, we have seen the important role of dialogue and relationships in coordinating innovative activity.[14]

With these ideas about the real economy in mind, we can turn to an analysis of the financial system. As we will see in the next chapter, a good financial system mirrors the features we have just discussed, both in how it interacts with individuals and businesses in the "real" economy (i.e., in the nonfinancial sectors) and in how financial firms are organized and managed.

Chapter 4

Reflections in the Financial Mirror

Financial institutions perform a wide range of functions and serve many kinds of customers. For convenience of exposition, however, I will focus on two emblematic financing activities: venture capital (VC) investments in new and start-up businesses, and the classical lending activities of a bank. The specific practices vary because of differences between the risks and returns of VCs and banks. Nonetheless, as we will see in this chapter, both types of institution incorporate subjective judgment, partially decentralized organization, dialogue, and ongoing relationships. A look at VCs and at bank lenders will help us understand why effective halfway houses of partial centralization tend to be more compact in finance than in many sectors of the real economy. Finally, we will look at the special—and important—case of life insurance: Its distinctive features will put in relief the nature of a good financial system.*

---

*Financial institutions also offer services such as check clearing and bill payments that do not involve credit or investment risks. Such activities are excluded from my analysis.

▨ VC Investing

The need for on-the-spot judgments by VCs derives from the nature of the innovative process that generates requests for funds. Consider how entrepreneurs conceive of the business propositions for which they solicit funding. In a decentralized system many individuals observe the same facts—the growing popularity of the iPhone or Facebook, for example—and several may think of similar ways to take advantage of these facts.* Of these individuals, some will choose to proceed and others, upon reflection, will choose not to. As no one is omniscient, either could be "right": Those who proceed may be overestimating their prospects, whereas those who don't may be underestimating them.

The VCs from whom entrepreneurs solicit funds, like the entrepreneurs themselves, therefore face a problem sometimes called the "winner's curse": Funding requests will, on average, be made by entrepreneurs who overestimated the prospects. Blindly backing all requests will not produce attractive returns to investors But, rejecting all requests means exiting the VC business. The challenge for the VC lies in selecting investments where the naysayers who did not proceed were likely to have been wrong or where there is an opportunity to produce an attractive return—even if the prospects have been overestimated by the entrepreneur because a less smashing success is good enough for the VC.

Thus, a big challenge for potential investors lies in catching honest mistakes in the judgments of entrepreneurs. Venture capitalists naturally expect serious applicants to have extensive knowledge of specific circumstances. But even well-informed entrepreneurs can have blind spots or gaps in their knowledge. These gaps, in conjunction with "known unknowns" (such as whether the technology can be scaled up) mean that the true prospects may be worse than the entrepreneur believes them to be. Assessing this likelihood—second-guessing entrepreneurs'

*The tale of how a January 1975 issue of *Popular Electronics* featuring the Altair 8080, the first personal computer, led Paul Allen and Bill Gates to start Microsoft has often been told. Allen saw the issue at a kiosk in Harvard Square, raced to his friend Gates's dormitory room (Gates was then a sophomore at Harvard), and told him, "Well here's our opportunity to do something with BASIC"—a popular programming language the two had worked with in high school (Wallace and Erickson 1993, 67). The two then worked nonstop for a month until they had written a version of BASIC for the Altair. What is not so well known is that nearly 50 other programmers were independently doing the same thing at about the same time (Wallace and Erickson 1993, 74).

judgments about their technologies, markets, and managerial capabilities—represents a difficult and time-consuming task. How well VCs make this assessment plays a significant role in the returns they earn. The problems of information asymmetries and misaligned incentives that arise in deciding whether to invest can be dealt with in a fairly routine way (see box).

Asymmetries and Incentives

Economists who study venture capital often focus on second-order problems of controlling information asymmetries and entrepreneurs' pursuit of "private benefits." In reality, whereas an unscrupulous dealer in secondhand cars may try to palm off a lemon as a good car, VCs face the more vexing issue of entrepreneurs who want to raise funding for a venture they sincerely and sometimes mistakenly believe is a sweet, succulent grapefruit. Similarly, many scholarly papers on VC attack the problem of entrepreneurs who knowingly solicit funds for bad ideas because of some "private benefit" (such as an emotional high) that they, but not their investors, will receive from undertaking the project. But in the real world, such "incentive misalignment" problems are easily controlled by ensuring that entrepreneurs have skin in the game by requiring they invest their personal wealth—including borrowing against their homes. Besides, VCs want entrepreneurs to have passion for their enterprise, so that when obstacles arise they will have the fortitude to confront them. In other words, some supposedly private benefits boost the likelihood of success.

Nor are the trendy concerns of behavioral economists—the cognitive biases and "overconfidence" of entrepreneurs—the main issue. It's true that entrepreneurs are optimists, especially about their capacity to deal with unforeseen problems. Without such a disposition, they would never get going, because a new enterprise will predictably throw up unforeseeable problems. But there is no evidence that entrepreneurs irrationally overrate their prospects or ignore information available to them. In fact, to the degree that a product is innovative—that is, novel and unlike what has been done in the past—it is impossible to conceive of an objective estimate of success. Against what rational benchmark, then, can we call an entrepreneur overconfident? This is not to say that entrepreneurs never have a reckless streak or a tendency to duck inconvenient facts. But such tendencies can be controlled by reference checks and by investing in founding teams with tried and tested individuals at the helm.

The VC's on-the-spot knowledge and subjective judgment play an important role. Individual venture capitalists often specialize in deals where they have prior experience and knowledge. Different VCs focus on different fields: biotech, telecom, semiconductors, software, or retail.

This specialization gives them the capacity both to understand the information provided by the entrepreneur and to identify and fill in blind spots. Although the entrepreneur and the VC operate in roughly the same category, and have a common vocabulary and knowledge of the field that facilitates conversation about the issues, their knowledge isn't the same. For instance, an entrepreneur developing specialized semiconductors for netbooks may have deeper knowledge about customers' requirements and about engineering problems; but the VC, who sees many kinds of semiconductor deals, has broader knowledge, and may be able to identify pitfalls that the entrepreneur is unaware of. VCs usually have a stable of industry experts with whom they can consult to get an even fuller picture of the pros and cons.

VCs often follow a structure and routine for making investment judgments. For example, many VC firms use a standard set of categories for collecting and cataloging information. One firm's "Investment Memorandum" starts with a summary (location, industry, number of employees, stage of the venture's development, deal amount, and so on) and has sections titled "Company Overview," "Product/Service Description," "Market Overview," "Competition," and "Management Team." These categories can help ensure that all bases are covered and provide a framework for a discussion about the merits of the investment. But checklists, however detailed, are not like quantitative models that provide an unambiguous answer. Venture capitalists' assessments of entrepreneurs' assessments are ultimately subjective.

A decentralized process that gives individual VCs considerable autonomy helps them make "on-the-spot" judgments. Although VCs organize themselves as limited partnerships that raise money from outside investors, those investors have no say in specific transactions—decisions are left entirely to the individuals who control the partnership. The VC partners divide up responsibilities among themselves according to their fields of expertise. Individual partners offer each other advice on their deals (further reducing the scope for blind spots), and the partnership as a whole ratifies investment proposals brought forward by an individual. But as long as a partner can make a persuasive case, proposals are ratified. This process conforms to the Hayekian idea about the benefits of autonomy: A more centralized procedure would be unable to digest quickly the mass of information that VCs must rapidly act on.

Dialogue plays a vital role. Just as an applicant for a research grant submits a written proposal, entrepreneurs may submit a business plan—but what happens afterward is quite different. A grant proposal is sent to anonymous reviewers who have no direct contact with the applicant. In contrast, business plans are just a "calling card," as one venture capitalist put it. The real information-gathering takes place in presentations and meetings. VCs learn about the business proposition and technology, and whether there is likely to be a good fit with the personalities and goals of the founders. Conversely, when founders can choose which VCs to raise money from, the meetings provide an opportunity to assess which one will best help them build their business. Due diligence requires VCs also have extensive conversations with target customers, industry experts, and the references provided by founders.

Investing also relies heavily on relationships. Venture capitalists prefer to back entrepreneurs with whom they have invested in the past; failing that or some other prior direct connection, an indirect connection—knowing someone who knows the VC—may be a must. As one investor says: "I know every important executive, scientist, and consultant in my space. If an entrepreneur can't get an introduction through someone in my network, he isn't credible or isn't trying." Furthermore, the initial connection is just the beginning of an ongoing relationship that evolves through the process of mutual courtship and the continued participation of the VC in the governance of the enterprise.

Ongoing relationships are especially valuable when, as is almost invariably the case, things don't go according to plan—unexpected technical problems arise, customer orders don't materialize, the funds start to run out. At that point, the investor has to make a judgment: Is there a fatal flaw in the business model or technology? Is the entrepreneur incapable? Or is it just a bump in the road that can be rolled over with more time and money? Such judgments are more reliable if based on learning accumulated through prior interactions.

Classical Bank Lending

Extending credit through old-fashioned bank loans provides another example of the real-world innovation game reflected in financial practice. The example is salient because bank lending and venture capital are bookends on the risk-return shelf. A top-tier venture capital fund usually invests in fewer than twenty businesses a year. The overall return depends on an even smaller number of big winners: One study of venture capital portfolios by Venture Economics reported that about 7 percent of investments accounted for more than 60 percent of the profits, while fully one-third resulted in a partial or total loss. In contrast, banks cannot afford many bad loans: A good loan provides a small gross spread—the difference between the interest a bank receives from a loan and what it must pay its depositors for the funds is a few percentage points a year. A bad loan can result in a total loss, however, thus erasing the profit from many good loans.

As we will see next, however, banks' lending practices also exemplify the dovetailing of the decentralization that sustains innovation with the decentralization in finance.*

Like VCs, banks face problems of misrepresentation and misaligned incentives with borrowers, perhaps to an even greater degree, for the universe of potentially credible borrowers is much larger. A single small bank may make more loans than the number of new businesses funded by the entire VC industry in the United States. Moreover, whereas VCs and company founders are roughly in the same boat—they prosper if the business does well and lose if it fails—with a loan the business owner keeps all of the upside. Thus, there is a stronger temptation to roll the dice with the bank's money. To protect against such eventualities, banks undertake credit and reference checks and demand contractual safeguards: Loans are secured by collateral whose value exceeds the amount of the loan; loan agreements have covenants to limit borrowers from rolling the dice; and, business owners are routinely asked to provide personal guarantees, effectively erasing the "limited liability" of an incorporated business.

All this, however, does not address the problem of honest mistakes—business owners may confidently sign a personal guarantee without knowing that a competitor with a superior technology is about to enter the market, or that a jump in oil prices is going to sharply reduce demand. Similarly, banks are also exposed to misestimates by business owners of their own resoluteness: When things go really wrong, despair may cause a good and capable owner to "give bankers back the keys," whatever the personal financial consequences may be. And while the

---

*To make the illustration concrete, I will focus on lending to small businesses, although the general principles extend to other kinds of traditional bank credit as well.

bank's loan may be fully collateralized on paper, managing a troubled business as it is wound down does not appeal to many bankers.

Bankers therefore put in a considerable effort to assess the judgments inherent in a loan application, not just the honesty of the borrower. The procedures are usually well structured and incorporate considerable data gathering and analysis. As with VC investing, however, subjective on-the-spot judgments of the banker are unavoidable and are, in fact, at the heart of the credit extension process (see box). (The degree to which a loan is based on judgment rather than mechanistic formulas does vary with the circumstances. Working capital loans to long-standing customers, for instance, are made largely on the basis of standardized ratios.)

Procedures for Extending Bank Credit

The process usually starts with a formal request from the borrower for a loan, although if the amount is small and well secured or the borrower's relationship with a bank is really solid, an oral request may suffice. In many banks, the banker may have to write her own loan application to go with the borrower's request.[1] Common elements include the following:

- overview of loan
- company funding requirements
- company background
- industry background
- risk analysis
- management background
- financial analysis: industry comparisons; historical and projected performance
- bank relationships

Once the requests and applications are submitted, procedures vary widely, but some version of the following is common: (1) A credit analyst analyzes the loan application, (2) the loan application and analyst's report are reviewed by a loan committee, (3) the banker returns to the applicant with a term sheet[2] outlining the terms and conditions of the proposed loan.

Bankers and loan committees often use the "five C's of credit analysis"—the character, capacity, capital, collateral, and coverage of potential borrowers—to evaluate a borrower's creditworthiness.

Character determines if a small business loan will be approved, for many bankers. The potential troubles involved in dealing with questionable characters—noncooperation with the bank, fraud, litigation, and write-offs—are a significant deterrent. The time, legal expense, and opportunity costs incurred because of a problem loan far outweigh the potential interest income derived.

(This factor, however, is less important with larger companies managed by a team of individuals.)

Capacity refers to the borrower's ability to operate the business and successfully repay the loan. An assessment of capacity is based on management experience, historical financial statements, products, markets, operations, and competitive position.

Capital structure with sufficient equity protects a bank's exposure. Bankers also view equity as an indication of the borrower's commitment and derive comfort from knowing that the borrower has much to lose if the business goes belly-up.

Collateral is the bank's claim on the borrower's assets in case the business defaults on the loan or files bankruptcy. The bank's secured interest generally gives it priority over other creditors in claiming proceeds from liquidated assets and provides an alternative source of repayment beyond cash flow. The bank may also require the borrower to pledge as collateral personal assets outside of the business.

Coverage refers simply to business insurance, or "key man" insurance, that is often required when management ability is concentrated in a few individuals. In the event of the death or disability of a key manager, such coverage ensures that the bank will be repaid if the business cannot meet its obligations.

Credit analysis is how the banker learns about the "five C's of credit."

The first step with a new borrower often involves assessing character. The lender will seek reference checks from individuals and organizations with which the borrower has had working relationships in the past. Data may be sought from credit files and personnel within the bank, lending officers at other banks, national credit agencies, suppliers, customers, competitors, former employers, colleagues and informal information networks.

The banker's intuition plays an important role. Most believe they have developed an ability to judge character through years of lending experience. Lenders often refer to the borrower's mannerisms, presentation skills, and "story" as telltale indicators of character.

The other elements of credit analysis are more systematic, although the banker's judgment remains an important component.

Capital structure is reviewed through an audited balance sheet, and insurance coverage is readily verifiable through the documentation. An analysis of collateral is conducted firsthand by the bank, independent auditors, or commercial appraisers of plant, equipment, or real estate.

Assessing the capacity—the firm's ability to prosper while meeting its loan commitments—is the most difficult challenge. Banks rely on a mix of quantitative and qualitative analyses. Spreadsheet analysis of up to five years of audited financial statements is conducted to identify historical trends that affect future operations. Key business ratios are analyzed to assess the historical profitability, efficiency, and solvency of the business and to compare the data with industry norms. The bank will then evaluate pro forma financial statements that depict the company's projected operations over the course of the loan based on established patterns and assumptions. Although each bank performs financial analysis in a unique manner with attention to specific parameters, the process is generally the same from bank to bank.

To supplement the quantitative analysis, bankers like to assess the company's operations and managers firsthand. By meeting with the managers, they are better able to predict growth rates, profit margins, depreciation schedules, and capital expenditures that are the key assumptions in projected financial statements. To make such assumptions, bankers must understand the firm's products, markets, operations, and competitive environment. They also form a more accurate estimate of the quality of the borrower's plant and equipment, the efficiency of the production process, and the nature of the workforce. Most important, they have the opportunity to evaluate the management team's experience and competence to run the business. It is this on-site analysis that allows bankers to gauge more accurately a lending opportunity beyond the financial statements.

Adapted from Bhidé, Stevenson, and Bilden 1990.

An extensive dialogue between bank and borrower is obviously integral to the process that I have described. Relationships that often start before a loan application is made also play an important role (see box).

How New Businesses Cultivate Banking Relationships

New businesses are rarely creditworthy at the outset: Banks usually don't lend to fund operating losses, R&D expenses, marketing campaigns, and the like; such needs have to be filled by equity financing. Banks are also reluctant to lend against a small firm's cash flows. The borrowing capacity of a fledgling enterprise is limited to the assets it can pledge as collateral. Furthermore, a bank is unlikely to accept as collateral all the assets on the balance sheet. A bank is unlikely to lend against specialized machinery that cannot be easily liquidated, an inventory of dresses that might go out of fashion or receivables due from shaky customers.

Nevertheless, my prior field research suggests, it is useful for entrepreneurs to cultivate a banker early, well in advance of an actual loan request. "Smaller, entrepreneurial companies" one banker said, "do not lend themselves to the same degree of factual analysis as the larger corporate clients, where a stream of data is available. A small business loan is unavoidably a bit like a personal loan to an entrepreneur. Trust is very important, and the only way you build this trust is to observe the entrepreneur in action over many years." All other things being equal, therefore, a known entrepreneur is more likely to get a loan and under less restrictive conditions than someone who has just walked in off the street. In fact, many bankers would regard an urgent request for a loan by a stranger as a "red flag" requiring caution.

Entrepreneurs said they found many ways to establish a relationship with banks they wanted to cultivate before they asked for money. They opened checking accounts and used the bank's cash management or foreign exchange services. This not only allowed bankers to get to know them better, but it helped create a sense of obligation because checking accounts and cash management fees are a source of low-risk profit for banks. And, as the relationship grew, they took the initiative to educate their bankers about their business, keeping them informed about important developments and encouraging visits.

Adapted from Bhidé, Stevenson, and Bilden 1990 and Bhidé 1992.

Relationships have value even after a loan is extended. Ongoing visits and reviews provide early warning signals to the banker—and may generate valuable advice for the business owner—before there is any explicit violation of the loan agreement. If the business grows faster than expected, the banker can move quickly to expand the size of the loan or modify its terms. Conversely, if the business runs into trouble and cannot meet its payments or satisfy all the loan covenants, the banker is better positioned to make a judgment—and it is a judgment rather than a preordained choice—about what to do: require the business to stick to the letter of the agreement, show forbearance, renegotiate terms, or, if the terms permit, call the loan. A lending officer walking in from the cold would lack the "knowledge of the specific circumstances," or even the confidence, to deviate from the contractual terms.

Halfway Houses

As with "real economy" businesses, there are advantages to agglomerating the activities of individual VCs and bankers into an organization—the limited partnership or bank. The most obvious of these advantages is in gathering funds. Financiers serve as intermediaries: VCs invest money raised from their limited partners, and bankers lend depositors' funds. The fixed costs of gathering the funds from many individuals and institutions, providing reports, and managing disbursements, make it prohibitive for individuals VCs and bankers to operate on their own. Investors are also reluctant to entrust funds to an individual financier who could be hit by the proverbial bus—or by reckless impulse. Banding together also helps VCs and bankers share information and get second opinions on their judgments. Economies of scale in the "back office" and other operational activities (such as generating periodic reports and handling disbursements) also benefit joint operations.

Forming organizations, in turn, limits the autonomy of individual financiers. When investors entrust their money to a VC, or depositors place funds with a bank, they expect a process that is to some degree centralized to oversee the activities of individual VCs and bankers. Typically the process entails ratification of individual judgments: VCs vote on each other's deals, and a banker's loan recommendations are vetted by loan committees. But the primary evaluation and structuring of deals isn't highly centralized. Thus, even though an organization makes the investments or loan, the individual financier's on-the-spot knowledge is put to its best possible use.

Beyond a point, however, the costs of managing large organizations outweigh the benefits—and that point is reached much sooner with finance than in many "real economy" industries. One important reason is that financiers have to make judgments about individual deals or loans, rather than about a large class of nearly identical situations or a high-volume process. As an analogy, think of the difference between the high-volume production of commodity semiconductors and making small lots of customized chips in a silicon "foundry." In both cases, judgment is necessary, for semiconductor manufacturing remains a black art. But in the former case, because all outputs and inputs are nearly identical, a single skilled operator's judgment can be used to produce a huge number of semiconductors, whereas making customized chips requires the judgments of many operators of many foundries.

Investing in start-ups or making loans is like producing customized semiconductors: VCs and bankers have to make judgments on a case-by-case basis, taking into account the individual circumstances. Technology—spreadsheets, email, online databases—may help an individual to make more judgments or manage more relationships. To a degree, this can increase centralization because the same amount of funds can be disbursed through fewer financiers. But because individual financing decisions cannot be lumped together, and relationships are necessarily one-at-a-time, improvements in the speed and accuracy of an individual's case-by-case judgments through the application of technology does not produce significant economies of scale and centralization. Since VCs have nurtured businesses that have made huge advances in information technology in the last few decades, they ought to be on top of opportunities to use IT to increase their own productivity. Nonetheless, the number of deals individual venture capitalists make, and the number of portfolio companies for which they serve on the boards of directors, has not changed much.

The distinctive problems of managing individual financiers also limit consolidation of finance into a few organizations. In industrial firms, bosses usually don't have to go too deeply into *how* subordinates make judgments. For example, the boss of the operator of a semiconductor plant doesn't have to delve into how the operator tweaks the dials; rather, the boss and operator negotiate objectives on what the production yield should be, perhaps by considering the historical performance of the plant and by benchmarking with other plants. The boss digs deeper only if the number of defective chips falls outside an acceptable range. Consequently, a boss can manage a relatively large number of operators who may, in turn, manage different types of plants.

In finance, because it can take many years to identify good output, this kind of management by objectives (MBO) and management by exception (MBE) is infeasible and possibly dangerous. Setting a quota of loans a banker must make encourages imprudent lending and waiting for widespread loan losses before intervening isn't sensible. Rather, managing a banker requires a laborious second-guessing of judgment, including a review of the facts and reasoning. This labor-intensive oversight, in turn, limits the number of financiers a boss can manage. And because bosses need to have a fairly detailed grasp of the judgments their subordinates make, the range of activities bosses can manage is also narrow. In other words, the cognitive limits of managers tightly restrict the scale and scope of healthy financial organizations.

Big Deal Trade-offs

There may be large projects where relationship-based finance does not work, such as building railroads and 3G wireless networks. A single financial institution won't have enough funds, and syndicates composed of many institutions will find it difficult to maintain a meaningful ongoing relationship with the enterprise receiving the funds. If funds are raised by selling small interests to the public at large, ongoing relationships are virtually impossible. The most investors can expect is periodic reports and votes on major decisions. Nonetheless, the gains from large projects due to, say, economies of scale may make it worthwhile to forgo the flexibility, understanding, and other advantages of close relationships.

In these cases, the limitations of arm's-length financing can be contained by due diligence and the clear specification of terms at the outset. Clear specification, in turn, means financing through debt rather than equity. A bond contract more or less precisely lays out the obligations of the borrower and the consequences of a default. A company's obligations to stockholders are necessarily broad. This is why historically railroads issued bonds to the public at large, whereas their equity was concentrated in the hands of a few active investors who provided close oversight and in some cases operating control.

In addition, when the immaturity of technologies or business models makes cash flows highly uncertain, debt financing is difficult to obtain. In such cases, entrepreneurs have usually had to temporarily forgo the advantages of scale and rely on capital provided by a small number of venture capitalists, wealthy individuals, or their own funds, until the major uncertainties were resolved. These historical patterns have been broken in the last few decades as the ownership of stocks, including those of highly immature companies, became widely diffused, whereas in the past the dispersed ownership of securities was usually limited to well-secured bonds of companies with predictable cash flows. In chapter 8, I will argue that this change is the unintended consequence of securities laws, not the result of the economic advantages of arm's-length equity financing.

We should also distinguish between arm's-length borrowing for large and truly indivisible projects such railroads and wireless networks, and large debt issues created by bundling small loans, such as mortgages and car loans, that could be made and held by a single bank. The economies of scale expected in this kind of "securitized" debt lie with the financier rather than with the borrower's technology or business. Supposedly, credit is more effectively extended through a centralized mass-production process than through the laborious case-by-case judgments of many lending officers. In other words, such synthetically large financing is both arm's length and robotic. Its growth over the last twenty or so years, as I will argue in chapter 13, is the result of regulatory changes, not an outcome of true advances in the automation of credit decisions.

The Life Insurance Exception

Life insurance stands in sharp contrast to VC and classical bank-lending in being centralized, robotic, and arms length, even for small transactions. But this is an exception whose special characteristics highlight the normal financial rule. Insurance companies employ a large cadre of frontline agents, yet, unlike VCs and bankers, these agents don't make subjective assessments of risk. Rather they are responsible for sales and personalized marketing: understanding their clients' needs, helping them select a policy, and then persuading them to write a check. Agents are now being replaced by websites; but, even before that, buying insurance through an employer only required checking a box in a benefits form.

The menu of policies and rates is set by centralized underwriting teams using quantitative models (actuarial tables) that don't require subjective judgment. The premium an individual pays depends on a relatively small number of objective risk-factors—age, gender, smoking habits, and so on. Insurance companies also protect themselves against adverse selection—the eagerness of individuals who expect to die soon to buy insurance—through stipulations in the insurance policies and medical exams.

No dialogue between underwriting teams and the person buying insurance takes place. As long as customers send in their premiums regularly, they don't need to have any contact, much less a meaningful relationship, with their insurance company.

There are significant advantages to large-scale operation in life insurance. Writing a large number of policies is necessary to diversify risk: Bad luck (or a few cases of adverse selection and fraud) could wipe out a company that insured a small number of lives. Standardization of policies and payment plans also creates economies of scale in data and payment processing. And because agents are not responsible for making risky judgments, they can be managed by numbers and quotas. So the managerial limits to growth are not as stringent as in bank lending.

Why not apply this objective, model-based, arm's-length approach of modern life insurance to all finance? As it happens, life insurance isn't exempt from the unavoidable pitfalls of predictive statistical modeling discussed in chapter 1. Inevitably, because the true models are unknowable and likely different for different individuals, actuarial tables will generate rates that are too low for some individuals and too high for others. But life insurance also has distinctive features that aren't found in other financial sectors that limit the problems of using quantitative models without sacrificing the benefits.

For starters, life insurance companies are not exposed to the misjudgments of their clients in the way that providers of debt and equity finance are exposed. Founders of start-ups that overestimate their prospects hurt their VCs, and borrowers who overestimate their capacity to repay hurt their lenders.* But people who buy too much or too little life insurance don't hurt their insurer. And if they can't pay their premiums, the insurance company merely cancels their policy. So the models of insurance companies don't have to second-guess anyone else's judgments.

Moreover, life insurance companies face more or less stable risks. The constant ebb and flow of the innovation game has little effect on the probability of someone dying. This is not the case with the risks of making equity or debt investments. Activities such as mortgage lending, which may seem shielded from the turbulence of innovation, are, in fact, heavily exposed. A sound mortgage loan in Detroit may turn sour because Japanese competitors figure out how to make better cars than GM, Ford, and Chrysler,† just as a dicey mortgage in East Palo Alto may become sound because of the booming fortunes of Silicon Valley companies. The mortgage of a pilot making $300,000 a year can become impaired because of the growth of no-frills airlines. Thus, models based on historic patterns cannot predict default rates with great accuracy.

Pricing and underwriting policies don't change the risks of life insurance. Charging lower premiums or offering more coverage usually does not make customers do things that will increase their chances of dying:

---

*The robotic model of finance can be used to extend credit that is extremely well secured, to the point where the loan is practically riskless, for example, in making margin loans against liquid stocks that are held as collateral by the lender. Such situations are not common, however. Competition between lenders willing to accept less collateral than their rivals—unless, as in the case of margin lending, or once upon a time, mortgage lending, restrained by regulation—is one important reason why.

†In October 2009, the average price of a home in Detroit had fallen to $15,000 from almost $98,000 in 2003 (*Economist,* December 19, 2009, 55).

Adverse selection is a greater issue in life insurance than the "moral hazard" problem of inducing risky behavior. In contrast, offering consumers more credit or lower rates can make them more reckless. In addition, as with the use of sabermetric *Moneyball* strategies in baseball, the successful use of credit-scoring models may be self-limiting. A model based on historical data that initially works better than subjective estimates may fail as competitors' use of the model changes borrowers' behavior.

The relative stability of the underlying risks protects life insurance companies against the inevitable errors of statistical modeling. Yes, actuarial tables over- and underestimate the longevity of particular individuals. But these errors aren't large or obvious to the prospective purchasers of insurance—they arise because no one can know the "right" model. Therefore, there is no reason for individuals whose premiums are too high (compared to an unknowable, true value) to avoid buying insurance. From the point of view of the insurance company, overcharging some buyers offsets undercharging others. Moreover, as long as the insurance company continues to sell insurance to the same kinds of customers using the same model, the offsetting of mistakes can continue year in and year out even if the insurer has no clue that its model is wrong.

The apple cart could be upset, of course, if insurers kept adjusting their models. For instance, if a few insurers start offering discounts to people who drink red wine, they will attract more red-wine drinkers—and alter the distribution of their competitors' customers and their aggregate risks. As it happens, though, a tradition of conservatism, actuarial training, and practices that are industry-wide rather than company-specific, along with tight regulation, has led insurance companies to use more or less the same models and to avoid changing their variables much.

Concluding Comments

Good financial practices should reflect the innovative game played in the real economy. Thus, the decentralized, subjective choices of venturesome developers and consumers of innovations call for decentralized, subjective judgments of their funding requests. To put it differently, financiers should play the role of English teachers helping to improve their students' essays, not of math teachers grading algebra tests, much less an automated SAT scoring machine. Moreover, forward-looking, case-by-case judgments by financiers are necessary throughout the economy. Like it or not, in a dynamic world the baker must remain ever alert to changes in technologies and tastes, and so must the baker's banker. Sensible home-buyers don't bid for properties without carefully analyzing the local market and their personal circumstances. Nor should their mortgage lender.

In fact, judgment is so central to its function that finance ought to amplify the features of the real economy we discussed in earlier chapters. We ought to see more decentralization and autonomy for individual financiers, and more of their time spent in conversations and building relationships. Financial firms ought to be smaller and less diversified than giant industrial corporations.

This sketch of what finance ought to be like remains an accurate portrayal of some sectors: venture capital and small and midsized commercial banks that focus on relationship lending. But, as I pointed out in the introduction, that's not where most of the growth in financing activity has occurred. In the last several decades, finance has become increasingly centralized, mechanistic, and arm's length. The capital invested by venture capitalists is tiny in proportion to the equity raised in public markets where stockholders fund companies "by the numbers," without on-the-spot evaluations or much dialogue with managers, and without ongoing relationships. Similarly, relationship lending has been displaced by arm's-length securitized credit, and the judgments of frontline loan officers have been replaced by centralized credit-scoring models. Like a central planner, these models have to abstract away from critical differences in "circumstances of time and place," to use Hayek's words. The displacement has occurred not through bonds issued to finance large projects (where securitization has always had some advantages over relationship-based loans) but mainly through the bundling of credit robotically extended to individuals and small borrowers.

In the next part of the book we will see how this circumstance came to pass.

WHY IT BECAME SO

"Absent fiat, the form of organization that survives in an activity is the one that delivers the product demanded by customers at the lowest price covering costs," wrote Eugene Fama and Michael Jensen in 1983.[1] This is a good rule of thumb, but stopping there can lead to Dr. Pangloss's view "that things cannot be otherwise than as they are; for as all things have been created for some end, they must necessarily be created for the best end . . . [T]he nose is formed for spectacles, therefore we wear spectacles. The legs are visibly designed for stockings, accordingly we wear stockings."

The principle that whatever survives must be for good reason, cannot be applied blindly to evaluate changes in a dynamic economy. Innovations—including those of organizational form—are often in play, and bad ones do not disappear immediately. The possibility is especially great when successful innovations, which are well suited for some narrow purposes, are extended broadly to inappropriate domains. And fiat is never ever fully absent in a modern economy, so we have to make a judgment about the extent to which the growth of an organizational form is the result of its natural superiority or the result of something else, such as a law or rule.

Among insiders, the dominant interpretation of the transformation of the financial system is that it was indeed for the best. The wholesale replacement of relationship-based finance by arm's-length securities was taken as proof of the superiority of securitization. The progressive consolidation of specialized financial firms into a few megabanks was extolled on the grounds that it helped realize economies of scale and scope. And the unprecedented mass production of new financial products and strategies was celebrated for reducing costs of capital and distributing risks into the hands of those best able to bear them.

Although the financial collapse in 2008 raises huge questions about the Panglossian view of modern finance, it alone does not prove the structure of finance was comprehensively wrong. The debacle could have been a freakish accident or the result of a weak link (regulation that failed to keep up is now a leading candidate) that can be repaired.

I have already laid out half of the argument that modern finance is deeply flawed because it conflicts with a decentralized, innovative real economy. But this is not enough. Why did bad finance become so dominant? What sustained its growth over so many decades?

To answer that question, I next trace the growth of centralized finance to two independent but often mutually reinforcing trends. One was a transformation of the theory of finance that provided technologies which seemed to dispense with the need for laborious, case-by-case financial judgment, just as the development of actuarial science had previously done in life insurance. The other was a subtle form of "fiat": changes in securities and banking laws that allowed the new technologies to proliferate even though that was not the primary aim of the changes.

Chapter 5

All-Knowing Beings

In a provocative article in the *New York Times* magazine, Paul Krugman, Nobel laureate in economics and celebrated columnist, combines a strong defense of Keynesian theories about fiscal stimulus with an attack on the methodology of modern economics. The economics profession has gone astray, he writes, "because economists, as a group, mistook beauty, clad in impressive-looking mathematics, for truth." The driver of the profession's failure "was the desire for an all-encompassing, intellectually elegant approach that also gave economists a chance to show off their mathematical prowess."[1]

Krugman's "Luddite attack on mathematics" is countered by John Cochrane of the University of Chicago, who argues that it offers "an incoherent vision for the future of economics": "I'm old enough to remember when Krugman was young, working out the interactions of game theory and increasing returns in international trade for which he won the Nobel Prize, and the old guard tut-tutted 'nice recreational mathematics, but not real-world at all.' He once wrote eloquently about how only math keeps your ideas straight in economics. How quickly time passes." What is the alternative, Cochrane asks? "Does Krugman really think we can make progress on his—and my—agenda for economic and financial research—understanding frictions, imperfect markets, complex human behavior, institutional rigidities—by reverting to a literary style of exposition, and abandoning the attempt to compare theories quantitatively against data? Against the worldwide tide of quantification in all fields of human endeavor (read 'Moneyball') is there any real hope that this will work in economics?"

The problem, according to Cochrane, is that we don't have enough math. "Math in economics serves to keep the logic straight, to make sure that the 'then' really does follow the 'if,' which it so frequently does not if you just write prose. The challenge is how hard it is to write down explicit artificial economies with these ingredients, actually solve them, in order to see what makes them tick." Krugman's article, he continues, proposes "a nonsensical future for economics" that only makes sense "if you don't regard economics as a science...a discipline that requires crystal-clear logical connections between the 'if' and the 'then.'"[2]

My analysis lines up with Krugman's methodological concerns.[3] Contrary to Cochrane's suggestion, the statistical decision-making of *Moneyball* is like a small planet at the periphery of the economic universe. If we believe in Hayek's analysis of a good economy (which Cochrane cites approvingly), that is where it will remain. Nor are mathematical formulations of logical propositions always the best. It is not clear that the legal arguments Supreme Court justices hear, and the opinions they write, are fuzzier or less logical than the discourse of economists or that the reasoning of the Court would improve by abandoning words in favor of math.

Crystal-clear logical connections between the "if" and the "then" are, of course, desirable, but we cannot neglect the choice of the "ifs." Picking "ifs" because they are best suited to mathematical modeling can be a recipe for great mischief.

In this chapter, I argue that the pursuit of mathematical representation has led to assumptions about how individuals cope with the unpredictable consequences of their choices that contradict crucial features of a decentralized economy. In the two chapters that follow, we will see how models based on far-fetched assumptions have fostered robotic, centralized, arm's-length—and dangerous—practices in the real world of finance.

▰▰▰ Risk versus Uncertainty

"The ability to define what may happen in the future and to choose among alternatives lies at the heart of contemporary societies," writes

Peter Bernstein in the introduction to his lively and engaging book *Against the Gods*. "The revolutionary idea that defines the boundary between modern times and the past is the mastery of risk: the notion that the future is more than a whim of the gods and that men and women are not passive before nature. Until human beings discovered a way across that boundary, the future was … the murky domain of oracles and soothsayers who held a monopoly over knowledge of anticipated events."[4]

"The story I have to tell," continues Bernstein,

> is marked all the way through by a persistent tension between those who assert that the best decisions are based on quantification and numbers, determined by the patterns of the past, and those who base their decisions on more subjective degrees of belief about the uncertain future. …
>
> The issue boils down to one's view about the extent to which the past determines the future. We cannot quantify the future, because it is an unknown, but we have learned how to use numbers to scrutinize what happened in the past. But to what degree should we rely on patterns of the past to tell us what the future will be like? Which matters more when facing a risk, the facts as we see them or our subjective belief in what lies hidden in the void of time? Is risk management a science or an art? Can we even tell for certain precisely where the dividing line between the two approaches lies?

As the chapters in Bernstein's book make clear, however, the systematic study of risk has been—with one brief interlude between the two world wars—principally about quantification (see box).

Mastering Quantifiable Risks

Bernstein's story begins with the Hindu-Arabic numbering system that reached the West seven to eight hundred years ago. In the 1650s, "The discovery of the theory of probability, the mathematical heart of the concept of risk," allowed people "for the first time to make decisions and forecast the future with the help of numbers."

Analysis of well-structured games of chance, with unambiguous outcomes and the repetition of identical events (differentiated only by "random" noise), provided both the impetus and the application for the theory of risk. Dice and the roulette wheel were "natural laboratories for the study of risk

---

because they lend themselves so readily to quantification; their language is the language of numbers."

As the years passed, however, mathematicians were able to transform probability theory from a gamblers' toy into a powerful tool for organizing, interpreting, and applying information. By 1725, mathematicians were devising tables of life expectancies and the British government was raising funds by selling life annuities. The eighteenth century also saw Bernoulli's invention of the Law of Large Numbers; the discovery of the concept of standard deviation, the structure of the bell curve; diminishing utilities (the next increment of something gives us less satisfaction than the last); and Bayes' theorem (which tells us how to revise our probability estimates as we get more information). In the nineteenth century, Gauss made foundational contributions to the measurement of risk, and Galton discovered regressions to the mean.

Not until chapter 13 of Bernstein's book do we encounter John Maynard Keynes and Frank Knight, who took seriously uncertainties that cannot be quantified and risks that cannot be measured, and questioned the degree to which we can rely on past occurrences to predict the future. Keynes's *A Treatise on Probability*, published in 1921, attacks traditional views and asserts that probability theory isn't relevant to real-life situations. He mocks what he calls the Law of Great Numbers, arguing there is no reason to believe that because similar events have been observed repeatedly in the past, they will probably occur in the future. Our perceptions of probability and risk are highly dependent on our judgment.[5]

Later, in the *General Theory*, Keynes writes:

> the extreme precariousness of the basis of knowledge on which our estimates of prospective yield have to be made. Our knowledge of the factors which will govern the yield of an investment some years hence is usually very slight and often negligible. If we speak frankly, we have to admit that our basis of knowledge for estimating the yield ten years hence of a railway, a copper mine, a textile factory, the goodwill of a patent medicine, an Atlantic liner, a building in the City of London amounts to little and sometimes to nothing; or even five years hence.[6]

We have already encountered Frank Knight, whose *Risk, Uncertainty, and Profit* was published in the same year as Keynes's *Treatise on Probability*. As it happens, Knight disliked Keynes—and many of the ideas Keynes advocated—intensely. But on the issue of predicting future events their views are quite similar. For convenience I will focus mainly on Knight's views.*

Knight divided unknown outcomes into three categories.[7] The first comprised "a priori" probabilities that could be deduced from mathematical laws, for instance, the odds of getting three heads in a row in a toss of a fair coin or getting two sixes in rolling a pair of fair dice. In the second category were "statistical probabilities" generated by evaluation of relative frequencies, as might be done by an actuary estimating life expectancies. The third category comprised estimates for which there was "no valid basis of any kind for classifying instances."[8] For the sake of simplicity, I will call the third category "one-offs."

Knight referred to the a priori and statistical probabilities as "risk" and one-offs as true "uncertainty." The uncertainty of one-offs is commonplace in business decisions and in many other walks of life, writes Knight:

> Take as an illustration any typical business decision.
> A manufacturer is considering the advisability of making a large commitment in increasing the capacity of his works. He "figures" more or less on the proposition, taking account as well as possible of the various factors more or less susceptible of measurement, but the final result is an "estimate" of the probable outcome of any proposed course of action. What is the "probability" of error (strictly, of any assigned degree of error) in the judgment? It is manifestly meaningless to speak of either calculating such a probability a priori or of determining it empirically by studying a large number of instances. The essential and outstanding fact is that the "instance" in question is so entirely unique that there are no others or not a sufficient number to make it possible to tabulate enough like it to form a basis for any inference of value about any real probability in the case we are interested in. The same obviously applies to the most of conduct and not to business decisions alone.[9]

*I have picked Knight over Keynes because Knight's views of risk and uncertainty are central to his life's work, whereas they comprise the lesser known half of Keynes's contribution, although they are crucial to his overall thesis, according to Robert Skidelsky (2009). Knight's focus on the entrepreneur-businessperson corresponds closely to the main unit of analysis of this book, whereas Keynes applied the idea of radical uncertainty to explain more "macro" phenomena such as why people hoard cash and the instability of aggregate investment.

Indeed, Knight's central thesis is that profit is a reward for taking responsibility for the uncertainty of one-off outcomes rather than for bearing a priori or statistical risks.

Knight allows that there is a continuum between statistical risk and the pure uncertainty of one-offs, because "nothing in the universe of experience is absolutely unique any more than any two things are absolutely alike. Consequently it is always possible to form classes if the bars are let down and a loose enough interpretation of similarity is accepted." In the case of the manufacturer thinking about expanding capacity, "It might or might not be entirely meaningless to inquire as to the proportion of successful factory extensions and the proportion of those which are not. In this particular case it is hard to imagine that anyone would base conduct upon a judgment of the probability of success arrived at in this way, but in other situations the method could conceivably have more or less validity."[10]

Moreover, the use of data from roughly similar past instances in most business situations is not at all like the use of actuarial tables in life insurance. A manufacturer might examine the track record of previous capacity expansions, but would usually not "regard the probability for *him* of success as that indicated by statistics of 'similar' instances" or, if lacking such data, would regard the odds of success as one-in-two. Rather, "his own estimate of the value of his own judgment would be given far greater weight than either sort of computation."[11]

Similarly, Knight notes a confusing superficial similarity in the language used to describe "statistical" probabilities and the estimates made in one-off situations: "We do estimate the value or validity or dependability of our opinions and estimates, and such an estimate has the same form as a probability judgment; it is a ratio, expressed by a proper fraction." For instance, a manufacturer may think that a decision to expand capacity has a 60 percent chance of being "right." However, insists Knight, such assessments "must be radically distinguished from probability or chance." More baldly, he observes that it is "meaningless and fatally misleading to speak of the probability, in an objective sense, that a judgment is correct."[12]

Knight's and Keynes's views enjoyed but a brief moment in the sun, however. Knight may be considered the father of Chicago school of economics but Chicago economists had little time for his central thesis after the Second World War. Milton Friedman's (1962) view is typical:

In his seminal work, Frank Knight drew a sharp distinction between risk, as referring to events subject to a known or knowable probability distribution, and uncertainty, as referring to events for which it was not possible to specify numerical probabilities. I have not referred to this distinction because I do not believe it is valid. I follow L. J. Savage in his view of personal probability, which denies any valid distinction along these lines. We may treat people as if they assigned numerical probabilities to every conceivable event.[13]

An article in the *Journal of Political Economy* (housed, perhaps coincidentally, at the University of Chicago) goes so far as to say that Knight himself didn't really mean the distinction he made, in the very title of his book, between risk and uncertainty: He was actually analyzing "moral hazard or adverse selection." The authors blame the widespread view that Knight was serious about his distinction to a writing style whose precision "leaves much to be desired." ("Almost all readers," they write, "will at times despair of extracting any core of original insight from the overripe fruit of Knight's prose.")[14]

Notwithstanding the revisionist view, I will argue next that there are profound differences in the real world, if not in the axiomatic universe of mainstream modern economics and decision theory, between the uncertainty of one-offs and the risks of quantifiable probabilities, and that much has been lost in ignoring these differences.

Consequential Differences

The modern approach usually maps all situations where the outcomes are unknown—whether or not they are one of a kind—into structured games of chance, typically a lottery, and infers a personal or subjective probability from the price a decision maker will accept for the lottery ticket. For instance, a person's willingness to pay $10 for a lottery ticket that will pay $100 if Osama bin Laden is captured or killed by end of the year implies a probability estimate of 10 percent.[15] If the event in question is one of a kind, the probability estimate is said to be subjective rather than objective. Apart from that distinction, decision making is, supposedly, exactly the same.

Individuals and businesses indeed do take bets on one-off events, and we can, in principle, infer a probability estimate from these bets. For instance, at the start of 2009, bookmakers in London (where such bets are legal) were offering five-to-one odds on Osama bin Laden being captured (corresponding to a probability of 16.67 percent) and fourteen-to-one on Queen Elizabeth II abdicating by the end of the year (a 6.67 percent probability).[16] Insurance companies similarly write policies on whether a diva's voice will hold up for a season and whether a rock concert will be rained out. These instances do not, however, establish that people can, do, or should make subjective probability estimates for all one-off situations. Nor do they erase crucial differences in how decision makers cope with the unpredictability of one-offs and recurring events.

To make a wager or to buy a lottery ticket requires unambiguous outcomes. Bin Laden is captured or not, or the queen abdicates by the end of the year or not. There is no middle ground. But consider, instead, the difficulty of betting on whether the war on terror will be won by a certain time: Because it is difficult to lay out specific objective criteria that must be met, victory lies in the eye of the beholder. It's also a moving target. Today we may regard the elimination of a defined set of terrorist groups as constituting victory. But what if the groups give way to free-standing individual terrorists?

Such instances are commonplace in one-off situations. Think of hiring decisions: There are many ways in which an employee can be good or bad, and it is hard to specify the criteria in advance—or ascertain whether they have been met afterward. Of course, organizations do define categories of performance that matter, but that definition of goodness rarely leads to unambiguous, measurable yardsticks of performance. Baseball pitchers or batters whose contribution can be reduced to a couple of statistics are exceptions. But without a clear specification of the conditions under which a lottery ticket pays off, how can an individual come up with an estimate of its fair price?

The challenges of forming a subjective estimate of probabilities—where it can be done at all—are also consequential. With one-off bets on whether bin Laden will be captured or a diva will lose her voice, the probability estimate may be no more than a wild or whimsical guess.* Contemplative decision-makers may think back to past situations when they had the same feeling in the pit of their stomachs that something

*As Knight (1921) put it: "The ultimate logic, or psychology, of these deliberations is obscure, a part of the scientifically unfathomable mystery of life and mind. We must simply fall back upon a 'capacity' in the intelligent animal to form more or less correct judgments about things, an intuitive sense of values."

would work out and, recalling that only half of them did, use this calibration to estimate probabilities. But given such a nebulous basis for forming estimates, it is hard to imagine that decision makers would rely on them in the same way they would use more objective estimates.

As Knight pointed out, with repeated events the law of large numbers practically eliminates unpredictability. A life insurance company that uses good actuarial tables can be pretty certain—if it writes a large number of policies—about the total number and amount of claims it will face each year. Not so with gut estimates. Imagine someone who makes numerous one-off bets thinking that each has a one-in-four chance of success. This does not at all ensure that a quarter will be successful or that a sensible decision-maker will expect that result. The main benefit of forming the one-in-four estimate is that it prompts the question: Will a successful outcome at least quadruple the initial outlay? The discipline of comparing estimates of the odds and payoffs of success (in situations where such estimates can be made) helps people come out ahead even if it does not eliminate unpredictability.

This is just one of the profound differences between choices about one-offs and those about repeated instances of the same category. The impossibility of mind reading makes it a mug's game to say how individuals make choices about one-offs, but observations of decision making by groups in a variety of settings—partners of a VC fund evaluating a new investment, loan committees deciding whether to extend a loan, recruitment panels deciding whether to hire a particular individual, and juries deciding legal cases—suggests some common patterns.

Little effort is made to quantify possible payoffs and probabilities associated with these payoffs. Venture capitalists and hiring committees do not argue over probability estimates of a successful investment or candidate. Nor do juries in criminal trials assess a numerical probability that someone is guilty. Rather, the goal is to decide which of a few, broadly defined categories of outcomes is more likely. In the case of criminal trials, this task is explicit: The jury has to decide whether the prosecution has proved its case beyond reasonable doubt. In other situations, the assessment is more implicit, for instance, whether a bank loan is likely to become troubled—a category that spans a range of possibilities of which complete loss is but one. Similarly, when VCs consider an investment proposal or recruitment panels a candidate, they may rank the likelihood that the investment or candidate will turn out to be a great success, adequate, or a failure.

The process of ranking likelihoods can be regarded as one of constructing and evaluating competing narratives, as John Kay[17] puts it. In a criminal trial, for example, the prosecution offers a story telling why and how the accused committed a crime. The story weaves together physical evidence from the scene of the crime, the opinions and interpretations of ballistic experts, the testimonies of witnesses, and so on. The defense tries to poke holes in the prosecutors' narrative. It secures acquittal by persuading the jury that the prosecution's narrative has weak links. A verdict of guilty "beyond reasonable doubt" means a story that has no weak links or large leaps of faith. In civil trials, where plaintiffs face lower standards of proof, the "preponderance of evidence" can be taken to mean that the story is more persuasive than alternative explanations, even if it isn't quite bulletproof.

The construction and evaluation of narratives also appears to be a sensible way of representing the venture capitalists' decision-making process: VCs do form a numerical estimate of the rate of return if the venture succeeds. But, more important, VCs look for a plausible story that leads to success—and the absence of a convincing story that dooms the enterprise to failure. The stories are certainly not "fictional" or purely "verbal" and impressionistic—they involve the gathering and analysis of considerable quantitative and qualitative data, and incorporate consideration of opinions as well as a review of scientific papers. But they do not remotely resemble a process of plugging numbers into a quantitative model.

Naturally there are variations in the process: Spreadsheets and fine-grained quantitative projections play a much more important role in real-estate deals than they do in VCs' investments in high-tech start-ups. Others who have observed decision making in these one-off contexts may provide a different account than mine. But I think there is little doubt that however we characterize the process, it is materially different from creating and using actuarial tables: First, it is holistic and hands-on, rather than reductionist and remote. Venture capitalists try to include as much on-the-spot knowledge as they can in "making a case" for or against an investment, whereas the life insurer uses a small number of variables that are the same for all instances.

Second, although history certainly matters, it is a starting point for decision making rather than the main basis for making predictions. For instance, a VC will take into account previous bad experiences with excessively egotistical founders, but it's in the context of the large number of idiosyncratic features of the investment under consideration.

In addition, a sensible VC will not ignore the fact that even after considerable due diligence, only a small proportion of its previous investments earned attractive returns—but the use of this fact is largely limited to setting a high bar for the return a venture must realize (if it works out) to be considered a worthwhile investment.

Third, probability estimates (to the extent they are made) often aren't "priced" to the same degree in one-offs as they are with recurring events. For example, the shorter life expectancy of a smoker does not preclude getting a life insurance policy—the insurer simply charges a higher premium. Venture capital firms will usually not, however, invest in businesses where the narrative suggests a high likelihood of failure even if they are offered shares at knockdown prices. Similarly, banks will not touch loans that analysis suggests are likely to become troubled, although lenders who specialize in such credits may.

The Ubiquity of One-offs

The obvious correspondence between how people cope with the Knightian uncertainty that arises in one-off situations, and the on-the-spot decision-making in a well-functioning Hayekian economy described in previous chapters, is not coincidental. Decentralized innovation makes Knightian uncertainty ubiquitous in several ways. One route is technological: A new product or process is, by definition, different from anything that has come before it, and there is no way of knowing whether it will work. This is true even for products that merely combine tried and tested components and have been designed in accordance with well-established scientific laws. Proven parts and principles, when put together, can interact in unpredictable and undesirable ways. Similarly, a technology that has worked under laboratory conditions can fail when scaled up for mass production. In the development of pharmaceuticals or medical devices, drugs or devices that appear safe and effective in animal experiments may fail in human trials. Previous experiences can suggest some do's and don'ts, but they cannot eliminate the Knightian uncertainty created by physical novelty.

Innovation also constantly alters the character of the economy. What happens tomorrow can be quite different from what happens today, and must therefore be considered at least to some degree a one-off rather than a draw plucked from a stable distribution. Furthermore, in an interconnected economy, a sector need not be at the cutting edge of innovation to feel its effects: As I argued earlier, housing prices in Detroit and Silicon Valley aren't insulated from innovations in the automobile and high-tech industries.

Decentralization also helps keep the pot stirred. In the aggregate, decentralization may help smooth and stabilize (with "B stepping in at once when A fails to deliver," as Hayek wrote). But from the point of view of an individual decision-maker, decentralization makes matters highly uncertain. In the absence of a supernatural mind-reading capacity, it is impossible to know what competitors plan to do (expand production or exit, introduce a new product or technology); whether there are new entrants lurking in the wings; or the intentions of customers. And even if a decision maker could somehow know what was on everyone else's mind, figuring out how the interactions would play out would represent another nearly insurmountable barrier to making an accurate forecast.

But if one-offs and Knightian uncertainty are such a pervasive and important feature of the modern economy, what accounts for their elimination from modern economics? Next we will see why many economists who extol Knight, Keynes, and Hayek in their popular writing ignore their ideas about uncertainty in their scholarly work.

▨▨▨▨ An Inconvenient Reality

The exclusion of one-off Knightian uncertainty from economic models can be compared to eliminating the vertical dimension on a map. All maps must simplify. Mountain ranges have valleys made gorgeous by carpets of poppies and hillsides dense with fir trees. Yet mountain climbers' maps rarely feature flower or fir: Representation of the flora on a map would be an unnecessary distraction, while excluding them frees up space for more valuable contour lines—a map that doesn't show how the terrain rises and falls is of little use to a climber. This vertical dimension also is crucial for pilots flying through mountains and navigators of ships in shallow waters, but not for highway maps—for a motorist, exit numbers are more valuable than contour lines. In other words, what should be left in and kept out depends on the intended use of a map or model.

What purpose might be served by excluding Knightian uncertainty? As it happens, the technical complexity of economic models restricts their direct use to economists. Unlike, say, the fields of engineering or medicine, practical utility isn't the primary goal of economic models. Rather, knowledge is primarily valued for its own sake, and, as is inevitable in a specialized field, that value is determined by the norms of the producers of the knowledge. As Paul Samuelson said, "In the long-run the economic scholar works for the only coin worth having—our own applause."[18] Therefore, choices of what to include and exclude in economic maps turn on what other economic mapmakers consider to be good maps.

Economics in the eighteenth and nineteenth centuries followed a verbal tradition, and, even in 1900 "there was relatively little mathematics, statistics or modeling contained in any economic work."[19] The use of mathematics increased over the next half century, but the discipline "remained pluralistic." After that, however, economics emphasized "formal treatments of rational, or optimizing, economic agents joined together in an abstractly conceived" world.[20] The increase in the proportion of pages in the *American Economic Review* that contained an equation illustrates this trend dramatically. In 1951, only about 2 percent contained an equation, but by 1978, 44 percent did.[71]

Why mathematical representation became so dominant in economics so quickly is a mystery: In the natural sciences, many important relationships are *not* captured in equations, as Richard Nelson points out. Darwin's theory was decidedly not mathematical. The structure of DNA and even "simple" organic compounds are represented as pictures. It's primarily in physics that equations rule. Perhaps it was the mathematical breakthroughs of a few extraordinary intellects, such as Kenneth Arrow, Gerard Debreu, and Paul Samuelson that created the momentum that pushed economics over some "tipping point."

It is easy to see, however, why Knightian uncertainty would fall by the wayside once economics had embraced math as its dominant mode of analysis. Mathematized economics placed immense value on tractable equations[22] that yielded unique "equilibrium" values of quantities of interest, such as at what price a market will clear or what mix of inputs will yield the most output at the lowest cost. Incorporating unquantifiable, Knightian uncertainties into tractable equations was extremely hard.[23] And even though the most applause goes to those who solve really hard problems, economists also had a common interest in adopting a methodology or paradigm that could support a large number of acceptable (read, mathematically sound) papers. Embracing the complications of Knightian uncertainty would have stood in the way.

The pursuit of tractable mathematical formulation not only required simplification—assuming away Knightian uncertainty—but also significant alterations in the representations of reality. Individuals were assumed to make decisions based on *identical* estimates of (quantified) probabilities. Modelers didn't really believe that there were no differences of opinion, but the math could not easily handle them: The most advanced game theory can just about cope with the interactions of two players with different views, and only after it makes heroic assumptions. Additional players make it impossible to find unique solutions. For all practical purposes, therefore, the economic game was assumed to be governed by a single mind and a single probability distribution. Competition between many was included in the models mainly to rule out monopoly power.

Further mathematical convenience was purchased by assuming that all decision makers always calculated the right odds because they knew everything about the current and possible future states of the world.* To be sure, the models didn't assume that decision makers knew exactly what would happen next; that assumption would eliminate modeling challenges, and while tractability was essential, solving equations that were too easy didn't secure much applause. The models also left open the possibility of exogenous shocks—meteor strikes from outer space, as it were, that could mess up the otherwise "correct" calculations of earthlings. But with these qualifications, decision makers in the models were all-knowing.

In a masterstroke of packaging, this widespread omniscience was labeled "rational expectations." In reality, the models developed under the rubric were rather like intelligent design theories of creationism: unfalsifiable but implausible. It is impossible to disprove the assumption that everyone has the right probability model. If a gambler bets on red and the roulette wheel comes up black, that doesn't mean the gambler miscalculated the odds: Losses aren't evidence of ignorance or mistake. Moreover, in most situations modeled, the true probability cannot be measured either before or after the fact.[24] The probability distributions that individuals act on are also unobservable: In a casino we might see

---

*Predictably, Knight was not a fan. His main complaint against economic models was their assumption of "practical omniscience on the part of every member of the economics system," the notion that everyone has all the information needed, and if the future is unknown, the laws of probability determine the outcome (Bernstein 1996, 220).

whether someone bets on black or red, but there is no way to know the odds the person had in mind. In addition, since both distributions are unobservable, it is impossible to know whether decision makers' distributions are "right." Finally, when the outcomes are in clear conflict with whatever probability distributions the players could possibly have had, there is the escape hatch of a meteor strike—an exogenous shock.

The assumption of identical, correct probability distributions, however, conflicts with a decentralized economy characterized by a high level of innovation. As I discussed at length in part 1, the independent subjective judgments and competing views of innovators are central to this process. Differences of opinions—and by extension of probability estimates (to the degree that innovators use quantified probabilities)—are an essential, not a peripheral or minor, feature of what goes on.

Furthermore, people have to make guesses about others' judgments in deciding what to do. In some cases, when an innovator tries to figure out whether customers will buy a new product, for example, uncertainty may be reduced by dialogue, but in other cases (in anticipating what competitors will do) this is not an option. Inevitably some guesses will be wrong. Trial and error is therefore a routine feature of modern business life. Doing the same thing over and over again, relying on the same model to produce a good overall result, is certainly not unknown, but not the norm. In the real world, people expect to make and correct mistakes; even after something does work, sensible people will be on the lookout for the possibility that it will start to go wrong. Such mistakes don't require an exogenous shock—they are a routine, inevitable consequence of a system of decentralized judgment. The assumption of universal omniscience is therefore a profound misrepresentation: It isn't like smoothening the jagged banks of a river on a map, but rather like representing its meandering path with a straight line drawn from its source to the sea.

▒▒▒▒ Risky Fantasies

Some economists defend unrealistic assumptions of "if, then" models on "as if" grounds: As long as the model yields accurate predictions, it's fine to represent the world as if it had the outlandish features.

Milton Friedman's essay "The Methodology of Positive Economics," published in 1953, has become an influential expression of this point of view (see box). The essay divides[25] economics into "positive" and "normative" components—the positive pertain to how the world works, and the normative to how it ought to work. The positive precedes (or, at least in Friedman's view, *ought* to precede) the normative: Whatever our values might be, we can't figure out how we should act unless we can predict the consequences of our actions. Moreover, Friedman argues that the accuracy or realism of assumptions used in the theories and hypotheses of positive economics is irrelevant—we should only care about good predictions. In fact, like maps, important hypotheses *require* assumptions that are to some degree inaccurate.

Other economists (such as Paul Samuelson) and philosophers (such as Jon Elster) reject Friedman's argument. In the opposing view, a positive theory should be based on sound, causal mechanisms and not merely on the quality of its predictions. But apart from these philosophical objections, there seem to be strong practical reasons for evaluating the correspondence of assumptions to the real world, especially if we want to turn positive theories into normative prescriptions (as I argue in the box). The nearly insurmountable challenges of testing the predictions should make us wary of putting into practical use what Elster might call "science fiction theories" that ignore Knightian uncertainty and assume widespread omniscience.

Why Assumptions Matter

According to Friedman, the goal of a "positive science" (which tells us how the world works, rather than how it ought to work) is the development of theory that yields predictions that are "meaningful" but not exactly right.

For this process of development, unrealistic assumptions are necessary and not a limitation. The assumptions of truly important hypotheses are, writes Friedman, "wildly inaccurate descriptive representations of reality." They must be so, because "a hypothesis is important if it 'explains' much by little" by abstracting "crucial elements from the mass of detailed and complex circumstances." Importance therefore requires that a hypothesis be "descriptively false in its assumptions."

Friedman cites the example of the wheat market:

A completely "realistic" theory of the wheat market would have to include not only the conditions directly underlying the supply and demand for wheat but also the kind of coins or credit instruments used to make exchanges; the personal characteristics of wheat-traders such as the color of each trader's hair and eyes, his antecedents and education, the number

---

of members of his family, their characteristics, antecedents, and education, etc.; the kind of soil on which the wheat was grown, its physical and chemical characteristics, the weather prevailing during the growing season; the personal characteristics of the farmers growing the wheat and of the consumers who will ultimately use it; and so on indefinitely. Any attempt to move very far in achieving this kind of "realism" is certain to render a theory utterly useless.

A good theory, Friedman argues, "cannot be tested by comparing its 'assumptions' directly with 'reality' and the question whether a theory is realistic 'enough' can be settled only by seeing whether it yields predictions that are good enough for the purpose in hand." Thus, even wildly unrealistic assumptions are okay as a convenience for making good predictions. Expert billiard players may never actually make complicated mathematical calculations; but if the hypothesis that expert players make their shots "as if" they did calculations yields excellent predictions, why not go with this fantastic formulation?

Theory, thus, is only to be judged by its predictive power. "Only factual evidence can show whether it is 'right' or 'wrong.'" Indeed, Friedman attacks—as fundamentally wrong—the view that conformity of the assumptions of a hypothesis to reality is "a test of the validity of the hypothesis different from or additional to the test by implications.... Far from providing an easier means for sifting valid from invalid hypotheses, it only confuses the issue, [and] promotes misunderstanding about the significance of empirical evidence for economic theory."

Let us concede the soundness of Friedman's argument that, in principle, we should be concerned only with the goodness of predictions and not assumptions. I would observe, however, that given how theories are actually developed, and the problems that arise in their testing, it behooves us, if we want to put these theories to practical use, to pay close attention to the realism of the assumptions.

First, unrealistic assumptions may well have value, as Friedman argues, in making positive theories concise. But when carried over into normative domains, they can produce dubious prescriptions. To claim that expert billiard players act as if they make complicated mathematical calculations may be a convenient way of describing how the world works. But cutting back on practice to learn complicated math is likely to lower—not increase—a player's performance. Or to take the matter immediately at hand: Assuming away Knightian uncertainty does indeed make for simpler, more compact mathematical representations. It is also possible (though I cannot think of any real instances) that this simplification leads to predictions that could not otherwise be made and that have been successfully tested.[26] But against this hypothetical benefit we should balance a real-world cost, as I argue in the next chapter.

Second, if the crucial assumptions of a hypothesis are totally far-fetched, it is impossible to derive sensible predictions. If expert billiard players who make good shots most of the time don't exist, and the world consists of duffers who rarely do, then the theory of how experts make their shots cannot lead to any testable predictions. Some smoothing and abstracting is certainly necessary for a good theory, but pure fantasy is something else.

Friedman's essay assumes away this problem. He posits a world in which positive theories have two parts.

One part consists of an abstract model that is simpler than the "real world" because it only contains "forces that the hypothesis asserts to be important." Friedman considers this a great virtue because it is also precise. This is where "mathematics and formal logic come into their own in checking its consistency and completeness and exploring its implications. There is no place in the model for, and no function to be served by, vagueness, maybe's, or approximations."

The second, and completely different, part comprises the rules that define the phenomena in the real world for which the model can be taken as a representation; these rules specify the correspondence between variables in the model and observable phenomena. Unlike the abstract model, these rules "cannot possibly be abstract and complete. They must be concrete and, in consequence, incomplete—completeness is possible only in a conceptual world, not in the 'real world.'"

Friedman asserts that although the two parts operate at different levels of abstraction and precision, they are inseparable. Rules that specify the circumstances under which the abstract hypothesis works and the "general magnitude of the error in its predictions under various circumstances" are "an essential part of the hypothesis."

In the idealized world postulated by Friedman, the abstract model is put to normative use only after it has been validated by testing its predictions—and then only in situations specified by the rules. No "off-label" use is permitted, to employ a term from the pharmaceutical industry (for drugs approved for one condition but prescribed for another).

If only.

In reality, the loudest applause goes to the first of the two parts posited by Friedman: Building abstract but highly precise and mathematical models wins a large proportion of the Nobel Prizes in Economics. The fuzzy second step has low status and is undertaken half-heartedly or not at all. Trying to tease out testable propositions from models far removed from reality is difficult[27] and also somewhat thankless because empirical falsification is so trivial. For instance, it is apparently no discredit to Akerlof's celebrated "market for lemons" theory, which demonstrates that information asymmetry makes markets for secondhand cars impossible, that there is a large and active market for such cars: Conditions in the real world do not satisfy the assumptions of Akerlof's model, but the existence of a real market does not disprove his theory.[28]

If there is any empirical content to highly abstract models, it is typically at the front end. Thus, a theorist starts with a specific incident or case said to illustrate a particular trade-off or choice to "motivate the model." The modeler proceeds to formalize the trade-off in mathematical terms and "solve" the model, making whatever assumptions are required to arrive at a unique solution. And there it stops. It is virtually unknown for theory papers to include the second part of Friedman's two-step and specify rules for using the model in the real world.*

To put it simply, although Friedman argues that abstract models ought not, by themselves, be used to guide real-world choices, in reality, they are often pressed into practical use without meaningful empirical testing. The prestige attached to models with mathematically brilliant and far from obvious construction, and the legitimacy this cachet provides to parties who have ideological or financial interests they wish to promote, is powerful. Akerlof's Nobel Prize–winning model was used in support of lemon laws even though it had no empirical validation; the plaudits earned by the model provided cover for laws that advocates had long wanted to enact.

Third, even when economists attempt to evaluate predictions, there are huge problems in gathering empirical evidence to determine whether a model generates "good enough" predictions for practical use. In most cases, it is next to impossible to run controlled experiments to test predictions. Here Friedman argues that historic data can be an adequate substitute. The predictions by which the validity of a hypothesis is tested, he writes, "need not be about phenomena that have not yet occurred, that is, need not be forecasts of future events; they may be about phenomena that have occurred but observations on which have not yet been made or are not known to the person making the prediction. For example, a hypothesis may imply that such and such must have happened in 1906, given some other known circumstances. If a search of the records reveals that such and such did happen, the prediction is confirmed; if it reveals that such and such did not happen, the prediction is contradicted."

The use of historical data to test hypotheses raises a number of practical difficulties, however. It is tempting to construct models that "predict" historical facts that are in fact known to the modelers or fish for facts that fit the model and ignore the ones that don't. Moreover, in a dynamic world, "Past performance is no guarantee of future results," as the standard Wall Street caution goes. (As Knight put it: "At the bottom of the uncertainty problem in economics is the forward-looking character of the economic process itself.")[29]

Historical data rarely directly confirms or contradicts most models. Rather, statistical models—which rely on what many consider to be unrealistic

*Maddy (2008) argues that a similar development has occurred in the relationship between mathematics and the natural sciences: "In Newton or Euler's day, the methods of mathematics and the methods of science were one and the same" as they both sought "to uncover the underlying structure of the world." The "correctness of a new mathematical method" was "established by its role in application." Now, "mathematics has been freed to pursue inquiries without application [and] encouraged to stock the warehouses with structures and leave the choices to the natural scientists. [E]ven the mathematical constructs that do function in application do so with a new autonomy as freestanding abstract models." (p.36).

assumptions—must be interposed between the hypothesis being tested and the data. As Friedman concedes, historical data is "far more difficult to interpret" than the results of controlled experiments. "It is frequently complex and always indirect and incomplete. Its collection is often arduous, and its interpretation generally requires subtle analysis and involved chains of reasoning, which seldom carry real conviction."

Then there is the issue of who decides whether predictions are "good enough," since they are never perfect. Because economists (who are brave enough to undertake empirical testing) all face the same difficulties, they have a common interest in setting the bar at a surmountable level. Furthermore, as Friedman points out, "The background of the scientists is not irrelevant to the judgments they reach": "The economist will be more tolerant than the sociologist" in judging the evidence favoring a hypothesis that assumes the "single-minded pursuit of pecuniary self-interest." But why should the relatively lenient standards of economists for testing economic theories represent a satisfactory screen for their practical use?

My bottom line is this: If models were carefully tested to a standard suitable for their practical use, then we might not have to care about the realism of their assumptions. In fact, many models just cannot be tested to this standard. Therefore, in making a judgment on whether to rely on untested models to produce their predicted results, we should assess the plausibility of the assumptions. And we should be particularly cautious about using models that are both untested and based on assumptions sharply at odds with the real world.

Concluding Comments

In an innovative, decentralized system, virtually all economic agents—businesses, consumers, homebuyers, investors, and lenders—face Knightian "one-off" uncertainty; they have to make decisions about situations that are to a large degree unprecedented. Decision makers cannot, therefore, rely on an analysis of statistical probabilities by looking at the distribution of what happened in similar past situations. Rather, they make choices based on a holistic consideration of the detailed circumstances at hand. But since mathematized economics cannot easily cope with Knightian uncertainty, it is almost always ignored in formal models. The models implicitly assume that each unique situation is, in fact, one of a large class of similar situations and that all the decision maker must do is to figure out the "vital statistics" of that class.

Many models go even further—they assume that all decision makers make the same guesses about the vital statistics and that these guesses happen to be the right ones. But such universal omniscience is utterly at odds with a decentralized, innovative economy where different individuals make different choices, depending on how they interpret the world around them and the facts that they uniquely observe. Worse, models based on universal omniscience, like theories of intelligent design, cannot be falsified; yet their results are often applied in the real world without empirical verification about whether and when such use is merited.

Of course, the assumption of universal omniscience isn't central to all of modern economics. Nor are all unrealistic models that cannot be empirically verified always put to bad use. Ricardo's theory of comparative advantage was based on the metaphor of "wool for wine" trade between England and Portugal. This highly simplified model did much good in promoting free trade and the repeal of the Corn Laws, designed to support high grain prices in Britain.

The use of unrealistic and untestable models in modern finance has not been benign, however. In the next two chapters, we will see how models that assume universal omniscience have fostered an overly centralized and robotic financial system.

Chapter 6

Judgment-Free Finance

Before the 1960s, the study of finance was dominated by texts and articles that followed the classical verbal tradition emphasizing institutional arrangements (how banks lent or how the New York Stock Exchange functioned) or recipes for picking stocks. Interesting, yes; exciting, hardly. Then, starting in the late 1950s, finance seemed to explode with brilliant ideas. Much applause was accorded to researchers who embraced the mathematical approach to build a set of wide-ranging, integrated models and used increasingly powerful computers and vast amounts of data on security prices to test hypotheses. Accordingly, over the last four decades, advances in the theory and practice of finance have been thought to exemplify the best that modern economics has to offer.

Finance was also ahead of many other branches of economics in its effect on practice. Many leading scholars were also profit-seeking entrepreneurs, not armchair theorists, offering consulting services to financial firms and raising funds from investors. Their indirect influence was even more profound: Their research transformed financial texts and courses in MBA and PhD programs, thus providing the financial industry with tens of thousands of recruits trained in methods of modern finance that were alien to many old-timers.

The interaction between research and practice was decisive. The success of the research enterprise garnered several scholars a Nobel Prize in Economics and brought great prestige to the leading journals in the field—providing even more legitimacy to the use of modern finance in practice.

This prestige and profit drew some good-natured ribbing by economists whose specialty wasn't finance. Lawrence Summers (writing in the *Journal of Finance*) compared financial economists to a fictitious group of "ketchup economists" who received much higher salaries than general economists. These ketchup economists, Summers wrote,

> have an impressive research program, focusing on the scope for excess opportunities in the ketchup market. They have shown that two quart bottles of ketchup invariably sell for twice as much as one quart bottles of ketchup except for deviations traceable to transaction costs, and that one cannot get a bargain on ketchup by buying and combining ingredients once one takes account of transaction costs. Nor are there gains to be had from storing ketchup, or mixing together different quality ketchups and selling the resulting product. Indeed, most ketchup economists regard the efficiency of the ketchup market as the best established fact in empirical economics.[1]

To what degree was the success of financial economics, especially in transforming financial practice, a good thing? In this chapter, I argue that the proliferation of modern theories has been, on balance, unfortunate. Assumptions of universal omniscience about probability distributions and the absence of Knightian uncertainty are at the heart of many breakthrough models. Yet these models have been widely used to replace forward-looking, case-by-case judgment with blind diversification and mechanistic processing of historical data. The participation of some of the leading scholars in practical finance has also been a mixed blessing. It may have educated them to institutional realities, but having to sell their models to clients likely encouraged them to downplay the limitations of the models, perhaps even to themselves.*

I focus on three major developments in this chapter: theories purporting to show the irrelevance of choices about debt and dividends;

---

*The late Fischer Black is a noteworthy exception. Although he spent the last part of his career as partner at Goldman Sachs, he cheerfully wrote articles such as "How to Use the Holes in Black-Scholes" (Black 1989).

the efficient market hypothesis (EMH); and models for constructing efficient portfolios and managing risk.

In the next chapter, I discuss the pricing of options and other such derivatives. Most of the problems highlighted in these two chapters are well known—and not just by a small circle of experts. In fact, almost everything in my relatively brief account has been covered in much greater detail in three excellent and highly accessible histories: Peter Bernstein's *Against the Gods*; Justin Fox's *The Myth of the Rational Market*; and Donald MacKenzie's *An Engine, Not a Camera*. The result of the combination of these problems is not, however, widely appreciated.

Debt and Dividends

Modigliani and Miller's theories on debt and dividends are a good place to start because they were the most direct early challenge to the traditional "predominantly descriptive and institutional approach to the academic study of finance."[2] Modigliani and Miller were at the time on the faculty of Carnegie's newly established business school, where, according to Modigliani, Herbert Simon was the decisive influence.[3] Simon heckled economists for "their ridiculous assumption of human omniscience."[4] Yet Modigliani and Miller's work used this assumption to break new ground. Apparently, for all the honors bestowed on Simon (he was awarded the Nobel Prize in Economics and the Turing Award for contributions to artificial intelligence, and concurrently held professorships at Carnegie in computer science, business, and psychology), his basic premise that no one can know everything was ultimately ignored by mainstream economists—just like Knight's and Keynes's closely related ideas about uncertainty.

Modigliani and Miller used economic reasoning to show "the essential irrelevance" of a company's decisions on how much to borrow or pay as dividends—"key matters from the viewpoint of an institutional or behavioral perspective on finance." Their 1958 paper argued that in a perfect market—and in world without taxes and bankruptcy—a company's debt-to-equity ratio would not affect its total market value (the sum of its debt and equity). The irrelevance of whether a company borrowed a lot or a little in relation to its equity was famously compared—by Miller, himself—to Yogi Berra's request to the pizza man to cut the pizza into eight pieces instead of the usual four because "I'm hungry tonight."[5]

A paper by Miller and Modigliani in 1961 made a similar argument about dividend policy: How much of its earnings a company paid out as dividends (rather than retained as equity) would make no difference to shareholders. Assuming that a firm's basic business activities remain the same, and investors behave rationally, paying more in dividends would reduce their capital gains by exactly the same amount. Conversely smaller dividends would be exactly offset by larger capital gains.

"Modigliani and Miller knew perfectly well that they were assuming a world that did not exist," MacKenzie points out. Taxes are a reality that seriously concern investors and companies, as is the prospect of bankruptcy, among other possibilities assumed out of existence by Modigliani and Miller. But their "intellectual strategy was to start with a highly simplified but in consequence analytically tractable world."[6] As Modigliani and Miller wrote in the conclusion to their 1958 paper on debt policy:

> Our approach has been that of static, partial equilibrium analysis. It has assumed among other things a state of atomistic competition in the capital markets and an ease of access to those markets which only a relatively small (though important) group of firms even come close to possessing. These and other drastic simplifications have been necessary in order to come to grips with the problem at all. Having served their purpose they can now be relaxed in the direction of greater realism and relevance, a task in which we hope others interested in this area will wish to share.[7]

As it happens, Modigliani and Miller's work on debt and dividends had little impact on choices made in the real world.[8] Nor, to my knowledge, did the many refinements that followed have such an impact, although they narrowed the gap between the assumptions and predictions of the models, on the one hand, and what we observe in the world, on the other. The indirect effect of Modigliani and Miller's work has, however, been enormous: They opened the door to a new style of theorizing in finance, and some of the models thus developed have had profound effects on practice.

The Modigliani and Miller papers (the first of which was published in the *American Economic Review*) legitimized, for finance, the axiomatic, deductive style of reasoning extensively used in economics especially after the Second World War. Equally crucial, they pioneered the use of a faux kind of arbitrage that later became the hallmark of many influential financial theories.

True arbitrage exploits clear, measurable, and unwarranted differences in prices. The difference in gold prices between New York and Riyadh, Saudi Arabia, ought not to exceed by a significant margin the cost of transporting gold between the two places. If the price of gold in Riyadh is lower than in New York by a margin greater than that cost, an arbitrageur can make a riskless profit by buying gold in Riyadh and selling it in New York.

Arbitrage can occur across time as well as distance. Think of a six-month "futures" price in gold: It should equal the cost of buying gold in the cash market plus the cost of holding (or "carrying") it for six months (which is principally the cost of storage and tying up capital in the inventory).

Another important property of true arbitrage opportunities is that they tend to be self-limiting, provided there is a sufficient supply of arbitrageurs with the knowledge and the means to take advantage of them. Given many well-capitalized traders with phone lines and easy access to shipping facilities, the difference in the price of gold between two locations will tend to remain within a range where no one can make a large profit from buying in one place and selling in the other.

Furthermore, we can use arbitrage calculations to estimate "fair" or "equilibrium" prices even in places where there is no active market, provided we can realistically imagine many knowledgeable and well-capitalized arbitrageurs between that place and a location where there is an active market. For instance, gold isn't actively traded in Boston. But we can reasonably think of a fair price of gold in Boston as equal to the New York price, plus the cost of transportation, because many people can easily shuttle information about prices and the gold itself between the two locations.

It is, however, hard to imagine a well-defined arbitrage price for gold in a pirate cove on the Somali coast. Yet the faux arbitrage pioneered by Modigliani and Miller involves the calculation of a fair price even though a crucial item of information necessary for true arbitrage is unknown or unknowable (such as the cost of transporting gold to a Somalian pirate cove). The artifice relied on in this approach is what Simon would call the "ridiculous assumption of human omniscience" or the equally miraculous stipulation that everyone forms exactly the same subjective estimate of the value of the unknown variable.

The landmark Modigliani and Miller paper on debt made the following argument: Suppose two firms, A and B, expected to generate the same cash flows from their operations (with identical risks associated with the cash flows), have different debt to equity ratios. If the total market value of the A's debt and equity is lower than B's, investors can earn a risk-free profit by buying the A "package" and selling the B package. Ergo, arbitrage will lead to identical values for the two packages, making the differences in their capital structure irrelevant. At the time Modigliani and Miller published their work, this was not a widely accepted mode of reasoning (see box).

Controversial Arbitrage

In 1952, a MIT professor observed:

> Economic theorists are fond of saying that in a perfectly fluid world one function of the market is to equalize risks on all investments. If the yield differential between two securities should be greater than the apparent risk differential, arbitragers would rush into the breach and promptly restore the yield differential to its proper value. But in our world, arbitragers may have insufficient funds to do their job because so many investors are deterred from buying stocks or low-grade bonds, either by law, by personal circumstance, by income taxes, or even by pure prejudice.[9]

The argument that inadequate capital may limit the ability of arbitrageurs to drive market prices to their correct values has been refined and expressed in the form of a mathematical model in a celebrated paper by Shleifer and Vishny published in 1997. It shows that "rational" or "informed" traders can go broke before they can correct "mispricing" in the market.[10]

Here I would like to emphasize basic cognitive limits to faux arbitrage. How can anyone, however rational or well informed, know the "right" absolute or relative prices of securities in a world shot through with Knightian uncertainty? Returning to the Modigliani and Miller arbitrage: A trader's valuation of company A's and company B's debt and equity (and thus of a package of the two) entails a subjective estimate of its future cash flows and the riskiness of these cash flows. It is an opinion, not a fact. Furthermore, different traders will have different opinions. One trader may believe that two packages should have the same value and will therefore buy the cheap package and sell the dear package; another may believe that the differences in price are merited by their prospects, and yet another that the difference should be greater than it actually is. The Modigliani and Miller arbitrage isn't at all like buying two four-ounce gold coins and selling an eight-ounce coin. Using the arbitrage reasoning pioneered by Modigliani and Miller to determine "correct" prices, or to solve for a unique equilibrium conditions, by assuming omniscience or identical estimates helps increase the output of "tractable" models, but it is not even an approximately right representation of the real world. As it happens, the misrepresentation in the Modigliani and Miller model was, by itself, harmless; but some of the theorizing that followed was more consequential, as we see later in this chapter.

Efficient Markets

The efficient market hypothesis (EMH) has become a lightning rod for criticism of modern financial theory and the practices derived from it. As I argue next, however, the central proposition of EMH—that market prices are highly unpredictable—does not require outre assumptions about omniscience or the uniformity of subjective beliefs. It is also consistent with the way a decentralized economy works. Moreover, sensible interpretations of EMH are well supported by the empirical evidence and provide reasonable guidelines for making investment choices. Unfortunately, because interpretations of EMH aren't always sensible, the investment rules that follow some interpretations are unreasonably extreme. In addition, EMH's well-founded claims about the high unpredictability of prices have become a stalking horse for dubious stipulations about how prices fluctuate "randomly."

Eugene Fama's seminal article about EMH in 1970 laid out "weak," "semistrong" and "strong" versions. The weak version of the hypothesis stipulates that one can't predict future prices from historical prices, the semistrong version that future prices can't be predicted by analyzing "public" data (as is contained in annual reports and newspapers), and the strong version that even access to confidential information (for instance, something known to insiders but not disclosed to stockholders) may not lead to a good forecast of what will happen to prices.

Several plausible mechanisms can account for the unpredictability that is at the heart of all three versions. One is that a competitive market encourages many traders to search for information or patterns that they expect will influence prices—and to act on this information quickly when they find it, before anyone else does. For instance, if a trader learns about good news that is not widely known so that a stock is underpriced, the trader will buy the stock until it becomes fairly valued. But if everything that is known is quickly incorporated into prices, then further price changes can only occur when surprising, unforeseeable news arrives. By definition, this fluctuation is unpredictable.

A second is that unpredictability can result even if trading is based on sentiment rather than hard news and fundamental analysis. Keynes had cuttingly likened professional investment to

> newspaper competitions in which the competitors have to pick out the six prettiest faces from a hundred photographs, the prize being awarded to the competitor whose choice most nearly corresponds to the average preferences of the competitors as a whole; so that each competitor has to pick, not those faces which he himself finds prettiest, but those which he thinks likeliest to catch the fancy of the other competitors, all of whom are looking at the problem from the same point of view. It is not a case of choosing those which, to the best of one's judgment, are really the prettiest, nor even those which average opinion genuinely thinks the prettiest. We have reached the third degree where we devote our intelligences to anticipating what average opinion expects the average opinion to be.[11]

This process should also lead to highly unpredictable prices because no one can reliably forecast what tomorrow's average expectation of the average expectation will be.

Finally, unpredictability of securities prices follows from the pervasive Knightian uncertainty of an innovative, decentralized real economy. Debt and equity securities are claims on the cash flows of businesses, and owners and managers of these businesses make judgments whose outcomes often turn on the independent judgments of customers, suppliers, and competitors that owners and managers cannot control or forecast. In other words, even insiders act on the haziest of forecasts or hunches about what will happen to their profits, rather than objective probability estimates. And forecasting what will happen to profits and cash flows only takes us part of the way to predicting stock and bond prices.

The unpredictably of prices is consistent with considerable empirical evidence. Statistical tests have found no evidence of "serial correlation" in prices—in other words, the tests suggest that prices have no "history" and there is no reliable way to predict prices by any formulaic extrapolation of past prices. The difficulty of making good predictions is also borne out by studies of the performance of professional investment managers, which show that the average manager does not beat a diversified market portfolio and winners don't repeat—managers who do better than their peers in one period often fall behind the pack in the next. Individuals, like Warren Buffett, who consistently outperform other investors and the broad market, are outliers. When anomalies that seem to offer surefire or low-risk returns are discovered and publicized, they tend to go away—possibly because when they become widely known, traders compete away the profits.

If the basic idea of EMH is sound and well supported by the evidence, then what is the problem?

One problem is the absence of good operating instructions for EMH. Recall Friedman's argument that hypotheses should have two parts: a complete and abstract model (that has no maybes and approximations) and more concrete and pragmatic rules for using the model. Such rules are not hard to imagine. We could say, for example, that EMH works best in markets where a large proportion of investors pay attention to valuations and profit opportunities; securities aren't "pumped" by dishonest stockbrokers; and prices aren't manipulated by spreading false rumors, engaging in fictitious transactions ("painting the tape"), or establishing "corners." We could further stipulate that prices usually (rather than always) reflect fundamental factors as they might be evaluated by knowledgeable experts and adjust rapidly (but not instantaneously) to new information, leaving enough time to provide a satisfactory reward to the traders who bring this information to market.

These are certainly somewhat ambiguous stipulations but, as Friedman pointed out, concrete rules—as opposed to abstract models—have to be incomplete: "Completeness is possible only in a conceptual world, not in the 'real world.'" Furthermore, however much we try to explicitly formulate the rules and "no matter how successful we may be in this attempt, there inevitably will remain room for judgment in applying the rules. Each occurrence has some features peculiarly its own, not covered by the explicit rules. The capacity to judge that these are or are not to be disregarded, that they should or should not affect what observable phenomena are to be identified with what entities in the model, is something that cannot be taught; it can be learned but only by experience and exposure in the 'right' scientific atmosphere, not by rote."

The absence of such rules—and accompanying sensibilities about the need for judgment in applying them—has led to a pointless argument, conducted with almost religious fervor, about whether the market really is always fully efficient. It has drawn attention away from more interesting questions, such as when markets are more or less efficient, to what degree prices reflect fundamental factors, or how quickly they adjust to new information.

A second and related problem pertains to the prescriptive lessons drawn from EMH.

Sensible interpretations of EMH suggest valuable rules for buying and selling securities. Don't overtrade: If the market is usually right, you won't get a better deal by switching the stocks in your portfolio very often, but you will certainly incur transaction costs. Don't buy a stock because you know that something good is going to happen to the company: Very likely, everyone else does too, and that prospect may already be reflected in the price. In fact, it can even be risky to trade on information that is not widely known. Suppose you have reliable "insider information" that a company is about to announce a doubling of its profits. Buying the stock can still be a losing proposition: If the market has guessed that profits will more than double, the price may fall after the company makes its announcement. It is also risky to buy a stock because it now pays a high dividend in relation to its price: As likely as not, the market has marked down the price because other traders know something you don't and have good reasons to fear that the dividend will be reduced or eliminated in the future. These possibilities are not, however, intuitively obvious to many individuals. Therefore, learning about EMH and its implications can be of great help in improving investors' returns.

But exercising great caution in trying to outguess the market does not mean having blind faith that the price is always right. In the long run, forsaking all judgment can be as dangerous as overtrading, as many individuals have recently discovered. Unfortunately, many EMH absolutists often endorse blind-faith investment, possibly because they have given little systematic consideration to practical operating instructions. Absolutists erroneously jump from the virtually incontrovertible evidence that it is hard to outperform the market to the erroneous prescription that all efforts to evaluate the correctness of market prices are useless. In fact, as we will now see, forsaking judgment is a bad idea even for investors who have no interest in rivaling Warren Buffett's investment record and merely wish to earn an acceptable return on their capital commensurate with the risk.

Clearly there are markets (usually in the "emerging" category) where manipulation, insider trading, fictitious accounting statements, and even ghost companies are commonplace. In such markets prices cannot be assumed to be close to right, either for individual stocks or for the market as a whole. In the United States and other developed markets, fictitious companies listed on stock exchanges are rare.* Serious accounting frauds (such as at Cendant and Enron) are also unusual. Low-grade manipulation of reported earnings is more common, but markets often see through such practices.

Yet even in advanced markets there are episodes, such as the Internet bubble of 1999–2000, where a modest level of analysis and due diligence suggest that securities prices are unhinged from any plausible valuation of the underlying business, and that shady underwriting practices, conflicts of interest, and puffery are rampant. Ignoring such signs can turn out to be costly even for investors who are not direct participants in the speculative mania. For instance, investors who didn't buy dot-com stocks were nonetheless exposed to the bursting of the Internet bubble if they owned index funds that contained larger than historically normal proportions of high-technology stocks whose prices had followed dot-coms into the stratosphere.

This is not to suggest that it is easy to predict when markets have reached a peak or to profit from such predictions (see box). Prudence is no guarantee of safety. Cautious drivers do get into accidents.

Right Call, Wrong Outcome

In January 2000, I published a book on how new businesses are started and how they evolve. The process I described was diametrically at odds with the dot-com fever that was raging at the time. This incongruity forced me to assert

---

*But not unknown: some readers may recall the case of the ZZZZ Best, an apparently immensely successful carpet cleaning company that went public in 1986, making its founder Barry Minkow the youngest person to take a company public in the United States up to that time. By early 1987 the market value of the company was nearly $300 million. The company was vetted by Citibank and a host of Wall Street firms. A Salomon Brothers team of investment bankers that conducted due diligence on the wunderkind Minkow pronounced him highly ethical and moral. A few months later the enterprise was revealed to be a gigantic fraud.

that my model was right and that there was something fundamentally wrong with the dot-com phenomenon. In an interview published in the March 6, 2000, issue of the *Industry Standard*, I declared that the bubble was going to burst.[12] By pure chance, the NASDAQ peaked four days later at 5132.52. I also thought it appropriate at the time to put my money where my mouth was, so to speak, and bought out of the money puts on the NASDAQ index; these puts gave me the right to sell the NASDAQ index at a price of 2900 on September 16, 2000. The puts were expensive—more than $13,000 a piece, but my timing could not have been better. The NASDAQ collapsed after March 10. Alas, although the index continued to decline rapidly for the rest of the year, it failed to fall below 2900 by September 16. I lost every cent I had paid for the puts.[13]

To put the point more clearly, consider the alternative: Investing without judgment is like driving blindfolded. As President Reagan once said, "Trust but verify." The market usually gets prices right, if certain conditions are met. Therefore, even investors who don't want to do their own analysis ought to assess whether these conditions are satisfied before trusting the market price. But, as Friedman's essay points out, such an assessment involves judgment—it cannot be done "by rote." Moreover, judgments about whether conditions are keeping prices in line with true values cannot be made once and for all. At a particular time the stock of Consolidated Telephones may attract a large number of competing traders whose transactions and research keep its price well aligned with its fair value. But if competition becomes so intense that the return from trading Consolidated Telephones becomes unsatisfactory, some traders migrate to the more neglected stock of Bicycles Unlimited. Accordingly, the price of Consolidated Telephones becomes less likely to reflect its fair value. Investors who want to free ride off market prices therefore have to make judgments about background conditions on an ongoing basis.

The argument that investment performance is all a matter of luck and therefore investment analysis isn't worth the effort is another lesson incorrectly drawn from EMH. It is claimed that extraordinary Warren Buffetts may earn their long-run records (Nobel laureate William Sharpe, whom we will soon meet, called Buffett a "three sigma event"),[14] but most others are merely the beneficiaries of lucky streaks: Imagine that the population of the United States is divided into pairs of contestants who call coin tosses, with each winner successively playing against other winners until the field is winnowed down to about two hundred people each of whom had made the right call twenty times in a row.[15] Of course any winner's claim to superior coin-toss calling skills is absurd.

In addition, there would be no point in practicing to play this game or in expending effort before making a call.

But now imagine a different game, say, professional tennis. It too has a few exceptionally dominant players like Roger Federer, but often within the top ranks, anyone can beat anyone. It wouldn't be outlandish therefore to say that winning a match or tournament is a matter of luck—as in a coin-tossing contest. But there is an important difference. In professional tennis, practice and effort matter a great deal, and a player who slacks off will soon fall out of the top ranks. In other words, winning close contests may require luck, but for any player to treat it as purely a matter of luck guarantees failure. As the Red Queen said, "It takes all the running you can do to stay in the same place."

Things are a bit easier in making investment choices since it is possible to take advantage of the efforts of other traders to set the right price. Even value investors rely on the eventual success of others' efforts to bring prices in line with values. But although hitching a ride may be relatively inexpensive, it isn't free. Unless you watch where the market is taking you, and make some effort to ascertain that it is operating normally, you run the risk of nasty—and possibly catastrophic—accidents. Moreover, diversification doesn't make the problem go away. Backing twenty thieves or buying a basket of 500 inflated bubble-stocks does not produce higher returns than going with a single Madoff or WorldCom.

Furthermore, the absolutist prescription to forsake judgment, to blindly trust market prices, not only puts those who follow it at risk, but also undermines the pluralism of opinions that help align prices and values. If many drive with their eyes closed, widespread collisions and injuries to those who do keep their eyes open become routine. When many simply pile on, so that prices reflect the judgments of just a few, the possibility of mistakes—and the opportunity for self-dealing—is great. Forsaking case-by-case judgment, like littering or not voting, is unsustainable en masse: If everyone eschews judgment, who will make market prices even approximately right,[16] or ferret out the offerings of thieves and promoters of worthless securities? Paradoxically, the efficiency of securities markets is a public good that can be destroyed by the unqualified faith of its believers.

A third problem with EMH lies in the company it keeps: The "unpredictability" of securities prices is tied to what is misleadingly called a random walk pattern of fluctuations. In reality, the "randomness" of prices under this construct is quite constrained. Price changes are assumed to conform to a normal or bell-shaped probability distribution. The center of the distribution—the most probable return—is supposed to be just enough to compensate investors for owning a risky security, rather than a riskless treasury bill. Probabilities on either side of the center are symmetric—prices are as likely to double as halve. And the distribution is assumed to be "stable": The shape of the bell remains constant and always has the same width.

The following image may be helpful in visualizing what this assumption implies: Imagine that the price of a stock is determined by a draw from an urn in the following way. The urn contains an equal number of red and black balls. The size of the balls is inversely proportional to their number—the urn contains many small balls and few large balls such that a plot of their diameters (or more properly the log of their diameters) against their frequency follows a bell curve. The change in price of a security depends on a random draw from "its" urn: If a black ball is drawn, the price increases by an amount commensurate with the diameter of the ball, whereas the draw of a red ball causes a fall in the price, again depending on the diameter of the ball.

Different securities have urns with different distributions—for instance, ball diameters for "riskier" securities will be distributed along a wider bell. But crucially, the contents of each urn never change. Therefore, although the result of each draw and price change is random and unpredictable, the long-run distribution of returns is completely predictable and fixed.

This predictable randomness stands in sharp contrast to EMH in terms of its theoretical plausibility and conformance to empirical evidence.

As I have argued, the unpredictability that is at the heart of EMH is well founded: In a competitive market all known information—and traders' subjective interpretations of this information—will be quickly reflected in market prices. Any change therefore requires some unforeseen information or an alteration of interpretations and sentiments. In addition, thanks to a decentralized system of innovation in the real economy, there are frequent unpredictable changes in the financial prospects of the businesses on which securities are based.

But this very kind of unpredictability flies in the face of the assumption of a stable normal distribution of price changes.

We may reasonably assume that the magnitude of the surprises that move prices will be inversely proportional to the frequency of their occurrence, with small surprises being more frequent than large surprises.

We should therefore expect to see more small changes in price than large changes. We can further imagine that the sum of positive changes, weighted by their true probabilities, equals a similar sum for negative changes. To put it differently, the area under the probability curve to the left-hand side of its center equals the area to the right-hand side. But the shapes of probability distributions (regular and irregular) that satisfy these two conditions is virtually infinite; and there is no reason to believe that the normal distribution is the right one.

More crucially, regardless of what the true shape might be, there is every reason to expect that it *won't* be stable and therefore that price changes *can't* be a draw from a fixed distribution. This logic can be most simply stated from the perspective of real economic changes: The distribution of price changes inarguably is different for different securities, presumably because of differences in their economic fundamentals. For example, IBM's stock price is likely to be less volatile than the stock of a small high-tech company because it is larger and more diversified. The unforeseen defection of a customer will have a smaller impact on IBM's financial prospects.

But in an innovative, ever-changing economy, IBM's fundamentals also change. Its stock today represents a claim on the cash flows of quite a different company than was the case a decade ago. Therefore, tomorrow's change in IBM's price must also be a draw from a different urn. In other words, the very factor that makes individual price changes unpredictable—the profoundly uncertain course of innovation—should also make patterns of price distributions unpredictable and unstable. Even if we ignore unquantifiable Knightian uncertainty, we cannot make a once-and-for-all determination of the quantifiable probabilities and risks.

In fact, in sharp contrast to the extensive empirical support for reasonable interpretations of EMH, data on price changes show no evidence of a stable normal distribution. It takes some imagination to see a bell shape in the plot of price changes of any stock or stock index. Although it has certainly become commonplace to calculate means and standard deviations of prices, under the assumption that they are normally distributed, that calculation has nothing to do with the reality. And the most casual observation of any price plot shows great instability from period to period: Even means and standard deviations show large fluctuations from month to month and year to year.

Yet the two discordant ideas—EMH and stable normal distributions—have been deeply intertwined. One reason is historical: EMH evolved from research that sought to model changes in stock prices as a normally distributed random walk, starting with ideas of Brownian motion drawn from physics. Second, normal distributions are mathematically convenient: The shape of the bell curve can be fully described by just two values—its mean and its standard deviation. Furthermore, assuming a normal distribution makes it easy to apply well-established probability theory. Conversely, representing distributions by other, more complex shapes and, even worse, allowing for changes in distributions, makes it hard to build "tractable" models.

In spite of the illogic and contradictory evidence, stable normal distributions have become entrenched in modern financial theory, possibly under the cover of what should really be their antithesis—EMH. For instance, in the early 1960s the polymath mathematician Benoît Mandelbrot made a plausible argument that price changes in financial markets were far better represented as "Lévy distributions" than as normal distributions. Mandelbrot's research initially sparked great interest but ultimately made no headway. Using Lévy distributions sharply limited the number of mathematical models that could be generated and solved. "The reason people didn't latch on to that stuff is it's not that tractable," said Eugene Fama, once a Mandelbrot fan and informal student. "It's not that easy to deal with those predictions in a systematic way."[17] Switching from normal to Lévy distributions would also mean abandoning a large corpus of models that had already been built. As Paul Cootner wrote in 1964, if Mandelbrot was right, "almost all of our statistical tools are obsolete.... Surely, before consigning centuries of work to the ash pile, we should like to have some assurance that all our work is truly useless."[18]

The flawed, but mathematically convenient, assumption of stable normal distributions also reshaped the practice of finance: It was central to the development of new technologies through which financial instruments and strategies could be robotically mass-produced, seemingly obviating the need for case-by-case subjective judgment, even of the quantifiable dimensions of risks and returns, as we will now see.

▓▓▓ Efficient Portfolios; or, Risk Redefined

Modern investment practice, reflecting modern finance theory, differs from traditional value investing (à la Warren Buffett) in important ways.

It focuses on portfolio composition: what proportion of assets to hold in stocks, bonds, cash, and alternative assets such as timberland, commodities, or private equity investments. The selection of individual securities—the principal preoccupation of the value investor—is left largely or entirely to the market. Moreover, portfolios are constructed in a mechanistic top-down way, with little or no case-by-case judgment.

Mechanistic modern practice also involves reducing risk—of portfolios and their individual components—to measures of the volatility of returns. Under the assumption of normally distributed returns, volatility is represented by a single number, the standard deviation of the distribution of returns (roughly, the width of the bell curve).

Harry Markowitz laid the foundations for focusing on the construction of portfolios, as opposed to individual constituents, with a seminal paper, "Portfolio Selection," published in the *Journal of Finance* in 1952. At the time, Markowitz was a twenty-five-year-old graduate student at the University of Chicago. Markowitz, who had no previous interest in the topic, had been drawn to study the construction of stock portfolios after a chance meeting with a broker. The broker urged him to apply techniques from the emerging field of linear programming to the stock market. Markowitz discovered that there was no existing work that systematically linked the risks of a stock portfolio to its returns.

Markowitz created a formula for constructing "efficient" portfolios of stocks that produces the highest returns per unit of risk rather than a single "best" portfolio. As Bernstein puts it, the formula generates a "menu" of portfolios—some with high returns and low risk, and others with low returns and high risk. The menu constitutes an "efficient frontier" of portfolios in that investors cannot get higher returns without taking on more risk (or reduce their risk without giving up return) than is offered by any portfolio on the menu. Any portfolio outside the menu is inferior, offering either lower returns or higher risk.

Markowitz defined the risk of a stock as a single number: the standard deviation (or "volatility") of its returns. This wasn't how most investors thought of risk at the time, but the definition made risk easy to calculate. Existing probability theory provided a formula for computing the volatility of a portfolio by combining the volatility and covariance (a measure of the extent to which the returns were in sync) of the components of the portfolio. Markowitz's calculation of the overall return was even more straightforward: It was just the weighted average of the return of the individual stocks.

But although the risk and return of any portfolio can be easily calculated, the ways in which a given set of stocks can be combined into a portfolio is infinite, and picking the most efficient set from a boundless number of possibilities was anything but easy. The problem, as MacKenzie puts it, "fell into a mathematical domain that operations researchers were only beginning to explore." Therefore, there was no off-the-shelf algorithm Markowitz could turn to: "It was difficult, innovative work." In fact, the technique that Markowitz developed was worthy of publication in an operations research journal.[19]

Markowitz's key insight for finance was "the strategic role of diversification," writes Bernstein. The mathematics of diversification, Bernstein argues, "helps to explain its attraction. While the return on a diversified portfolio will be equal to the average of the rates of return on its individual holdings, its volatility will be *less than* the average volatility of its individual holdings. This means that diversification is a kind of free lunch at which you can combine a group of risky securities with high expected returns into a relatively low-risk portfolio, so long as you minimize the covariances, or correlations, among the returns of the individual securities."[20]

Markowitz's paper on portfolio selection, and the book he published in 1959, remarks Bernstein, "provided the groundwork for just about all of the theoretical work in finance that followed." The publications also "revolutionized the profession of investment management by elevating risk to equal importance with expected return" and supported many practical applications, such as portfolio allocation between stocks and bonds and the "valuation and management of options and more complex derivative securities."[21]

But not all revolutions, even ones that spread widely and survive for decades, are for the better. As Bernstein notes, critics "have turned Markowitz's work into a punching bag, attacking from every side the entire set of assumptions that support it."[22]

An obvious target is the assumption that stock returns follow a smooth, bell-shaped distribution. Without this assumption, Markowitz's already challenging operations research problem would have been impossible to solve. The assumption is nonetheless clearly false. That in and of itself wouldn't be a problem (at least from the perspective of Friedman's essay) if its predictions could be empirically shown to be reasonably accurate. But the Markowitz model, unlike EMH, doesn't purport to explain how the world works. It is a prescriptive formula that tells investors how they should construct efficient portfolios if X, Y, and Z conditions hold. Markowitz himself described his book as "really a closed logical piece."[23]

Unfortunately, it's virtually impossible to test whether a portfolio is or is not efficient either before or after the fact. Therefore, we cannot know whether making the erroneous assumption that returns are normally distributed matters a lot or a little. Seemingly efficient diversification might be a free lunch—or it could come with a ruinous price tag at the end.

Another important issue lies in a practical problem that Bernstein calls technical. Using the Markowitz method requires values for the expected return and volatility of each security in the portfolio, as well as the covariance of the returns for every pair of securities. Furthermore, the formula is highly sensitive to these values, so if the numbers for returns, volatilities, and covariances are a bit "off," the formula will generate portfolio compositions very different from ones generated with the "right" numbers. Of course, an omniscient being would know the right numbers, but what about flesh-and-blood investors?

In his 1959 book, which was intended to be a practical guide for investors, Markowitz assumed that estimates "would come from security analysts," as he told Justin Fox. "My job as an operations research guy is, you give me the estimates, and I'll compute the portfolios faster than the next guy."[24] In principle, therefore, the Markowitz method had some room for case-by-case judgment, albeit not of the full-blown "investment case" or narrative style.

But actually using case-by-case judgment to estimate the numbers required by Markowitz's formula was practically impossible. Yes, security analysts can and do estimate rates of return from buying a stock. They may, for instance, try to calculate how a company's earnings will grow over the next five years, estimate what will happen to the ratio of its stock price to earnings, and thus project its future stock price. Comparing this price to the current price yields an estimate of the rate of return. But how can anyone estimate the volatility of returns? This entails forecasting not where a stock's price will be at the end of a period, but rather the degree to which it will fluctuate because of surprising news that will arrive along the way, unpredictable changes in the opinions and moods of buyers and sellers of the stock, or both. And how does anyone begin to think about estimates of covariances—the degree to which a stock will fluctuate in tandem with some other stock?

Inevitably, because people can't, they don't. Instead they rely on historical volatility, covariances, and often, rates of return: It's easy, quick, and seemingly objective and unbiased. But historical values are also bad predictors of future values, and often by a meaningful margin. As I mentioned earlier, the volatility of returns is as unstable and unpredictable as the returns themselves, and for precisely the same reasons. Nor is there any reason for the covariance of the returns of pairs of prices to be stable—and they aren't.

The problem of using historical data is made particularly acute by the Markowitz model's use of the volatility of returns as a principal measure of risk. Bernstein writes that standard deviations have "an intuitive appeal as a proxy for risk," because "our gut tells us that uncertainty should be associated with something whose value jumps around a lot over a wide range. Most assets whose value is given to springing up violently tend to collapse with equal violence."[25]

Undoubtedly, the volatility of the price of an asset represents an important facet of its risk: Investors who buy securities whose prices fluctuate a lot face the risk that prices will plummet just when they need the cash. And even long-term investors, who don't worry about having to raise cash at an inopportune time, will worry that a stock which has shot up will fall abruptly. But now consider Bernstein's further argument that "statistical analysis confirms what intuition suggests: most of the time, an increase in volatility is associated with a decline in the price of the asset."[26]

Historic, or backward looking, volatility does indeed jump when prices collapse, as we saw most recently in the fall of 2008. Famously, the bankruptcy of Lehman Brothers on September 15, 2008, triggered a financial panic, including a steep decline in the Standard and Poor's 500 stock index (the S&P 500). In the following six months, the index lost about 40 percent of its value, compared to a 3 percent drop in the previous six months.[27] Average historic (sixty-day trailing) price volatility in the six months after mid-September was likewise more than double what it had been in the prior six months.[28]

But past volatility is a poor predictor of future volatility. Even if one equates volatility with risk, it is hard to believe that stocks were much riskier looking *forward* in mid-March 2009 than they were the day before Lehman Brothers collapsed—and, in fact, volatility did fall sharply, by more than half, after mid-March.[29] In other words, an investor who had relied on historic data would have predicted stock prices to be twice as volatile as they turned out to be. Also think of the issue from the perspective of an old-fashioned investor who is concerned about losses rather than volatility: Were stocks in mid-March 2009 twice as risky as they had been the day before Lehman fell, *after* prices had fallen by nearly half?[30] Surely stocks are less likely to collapse further after a historic battering and therefore ought not to be regarded as more risky.

Conversely, the mechanistic use of historical price volatility as the principal measure of risk can lead to a dangerous underappreciation of the downside. After long periods of price stability—dull markets are as much a feature of an unpredictable world as is unexpected chaos—risk, as measured by the backward-looking volatility of returns, all but disappears. This encourages widespread buying, sometimes with the use of leverage, because the asset is considered low risk. But when volatility returns to more normal levels, mechanistic rules that cap the total risk permissible in the asset lead everyone to trim back. And if everyone tries to do this at once, a selling cascade can ensue.

Why, then, in spite of all these problems—ranging from the erroneous assumption about the normal distribution of returns, to a one-dimensional, backward-looking view of risk, to the hazards of herding behavior—has the Markowitz approach to constructing portfolios become so popular?

I believe one reason is the visceral reactions it evokes, both in the people who can handle the math and in those who can't. For those who can, the approach offers provides a seductive rush, possibly admixed with a *Revenge of the Nerds*–like sentiment.* And those who can't handle the math are often awed by those who can, or possibly are too insecure to admit that they don't understand how the technology works.

This awe and insecurity, in turn, has commercial value to purveyors of asset allocation services, seemingly rooted in objective science, that help clients maintain an "efficient" mix of stocks, bonds, and cash.[31] Asset allocation models have also been used for the even more lucrative activity of selling alternative or nontraditional assets, such as limited partnerships that invest in oil and gas and timberland, and, recently, commodity indexes. As the commodity example illustrates, efforts to sell a new asset class usually follow a run-up in its price. Clients can be sold on the high

---

*This interpretation is perhaps an unwarranted generalization from personal experience: Around 1996 I constructed (with a great deal of effort and without the grasp of its limitations that I now have) a Markowitz-style model to trade government bond futures. Fortunately, I incorporated safety features, so that it wasn't really capable of losing (or making) a lot of money. After a few years of trading with results akin to spinning wheels, I wound up the enterprise.

historic rates of return of the class *and* its low correlation with traditional assets: Investors can therefore trade up to a more advanced "efficiency frontier." Or so they are told.

Unfortunately, by the time a new asset class becomes popular, prices are not far from the peak. Moreover, when a large amount of passive money enters a market to buy into an asset class, it can at least temporarily distort prices (see box).

Roiling Commodity Prices

According to one Wall Street veteran, commodities markets used to be the province of specialists, so prices reflected the aggregated opinion of knowledgeable traders. For instance, corn traders kept abreast of the factors (such as Department of Agriculture reports on acreage planted) that would affect the supply and demand for corn. The influx of investors who treated commodities as an asset class untethered prices from judgments of actual supply and demand. Purchases of the asset class sort in the first half of 2008 thus helped drive commodities prices, notably those of crude oil, to unsustainably high levels, setting the stage for a dramatic collapse later in the year.

"Normally one would expect knowledgeable traders to stabilize the market," this expert observes,

> by shorting to the passive investors whatever amount of a commodity they would want and profiting later when the fundamentals reassert themselves. The fundamentalist never knows, however, the size of the buying wave he is selling into. Solvency considerations dictate that he will conserve capital and at some point actually withdraw from the market. Once the passive buyers have gone through the first round of fundamentalist selling, the price may have to rise to extreme levels before new capital has the incentive to learn the fundamentals and join the sellers. This is a phenomenon I have seen any number of times over the past 30 years. The normal experts are overwhelmed and prices go to an extreme until new capital enters the market.[32]

Finally, financial firms have also found Markowitz models attractive for internal use. As mentioned in chapter 4, the size of a financial firm and the scope of its activities are limited by the inability of bosses to manage subordinates "by the numbers." They cannot, for instance, monitor the quantity and quality of output, as a vice president of manufacturing might do in a semiconductor factory. Rather, in the financial industry, bosses face the labor-intensive task of second-guessing the judgments of subordinates. Using the Markowitz approach gets around this problem: Bosses no longer need to get into the whys and wherefores of their subordinates' decisions and positions. They can instead focus on monitoring the overall risk of their organization's portfolio, limiting what they need to know about individual positions to a matrix of numbers (comprising volatility and covariance estimates).

As it happens, this reductionist, quantitative approach has been the undoing of many a financial enterprise. Yet its use remains pervasive in organizations where bosses get a share of the profit without having to invest much of their own capital because it provides a respectable cover for assembling large conglomerations of risk-taking. And, possibly for this reason, learning from failure is also limited. Standard operating procedure after a debacle is for the principals to admit having underestimated the possibility that previously uncorrelated positions might all fall together in times of stress, and to resolve not to make this mistake next time around. What is not acknowledged is that the entire risk-management procedure relies on several unrealistic assumptions and is not a good substitute for careful scrutiny of individual positions. Therefore, as the case of John Meriwether shows, the second time around can reprise the first.*

In spite of the broad diffusion of the Markowitz model into many areas of financial practice, it did not make any headway in the application for which it was originally designed—constructing efficient stock portfolios—because of computational problems. One issue lay in having to calculate a large number of covariances: For a 1,000-security portfolio, 499,500 pairs of covariances were necessary,[33] in addition to the estimates of volatility and returns for each security. These inputs also had to be processed through the algorithm that Markowitz had developed. The state of the art for mainframe computers in the early 1960s could not handle more than 249 securities.[34]

In the domain of theory, Markowitz's model belonged more to the field of operations research than to mainstream economics. In fact, when Markowitz defended his PhD thesis (about two years after the publication of his *Journal of Finance* article in 1952) Milton Friedman, who was one of the examiners, took the view that Markowitz's dissertation was

*Meriwether founded Long-Term Capital Management (LTCM), which collapsed spectacularly in 1998, four years after it was started. In 1999 Meriwether founded JWM Partners, promising to use more conservative correlation estimates in its risk management system than had been done at LTCM. Nonetheless JWM Partners was battered in the 2008 crisis. In July 2009 Meriwether closed JWM.

a "mathematical exercise, not an exercise in economics."[35] (Markowitz did get his degree, however and, a quarter century later, a Nobel Prize in Economics.)

Markowitz had sketched out a possible solution to the computational problem. In his 1959 book he had suggested that instead of calculating the covariance for every pair of securities in a portfolio, we could assume that they were all correlated with "one underlying factor, the general prosperity of the market as expressed by some index."[36] Instead of calculating nearly half a million pairs of covariances for a thousand-security portfolio, the simplifying assumption would require only a single estimate for the correlation of each security with the "one underlying factor."

In 1960, William Sharpe, then an economics doctoral student at UCLA, approached Markowitz for advice on a dissertation topic. Markowitz suggested that Sharpe develop an algorithm that implemented his proposal to make efficient portfolios easy to compute. Sharpe did just that. The time taken to analyze a 100-security portfolio fell from thirty-three minutes on an IBM mainframe to thirty seconds, using a method that used the covariance of each security with returns for the stock market as whole, rather than with all the other ninety-nine securities in the portfolio.[37] Sharpe's solution became the first part of his doctoral thesis and was published in 1963 in *Management Science*.

But this was still operations research, not economics. Sharpe, who was "at root" an economist, then "asked the question that microeconomists are trained to ask. If everyone were to behave optimally (that is, follow the prescriptions of Markowitz's portfolio theory), what prices will securities command once the capital market has reached *equilibrium?*"[38] According to the model that Sharpe developed, equilibrium would be reached (the supply of all stocks would match their demand) when the expected return of a security was proportional to its "beta"—the security's covariance with the rate of return of the overall market.

This model is now known as the capital asset pricing model (CAPM). Versions of CAPM were independently developed about the same time by Harvard's John Lintner, by Jan Mossin from the Norwegian School of Economics and Business Administration, and by Jack Treynor, a California-based money manager. In 1990, when Sharpe was awarded the Nobel Prize in Economics,* the presentation speech noted

---

*Lintner and Mossin were deceased by then, and Treynor may have been passed by because he was a practitioner.

that CAPM had "become the backbone of modern price theory of financial markets."[39]

But Sharpe's CAPM required assumptions that went beyond even the considerable simplifications of Markowitz's model. All investors were assumed to be able to borrow or lend at the "riskless" or treasury bill rate, for instance. Even more audacious was the assumption that all investors had exactly the same forecasts for returns, risks, and correlations. This assumption allowed Sharpe to use the faux arbitrage approach to identify equilibrium conditions[40] that had been pioneered by Modigliani and Miller. But the assumption was just as self-evidently false: Without buyers who believed IBM's shares were cheap and sellers who thought them dear, there would be virtually no trading of IBM's stocks. And indeed, a referee at the *Journal of Finance*, where Sharpe had submitted a paper containing his model, thought his assumptions were "absurdly unrealistic." But Sharpe "stubbornly resubmitted the piece, writing a letter that cited Milton Friedman's 'Methodology of Positive Economics' arguing that it was the implications of his theory that mattered, not the assumptions."[41] The editor of the journal had changed by the time Sharpe's resubmission arrived, and the paper was published in 1964.*

As it happens, CAPM failed to meet the criteria that Friedman had laid out for making unrealistic assumptions acceptable—that they produce predictions borne out by the evidence. The model clearly flunked this test. For instance, one of its testable implications was that low "beta" stocks—ones whose returns were weakly correlated with the returns of the overall market—should provide lower returns than high-beta stocks. In fact, Michael Jensen, Myron Scholes, and Fischer Black, who studied New York Stock Exchange listed stocks from 1931 to 1965, found that portfolios comprising "low beta" subsets had higher returns and "high beta" portfolios had lower returns that CAPM predicted.[42]

Similarly, Eugene Fama and Kenneth French found higher betas produced higher returns in the period 1941–65, but not afterward.

---

*In the final version, Sharpe acknowledged that his assumptions were "highly restrictive and undoubtedly unrealistic." But because the assumptions implied "equilibrium conditions which form a major part of classical financial doctrine," the formulation ought not be rejected, "especially in view of the dearth of alternative models" (Sharpe 1964, 434). In other words, "science fiction" theory, as Jon Elster might call it, was better than nothing.

Moreover, even for 1941–65, the relationship between beta and return disappeared when controlled for firm size.[43] CAPM, Fama has come to believe, "is atrocious as an empirical model."[44]

In a different kind of critique, UCLA economist Richard Roll argued that it is not possible to test CAPM. Estimating the "beta" of a security requires measuring the correlation of its returns with the returns on the market portfolio. But what is a market portfolio? Roll argued that an index of U.S. stocks is a poor proxy. A true market portfolio ought to be global, encompassing all assets including real estate and human capital. Because the returns of such a portfolio cannot be observed, we cannot set up an empirical test of CAPM. Sharpe apparently endorsed Roll's view, telling an interviewer, "We'll never be able to say definitively the CAPM holds. We'll probably never be able to say definitively the CAPM doesn't hold as well."[45] But if the model cannot be tested *and* the assumptions are completely at odds with reality, then, by Milton Friedman's argument, it is just a "structure of tautologies"[46] and ought not to be pressed into practical service.

Yet prescriptions drawn from CAPM have become pervasively influential. The model purportedly shows, for example, that the efficient frontier for stocks comprises just the market index souped up with leverage (for investors willing to face higher risk for higher returns) or diluted with cash (for investors with low risk-tolerances).* While this prescription is not universally followed, it has made deep inroads.

The use of "beta" as the principal measure of the risk of security has had even greater impact. Every MBA is now taught that systematic risk—the degree to which a stock tracks the overall market as measured by its beta—is paramount because investors can diversify away idiosyncratic (or "unsystematic" risk). Such beliefs obviously devalue the importance of company- and context-specific analysis. Moreover, the beta view—like the Markowitz method from which it descends— encourages the often self-serving belief that the risks of very large portfolios can be managed in a mechanistic, top-down way.

---

*In the original Markowitz model (and in the early version of Sharpe's model) portfolios with a wide variety of compositions (not just the market basket) could be efficient.

Concluding Comments

Eugene Fama's article on EMH, according to MacKenzie, can be regarded "as the capstone of the transformation of the academic study of finance that had occurred in the U.S. in the 1950s and 1960s. What had started as separate streams—the Modigliani-Miller "irrelevance" propositions, portfolio theory and the capital asset pricing model, the random-walk model—were, by 1970, seen as parts of a largely coherent view of financial markets."[47] But the practice of finance had not yet been altered. Just as life insurance companies in the eighteenth century continued to rely on subjective estimates even though statisticians had developed mortality tables, most practitioners continued to be use traditional methods. For example, CAPM was "still only an academic theory" in 1971.[48]

But in the 1970s practice rapidly caught up with theory.

In 1974, Peter Bernstein founded the *Journal of Portfolio*, intended to present the practical implications of modern research to practitioners of finance. Virtually everyone I have mentioned in this chapter has been published in the journal. In its very first issue, Paul Samuelson, who had spearheaded the theoretical triumph of mathematical economics, issued investors a "Challenge to Judgment." The world of "practical operators," Samuelson wrote, was giving way to a "new world of the academics with their mathematical stochastic [probabilistic] processes." Academics understood that valuing individual securities was a wasted effort: "Most portfolio decision makers," Samuelson suggested, "should go out of business—take up plumbing, teach Greek, or help produce the annual GNP by serving as corporate executives."[49] Ordinary investors should understand the futility of stock picking, too, Samuelson counseled. Just buy the diversified market portfolio and throw away the key.

Samuelson's message resonated. Reading "Challenge" inspired John Bogle to launch the first stock index fund in 1976, and by November 2000, it had become the largest mutual fund ever, with $100 billion in assets. Case-by-case investing didn't completely disappear, of course. Venture capitalists who invested in young, unlisted companies continued to use the "common law," due diligence approach and maintain close, ongoing relationships with the companies in their portfolios. But this style of investing was progressively banished to the margins, especially in listed securities. The standard formula for institutional investors comprised a core holding of the Standard and Poor's 500 stock index, with peripheral investments in venture-capital funds and other such alternative assets.

The use of blind diversification as a substitute for case-by-case analysis took off in the credit markets as well. Bruce Bent launched the first American money market fund in 1970. Now nearly 2,000 funds manage about $3.8 trillion. Like stock-index funds, money market funds eliminate the costs of case-by-case judgment and of maintaining ongoing relationships: They simply buy a diversified portfolio of short-term instruments, certified as high quality by a rating agency.

The eventual emergence of ingenious schemes to take advantage of money market funds that depend entirely on free double- or triple-A certification by Standard and Poor and Moody's (which, themselves, have come to rely on stochastic modeling processes rather than on costly shoe-leather due diligence) was also unsurprising. Losses on debt issued by Lehman Brothers broke Bent's pioneering Reserve money market fund in September 2008. The debt was rated investment grade but, as we now know, not all highly rated securities are really safe.

Next we look at the breakthrough development in financial theory of the 1970s—the Black-Scholes model (or more properly, the Black-Scholes-Merton model) for pricing options. The model built on many of the assumptions and approaches we have discussed in this chapter—crucially, turning unpredictability into unvarying normal distributions and the use of arbitrage arguments. It also broke new conceptual ground, and its practical consequences were revolutionary. Whereas the pre-1970 theories helped mechanize the traditional financial activity of investing in equities and extending credit, Black-Scholes-Merton helped financiers mass produce and trade derivatives—instruments that had not previously been an important feature of the financial landscape.

Chapter 7

Storming the Derivative Front

Derivatives, writes Peter Bernstein, "go back so far in time that they have no identifiable inventor."[1] He speculates that they originated centuries ago, down on the farm. Farmers incur heavy expenses when they plant their crops and, often being in debt, cannot bear the risk that prices will wilt by harvest time. Options can limit this risk: Selling a futures contract or buying a put locks in a fixed price. But derivatives also have a long history as vehicles for speculation. The Dutch tulip mania of the seventeenth century involved more trading in tulip options than in the tulips themselves. Speculators bought "call" options—the right, but not the obligation, to buy tulips by a particular date—because the options provided more leverage than just buying the tulips.

While futures and options may not be new, the large-scale trading of derivatives—financial claims based on underlying assets, like stocks, bonds, or currencies—is. Financial futures and options began trading in Chicago in the early 1970s, sandwiched between the launch of Bruce Bent's pioneering money market fund and John Bogle's S&P 500 index fund. The Chicago Mercantile Exchange ("Merc") started trading futures on seven currencies in May 1972. Trading in stock options on a modern, organized exchange was launched in April 1973 by the Chicago Board of Trade's offshoot, the newly established Chicago Board Options Exchange (CBOE).

Exchanges quickly expanded. The Chicago Board of Trade started trading futures on mortgage-backed bonds (Ginnie Mae contracts) in October 1975 and on U.S. Treasury bonds in August 1977. The Board's neighbor and rival, the Merc, initiated trading in treasury bill futures in 1976. Trading in stock index futures started in 1982 with a contract on the Value Line index on the Kansas City Board of Trade. A few months later, the Merc introduced futures on the Standard and Poor's 500 stock index, which soon became the dominant equity futures contract. All these futures also had accompanying options, although they were not necessarily traded on the exchange hosting the future itself.

Trading in the new instruments soared. On the first day that stock options were traded on the CBOE, in April 1973, 911 transactions on sixteen stocks were recorded; five years later, the average daily trading volume had grown to 100,000 options with another 300,000 options trading on four other exchanges around the country. Since an option represents the right to buy or sell 100 shares, the daily trading volumes were significant compared to trading in the underlying shares on the stock exchanges.

Growth in the trading of financial futures was also explosive. The early 1980s saw the development of "over the counter" (OTC) financial derivatives, largely based on interest rates and exchange rates, that weren't traded on an exchange.

A pivotal role in this explosion was played by the Black-Scholes-Merton (BSM) model. The model was published in May 1973, right after options started trading on the CBOE and later won two of its developers* a Nobel Prize in Economics. "Today's huge volumes of derivatives trading would scarcely be possible without the calculative resources" it provided, MacKenzie writes.[2] The BSM formula for pricing options and "its associated hedging and risk-measurement techniques, gave participants the confidence to write options at lower prices" than they would have been willing to under older, more ad hoc pricing methods. This, in turn, helped "options exchanges to grow and to prosper"[3] by creating a virtuous cycle. Lower prices attracted buyers, increasing the volume of trading and reducing trading costs. Lower trading costs attracted even more buyers and sellers.

The growth of the over-the-counter derivatives similarly owes much to the model's capacity to generate theoretical prices. Many OTC derivatives are so highly specialized that sometimes no liquid market, or easily

*The third, Fischer Black, passed away in 1995 before the prize was awarded.

observable market price, exists for them. However, BSM allowed both vendors (most usually commercial and investment banks) and at least the more sophisticated purchasers to calculate theoretical prices, and thus have a benchmark "fair" price."[4]

Although the practical consequences of BSM are indisputable, it is an open question whether these consequences are good or bad. This chapter offers a skeptical perspective. The BSM pricing formula certainly enabled the mass production and use of derivatives: A trader with a handheld calculator could easily price a stock option traded on the CBOE, and wizards using large computer systems could quickly price and—in principle—manage the risks of complex OTC derivatives. But, I argue, the mathematical elegance of BSM (and its successors), which makes perfect sense in an idealized world (or what Merton calls the "super-perfect market paradigm"),[5] is poorly suited to the unpredictability of a decentralized, dynamic economy, where it systematically produces erroneous results.

A Paradigmatic Breakthrough

Pricing the financial futures that started trading in Chicago in the early 1970s was easy. Simple arbitrage reasoning could be used to calculate the right price: The future price had to equal the current cash price (of a bond, stock index, or foreign currency) plus the carrying cost (the net cost of tying up capital till the futures contract terminates).* This is not just a theoretical construct: Futures markets have flesh-and-blood arbitrageurs who make their living trading futures against their underlying instruments when relative prices stray from their proper relationship.

Pricing options (the right to buy or sell for a specified "strike" price until its expiration date) was, however, challenging. A call option on a stock should not cost more than the price of the stock—no one will pay more for the right to buy something than the cost of its outright purchase. Nor should a call option cost less than the difference between the stock price and the option's strike price; otherwise, shorting the stock and buying the option will yield an easy arbitrage profit. For the same

---

*For stocks this cost equals the borrowing cost less the dividend yield. For bond futures the carrying cost is usually negative because the borrowing cost is less than the interest earned while the bond is held in inventory. The futures price is therefore usually less than the cash price.

reason, call prices should be higher the longer the time left to expiration, but then converge to the difference between the strike price and stock price as expiration approaches.

Going beyond these obvious limits and rules to a precise mathematical formula proved extremely hard. Even the redoubtable Paul Samuelson failed to pull it off. Instead, market practitioners relied on rough-and-ready rules of thumb that "did not add up to a precise or comprehensive theory."[6]

The problem was ultimately solved by Fischer Black, Myron Scholes, and Robert Merton, with Merton providing both the crucial conceptual breakthrough and the mathematical know-how to turn the breakthrough into a formula. The conceptual breakthrough was a "replicating portfolio." Merton showed that the returns on a stock option could be perfectly replicated—and therefore perfectly hedged—by a combination of the stock and holding or borrowing of cash, if the composition of the combination could be continuously adjusted (as the price of the stock changed). And a perfectly hedged, that is, "riskless," portfolio can only earn a risk-free rate of return because otherwise arbitrageurs would buy the cheap side of the hedge and sell the dear side.

This reasoning implied that determining the right price of an option was equivalent to pricing its replicating, continuously adjusted combination of stock plus cash. Reducing the price of the latter to a formula, it turned out, was challenging. Standard calculus wouldn't do. In the end, Merton used stochastic calculus drawing on techniques developed by the Japanese mathematician Kiyosi Itô.

The BSM model became "an exemplary problem solution that could be developed and extended imaginatively," writes MacKenzie.[7] Financial economists used it to value complicated options, analyze decisions that had "option like" features, and build asset-pricing models based on arbitrage. But, according to MacKenzie, "for all the diversity and elaboration of option pricing theory after 1973, the work of Black, Scholes, and Merton remained paradigmatic. None of what followed contradicted their approach: It was all consistent with it."[8]

The Catch

As with the models we examined in the last chapter, BSM made a number of assumptions. One was the standard stipulation that changes in stock prices followed a stable, bell-shaped distribution. It also assumed that stocks and options could be traded without any transaction costs, that there were no obstacles to short-selling, and that it was possible to borrow at the riskless interest rate. At the time, these assumptions were "wildly unrealistic."[9] High brokerage commissions made buying and selling stocks and options expensive. Short-selling was tightly regulated and practically difficult, and borrowing at the riskless rate was the prerogative only of the U.S. government.

But inaccurate assumptions about trading costs, short sales, and borrowing may have been the less consequential of BSM's approximations and simplifications. As options trading picked up steam, market conditions became closer to the ones assumed in the BSM model: Trading costs fell sharply in the 1980s, and stock index futures made it easy to go short. Here, I want to focus on a problem that did not—and cannot—diminish and that makes the model unfit for the broad industrial-strength uses to which it has been put.

For all its stochastic calculus and Itô lemmas, the replicating portfolio paradigm, like its primitive Miller-Modigliani ancestor, is essentially faux rather than real arbitrage.

Imagine trying to calculate the price of bronze through the "replicating portfolio" of its components, tin and copper. Arbitrage calculations can provide a good estimate—if you happen to know the price of tin and copper, the proportions of the two metals used to make bronze, and the cost of combining and separating the two metals. But suppose you don't know one of these variables, say the proportions of tin and copper. Then all you can say, using the logic of arbitrage, is that the price of bronze must lie between the price of tin and copper, with due allowance for the costs of separating and combining the two metals. Anything beyond that is just a wild guess.

BSM not only assumes that the distribution of stock prices is bell-shaped (which is empirically false) but also that the volatility of this distribution (the width of the bell) is known. Without this knowledge, there can be no true arbitrage between an option and its replicating portfolio. But only an omniscient being can know the true value of volatility. The rest of us can only guess.

And making good guesses is hard. As I argued in the last chapter, forecasting volatility is more challenging than forecasting a range of prices: There are several sensible ways to think about the possible prices of a stock in sixty days, but not how much a stock will fluctuate over the next sixty days. The path of least resistance, if we are forced to forecast volatility, is to assume that future volatility will be the same as historic volatility—or at least to use historic volatility as a starting point and then, somehow, shade it up or down. But in fact, the volatility of prices is also volatile, so historic figures aren't good predictors (see box).

How Bad Is Historic Volatility as a Predictor of Future Volatility?

Think of the error that arises if we use the volatility of returns on the S&P 500 index for the past sixty days as a forecast for the next sixty days. On the first trading day of 2009 (January 2, 2009), the "historic" sixty-day volatility was 67.9 percent. But the volatility for the next sixty days was actually 42.1 percent. Thus if we had used the historic volatility as a forecast on January 2, 2009, the percentage error, defined as the difference between "historic" volatility (67.9) and the "true" volatility (42.1) divided by the "true" volatility, would have been 42.1 percent. Repeating this calculation for each trading day from January through May 2009 shows that the percentage error would have averaged 48 percent. In the second half of 2008 the average error would have been about 55 percent and in the first half of 2008, 17 percent.

Option traders do "shade" historic data for their estimates, and we can back out these shaded estimates using the BSM formula to calculate the volatility "implied" by option prices. These implied volatilities are closer to actual volatilities, but they are far from an accurate forecast. For instance, the "implied" volatility on January 2, 2009, was 33 percent. Thus the percentage error in using implied volatility as a forecast for the next sixty-day volatility would have been 20.4 percent (33 minus 42.1 divided by 42.1). Repeating this calculation for each trading day from January through May 2009 shows that the percentage error would have averaged 23 percent. In the second half of 2008 the average error would have been about 40 percent and in the first half of 2008, 16 percent.

How inaccurate are BSM prices? This is difficult to judge. Out-of-the-money call options (where the strike price is greater than the price of the stock when the option is sold) are typically worthless when they expire. This does not mean, however, that out-of-the-money call options are systematically "overpriced" when they are sold. With life insurance we can compare actual numbers of insured people who die, or claims paid out by the insurance company, against mortality tables and payout forecasts to assess whether insurance premiums were too high or too low. But with options, there is no similar benchmark, so it is impossible to know whether an option was priced correctly even after the fact.

We can say, however, that after decades of use and refinement of BSM, options still periodically trade at prices reasonable people would consider odd, especially in turbulent periods when demand for the kind of risk-control that options are supposed to offer is great (see box). Very likely, the oddness arises because of the widespread use of a model that demands knowledge of a value that no one has or can make a sensible guess about.

A Tale of Two Option Prices

"Out of the money" put options (rights to sell stock at a price below the current price) are often purchased as an insurance policy against price declines). As stock prices fell in 2008, the demand for such puts increased, as did their prices. On September 12, 2008, the day before the Lehman bankruptcy, a put representing the right to sell the S&P 500 at a price of 1,000, compared to the then prevailing price (of 1251.7), for roughly three months cost about $6. In other words, investors who owned the S&P 500 index could insure against a price decline of greater than 20 percent (their "deductible," as it were) for a premium representing slightly under 0.5% of the value of the stocks insured.

On March 13, 2009, when the S&P index had fallen to about 750, a put representing the right to sell the S&P 500 at a price of 600 for roughly three months cost $14. In other words, the cost of insurance against a 20 percent price decline jumped to 2.33% of the value of the stocks insured from less than 0.5%—a more than fourfold increase.

The more than fourfold increase in the cost of insurance is puzzling from the point of view of true believers in the unpredictability of prices: If prices reflect all available information, good and bad, why should the possibility of a 20 percent fall in prices be any greater in March 2009 than it had been six months earlier? And for those who think about fundamental values, the jump in insurance cost makes no sense at all. Shouldn't the prospect of a further 20 percent fall in prices be lower when the S&P is at 750 than when it is at 1250?

The anomalous pricing is, however, consistent with the mechanistic use of the BSM formula. Historic (sixty-day) volatility had jumped from to 39.4 percent in mid-March 2009 from 22.4 percent in mid-September 2008. Traders had no way of knowing what future volatility would be—whether it was now permanently or temporarily elevated. So they used an estimate of 37.5 percent, which was a shade lower than the sixty-day historic number but much higher than the 24.2 percent they had used to price options six month ago.

We can also make a rough calculation of how much misestimates of volatility matter, assuming that everything else about the BSM model is "right." These errors are not trivial (see box)

How Misestimates of Volatility Lead to the Mispricing of Options

Let us define the "pricing error" of a call as the difference between the market price and the "true" price divided by the "true" price, where the true price is calculated by an omniscient being who knows what the volatility of prices will be for the next sixty days. On January 2, 2009, an "at the money" S&P 500 call (where the strike price equals the market price) with sixty days left to expiry, would have been mispriced by 20.4 percent. Repeating this calculation for each trading day from January through May 2009 shows that the percentage error would have averaged 22 percent. In the second half of 2008 the average error would have been about 38 percent and in the first half of 2008, 14 percent.[10] All this assumes that the BSM is right in every other way—no errors occur because, contrary to the theory, price changes aren't distributed along a bell shaped curve, for instance.

Faux Testing

The folklore asserts that BSM was "*spectacularly* good at predicting options prices"[11]—and that traders who used it made more money than those who used other methods. But MacKenzie's analysis suggests a different interpretation. The volatility numbers that the early traders plugged into the BSM formula may or may not have been right, but they did lead to option prices systematically lower that the ones produced by other pricing methods. Therefore, traders using BSM were more likely to find buyers for the options they offered for sale. Furthermore, selling (also called "writing") options is usually a profitable business since options often expire unexercised—except in bull markets. But the decade of the 1970s was far from a bull market. For many years after the CBOE opened for business, the stock market treaded water—a perfect environment for selling options.

Then there are seemingly more systematic econometric tests that are also said to support the reliability of BSM. The best known of these tests was conducted by Berkeley economist Mark Rubinstein, one of the leading scholars in the field of derivatives and closely involved in its commercial practice, as we will later see. Rubinstein tested an implication of BSM—that the implied volatilities backed out from the prices of all options on the same stock with the same time to expiration would be the same, regardless of their strike price. In the early 1970s, there were considerable differences in these implied volatilities, but by 1976–78 they had largely disappeared. Rubinstein therefore declared that BSM had passed its test "with remarkable fidelity."[12] This and similar research led another leading derivatives researcher, Stephen Ross, to claim in 1987 that "judged by its ability to explain the empirical data, option pricing theory is the most successful theory not only in finance, but in all of economics."[13]

But showing that implied volatilities of different options on the same stock are virtually identical doesn't establish that the model generates the right option prices. No test, as I have argued, can ever do this. The rapid disappearance of differences in implied volatilities that existed when options were first traded very likely reflects the fast and widespread adoption of BSM, as MacKenzie and others have suggested. When everyone started using the same formula—and using the same historical data to anchor their estimates of volatility—differences in implied volatilities naturally disappeared. In fact, as MacKenzie points out, "spread traders" who used BSM to sell options with high implied volatility, while buying options on the same stock with the same time to expiration, helped ensure that the differences would be negligible. To put the point simply, Rubenstein's research was a faux test of a model based on faux arbitrage.

Reasons for Dominance

Unlike the formulas for pricing treasury bond or stock index futures, BSM is not transparent or intuitively obvious. For most users, the formula is a black box: They enter values of a few variables (such as the stock price, strike price, time to expiration, and volatility) and use the option value that comes out on the other side—with no clue about what goes on inside the box.

There are easier and more transparent ways to calculate option prices from historical data that produce results just as good as the ones generated by BSM and with fewer unrealistic assumptions (see box).

A Simple System

In 1983, I developed and implemented a simple computer program to trade newly launched options on the S&P 100 index. Several practical considerations precluded using BSM. Instead, my program used a "pot" containing every one-day percentage price change in the index that had occurred over past five years; thus the pot contained about 1,250 price changes.

The program used this pot to value options in the following manner. Here is how it would handle a thirty-day time-to-expiration call with a strike price of 130, when the S&P 100 index was at 110.

It would first "randomly" draw thirty percentage price movements from the pot. These might be +1.1%, +0.68%, −.22%, and twenty-seven other such numbers. From these numbers the program would calculate one possible "end point" for the index after thirty days. This would equal the current price of the index, 110, multiplied by $(1 + .011) \times (1 + .0068) \times (1 − .0022)$ and by twenty-seven similar numbers.

Suppose that index end point was greater than the strike price: Then the corresponding value of the option would be the end point minus the strike price. For instance, if the calculated end point was 135.3, then the corresponding value of the option would be 5.3 (= 135.3 minus 130). If, however, the calculated end point of the index was less than the strike price (130), the value of the option would be zero.

The program would then calculate 499 other possible end points for the index and their corresponding option values. A simple average of the 500 options values provided a "fair value" for the option. No fuss, no muss, and no calculus.

Besides calculating option values, the same procedure provided "fair values" of spread trades—for instance, of buying a 130 strike price call and selling a 140 strike price call—and the probability of making a profit on such a trade (i.e., what proportion of the 500 possible end points would yield a profit).

For about half a year, the system produced attractive trading opportunities. Then, as the market became more actively traded, profitable spread trades went away. And since I did not want to move to Chicago to become a professional options trader (which the tighter markets made necessary if I wanted to continue using the program), I stopped using the system.

As far as I can tell, the method was and remains as good as BSM for valuing options and spread trades. It certainly is backward looking in relying on historic returns, but it does not assume that they follow a bell-shaped distribution. Its main "unrealistic" assumption is that future price changes are independent, eqi-probability draws from a historic pot; and even this is not seriously problematic for spread trades.

Why then did the BSM model (and its descendants) displace existing methods of the early 1970s and then establish and maintain hegemony?

One reason BSM rapidly secured market share, as I have already mentioned, is that it generated lower prices than prevailing methods. MacKenzie cites several other reasons for its quick and continued dominance. It was grounded in economic theory and inherited the "cognitive authority of financial economics in a political culture in which economics was a useful source of legitimacy, and in which, in particular, the status of financial economics was rising fast."[14] Some other pricing services offered "option values based not upon theoretical reasoning but upon econometric analyses of observed option patterns."[15]

Moreover, BSM was "publicly available in a way many of its early competitors were not."[16] For instance, Gary Gastineau developed a model that he believed remedied the deficiencies of Black-Scholes-Merton, but he only published an outline of his model, keeping the details private so that he could sell the results to a select number of clients.

Traders could easily talk about BSM's "one free parameter—volatility,"[17] whereas models offered by other financial economists often involved required estimating three or more free parameters. Reducing the complexity of options to a single metric also allowed trading firms to coordinate the activities of many individual traders. The firms believed they were essentially buying and selling volatility; therefore, strategies involving many different transactions could be discussed and evaluated simply in terms of whether they would add to or reduce the firm's exposure to this variable.

BSM, like the Markowitz model discussed in the last chapter, offered a seemingly objective, top-down way to control and manage risk. Besides generating an option price, the BSM formula projects the sensitivity of that price to changes in the values of the key variables. Most notably, the formula predicts how much the price of the option will change for a given change in the price of the underlying stock—the so-called delta. And delta became a crucial risk-management tool. For instance, if a trader bought a call option, the firm that employed the trader could use its delta to short the underlying stock in amounts that would insulate the overall position (the option plus the short stock position) from subsequent changes in the stock price.

Such delta hedges provided reassurance, not just to the management of the firms trading the options, but to other parties as well. Firms that provided "clearing" services were exposed to the bankruptcy of the trading firms, and they, too, received comfort from delta hedging. If all options are properly offset by long or short positions in the underlying stock, there is no reason to worry about movements in the stock price. In principle, the simple alternative method (described earlier in a box) could also be used to construct the equivalent of a delta hedge. But explaining such a hedge to a boss or a third party, such as a clearing firm, would be harder than with a well-standardized BSM approach.

The risk management capabilities of BSM and its offshoots played a crucial role in the growth of OTC derivatives in the 1980s and beyond. Here's how: Futures and options exchanges, such as the CBOE, impose "position" limits on traders and trading firms. In other words, any one trader or trading firm cannot be long or short a particular option contract in amounts exceeding the position limit established by the exchange. This protects everyone who trades on an exchange in two ways: It makes "cornering" the market difficult and contains the ripple effects of the collapse of a trader or firm. As a side effect, capping the size of positions also protects the traders and trading firms from their own mistakes.

In OTC derivatives, however, there are no externally imposed limits. Banks and other financial institutions dealing in these instruments can enter into contracts with enormous exposures if they are not properly offset or hedged. Furthermore, OTC derivatives are usually far more complex than the options and futures traded on an exchange. Therefore, rules of thumb or simple models cannot be used to hedge exposures or even estimate the magnitude of the risks. But BSM provided the necessary tools, at least on the surface, to deal with that risk.

In reality, however, even basic delta hedging of a simple stock option is only as reliable as the formula used to calculate delta, and that formula is only as reliable as estimates of the volatility of the stock. In other words, not very. With complex OTC derivatives, the reliability of hedges crafted using BSM models is even more questionable. But the top bosses of financial firms often don't have the expertise to grasp the fragility of their hedges and risk management systems. And since most of the time OTC derivatives provide large profits, bosses have little incentive to dig too deeply.

The entrepreneurship of its developers—in the commercial and not just the intellectual domain—also likely contributed to the eventual domination of BSM. The zeal and salesmanship of the principals typically plays an important role in the success of many new technologies. Inventing a product that the inventor believes to be great is usually not enough because others tend to be skeptical. Thus, inventors have to become innovators, turning their ideas into commercial products and services. At the outset, they have to sell their products personally: Professional salespeople don't have the same fervor and credibility.

The success of BSM fits this pattern.

Fischer Black started an options-pricing service. He sold subscribers computer-generated pricing sheets "of theoretical prices for all the options traded on U.S. options exchanges." But to generate these "theoretical prices," Black had to go beyond the theory. Recall that the model requires knowledge of the true value of volatility that only an omniscient being can have. To generate his sheets, Black took a pragmatic approach. "My initial estimates of volatility," he wrote in 1975, "are based on 10 years of daily data on stock prices and dividends, with more weight on more recent data. Each month, I update the estimates. Roughly speaking, last month's estimate gets four-fifths weight, and the most recent month's actual volatility gets one-fifth weight. I also make some use of the changes in volatility on stocks generally, of the direction in which the stock price has been moving, and of the 'market's estimates' of volatility, as suggested by the level of option prices for the stock."[18]

This arbitrary goulash of assumptions had none of the mathematical elegance of BSM. The method also had elements of circularity—current market prices of the options were at least partially assumed to be fair and were used to calculate a fair price. But this was irrelevant from a business point of view: how many traders who bought Black's sheets knew or cared how he estimated volatility?

Scholes and Merton also transcended their role as financial theorists, although their commercial reach was not as broad as Black's. While Black sold his sheets to anyone who was prepared to pay (in 1975, his basic service cost $15 a month),[19] Scholes and Merton contracted with Donaldson, Lufkin & Jenrette (DLJ), a New York–based brokerage and investment bank, to provide theoretical prices. Mathew Gladstein of DLJ told MacKenzie in an interview that on the day the CBOE opened for trading: "I looked at the prices of calls and I looked at the model and the calls were maybe 30–40 percent overvalued! And I called Myron [Scholes] in a panic and said, 'Your model is a joke,' and he said, 'Give me the prices,' and he went back and he huddled with Merton and he came back. He says, 'The model's right.' And I ran down the hall...and I said, 'Give me more money and we're going to have a killing ground here.'"[20]

Scholes and Merton, like Black, had to go beyond their theory: Their claim that the market prices of calls were 30–40 percent overvalued turned on a market judgment about volatility. As it happened, Merton had a long history in making market judgments. He had traded stocks as a ten- or eleven-year-old. When he was a graduate student in applied mathematics at the California Institute of Technology (before transferring to MIT for a PhD in economics) Merton "went to a Pasadena brokerage most mornings at six thirty and traded until nine thirty, when he left for class."[21] But as with Black's subscribers, it is not obvious that DLJ knew they were buying into a market judgment as much as they were buying into a theoretical model—or that they cared.

Financial economists were attracted by the "elegance" of the Black-Scholes-Merton solution because its arbitrage-based reasoning did not require knowledge of an "unobservable variable"—investors' expectations of the returns of the underlying stock—that was required by other methods for valuing options. But BSM did require knowledge of another unobservable variable—expected volatility. Black claimed that estimating variances was "orders of magnitude easier than estimating...expected returns."[22] To what extent was this true, as opposed to Black talking his book, so to speak?

Forming reasonable, subjective estimates of a stock's return can be a challenging exercise. Predicting whether and by how much IBM's price will appreciate requires researching and thinking about several factors such as its product plans, relationships with customers, existing and potential competitors, exchange rates, and the strength of the economy. With volatility, because there is no sensible way to think about what it should be, there is almost no choice but to take the "easy way out": Calculate historic volatility. Shade to taste.

Invisible and Visible Consequences

With everyone taking the same easy way out, however, estimates of volatility tend to be similar. And because of the dominance of BSM, everyone has similar valuations of options prices. Therefore, without any centralized authority dictating prices, and thanks to the seemingly easy, robotic approach to valuing options, the diversity of opinion that is supposed to be the hallmark of a decentralized market is supressed. Furthermore, anchoring volatility estimates to historic data inevitably leads to bad forecasts and, presumably, to consensus valuations that are almost always wrong, sometimes by wide margins. Individual estimation errors don't cancel each other out. Rather, they add up to a single, market-wide mistake. Similarly, the hedging formulas that come out of BSM also tend to be wrong because they are also based on erroneous estimates of volatility. And here, too, everyone tends to make the same mistake.

That said, the harm caused by such mistakes was contained as long as the buying and selling remained limited to exchanges. The trading of options on exchanges is, to a large degree, a closed zero-sum game—even if everyone makes the same mistake, buyers and sellers who happened to be on the right and wrong sides gain or lose at each other's expense. Those who don't trade aren't affected. Moreover, because the number of participants is large (and exchanges impose position limits), the losses are widely dispersed.

But matters became more serious in the 1980s when BSM models extended their reach to products and strategies beyond exchange-traded options. Options—and the problem of pricing them—became ubiquitous. Options became a common and important component of compensation, especially in high-tech companies, where they are now granted to employees at every level. And options had long been implicitly embedded in mortgages, in the form of the right of borrowers to prepay their loans. As these mortgages were securitized, buyers of the securities became the de facto sellers of prepayment options. The BSM model was so well established that it became the pricing mechanism of choice even in conditions that weren't remotely close to its crucial assumptions. For instance, it was used to value option grants in companies that were not publicly traded, even though the arbitrage reasoning of the model assumed completely frictionless trading.

Thus, there is every reason to expect that the mispricing of exchange traded options—which I have argued is inevitable and frequently significant—would be at least as common under conditions far removed from BSM's idealized "super-perfect market paradigm." But now it wasn't just option traders who were taking their chances with pricing and hedging mistakes. Everyone who took out a mortgage with an embedded option, and the pension funds who invested in mortgage-backed securities, was exposed to mispriced options. So were administrative assistants at high-tech companies, investors in these companies, and even the IRS, which also relied on BSM to calculate taxes on option grants. Moreover, if we believe that good prices are necessary for the efficient allocation of resources, then we must conclude that miscalculations of employee compensation and mortgage rates that followed from errors in the mispricing of options injured the economy as a whole. No one, in other words, was sheltered when the misapplication of BSM became widespread.

It could be argued that because there was no better model, there was no other choice. This is not the case. There are simpler ways to value options that require explicit case-by-case judgment, most crucially about "final values." A sensible person who goes through the process of making these judgments, therefore, becomes aware of the errors that the judgments are likely to contain and will use the end result with due caution. Prudent bridge designers who are aware that they don't know the tensile strength of the steel they have available will shy away from building long-spanned bridges for four-lane traffic. Similarly, a start-up company that recognizes it cannot figure out how much an option grant is worth, within an acceptable margin of error, might decide to rely on cash compensation and stock grants. But users of BSM are often blissfully unaware of—or sometimes cynically ignore—the magnitude of errors it produces.

Usually, however, just as the reasons for the bad valuations produced by BSM are hidden from public view, so are the consequences of the mistakes. Misevaluations of employee stock options almost certainly distort the labor market, and the options embedded in mortgages distort the housing market and the bond market. But the magnitude of these distortions, and the economic harm that results from them, is impossible to measure. They are like a hidden tax that everyone pays; we just don't know how much.

On occasion, though, problems caused by the use of BSM have led to spectacular and very public blow-ups. "Portfolio insurance" provided an early taste. This product was created and marketed by two Berkeley finance professors, Hayne Leland and Mark Rubinstein (whose empirical tests BSM had passed with flying colors) in collaboration with an industry veteran, John O'Brien. The scheme was the mirror image of BSM: Instead of using hypothetical, constantly adjusted, replicating portfolios to price actual options, portfolio insurance constantly rebalanced actual portfolios of stocks and cash to replicate hypothetical put options. As mentioned, put options can be used to insure stockholding against price declines; but pension funds and other large institutional stockholders can only use exchange-traded puts for this purpose to a limited degree. One reason is that the number of puts needed to insure very large stock portfolios exceeds the position limits imposed by exchanges. And, since long-term puts traded on an exchange are not very liquid, long-term insurance would require the frequent—and costly—rolling over of short-term puts as they expired. Puts synthesized by portfolio insurance got around these limitations. In principle, at least.

Leland O'Brien Rubinstein Associates (LOR) was formed in 1981 to commercialize the scheme. By early 1987, LOR (and licensees of its technology) had insured about $50 billion of stock,[23] and unaffiliated imitators insured roughly the same amount.[24] These large amounts increased the gap between the assumptions of BSM and portfolio insurance, on the one side, and conditions in the real world, on the other. In particular, the assumption that trading would always be continuous, and that the transactions of hypothetical arbitrageurs constantly rebalancing their portfolios would have no effect on prices, became especially far-fetched.

The rapid fall in stock prices that started in mid-October 1987 made it nearly impossible to rebalance the replicating portfolio smoothly. The strategy called for selling as markets fell and buying as markets rose. By many accounts, the mechanical selling triggered a downward cascade; other traders who knew that portfolio insurance models required large sales after a price decline, jumped ahead and sold stock first, thus accelerating the price declines. This caused a stock market meltdown on Black Monday, October 19, 1987. Ironically, the meltdown also nearly caused the futures and options exchanges, whose limitations portfolio insurance was supposed get around, to "go down the tubes" forever, in words of Leo Melamed, the long-standing chairman of the Merc.[25]

Memories of Black Monday and the harm to innocent bystanders by mechanistic models used outside the closed environment of exchanges didn't last long.* Over the next two decades, complex OTC derivatives—also designed and managed with BSM-based technologies—grew to a size that dwarfed the $100 billion that had been covered by portfolio insurance. Worse, the problems of mispricing the derivatives and mismanaging the risks were concentrated in a handful of megabanks, as we will see in later chapters. The financial health of these banks had, by then, become vital to the well-being of the economy as a whole; therefore the megabanks' derivative problem became, in the crisis of 2008, everyone's problem—on a scale that could not be missed.

Advancing Arm's-Length Finance

In this and the last chapter, I discussed how financial economists developed technologies for mechanistic decision-making that rely on historic

---

*Rubinstein was named "Financial Engineer of the Year" and elected president of the American Finance Association for 1993.

statistical data and how these technologies replaced forward-looking case-by-case judgments. Earlier in the book, I argued that the modern financial system has another dysfunction: an excessive reliance on arm's-length and so-called market transactions, instead of ongoing relationships. How, if at all, did finance theory help arm's-length finance displace relationships?

One effective driver was to deprive traditional financing practices of attention and interest. Modern theory not only transformed how finance was treated in textbooks and academic research, but it also changed the topic.[26] Descriptive work, the heuristics, and rules of thumb that pervaded books like Graham and Dodd's *Security Analysis* were replaced by mathematical treatments and models. Concurrently, *what* was talked about also changed: Finance became concerned about securities and derivatives markets, and the decisions made by participants in these markets, rather than the choices faced by, for instance, lending officers in banks and the corporate treasurers who borrowed from them, or by investors in privately held companies.

The focus on securities markets was not unrelated to the shift to mathematized economics: (idealized) markets were easier to model. As MIT's Paul Cootner pointed out, researchers at business schools who studied finance had "found [themselves] on the road to academic prosperity," compared to those who studied marketing and organizational behavior, because they focused on markets rather than firms. Moreover, within finance, the slowest progress had been made in areas that were "internal to the firm and most immune to market constraint, or those in which financial institutions' very *raison d'être* arises from the imperfection of markets."[27]

A second driver was how finance scholars and other economists looked at markets. They implicitly and explicitly extolled the benefits of liquid markets. Frictionless trading was more than just a useful assumption of their models. It was also reflected beliefs about how things ought to be. Like diversification, market liquidity, which enabled everyone to trade without affecting prices, was considered a free lunch. Liquid markets were an unqualified good because they lowered the costs of capital—and made it easier to diversify away "firm specific" risks that, CAPM taught, no investor should bear. The notion that sticky relationships facilitated dialogue, or that too easy "exit" might discourage the exercise of "voice," as Albert Hirschman might have put it, did not enter into the equation. This is not a bias, incidentally, peculiar to financial economics: In many other branches of economics, the notion of being tied to a particular relationship is regarded as a minus, a drag on the efficient redeployment of resources, and an invitation to the exercise of monopoly power.

The breadth of markets was also held in high regard. Models created by Nobel laureate Kenneth Arrow and Gerard Debreu highlighted the benefits of "complete" markets in contingent claims that would allow everyone to ensure against all possible risks—and the inefficiencies that result because markets are incomplete.[28] This work helped create the belief that new derivatives markets could only further the public good.[29] Arrow's student, Stephen Ross, now a leading figure in derivatives research, argued in 1976 that although creating contingent claims markets did entail costs, it was "difficult to believe that such costs would be so prohibitive as to prevent the formation of nearly all contingent claims markets. Yet with the exception of some insurance examples, contingent contracts are difficult to find in actual markets," creating potentially significant inefficiencies.

Ross proposed that options and other such derivative contracts could "complete" markets: "Although there are only a finite number of marketed capital assets, shares of stock, bonds, or as we shall call them 'primitives,' there is a virtual infinity of options or 'derivative' assets that the primitives may generate. Furthermore, in general, it is less costly to market a derived asset generated by a primitive than to issue a new primitive."[30] In other words, markets in options had value not just for hedging stock holdings against price declines, but for making the economy as a whole much more efficient.

MacKenzie describes concrete ways in which the conviction of many economists that the world is better off with more complete and liquid markets helped nudge the world in that direction. When the Chicago futures exchanges tried to expand from agricultural commodities into financial futures and options, regulators were suspicious. Futures and options were regarded as instruments for speculation: Why create more opportunities for gambling? Therefore, when Merc chairman Leo Melamed sought to launch currency futures in the early 1970s, he sought a "stamp of authenticity" from his hero, Milton Friedman. The Merc commissioned Friedman to write a paper, "The Need for Futures Markets in Currencies," that it published in December 1971.[31] Melamed then met with key regulators, such as Arthur Burns, chairman of the Federal Reserve (and Friedman's mentor), and George Shultz, secretary of the Treasury, to ease concerns about the new instruments, sending out Friedman's paper before these meetings. Shultz told Melamed: "If it's good enough for Milton, it's good enough for me."[32]

Similarly, when the Chicago Board of Trade sought permission from the SEC to trade stock options in the late 1960s, it faced "instinctual hostility" because of memories of "the role that options had played in the speculation and malpractices of the 1920s." So the Board of Trade also turned to economists for legitimacy. Three respected economists from Princeton provided a report showing how an options exchange could serve the "public interest."[33] BSM was even more effective in legitimizing options trading. As Burton Rissman, a former counsel of the CBOE told MacKenzie, "We were faced in the late 60s–early 70s with the issue of gambling." The issue went away, according to Rissman, because of BSM: "The SEC very quickly thought of options as a useful mechanism in the securities markets.... I never heard the word 'gambling' again in relation to options."[34]

Cynics may question how much the beliefs of economists about what is right can affect public policy in the face of lobbying by interested parties. Certainly lobbying by vested interests can block policies that are widely regarded by economists to be good, and advance ones that are regarded as bad. Restrictions on imports are an example of the former, and tax breaks and subsidies aimed at specific companies are examples of the latter. But that's not the end of the story. Interests often compete, with some lobbying for a particular policy and others against. Strongly held beliefs of even a small number of idealists can therefore tip the outcome. In the early 1900s, the Populist alliance with entrepreneurs in the emerging automobile industry who were at the time far from powerful destroyed the mighty railroad barons in just a few decades. In the late 1970s and early 1980s, the arguments of a bipartisan group of economists led to the abolition of the Civil Aeronautics Board, which had regulated airfares, routes, and schedules for nearly half a century. In other words, the tyranny of the status quo (to borrow the title of a Milton and Rose Friedman book) can be toppled by ideas and idealists.

Second, even where individuals and businesses are bent on pursuing their self-interest, they often don't know where their self-interest really lies. As we will see later in this book, commercial banks opposed the institution of national deposit insurance in the early 1930s, but didn't lobby against money market funds in the early 1970s. The former turned out to be a great boon for commercial banking, whereas the latter became a mortal threat. Similarly, investment banks opposed the deregulation of brokerage commissions in 1975—a move that eventually sparked huge increases in trading volumes and industry profits.*

To put it simply, choices about what to lobby for or against are fraught with uncertainty and ambiguity. In the face of this uncertainty, the prevailing economic wisdom can tip the balance. A particularly important instance, which we will discuss later, was the attitude of commercial banks toward securitization of credit. They could have opposed it, or they could have lobbied for powers to participate in securitization. Banks chose the latter course. The influential leaders of top banks, most notably Bankers Trust and J.P. Morgan, embraced the arguments of financial economists that securitization would be a great boon for the economy, and their endorsement helped persuade more traditionally minded bankers to go along.†

Concluding Comments

The principal ways, discussed in the last three chapters, by which modern theories of economics and finance promoted robotic, top-down financial practice are summarized in the box below. Modern financial theory helped transform financial practice in the same manner that actuarial methods based on probability theory had earlier revolutionized the life insurance industry. This time around, however, the theory was based on implausible assumptions and was pressed into service without serious empirical testing or even after-the-fact evaluations. The results have been much less than desirable: They have created a financial system that is at odds with the needs of an innovative real economy.

The Evolution of Mechanistic Finance: A Summary

In chapter 5, we saw how modern economic theories assumed away unquantifiable, multifaceted uncertainties that are arise in one-off situations.

---

*Barra (2009) similarly points out that owners of professional baseball teams accepted a long (232 day), ugly strike by players and fought a complaint by the National Labor Relations Board. The owners' goal was to hold down player salaries. Eventually the owners were forced to bargain in good faith over salaries—this helped baseball go from a $1.3 billion to a $7.5 billion business.

†In a twist of fate, Bankers Trust was felled in the 1990s by its involvement in selling derivatives.

Such situations are ubiquitous: Even a seemingly routine problem, such as whether or not to hire a particular individual for a position, inevitably involves a unique combination of circumstances. The uncertainty of one-offs encourages a narrative or case-based style of decision making that incorporates a holistic view of the specific circumstances, rather than relying on the extrapolation of historical data. Assuming away this kind of "Knightian" or "Keynesian" uncertainty facilitated the mathematization of economic theory. It also paved the way for robotic decision-making based largely on statistical analyses of historical data that pay no heed to case-by-case differences.

In chapters 6 and 7, we examined financial models and practices based on mathematized approaches to uncertainty and decision making. Chapter 6 started with a discussion of the Modigliani-Miller propositions about the irrelevance of debt and dividend policies. The propositions relied on arguments involving "faux" arbitrage—the equilibration of prices through buying and selling that only an omniscient being could do. By themselves, the Modigliani-Miller propositions were practically inconsequential, but the faux arbitrage reasoning they pioneered inspired models that did have great effect on financial practice.

Then we looked at the efficient markets hypothesis (EMH). My critique did not join in the popular sport of bashing the hypothesis. Within sensible limits, I argued, EMH is a good description of how the world works, as well as a guide to practical decision making. Unfortunately, it has been both overextended and not taken seriously enough. It is used by EMH absolutists to claim that investors should forgo case-by-case judgments and rely on market prices, a prescription, I argued, that goes far beyond the evidence and the theory that undergirds EMH. The hypothesis has also been yoked to the assumption of an implausible sort of randomness: While price movements are unpredictable, they are drawn from a fixed, normal distribution. This assumption is inconsistent with the evidence—and with the theory on which EMH is based. Yet its mathematical convenience has been irresistible for the developers of what have become basic models and practices of modern finance.

One such model, as we also saw in chapter 6, is the Markowitz method of constructing efficient portfolios and of managing risk through a top-down, statistical, rather than judgmental, approach. The method, which requires the assumption of fixed normal distributions—and several other far-fetched stipulations—cannot be empirically tested. In fact, its use is closely linked to spectacular blow-ups. Yet it has become a basic risk management tool for institutional investors, large financial institutions, and the regulators of such institutions.

The Markowitz method (and the assumptions it embeds) was also the starting point for the capital asset pricing model (CAPM). This model provides stock investors with a specific prescription for how they can most efficiently forgo case-by-case judgment: Buy the market portfolio. The prescription has now been widely adopted. The core equity holdings of most large pension funds and endowments now comprise a market index. CAPM "betas" have also become a standard risk-management tool.

In this chapter we analyzed BSM, described by Eugene Fama as "the biggest idea in economics of the century." Like the Modigliani-Miller propositions, BSM is based on faux arbitrage, albeit of a sophisticated and mathematically complex sort. It generates the right values for pricing options and for hedging the risks—for omniscient beings who can accurately predict the volatility of the underlying security. Actual buyers and sellers, who aren't omniscient, have to rely on historic volatility. This virtually guarantees option prices and hedges that are wrong, sometimes by a wide margin. The consequences of BSM miscalculations did not harm the public interest, however, as long as the model's use was confined to options exchanges. Now that BSM is extensively used, its mistakes lead to widespread distortions and misallocations of resources. These problems are usually hidden and diffused, but they can explode to the surface, as happened in the stock market crash of 1987 and in the 2008 financial crisis.

We also saw in this chapter how modern theories and their assumptions have influenced the adoption of public policies that favor complete, liquid, arm's-length securities markets rather than ongoing relationships. As I will argue next, however, economists' theories, beliefs, and public advocacy did not create a highly mechanistic and securitized system of finance on their own; they played an important supporting, but not determining, role. Other ideological preferences and political calculations were at least as crucial in establishing rules and regulations that helped arm's-length securitized finance displace ongoing relationships and marginalize decentralized financial judgment. In the next six chapters we will see how this shift occurred.

Chapter 8

Liquid Markets, Deficient Governance

In 1984, the Securities and Exchange Commission (SEC) celebrated its fiftieth anniversary.* Its chairman, John Shad, commented that when the agency had been created in the depths of the Depression, the nation's securities markets were demoralized. "Today," he observed, "they are by far the best capital markets the world has ever known—the broadest, the most active and efficient, and the fairest. The Securities and Exchange Commission has played an important role in the restoration of public confidence...[and] has discharged with distinction its mandate to protect investors and maintain fair and orderly markets."[1]

This was no empty assertion. The limited liquidity and breadth of many European markets, where securities regulation was relatively weak, bore out Shad's claims. "For years," the *Economist* reported in 1991, investors had complained that the Swiss markets were "too fragmented, too illiquid, opaque and too expensive." Companies did not reveal quarterly or line-of-business results. They could "refuse share

*This chapter draws heavily on my prior articles in the *Journal of Financial Economics* (1993) and the *Harvard Business Review* (1994a) and an April 1994 lecture at the Royal Society of Arts in London.

registration, and so voting rights, to anyone they do not like," and the resulting "tiered share structure...limited the market and depressed prices."[2] Transaction costs in the United States through the 1980s were half the level of Germany, Italy, and Japan, which were the next most liquid markets. The block traders of Wall Street, who could execute trades of millions of shares in a few minutes without significant impact on market price, had few counterparts.

The apparent success of U.S. market regulation led regulators in Europe to establish disclosure requirements, one-share, one-vote rules, and sanctions against insider trading. Rules in the United States also provided a model for Eastern Europe, India, and other countries seeking to establish active stock markets. Although U.S. stock markets continued to offer unparalleled liquidity and breadth, the gap with other markets narrowed, pointing to the efficacy of the SEC model.

Policymakers in the United States and abroad may not have fully appreciated the costs, however.

Regulation in the United States, as we will see in this chapter, involves a subtle trade-off. Rules to protect small investors, starting with New Deal securities legislation, have made U.S. stock markets highly—and unnaturally—liquid. They have also promoted diffused, arm's-length stockholding and discouraged investors from establishing ongoing relationships with managers. Therefore, while the stocks of publicly held companies are highly liquid, their governance is impaired because, without ongoing relationships, stockholders cannot provide proper oversight or secure the loyalty of the executives of the companies they invest in.

These governance problems are in addition to those faced by large businesses under any regulatory regime. Modern technology offers opportunities to realize significant economies of scale and scope. Realizing these economies often requires large businesses with many stockholders. But fragmented stockholding creates a collective action problem: Individual stockholders lack the incentive and ability to play an active role in governance of the firm,[3] leaving managers free to disregard their interests. This was pointed out by Berle and Means in their 1932 classic, *The Modern Corporation and Private Property*, before New Deal securities legislation was enacted. This legislation, as we will see, provided a powerful impetus to the natural fragmentation of stockholding in publicly traded firms, and amplified governance problems.

Securities Acts

Congress passed the Securities Acts in the wake of the Great Crash. Between September 1, 1929, and July 1, 1932, stocks listed on the NYSE lost 83 percent of their total value, and half of the $50 billion of new securities that had been offered in the 1920s proved to be worthless.[4] The Crash, according to the SEC, brought the "country's business and financial systems to the verge of disaster"; it followed a decade in which some 20 million shareholders "took advantage of the postwar prosperity and set out to make their 'killing' on the stock market," but gave little thought to the inherent dangers.[5]

The Crash led to landmark securities legislation in the form of the Securities Act and Securities and Exchange Act, as well as the creation of the Securities and Exchange Commission. A legal expert at the time observed that "until the advent of the New Deal, the law relating to security markets has been characterized by gradual growth rather than by abrupt change...[W]hat has heretofore been evolution has become revolution."[6]

The primary reason offered for securities regulation was to protect small investors and restore their faith in the stock market.[7] Federal intervention was necessary not only because of "the outraged feelings of voters," proclaimed a SEC pamphlet, but because "America's economy was crippled without investor confidence."[8] "A very numerous and widely dispersed class of small individual and small institutional investors" had become, suggested the special counsel to a House subcommittee on securities acts, an essential source of investment capital.[9]

The new legislation had a revolutionary preemptive orientation; the response to earlier stock-market panics had been to let the victims bear the consequences and prosecute frauds and cheats. The Securities Acts, however, sought to protect investors *before* they incurred losses in three ways: ensuring adequate disclosure by firms to their investors, discouraging the unfair use by insiders of information that is not made public,[10] and eliminating "manipulation and sudden and unreasonable fluctuations of security prices" (see box).[11]

How Securities Acts Seek to Protect Investors

Disclosure Requirements. To help public investors make informed trading decisions, the 1934 act required the registration of publicly traded securities.

The registration statement required information about the directors, officers, underwriters, and large stockholders (and their remuneration), the organization and financial condition of the corporation, and certain material contracts of the corporation. Issuers were also required to file annual and quarterly reports, whose form and detail could be prescribed by the SEC.[12] Over the years, the SEC substantially increased the types of reports required; examples of this expansion include disclosure of management perks, overseas payments, replacement cost accounting, and segment or line-of-business accounting.[13]

Another objective of regulating disclosure, especially in the area of proxy solicitations, was to give small stockholders more information about the election of directors and other issues put to shareholder vote. Section 14a of the 1934 act gave the SEC broad powers over any person soliciting a proxy or consent from another security holder. In its report recommending the adoption of the section, the Committee on Interstate and Foreign Commerce of the U.S. House of Representatives stated:

> Fair corporate suffrage is an important right that should attach to every equity security bought on a public exchange. Managements of properties owned by the investing public should not be permitted to perpetuate themselves by the misuse of corporate proxies....Insiders have at times solicited proxies without fairly informing the stockholders of the purpose for which the proxies are to be used and have used such proxies to take from the stockholders for their own selfish advantage. Inasmuch as only the exchanges make it possible for securities to be widely distributed among the investing public, it follows as a corollary that the use of the exchanges should involve a corresponding duty of according to shareholders fair suffrage.[14]

The SEC's first rules, adopted in 1935, were, according to testimony by SEC chairman Ganson Purcell in 1944, "extremely rudimentary in nature" and "merely prohibited falsehoods in proxy solicitations."[15] In 1938, the SEC adopted rules requiring affirmative disclosure. The proxy statement had to show who the candidates were for directorship, their security holdings, and some of their transactions with the corporation.

In spite of opposition from representatives of industry and the financial sector, and complaints about usurping the powers of Congress,[16] the SEC continued to expand its regulation of proxy statements. Revisions of the rules in the 1940s required companies to give the commission an opportunity to examine proxy statements for ten days before they were sent, and broadened the privilege of stockholders to present proposals and to have them set forth in the management proxy materials. The revised rules also required disclosure of the compensation of all officers and provided for more complete information regarding the compensation, dealings, associations, and principal business of all directors.[17]

The disclosure regulations were backed by a variety of enforcement devices. The 1933 and 1934 securities laws provided criminal penalties for willful material false or misleading statements, and empowered the SEC to suspend or withdraw the registration of securities for failure to comply with the reporting provisions of the acts. Restitution for wrongs was also expected to be obtained through derivative suits. Here SEC officials observed that although the commission usually had no official interest in class or derivative actions, the "Commission has had occasion…to advise the courts that the purposes of the statutes it administers can be subserved by a liberal attitude towards class suits for the enforcement of statutory obligations…[The commission] recognized the abuses of 'strikers' and their raids on the corporate treasury, but emphasized the general prophylactic and deterrent effect of the stockholders' suit."[18]

Insider Trading Rules. Section 16 of the Securities Exchange Act seeks to prevent "the unfair use of information" that an officer, director, or major stockholder may have obtained "by reason of his relationship." Accordingly, Section 16(a) requires every officer, director, and 10 percent equity owner to periodically file statements showing their ownership of all equity securities. Section 16(b) provides that any short-term profits realized by such persons (i.e., due to purchases and sales within any six-month period) shall "inure to and be recoverable by" the company. The law provides criminal sanctions for failure to report such transactions.

By most accounts, the SEC has zealously prosecuted the insider trading provisions of the 1934 act, and, arguably, has expanded the scope of its provisions. For example, in the 1966 Texas Gulf Sulfur case, the SEC first asked a federal court to order *outsiders* to make restitution to shareholders who sold them stock.[19] In the 1980s, the SEC began to seek jail terms for insider trading (whether by insiders or outsiders), and the 2009 Galleon case broke new ground through the use of wiretaps.

Rules to Eliminate Market Manipulation. Section 9 ("Prohibition Against Manipulation of Security Prices") and Section 10 ("Regulation of the Use of Manipulative and Deceptive Devices") of the 1934 act prohibited several practices outright and subjected others (such as stop loss orders and short sales) to regulation by the SEC. Section 6 required stock exchanges to register with the SEC, to agree to comply with the act, and to help enforce compliance by exchange members. The SEC could deny registration to an exchange following an inquiry into the exchange's ability to comply with the act, and into the adequacy of its rules. The SEC soon used its powers to close nine exchanges, and, in the late 1930s, Chairman William O. Douglas virtually threatened the NYSE with takeover by the SEC if reforms were not instituted.[20]

In its public relations, the SEC emphasized its role in maintaining honest markets. "The early years of the SEC," write Phillips and Zecher, "were marked by [Chairman] Kennedy's speeches and efforts to support and encourage the mainstream of the flagging financial markets. He touted the SEC's better business bureau role and suggested the SEC could protect the honest exchanges, traders and investors from the fraudulent dealers."[21]

▮▮▮▮▮ Promoting Liquidity

The liquidity of a securities market refers to the extent to which it is "continuous," that is, without large price changes between trades, and "deep," that is, with many buyers and sellers willing to trade just below or just above the prevailing price.[22] Stockholders value liquidity because it enables them to buy and sell quickly without incurring large transaction costs; in contrast, the owners of illiquid assets cannot turn their holdings into cash quickly—or may have to accept a large reduction in price in order to do so.

Although increasing the liquidity of stock markets wasn't a goal of the Securities Acts, the measures intended to protect investors from shady practices had an unintended consequence of promoting market liquidity.

As mentioned in the box, in its early years the SEC closed nine exchanges, and threatened to take over the NYSE if it didn't clamp down on "Manipulative and Deceptive Devices." Thanks to the SEC's ongoing efforts, practices such as "painting the tape" and the "parking" of stock (to create the impression of active trading or rising prices), or the formation of rings to drive stocks up or down, are now confined to the netherworld of penny stocks. The SEC's certification of the integrity of exchanges, in turn, reassures buyers and sellers, and especially the short-term traders whose transactions are essential to maintain the liquidity of markets. Even compulsive gamblers don't like to bet on rigged games.

Penalties for insider trading similarly undergird a liquid market in which many buyers bid for stocks offered by anonymous sellers. The fear of trading against better-informed insiders would otherwise lead buyers to demand access to the company's books and investigate the motivation of the sellers: Do they know something bad about the business, or do they just need money? Without insider trading rules, stock trades, like used-car or real-estate transactions, would probably require negotiation between known parties, undermining what the economist Harold Demsetz calls the distinguishing characteristic of trading on organized exchanges: the willingness of customers to "let others buy and sell for them...[and] conclude an exchange without a personal prior examination of the goods."[23]

Similarly, disclosure rules facilitate trading of the stock of companies that neither buyer nor seller has examined from the inside. The SEC's vigorous and well-publicized prosecutions of inaccurate or incomplete statements reassure traders that they can buy stocks without independent, time-consuming audits.

Furthermore, the liquidity sustained by the rules tends to be self-reinforcing because it promotes diversification. Almost all businesses have highly concentrated stockholding when they go public. A liquid market then makes it easy for stockholders to diversify their holdings. This diversification also increases fragmentation: A company's stock becomes dispersed across many stockholders. In addition, fragmented stockholding promotes liquidity by increasing the odds of a trade because someone needs the money or believes that a stock is mispriced. When stock is held in a few hands, trading is more episodic, and the continuity and depth of markets is impaired.[24]

Arm's-Length Stockholding

A second unintended consequence of the Securities Acts has been to discourage close, ongoing stockholder-manager relationships and to encourage arm's-length stockholding.

As I have mentioned, insider-trading rules place special restrictions on investors who hold more than 10 percent of a company's stock, serve on its board, or receive any confidential information about its strategies or performance; they are required to report their transactions, forfeit short-term gains, and try to avoid any hint of trading on inside information. But why should investors want to become insiders and be subject to these restrictions just so that everyone else can enjoy the benefits of a level trading field? They don't: Institutional investors with fiduciary responsibilities usually refuse to receive any private information from managers. They may grumble about a firm's performance, but they will not sit on its board for fear of compromising the liquidity of their holdings. Institutions also make sure they stay below the 10 percent ownership limit that puts them under the purview of insider-trading restrictions. The rules thus make large investors resolute outsiders. In a free-for-all market, the same institutions would likely demand access to confidential information before they even considered investing.

Disclosure requirements also encourage arm's-length stockholding. For example, rules that mandate the disclosure of transactions with insiders make a firm's banks, suppliers, and customers less willing to hold large blocks of stock or serve on boards. Disclosure rules also make anonymous shareholding safe. If companies' reports were sketchy or unreliable, shareholders would likely demand an inside role and ongoing access to confidential information.

Furthermore, the two unintended consequences of investor protection measures—more liquidity and more arm's-length stockholding—reinforce each other.

Market liquidity weakens incentives to play an inside role. All firms with more than one shareholder face what economists call a free-rider problem. The oversight and counsel provided by one shareholder benefits all others, with the result that all of them may shirk their responsibilities. This is particularly relevant if a company faces a crisis. In illiquid markets, shareholders cannot run away easily and are forced to pull together to solve any problem that arises. But a liquid market allows investors to sell out quickly and cheaply. In economist Albert Hirschman's terms, investors prefer a cheap "exit" to an expensive "voice."

Conversely, investors who don't have long-term relationships can diversify their holdings easily. Managing relationships takes time, and having too many means that an investor cannot pay proper attention to any one relationship. Such limits do not apply to arm's-length stockholding. But widespread diversification by investors also leads to fragmentation in the stockholding of individual securities. And greater fragmentation leads to more trading and liquidity.

Developments in common and statutory laws governing corporate structures, many predating the Securities Acts, have also encouraged arm's-length shareholders to rely on "exit" rather than "voice." Through the nineteenth century (and in some states, including Ohio, as recently as 1927), corporate charters were granted for a single, closely defined business, often after a negotiation between the legislature, the promoters, and the investors.[25] Currently, there is no negotiation, and off-the-shelf charters allow a corporation to enter any legitimate business. In the past, major corporate decisions relating to dividend policies, capital structure, or diversification had to be unanimously approved by stockholders; now, however, with the expanding "business judgment" rule, the courts give directors wide latitude in these matters.

Unless they are prepared to play an inside role by, for instance, serving on boards, the law doesn't give outside stockholders much influence. As Robert Clark, the former dean of Harvard Law School put it: "As a matter of statutory law, stockholders' powers in a public corporation are extremely limited.... To influence corporate managers...stockholders can vote for directors and approve or veto director-initiated organic changes, but cannot do much else."[26]

Regulating Intermediaries

The unintended consequences of the Securities Acts were reinforced by laws regulating financial intermediaries. These laws reflected "popular mistrust of large financial institutions with accumulated power," according to Mark Roe. "Main Street America did not want to be controlled by Wall Street. Congress responded to Main Street, not Wall Street; laws discouraging and prohibiting control resulted."[27] The laws also reflected concern about the safety of the funds the public entrusted to the intermediaries.[28]

Banks' ownership of Main Street stocks had been restricted as far back as 1863 when the National Bank Act was passed.[29] In 1933, Congress passed the wide-ranging Banking Act (better known as the Glass-Steagall Act). I will have much more to say about this act in later chapters; here it is sufficient to note that the act prohibited banks from owning equity in Main Street companies altogether. In countries like Germany and Japan, where big banks have held large blocks of the stock of industrial companies on a nearly permanent basis, the banks have maintained close relationships with their managers; Glass-Steagall eliminated this possibility in the United States.

In the 1930s, Congress asked the SEC to study the operations of mutual funds (or investment trusts) because it was "suspicious" of their "power to control industrial companies." In 1934, a Senate investigation, culminating in the Pecora report, urged Congress to "prevent the diversion" of investment trusts "from their normal channels of diversified investment to the abnormal avenues of control of industry."[30] After extended study of the Pecora report, the SEC drafted a bill that became the Investment Company Act of 1940. The act set minimum levels of diversification for mutual funds and effectively precluded them from holding more than 10 percent of a firm's stock. It even made holding 5 percent of the stock of a company problematic.[31] As I have mentioned, diversification tends to increase liquidity[32] and makes it difficult for managers to maintain close relationships with managers.

The New Deal legislation set the stage, but its actual impact on market liquidity and active stockholding was muted for several decades because, until the 1960s, 80 percent or more of equities were directly owned by individual stockholders.[33] Individual stockholders not only faced high transaction costs on their trades, but also federal and state tax rates in excess of 70 percent on short-term gains and 50 percent on long-term gains. Annual deductions for losses were then limited to $2,000 a year. These high selling costs made restrictions on insider transactions and other market regulations of little concern. Individuals and families, who often acquire controlling blocks through inheritance or entrepreneurial activity, were more likely to hold on to them. As we will see, however, institutional stockholding by pension funds, endowments, and the like replaced the more concentrated individual stockholding. The share of outstanding equities held by institutional investors grew from 19 percent of listed stocks in 1960 to 42 percent by 1988, thereby increasing the amount of fragmented and transitory stockholding. At the same time, legislative and regulatory initiatives helped reduce trading commissions that magnified the naturally higher propensity of institutions to turn over their portfolios.

The Institutionalization of Stockholding

Wage controls and a 93 percent tax on excess profits instituted during World War II had encouraged U.S. companies to set up pension plans that allowed employers to increase compensation—and thus retain employees—without violating rules against wage increases. And because contributions to pensions were deductible, their after-tax cost (at a 93 percent tax rate) was small. At first, pension assets were invested mainly in government and high-quality corporate bonds.

The typical plan of the time was of the "defined benefit" variety, promising retired employees a fixed pension. However, if companies did not put enough money in their plans to meet their pension obligations—or had the plan invest mainly in their own stocks—a company failure meant that retirees lost their pensions. Thanks, in part, to the media coverage of mismanaged pension plans, Congress passed the Employee Retirement Income Security Act (ERISA) in 1974. This legislation increased the amounts that employers put into retirement plans by mandating their proper funding and prohibiting plans from holding more than 10 percent of the sponsor's own stock. By redefining the duties of trustees, ERISA also encouraged pension plans to invest in listed equities rather than sticking to bonds. Previously, trustees often avoided stock investments "for fear of running afoul of the legal requirement to behave according to the 'prudent man' standard." Prudence in ERISA, however, followed the Markowitz model discussed in chapter 6: "By stressing the performance of an entire portfolio," ERISA emboldened pension fund managers to purchase stocks that might have been individually regarded as excessively risky.[34]

Employers were also attracted to equities by their expected returns, which were higher than those of bonds; the greater the return, the less an employer would have to put into a plan to meet pension obligations. Furthermore, proper funding of a plan required some guesswork since no one could know either the precise amounts that would have to be paid to retirees or how much money the plan would have to meet its obligations. From an employer's point of view, the more uncertain return from stocks, as compared to bonds, had an attractive feature. It provided the wiggle room to make aggressive assumptions of future returns and thus helped reduce current contributions to pension plans.[35]

Although ERISA only covered corporate plans and did not apply to public pension funds and endowments, it "psychologically liberated all institutional money to be invested more creatively and aggressively"[36] in equities. Until 1968, for example, public funds in California and fifteen other states did not own any stocks.[37] But thanks in part to the example set by ERISA, public pension funds and nonprofit endowments abandoned traditional policies against investments in equities. State and local pension funds that had bought just $5.7 billion in equities during the 1960s increased their purchases to $30.9 billion in the 1970s and to $173.4 billion in the 1980s.[38] By 1991, 43 percent of public funds were invested in stocks.[39]

Institutional investors were more prone to trading their holdings than were individual investors. Unlike individual investors, tax-exempt pension funds and endowments do not face high taxation of trading gains and low deductibility of losses. Size allowed institutions to negotiate attractive commission rates after they were deregulated in 1975, as we will see. Consequently, institutions took greater advantage than did individuals of the fair and orderly markets that the SEC sought to maintain, and their share of trading grew even faster than their share of stockholding. Trading by institutions that accounted for between 17 and 28 percent of total NYSE volume in the period from 1945 through 1963, rose to 52 percent by 1969[40] and 70 percent by 1988.[41]

The rules governing pension funds also encouraged institutions to contribute to market liquidity and maintain arm's-length relationships with the companies they invested in. For instance, ERISA, like the

Investment Company Act of 1940, encouraged pension funds to diversify and avoid any active role in corporate governance (see box). Pension funds also faced political pressures to avoid involvement in controversial governance issues.

How ERISA Promotes Market Liquidity and Arm's-length Investing

ERISA requires pension plans to hold a diversified portfolio unless it can be shown that it is "clearly prudent" not to do so. Furthermore, plans are supposed to follow prevailing investment practices in the extent of their diversification; and prevailing practice entails spreading holdings over hundreds of securities, not just the fifteen or twenty.[42] Diversification, in turn, contributes to market liquidity and limits the capacity of pension funds to maintain close relationships with portfolio companies.

Concerns about being held liable for imprudence also may encourage pension fund managers to keep their distance. For instance, if they sit on a board of a company where the investment goes bad, pension managers face the risk that Labor Department regulators will make them prove they had expertise in the field of the firm's operations and were capable of serving on its board.

Conversely, ERISA rules encourage wide diversification (and frequent trading) by absolving pension managers from the responsibility of case-by-case analysis of the stocks they purchase. Under the standard prudent-man rule of personal trusts, a fiduciary must ensure that every single item of investment is prudently made. Apparently, in "a direct response to modern portfolio theory,"[43] the Labor Department's interpretation of ERISA requires only that an entire portfolio meet prudent-man responsibilities. This interpretation not only encouraged investment in stocks, it also made due diligence on individual securities unnecessary: As long as the portfolio is adequately diversified, due diligence is not necessary. Pension funds can trade baskets comprising hundreds of stocks, treating individual securities merely as fragments of systematic risk whose fundamentals need not be investigated.

Unfixing Trading Commissions

Institutional trading both helped catalyze and got a boost from rules that ended the system of fixed brokerage commissions. Essentially, the NYSE had operated a legalized cartel since the Buttonwood Tree Agreement of 1792. There was no price competition among NYSE members—they all charged their clients brokerage commissions at rates fixed by the exchange. And there were no price breaks for large orders. As trades by institutions—which were generally larger and more frequent than trades by individuals—grew in importance, institutions demanded lower commissions on large orders. The NYSE refused to budge, however.

In 1958, the SEC, which had to approve the NYSE's commission schedule, suggested that the NYSE study the issue of quantity discounts. The NYSE agreed but did not conduct a study.[44] In 1966, an NYSE committee proposed modest discounts, but the broader membership was opposed and the proposal was never submitted to the SEC. In 1968, SEC commissioners voted to require the exchange to abolish fixed rates for orders greater than $50,000 or establish quantity discounts. The exchange agreed to a 30 percent discount for orders larger than 10,000 shares, but not to the abolition of fixed rates (regardless of the size of the trade.)[45]

In 1970, echoing a decision by the Supreme Court that the NYSE was only exempt from antitrust laws when this exemption was necessary to "make the Securities Act work," the SEC sent a letter to the exchange opining that fixed rates for orders greater than $100,000 were "neither necessary nor appropriate to make the Securities Act work." In the face of opposition from the exchange, the SEC agreed to raise the threshold for competitive commission to orders of $500,000.[46]

In February 1972, the commission proposed reducing the threshold to $300,000, and two months later the exchange agreed.[47] Meanwhile, federal legislation to make all commissions negotiable was gathering momentum, and the Justice Department was gearing up to challenge the NYSE's antitrust exemption. Nonetheless, the exchange requested a rate increase in 1973—and a delay in reducing the $300,000 threshold for freely negotiated rates—which the SEC agreed to.[48] This was a temporary reprieve: Congress passed amendments to the Securities Acts that eliminated all fixed commissions by May 1, 1975, ending a practice that had lasted 183 years. Large investors were able to negotiate fees down from an average of 26 cents a share in 1975 to 7.5 cents in 1986.[49]

In 1974, the chairman of Morgan Stanley had referred to the date of the unfixing of rates as "Mayday," an international distress call signal, and predicted that cutthroat competition would cause 150 to 200 NYSE member firms to fail. Some 100 firms did go under,[50] but overall, the unfixing turned out to be a great boon for stock trading and the securities industry. On the tenth anniversary of Mayday, John Phelan, the NYSE chairman, described the abolition of fixed rates as "the best thing that ever happened to the industry."

▓▓▓▓ Historical Evidence

Although it is impossible to quantify the effects of the securities laws we have been discussing, historical evidence suggests that, without regulation, stock markets would be marginal institutions.

Financial markets in Europe and the United States developed around *debt,* not equity. "Prior to 1920," Jonathan Baskin writes, "there were no large-scale markets in common stock....Shares were viewed as akin to interests in partnerships and were simply conveniences for trading among business associates rather than instruments for public issues."[51] Promoters of canals and railroads—the few businesses organized as joint-stock companies—restricted ownership to known investors whom they believed to be "both wealthy and committed to the enterprise." The public at large perceived equities as unduly speculative, and "tales of the South Sea fiasco evoked instant horror."[52]

Carol Vinzant similarly observes that for much of America's history, "the public reaction to the stock market was one of general distrust." Shady activities were rampant through the nineteenth century, and in the early twentieth century the stock market was still "a shadow world in which only the initiated could find their way." Most companies raised money from the public through bonds: Of the 1,200 public issues listed in 1900, "fewer than a quarter were stocks, and nearly half of those were railroads."[53]

Public markets for sovereign or high-quality *bonds*, however, can be traced back to the 1600s. The first financial instrument to be actively traded in Britain was the national debt, and in the United States, as well, most publicly traded securities consisted of government issues until 1870. The first insider trading scandal, implicating William Duer, an assistant secretary of the Treasury in the 1790s, involved government bonds. Later, railroad debt became popular and, at the turn of the century, preferred issues financed the great merger wave. It is noteworthy, too, that, unlike the public equity markets, which would evaporate for long periods following speculative bubbles, debt markets bounced back from serious crises. Furthermore, until the recent securitization boom, the debt of "risky" or small borrowers— most private debtors, as a matter of fact—has historically not been traded either. Banks, insurance companies, and individual money lenders who had ongoing relationships with borrowers, not arm's-length purchasers of bonds, dominated the extension of credit to most companies and individuals.

The contribution of U.S. regulators to the growth in equities markets can also be inferred from the historic illiquidity of European markets, where restraints on insider trading, disclosure requirements, and manipulative practices were traditionally weak. In the Belgian market, described in 1984 as "a sad, largely deserted place,"[54] insider trading was considered unethical but not illegal. Most other countries in Europe did not have statutes against insider trading until the mid-1980s, when the European Community directed member countries to adopt a minimum level of shareholder-protection laws. American occupation forces instituted laws against insider trading in Japan after World War II, but officials exercised "benign neglect" of the rules. As American-style securities regulation and enforcement caught on in the rest of the world, however, the liquidity of global stock markets also improved.

Historical and comparative evidence also points to the important role that the rules have played in promoting arm's-length stockholding. Transient outsiders now own a significant share of most publicly held stocks in the United States. The typical institutional investor's portfolio contains hundreds of stocks, each of which is held for less than a year. Institutional investors follow the so-called Wall Street rule: Sell the stock if you are unhappy with management. In countries where American-style rules don't exist, aren't enforced, or have been adopted relatively recently, the situation is different. There we see large investors whose holdings are immobilized by special classes of stock, long-term financing, or other business relationships.

Outside the United States, as former SEC commissioner Joseph Grundfest has observed, "Corporate investors and intermediaries are able to reach deep into the inner workings of portfolio companies to effect fundamental management change.... In the U.S., in contrast, when large institutional investors suggest that they might like to have some influence on management succession at General Motors—a company that has hardly distinguished itself for skillful management—they are met with icy rejection and explicit warnings that presumptuous investors had better learn their place."[55]

Richard Breeden, a former chairman of the SEC, claims that the "closed nature" of foreign governance systems "contradicts U.S. values of openness and accountability" and is "not appropriate to U.S. traditions."[56] However, the historical evidence suggests that investor-protection rules, not deep-rooted traditions or values, have fostered the unusually fragmented and anonymous stockholding that we find in America today.

Before the New Deal, investors who took an active inside role in governance played a major role in financing U.S. industry. DuPont family money helped William Durant—and later Alfred P. Sloan—build General Motors. Investors represented by J. P. Morgan helped Theodore Vail build AT&T and enabled Charles Coffin to create the modern GE. These investors were in it for the long haul, too, and they played an important oversight role. Pierre DuPont watched over the family investment in GM as chairman of its board; he reviewed "in a regular and formal fashion" the performance of all its senior executives and helped decide on their salaries and bonuses. Although he left the details of financial and operating policy to executives, DuPont "took part in the Finance Committee's critical decisions on important capital investments."[57]

Even today, investors in *private* companies continue the DuPont tradition. Partners in venture capital firms, for instance, serve as active board members of their portfolio companies, help recruit and compensate key employees, work with suppliers and customers, and help develop strategy and tactics.[58] But, unlike the DuPonts, modern venture capitalists are not long-term investors: They expect to sell out in five to seven years. Moreover, thanks to U.S. public policies, the holdings of venture capitalists (and other founders) are more likely to be sold to diffuse stockholders. Liquid markets and passive institutions pave the way for founding stockholders to cash in through one-time public issues, gradual market sales, or a negotiated sale to a company with diffuse stockholding, instead of selling their interests to other active investors.

The investment strategy of Berkshire Hathaway's Warren Buffett also suggests that Pierre DuPont's careful overseer approach conflicts more with U.S. regulations than with the traditions or values that Breeden invokes. Buffett isn't subject to the same regulatory pressures to diversify as is the typical pension-fund manager: He and his long-term partner and vice chairman, Charlie Munger, own well over half of Berkshire's stock. Berkshire seeks to "own large blocks of a few securities we have thought hard about," writes Buffett.[59] Buffett serves as a director of the companies that constitute Berkshire's core holdings and will, in a crisis, intervene to protect his investments. For example, in the scandal over government bond auctions at Salomon Brothers, he stepped in as chairman to help effect sweeping changes in management. Apparently, Buffett's large holdings of Berkshire's stock (and the tax consequences of realizing gains) make him more willing than other institutional investors to submit to the liquidity-reducing rules that insiders face. His favored holding period is "forever.... Regardless of price, we have no interest at all in selling any good businesses that Berkshire Hathaway owns, and are very reluctant to sell sub-par businesses.... Gin rummy managerial behavior (discard your least promising business at each turn) is not our style."[60]

The Hidden Costs

The absence of close, long-term manager-shareholder relationships that has become the norm in publicly traded companies in the United States has impaired their governance. The basic nature of the work of top executives calls for intimate relationships; anonymous masses of shareholders cannot provide good oversight or counsel and often evoke mistrust and hostility.

Stockholders should have to make ongoing, case-by-case judgments about top executives, as I argued in chapter 3. Top executives aren't like agents who execute specific tasks under the direction of their principals. Like doctors or lawyers in relationship to their patients or clients, they have a broad responsibility—a fiduciary one—to act in the best interests of stockholders. Moreover, because crucial top executive choices involve one-off Knightian uncertainty, their performance cannot be assessed according to a mechanical formula. Shareholders have to make judgments about executive judgments, weighing outcomes against their guesses about what would have happened if executives had followed other strategies. Losses do not necessarily establish incompetence because the alternative strategies might have been worse. If concrete performance objectives are set, shareholders have to judge whether executives are playing games with the targets: for example, if they are meeting cash-flow goals by skimping on maintenance.

To make fair evaluations, therefore, shareholders must maintain a candid dialogue with executives, as discussed in chapter 3. But a candid dialogue between top executives and arm's-length shareholders is impossible. Practically speaking, diffused shareholders cannot have much contact with senior executives: In the typical public company, most retail shareholders have no idea who is running the company, and most institutional investors catch, at best, only an occasional glimpse of the CEO in a carefully staged road show or a presentation to analysts. Nor can executives share sensitive data with shareholders at large; indeed, executives must *conceal* strategic information from them. If a company wants to convince potential buyers that a new product is here to stay, its CEO cannot reveal to stockholders that early sales have been disappointing. Chief executives are forced to be circumspect; they can't discuss critical strategic issues in public, and insider-trading rules discourage private communications. Almost inevitably, their dialogues with the investment community revolve around estimates of quarterly earnings per share, even though both sides know well that those figures have little long-run significance.

How wholeheartedly top executives advance the interests of anonymous shareholders is also questionable. Basic honesty and concern for their own reputations, as well as fear of public censure, inhibit flagrant disloyalty and fraud; but the abuses that shareholders must worry about are often more subtle. CEOs who use corporate jets to fly their dogs around patently abuse shareholders. But having CEOs wait in airports for standby seats more subtly ill-serves shareholders. Where and how do executives draw the line?

The identity and values of the particular people whose approval executives seek has a great influence on these choices. CEOs who want to impress other CEOs, and who have no contact with shareholders, will find it easier to convince themselves that well-appointed corporate jets make them more productive. Executives who know their stockholders, and value their esteem will probably provide more careful stewardship.[61] Similarly, shareholders are more likely to ascribe poor performance to incompetence than to bad luck if their perceptions have been shaped by colorful reports in the press, instead of personal relationships with a company's executives.*

Unfortunately, thanks to the rules, executives and shareholders now regard each other with suspicion. Some CEOs complain that investors are fixated on quarterly earnings and are ignorant of companies' markets, competitive positions, and strategies. Investors see many CEOs as entrenched, overpaid, and self-serving. As Peter Lynch, the former manager of Fidelity's Magellan Fund, half-jokingly remarked, "I only buy businesses a fool could run, because sooner or later one will."

---

*Close relationships can, of course, be abused and do not ensure mutual understanding and goodwill. We make mistakes with people we have known for a long time. Those we believe are steadfast get tempted; those we think are well disposed turn out to have harbored secret grudges. But note also the normal response to mistakes: we look for more personal data and more shared experiences. We proceed more slowly as we venture into ambiguous agreements, not more quickly. The issue is not whether our judgments of the people we know and relate to are always right. Rather, the question is whether we can think of getting into fiduciary relationships with strangers or people who make us uncomfortable.

Conversely, CEOs could well have asked how Lynch even remembered the names of the 1,000 or so stocks in which his fund invested.

The alienation of stockholders and top executives makes public-equity markets an unreliable source of capital. The exceptional liquidity of U.S. markets apparently does not compensate for the problems that come with issuing equity shares. Thus, American corporations are like the large public corporations of other major industrialized nations in issuing common stock to raise funds "only in the most exigent circumstances," and "the quantity of funds raised by new equity issues—especially by established firms—appears to be relatively insignificant" in all countries, regardless of the liquidity of their stock markets.[62] The stock market does, on occasion, allow firms in fashionable industries to issue stock at lofty prices. But such instances usually represent episodes of market mania, which underwriters call "windows of opportunity." When the window closes, investors dump the stocks wholesale and don't give the category another chance for a long time.

Arm's-length stockholding subjects executives to confusing signals from the stock market. It isn't that Wall Street is shortsighted—in fact, the market often values favored companies at astonishing multiples of their future earnings. But companies fall in and out of favor unpredictably: The market abruptly switches from taking a rosy long-term view of biotechnology to a fascination with Internet companies. Understandably so, for without inside knowledge of companies' strategy and performance, investors have little choice but to follow the crowd.*

Executives, in turn, pursue strategies to protect "their" companies against apathetic or fickle investors. Uncertain about access to capital when the firm might need it, executives avoid paying out earnings to stockholders even when it does not. They reinvest profits, sometimes in marginal projects, and outside shareholders can do little about the situation.

In the 1960s, for example, managers of cash-rich companies in mature industries made acquisitions in businesses that were unrelated to their core capabilities. The result was many conglomerates of unmanageable size and diversity. As historian Alfred Chandler observes: "Before World

*SEC surveillance may make the market "efficient" in the EMH sense of discounting all available information and prices "unpredictable," i.e., as likely to rise as fall. But because the information about plans and prospects that executives can make public is limited, market prices may be far removed from those estimated by an expert who knows the true state of affairs.

War II, the corporate executives of large diversified international enterprises rarely managed more than 10 divisions.... By 1969, many companies were operating with 40 to 70 divisions, and a few had even more." Top management often had "little specific knowledge of or experience with the technological processes and markets of the divisions or subsidiaries they had acquired."[63] In more recent periods, the managerial propensity to retain earnings has led to investment in businesses that should shrink. In industry after industry with excess capacity, Michael Jensen writes, managers "leave the exit to others while they continue to invest," so that they will "have a chair when the music stops."[64] Thus, the workings of a stock market that supposedly facilitates capital flows actually helps immobilize capital within companies.

Investors' indifference and hostility are also reflected in operating inefficiencies. Apparently, many managers don't try very hard for anonymous shareholders. Several studies have documented dramatic improvements in profit margins, cash flows, sales per employee, working capital, and inventories and receivables after leveraged buyout transactions that replaced diffused public stockholders with a few private investors.

What about the so-called market for managerial control? How can CEOs who provide poor stewardship survive the unsolicited tender offer, which supposedly represents "the most effective check on management autonomy ever devised"[65]?

Actually, unsolicited tender offers comprise a tiny fraction of takeover activity. Most mergers are friendly affairs, negotiated by executives of established companies seeking well-managed, profitable targets for which they are willing to pay premium prices. The managerial club frowns on hostile offers. A few profit-motivated raiders serve as a check only against flagrant incompetence and abuse. Raiders, in fact, operate under significant constraints: They have to raise money, much of it in the form of high-yield debt, deal by deal, making their case from publicly available data. Even at their peak, in the mid-1980s, raiders posed a threat to only a small number of targets: those diversified firms whose breakup values could be reliably determined from public data to be significantly higher than their market values. They could not, and did not, go after turnaround candidates any more than friendly acquirers do.[66]

Outside shareholders, analysts, and takeover specialists cannot easily distinguish between a CEO's luck and ability. Again, Warren Buffett, because he was a director and major investor in Salomon Brothers, could much more easily assess the culpability of Salomon's CEO and the consequences of replacing him than outside shareholders could. Judgments *by* executives, and therefore *of* executives, are necessarily subjective, and require considerable confidential and contextual information.

The case of IBM dramatizes the inadequacies of external scrutiny. Between the summers of 1987 and 1993, IBM's stock lost more than 60 percent of its value while the overall market rose by about the same degree. The magnitude of IBM shareholders' losses was comparable to the GDP of several OECD countries. But while its stock price relentlessly declined, IBM's management did not face the least threat of a hostile takeover or proxy fight. Outsiders had no way of knowing whether or not IBM executives were struggling, as competently as they could, with problems beyond their control. Ultimately IBM's fortunes turned after the fortuitous appointment of Lou Gerstner as its CEO, and not because of a new strategy demanded or imposed by a raider.

Concluding Comments

Wall Street's traders, who reflexively resist any form of regulation, in fact owe rules to protect the small shareholders a great and unacknowledged debt. As we saw in this chapter, New Deal Securities Acts designed to protect small investors have been crucial to maintaining the depth and liquidity of stock markets.

Furthermore, the Securities Acts, revolutionary as they were in the 1930s, were just a starting point. The SEC, created to enforce these acts, broadened their scope by taking an increasingly expansive view of insider trading and ramping up disclosure requirements. Congress also continued to pass laws: For instance, the Investment Company Act of 1940 and ERISA in 1974 regulated the investments of mutual funds and pensions, and amendments to the Securities Act in 1975 forced the NYSE to unfix brokerage commissions. These changes helped the stock exchanges approach the Nirvana of nearly frictionless trading. The same rules, however, impaired the governance of listed firms by encouraging their increasingly institutional stockholders to fragment their holdings and avoid close ongoing relationships with managers. The much-vaunted liquidity of stock exchanges helped make corporate executives less diligent fiduciaries and sensible allocators of their stockholders' capital.

The drag on the performance of publicly traded companies created by inadequate oversight is, however, often not noticeable because the dynamism of the real economy more than compensates. Indeed, the invisibility of the costs has encouraged many to see the hyperactivity of the equity markets as an unmitigated good and ignore the possibility that the real economy has done well in spite of this hyperactivity, rather than because of it. In the financial sector, however, poor governance of publicly traded firms can have a large downside, as in the 2008 crisis. This we will now examine.

Chapter 9

Financiers Unfettered

The basic nature of the activities that many financial organizations undertake makes them particularly unsuited for arm's-length stock-holding. Despite this, most of the important financial firms now have widely dispersed, and intentionally uncommitted, ownership.

As we saw in chapter 4, short-term outcomes are poor indicators of the quality of the subjective judgment that is at the heart of much of finance. Unlike bosses at industrial firms, where measures of short-term results (like the yield of a semiconductor plant) are somewhat more reliable indicators of performance, bosses at financial firms have to make case-by-case judgments about their subordinates' decisions to a much greater degree. They cannot manage subordinates just by comparing their performance against numerical profit targets or by examining "value at risk" metrics.

The same logic carries through to stockholder-executive interactions. The overall profits of a financial enterprise are particularly poor measures of its long-term performance. It is easy for top executives to inflate profits by prodding subordinates to take large risks, or at least to look the other way when subordinates take risks to meet aggressive profit targets. This can happen in industrial companies, of course, but the process is not as straightforward or quick. And the imprudence or chicanery of a handful of individuals can cause large financial firms, such as AIG and Lehman, to unravel quickly. Therefore, it is crucial for investors to provide close, ongoing oversight. Arm's-length stockholders represented by directors with little skin in the game (even if their credentials are impeccable, as was the case with AIG's directors) cannot provide it.

In fact, whether or not they are arm's-length, outside stockholders cannot properly watch over many kinds of financial activities, such as trading. Historically, thus, firms that engaged in such activities were organized as partnerships whose capital was provided entirely by individuals who were also engaged, full-time, in the work of the enterprise. Individual partners had a strong incentive to monitor each other's activities because the mistakes or imprudence of a few could wipe out the wealth of all. Active partners could also provide effective oversight because they could easily keep an eye on who was doing what.[1]

Currently, however, there are no large financial firms organized as partnerships; arm's-length stockholding has become the norm. In this chapter, we will see how this arrangement came to pass and consider the salient consequences of the change.

The Growth of Arm's-Length Stockholding

The evolution of the stockholding of large commercial banks, such as Citibank and J.P. Morgan, has paralleled changes in large industrial companies. Banks were among the first businesses in the United States to receive corporate charters (instead of operating as partnerships or sole proprietorships) and to raise equity from outside investors. Initially, as with industrial corporations, stockownership was concentrated in the hands of individuals who played an active role in governance.

In 1872, the First National Bank of the City of New York, which merged into Citibank in 1955, had just twenty stockholders, and its directors held "*4630* shares out of 5000!" as a bank examiner with enthusiastic punctuation noted in his report.[2] A cofounder, George Fisher Baker, elected president in 1877 and chairman of the board in 1909, became its largest stockholder. Baker's initial $3,000 investment in the bank grew to be worth more than $20 million. The National City Bank—another forerunner to Citibank—had similarly concentrated stockholding. James Stillman, who became president in 1891 and ran National City till 1918, was also its controlling stockholder.[3]

Arm's-length stockholding in commercial banks was discouraged by the "double liability" provisions of most state banking laws, and was included in the National Bank Act of 1863.[4] Under "double liability," which remained in force until 1937,[5] stockholders of a failed bank stood to lose more than just the value of their shares. They were personally liable for depositors' losses in amounts equal to the full or par value of their stock. In addition to providing another source of funds to make depositors of a failing bank whole, the additional liability encouraged stockholders to exercise close oversight and discouraged buying bank stocks without investigating the risks. The elimination of double liability, as economist Homer Jones observed in 1938, effectively meant that "the capital of the banks of the country was suddenly reduced by a large amount on July 1, 1937." The argument for abandoning the rule was "the belief that bank stock would be more popular and the capital ratios of the banks would be raised."[6] Jones was skeptical; and, indeed, capital ratios are now about half of what they were in 1937.

But the elimination of double liability did affect the nature of stockholding and helped pull banks, and especially the larger "money center" ones, into the overall trend of diffused, arm's-length stockownership that we discussed in the last chapter. Many of the smaller and regionally based banks continued to have large stockholders who were also active in management. However, when restrictions on interstate banking were eased, starting in the 1980s and especially after the Riegle-Neal Interstate Banking and Branch Efficiency Act was passed in 1994, large banks went on an acquisition spree. Thanks to these acquisitions, commercial banking became concentrated in the hands of fewer institutions with widely diffused, arm's-length stockholding. The share of deposits held in the ten largest banks in the United States grew from 12 percent in 1994 to over 40 percent in 2008.* None had large, active stockholders.

From Partnerships to Public Companies

Unlike commercial banks, which were usually organized as corporations from the get-go, investment banks started as partnerships with no outside stockholders. Their path to diffused arm's-length ownership was likewise different.

---

*And concurrently, as we will see in later chapters, weakening of banking rules also significantly reduced the regulatory constraints faced by large banks.

During the 1980s and 1990s, the reassurance provided by the Securities Acts and other investor protection rules, academic theories encouraging investors to own a slice of the overall market regardless of what stocks it contained, and the relaxation of standards by exchanges and underwriters, all helped increase what is euphemistically called market "breadth." To put it differently, in the 1980s and 1990s the ranks of listed companies were swollen by businesses that were previously considered unsuitable for public ownership. After 1979, IPOs (initial public offerings) increased from about 140 to nearly 600 per year, report Fama and French. The character of firms going public also changed: Before 1978, the profitability of newly listed firms was higher than the profitability of seasoned firms: Between 1973 and 1977, the return on equity of newly listed companies was 18 percent, compared to 14 percent for all firms. The profitability of newly listed firms then fell for the next twenty years—from 1993 to 1998 their return on equity was just 2 percent, compared to 11 percent for all firms.[7] This process culminated in the Internet bubble—when companies with no profits and tiny revenues famously went public.

But the increase in market breadth wasn't just due to the listing of unprofitable or immature companies. Before 1970, brokerage firms operated as partnerships because NYSE rules forbade members of the exchange from being publicly traded companies.[8] This prohibition was based on the feeling of both the SEC and the exchange that if brokerage firms were publicly held, "the exchange would be unable to police adequately the activities of its members." NYSE rules "require[d] approval by the board of governors before any individual [could] be admitted as a partner or stockholder of a member firm. Such approval obviously would be impossible to enforce if stock in member firms were made widely available to the public."[9] In other words, a public listing would allow undesirable characters to purchase the stocks of NYSE member firms and perhaps exercise undue influence over their activities.

But in 1969 and 1970, the securities industry suffered financial setbacks. The brokerages found that the size, scale, and nature of their operations limited the advantages of mutual monitoring by the partners. In addition, lack of automation in many brokerage houses created an operational crisis in their back offices; trading volumes—and brokerage commissions—fell. This pressured the companies to look for more dependable sources of capital, starting the "process of transforming the old New York houses from private partnerships to publicly held corporations."[10] Donaldson, Lufkin & Jenrette (DLJ), then regarded as

"Wall Street's most aggressive and best known institutional brokerage house,"[11] forced the NYSE to change its rules. The SEC approved, and, after DLJ went public in 1970, the "wire-houses"—large brokerages with national reach—soon followed (see box).

The Pioneers

DLJ, the first NYSE firm to go public, was also the "first major Wall Street firm started from scratch since the Great Depression." Founded in 1959 by "three brash young Harvard Business School graduates" who "pooled some $100,000 of their families' savings," DLJ "flouted Wall Street traditions" by providing brokerage services and investment research to banks, mutual and pension funds, and insurance companies and other such institutions rather than to the general public.[12]

In May 1969, DLJ challenged the NYSE rule against public ownership of member firms when it filed a registration statement with the SEC covering the public offering of 800,000 of its shares. Richard H. Jenrette, chairman of DLJ's executive committee, noted that "the lack of access by exchange members to permanent, public capital has begun to erode the exchange's historic role as the nation's central auction market." DLJ's prospectus acknowledged the risk that the company could lose its NYSE membership; but it hoped that "means may be found whereby such membership may be retained" given "the substantial portion of the company's total revenues attributable to exchange commissions." And DLJ's Dan W. Lufkin, who was also a governor of the NYSE, proposed amendments to the exchange's constitution that would provide "the mechanism and safeguards for public ownership."[13] As mentioned in the text, an important reason for keeping NYSE member firms private was the desire by the exchange and the SEC to exclude stockholding by undesirable characters.

The DLJ announcement included a veiled threat. If deprived of membership, DLJ would make greater use of regional exchanges and the over-the-counter market. The NYSE, which was "deeply fearful" that the "desertion of the stock exchange by a firm as influential as D.L.J. could trigger similar moves by other houses," offered a cautious response. Robert Haack, the president of the exchange, noted that the NYSE had already asked the SEC to allow member firms to issue publicly traded bonds. The issue of member firms also selling an equity interest to the public was "extremely complex by reason of its being closely woven into the matter of institutional memberships on stock exchanges, as well as the regulation and surveillance of its members," said Haack.[14] Ultimately the exchange blinked. The SEC approved to the change in its rules, and DLJ went public in 1970.

Merrill Lynch, the leading national brokerage, quickly took advantage. Bond salesman Charles Merrill, who became known "as the man who brought Wall Street to Main Street," started the firm in 1914. The firm divested its retail

The premier investment-banking partnerships that focused on underwriting, mergers and acquisitions, and trading were more hesitant to go
public. They were smaller and, in good times, highly profitable. Going
public would require sharing these profits with outside investors. This
was of particular concern to the younger partners and employees who
hoped to become partners. Senior partners were, however, often more
keen—going public would allow them to cash in their interests at two or
three times their book value: Under typical partnership rules they would
only be allowed to withdraw their capital in stages after they retired.
And, because withdrawals were typically at (or slightly above) book
value, retiring partners could not capture the true economic value of their
partnership interest—that would be a "gift" to incoming partners (until
they in turn retired). In addition to these intergenerational conflicts, there
was concern that giving up the partnership form of governance would
undermine their external prestige and internal cohesiveness. Nonetheless, the desire of senior partners to sell, the argument that public listing
would provide access to capital, and conflicts among partners over sharing profits, ultimately led all top-tier investment banks to become public
companies—or subsidiaries of public companies (see box).

Joining the Parade

Most of the premier trading and investment-banking houses did not start going
public till the 1980s. In 1981, Salomon Brothers merged with a publicly held
commodities trading firm, Phibro Corporation (which had been recently spun out
of Engelhard Minerals & Chemical Corporation). Salomon, which was founded
in 1914, had become, according to Michael Bloomberg, who was then a partner,

"the country's most successful securities trading firm"[15] The decision to sell to Phibro was "thrashed out among Salomon's partners during a stormy, weekend-long, locked door meeting" and "left many younger employees bitter. They no longer had a path upward to partnership" that had previously "meant becoming an 'instant millionaire.'"[16] But every existing partner, Bloomberg (who was then thirty-eight years old) recalls, "was now wealthy beyond his dreams. Previously, partners' money had just been numbers in a capital account ledger book, 'funny money'.… All of a sudden, it was real. And ours. In our pockets. In cash!"[17]

Lehman Brothers was acquired in 1984 by the publicly held American Express Company. The acquisition of the 134-year private partnership was apparently triggered by a power struggle at Lehman. Pete Peterson, a former secretary of Commerce, had become chairman in 1973, and proceeded to save Lehman from near bankruptcy. Ten years later Lewis Glucksman, supported by Robert Rubin, deposed Peterson. As the new CEO, Glucksman quickly "installed his own men at the head of most departments of the firm." Glucksman made his thirty-seven-year-old protégé, Richard Fuld, head of equities, one of Lehman's two largest divisions. When Glucksman also changed bonuses, increasing his own and those of his allies and slashing others, "the battle lines were drawn." A "contentious board" held a meeting without him, and by the end of the meeting Glucksman had lost control of Lehman Brothers.[18] In April 1984, less than ten months after Glucksman had taken Peterson's place, the sale of Lehman to American Express was announced. Ten years later American Express spun out Lehman as a freestanding publicly traded company.

Morgan Stanley went public in 1986 without much fuss. It had been formed by employees of J.P. Morgan and Company in 1935 when the Glass-Steagall Act required J.P. Morgan to stop its investment-banking activities. The connections and reputations of Morgan Stanley's founders allowed the new firm to secure a 24 percent share of public offerings in its very first year. The firm established a blue-chip clientele, including nearly half the nation's fifty largest corporations. Until the 1970s, "Morgan Stanley men were bankers, not traders or brokers," and "more than any other investment house" the firm "was 'white shoe,' projecting a WASP, Ivy League image."[19] Robert Baldwin led the transformation of Morgan Stanley after he was elected president in 1973. The firm created a research department, started selling securities to institutional investors, became a pacesetter in corporate takeovers, and established intentional operations.[20] In the mid-1980s, Morgan Stanley became active in leveraged buyouts, not just as an advisor, but also putting up its own capital to take equity stakes and to provide temporary bridge loans. To raise funds for such activities, Morgan Stanley sold 20 percent of its shares to the public in 1986.[21] By 2009, shares owned by insiders had dropped to 0.25 percent of the total.[22]

Kidder, Peabody & Company was acquired by the General Electric Corporation in 1986—the same year in which Morgan Stanley sold shares to the public. Kidder, which traced its origins to 1865, had collapsed after the 1929 stock market crash. In 1931, its name and physical assets were purchased by a new partnership that moved its headquarters from Boston to New

York. Albert Gordon, who had been part of the founding group of partners in 1931, led the firm for many decades. Unlike Morgan Stanley, which focused on blue-chip clients, Kidder sought the investment-banking business of smaller companies: "No issue was too small, no participation was too insignificant."[23] Kidder doubled its earnings and earned about a 20 percent annual return on shareholders' equity in the five years before it sold out to GE. Nonetheless, Ralph DeNunzio, who had succeeded Gordon as the head of the firm, was thought to have "allowed Kidder to lag behind its peers," and senior partners "began muttering darkly about the need for change." By 1986, DeNunzio admitted that "Kidder needed more capital" and, while discretely shopping the firm, received "an astonishingly high bid from GE." Kidder's partners received an average of $1.2 million and DeNunzio an estimated $30 million.[24]

Goldman Sachs, whose partners had started debating the merits of going public in the late 1960s, was the last holdout among large investment banks. Like several of its peers, it had secured outside capital in the 1980s—but not by going public. Rather, it raised more than $500 million from Sumitomo Bank (which received a 12.5 percent nonvoting interest for its $430 million) and the Kamehameha Schools / Bishop Estate of Hawaii, an educational trust. In June 1998, the partners of the 129-year-old firm voted to issue stock to the public. The move "exacerbated, and brought out into the open, divisions within the firm." The firm officially declared that going public would "match our capital structure to our mission." But John Whitehead, who had previously retired as cochairman, wrote that the decision of many of the partners was "based more on the dazzling amounts to be deposited in their capital accounts than on what they felt would be good for the future of Goldman Sachs."[25] As it happened, the LTCM-triggered financial crisis caused Goldman to scuttle its IPO. The firm ultimately went public the following year in May 1999 in a deal that valued the firm at $3.6 billion.[26]

Bankers Unbound

As partnerships gave way to arm's-length public ownership, restraints on their risk-taking declined. Bankers now had much less skin in the game. Yes, Richard Fuld, the former CEO of Lehman, lost all his shares and options—worth about $1 billion at their peak—when the company went bankrupt in September 2008. But between 2000 and 2007, Fuld and four other top-paid Lehman executives received more than $100 million in cash bonuses and sold more than $850 million in stock. Similarly, at Bear Stearns, which also blew up in 2008, its CEO and four top executives had received more than $326 million in bonuses and sold more than $1.1 billion in stock between 2000 and 2007.[27] If Lehman and Bear Stearns had gone bankrupt as partnerships, their CEOs and all other partners would have been almost completely wiped out.

The loss of mutual monitoring was equally important. A CEO of a publicly traded company—with arm's-length stockholders represented by deferential boards of directors—has enormous power. In a partnership, however, the managing partner's power is much more circumscribed. The heads of large investment-banking partnerships were "first among equals" with more clout than the other partners, but they did not have the authority to bet the ranch to the same degree as CEOs of public companies. A hundred or more strong-willed partners, each with virtually all their personal wealth at stake, had a great interest in controlling the recklessness of any one partner, including the head of the partnership. Furthermore, because partners could not easily move to other firms, they were unwilling to let anyone jeopardize the long-term success of the partnership for short-term returns. Partners at Goldman Sachs, for instance, took pride in being "long term greedy" (see box).

Focused on Risk

Peter Weinberg, a former Goldman Sachs partner, recalls:

> When elected a partner, you were required to make a cash investment into the firm that was large enough to be material to your net worth. Each partner had a percentage ownership of the earnings every year, but the earnings would remain in the firm. A partner's annual cash compensation amounted only to a small salary and a modest cash return on his or her capital account. A partner was not allowed to withdraw any capital from the firm until retirement, at which time typically 75%–80% of one's net worth was still in the firm. Even then, a retired ("limited") partner could only withdraw his or her capital over a three-year period. Finally, and perhaps most importantly, all partners had personal liability for the exposure of the firm, right down to their homes and cars.
>
> The focus on risk was intense, and wealth creation was more like a career bonus rather than a series of annual bonuses.[28]

Before Goldman went public in 1999, its 220 partners "took good care of their pot of gold," John Gapper observes. The firm's "trading and principal investing division—the part that took the most risks with partners' capital—was balanced with its fee-based investment banking and asset management divisions. Trading contributed about a third of its revenues in the two years leading up to its 1999 initial public offering." But "after Goldman sold shares in the IPO to outside investors—pension and mutual funds [now] hold about 80 per cent of its equity—it steadily increased its appetite for risk. Its fixed income and currency division has become dominant, bringing in two-thirds of Goldman's revenues in 2006 and 2007 (and 78 per cent in the first nine months [of 2009])."[29]

Hither and Anon

The incentives and leeway that top executives of financial firms with arm's-length stockholding had to encourage or condone recklessness went beyond simply scaling up the magnitude of the risks. The leverage of commercial and investment banks multiplied, but not merely because they borrowed more to increase purchases of the kinds of assets they previously owned or traded. Rather, risk was added by diversifying into new, nontraditional arenas that top executives could not easily control.

Recall the argument about the limits to diversification made in chapter 4. Proper control in financial firms requires bosses to evaluate the judgments of subordinates and not just monitor quantifiable indicators of outcomes. Evaluating subordinates' judgments requires knowledge of the activity undertaken; acquiring such knowledge requires time and effort. The range of activities that bosses of financial firms can oversee is therefore narrower than the range in industrial companies, where bosses can more easily manage by the numbers. Indeed, conglomerates operating, more or less successfully, in a wide range of business have failed to digest acquisitions of large investment and brokerages banks (see box).

Indigestible Acquisitions

General Electric's legendary CEO Jack Welch successfully managed, by many accounts, "a business empire with $304 billion in assets, $89.3 billion in sales, and 276,000 employees scattered in more than 100 countries"[30] ranging from plastics to jet engines to network television. Yet GE failed to digest Kidder Peabody. At Kidder, Joe Jett, who would later be described by Welch as a "rogue trader," single-handedly executed "an elaborate scheme to create…phantom profits."[31] In 1993, the scheme secured Jett a $9 million bonus in 1993—an amount so large that it had to be approved by GE's board. When the scheme unraveled in the following year, GE had to take a $350 million charge to earnings.[32] Other acquisitions of brokerages and investment banks by firms from outside the industry—of Dean Witter by Sears, of Bache by Prudential, and of Lehman by American Express—also didn't work out and were eventually unwound.

Diversification into businesses that top management did not have the expertise to control was a noteworthy feature of the 2008 crisis. The so-called monoline insurers, Ambac Financial and MBIA, were early dominos to fall in this manner (see box), although subsequent events pushed their problems out of the limelight.

Melting Monolines

Monoline insurers were founded in the early 1970s to insure municipal bonds against default. Bonds could secure high ratings from credit-rating agencies if they were insured by a highly rated monoline. This allowed municipalities to issue debt at lower rates. Municipal bonds rarely defaulted, however, and since that was the only risk the monolines insured, they almost never had to pay out claims and did not have to hold much capital to maintain their own credit ratings. But then the monolines branched out into insuring bonds backed by real estate and collateralized debt obligations. In the new millennium, most of the growth of monolines came from such "structured" products. By 2006, "the total outstanding amount of paper insured by monolines reached $3.3 trillion," with guarantees amounting to 150 times their capital.[33]

Until 2007, no monoline had ever defaulted on its guarantees or even been downgraded by ratings agencies. But insuring structured products backed by residential real estate was a different proposition from insuring municipal bonds; it required much more care and capital. When housing prices began to fall, the monolines suffered large losses. In December 2007, one month after a monoline had suffered a loss that wiped out its equity, credit-rating agencies placed the others under review.

By January, Ambac, the largest (and now not quite) monoline, was "a company in free fall," having just reported a quarterly loss of $3.3 billion. It had "a staggering $67 billion in CDO exposure," of which $29.1 billion comprised "asset-backed CDO's of increasingly dubious credit quality." Overall it had just "$14.5 billion of claims-paying resources to support a $524 billion guarantee portfolio." MBIA, Ambac's nearest competitor, had even larger credit exposures and insurance guarantees. The traditional business of the monolines—insuring municipal bonds—remained "profitable and relatively safe." But because the guarantees of the monolines were now regarded as worthless, issuers of municipal bonds were "increasingly forgoing insurance" and accepting higher interest rates while saving on insurance fees that could amount to half a point of interest.[34]

The pattern was repeated in the failures and near-failures that followed the monoline debacle. These spanned, as John Kay notes, a wide range of institutions: large bank holding companies such as Citigroup, investment banks such as Lehman and Bear Stearns, public agencies such as Fannie Mae and Freddie Mac, and the largest U.S. insurance company, AIG. In almost every case, Kay writes, "The failure was the result of losses in activities that were peripheral to their core business. Otherwise they had little in common."

Why did these companies court disaster outside their core businesses?

Diffused public ownership provided a strong temptation to CEOs. In public companies, CEOs' shares of the gains and losses are asymmetric, as I have mentioned. This creates incentives for them to take on more risk than they otherwise would. (I don't want to exaggerate: CEOs are concerned about the downside. Serious failure can be career-threatening and humiliating.) Diversification into uncorrelated activities supposedly offers, as in Markowitz's theory, a free lunch of higher returns with little additional overall risk. Of course increasing the number of activities also strains the managerial capacity of the CEO—and increases the odds that a poorly supervised unit will bring down the entire enterprise. But CEOs aren't selected for their diffidence, and the likelihood that they will fail to stay on top of each business is considered, by the CEOs, remote. Furthermore, in the typical public firm there are no strong outside stockholders or partners to restrain the CEO's hubris.

The "before" and "after" contrast at Goldman Sachs is instructive. As a partnership, Goldman was notoriously conservative about entering new businesses.* One observer noted in 1984 that Goldman Sachs "remains the epitome of an old-line house. In an era when the hot shops are the mergers-and-acquisitions departments, Goldman has been curiously unaggressive. Almost alone among major investment banks, it will not represent a raider on a hostile offer. Goldman Sachs was also slow getting into foreign markets, which accounted for less than 10 percent of its business."[35] Similarly, Paul DeRosa, a pioneer of the swaps market, recalls that in the 1980s, the partners at Goldman Sachs were suspicious of risks that might be hidden in what are now regarded as elementary interest-rate swaps (allowing borrowers with floating rate obligations turn them into fixed rates and vice versa). Traders at Goldman were therefore not permitted to put swaps on their books and had to work late into the night to find a counterparty for the other side of transactions. Every night.[36]

---

*The reluctance of partnerships to enter new fields is not confined to financial services. Marvin Bower, cofounder of the consulting firm McKinsey & Co. and for many decades its larger–than–life leader, took more than six years to persuade his partners to open its first overseas office (Bhidé 1996).

As a public company, however, Goldman became one of the leading players in derivatives market, trading instruments far more complex than 1980s-style swaps and enthusiastically embracing the models and technologies discussed in chapters 6 and 7. Under new ownership, the old prejudice against taking unfathomable risks was gone—along with personal liability for things going wrong. At the end of 2008, Goldman was the fourth largest U.S. dealer in derivatives, with nearly 30 trillion dollars in notional value of contracts on its books.[37]

Goldman was also one of AIG's larger derivative counterparties, receiving $13 billion in government funds as settlement of its obligations after AIG was bailed out. Goldman has repeatedly asserted that it did not need the bailout funds because it was "always fully collateralized and hedged."[38] Even if we assume that the hedging models are robust—in chapter 6, I argued they are not—the question remains: fully hedged against what? Almost certainly not against a widespread breakdown of the derivatives market that was likely without a bailout. Even if Goldman had legal claims to amounts greater than its liabilities, given the size of its derivatives exposure, the firm would probably have ceased to operate. And, if Goldman had not gone public, how likely is it that its partners would have permitted the firm to get into this position?

It is worth noting that Goldman was widely regarded as the one investment bank that was—however briefly—run with the culture and prudence of a partnership. Large commercial banks don't have this culture—they were never partnerships. Rather, they have a tradition of decisive, strong-minded CEOs and docile boards of directors. Unsurprisingly, when legal restraints were removed after the 1990s (which we will discuss in later chapters), the megabanks rapidly entered virtually every financial activity imaginable. Furthermore, their willy-nilly diversification was not limited by the "market for corporate control."

As discussed in the last chapter, corporate raiders were never as potent as they were made out to be. Although they did represent a check on unwarranted diversification, raiders posed no threat to the diversification of banks for practical and regulatory reasons. Raiders use high-yield debt (aka "junk") to finance their takeovers. But relying on a bank's "unused" debt capacity to take it over is difficult, because most banks are already highly leveraged. The takeover of a financial institution also has to be approved by bank regulators, and they will not approve a transaction that involves loading on more debt. Moreover, one of the long-standing goals of financial regulation has been to separate the ownership of "real" businesses and "financial" businesses. Thus, just as regulators try to prevent banks from investing in real businesses, they are also loath to let a nonbanking entity take over a bank.

As a result, there are no recorded instances of a large U.S. financial institution that has been the target of a serious tender offer by a raider. Bank CEOs usually lose their jobs only when calamitous performance has forced their boards of directors into action, never because of a bust-up takeover.

Concluding Comments

In the last chapter, we saw how tough New Deal investor protection rules—which became tougher over time—both helped liquefy U.S. stock markets and impair the governance of publicly listed companies by encouraging arm's-length stockholding. The impaired governance took its toll, albeit in a well-hidden way, on the performance of enterprise throughout the economy.

In this chapter, we focused on the governance problems of financial firms. As in other large industrial companies, active, concentrated stockholding in large commercial banks gave way to fragmented, arm's-length stockholding. As the "breadth" of stock markets widened, investment banks such as Salomon Brothers, Morgan Stanley, and Goldman Sachs, which had flourished as private partnerships, also went public. Both commercial and investment bankers were therefore free to play "Heads we win, tails public stockholders lose," with boards of directors (whose own personal stakes were negligible) providing little restraint. Calculated carelessness became the order of the day.

I also briefly suggested that the weakening of internal oversight was especially damaging because it coincided with a relaxation of external restrictions imposed by banking regulators. The next four chapters focus on how this came to be. We will see that the New Deal brought tough banking laws as well as tough securities laws. The banking laws stabilized and expanded the role of relationship-based lending, while the securities laws encouraged arm's-length stockholding. Whereas the securities laws became tougher over time, banking rules became weaker. Weaker banking rules made lending more arm's length and removed important restraints on the recklessness of bankers. This change in banking practices hurt the allocation of credit even in normal times: Those who shouldn't have borrowed received large sums, while worthy borrowers were stranded. It also helped trigger the 2008 financial crisis.

Chapter 10

The Long Slog to Stable Banking

The evolution of banking regulation followed quite a different path than did securities regulation. As we saw in chapter 8, there was virtually no federal securities regulation till the New Deal—or even the clamor for such regulation. Securities markets evolved more or less spontaneously, and, even though they weren't broad or liquid, securities issuance did play a useful role in financing capital-intensive enterprises such as the railroads. My analysis also suggested that the real economy might not have paid much of a penalty if securities laws hadn't been passed.

Banks, however, were tightly controlled long before the New Deal, as we will see in this chapter. In fact, they were regulated from the get-go. In a time when the regulation of commerce was lighter than it has ever been, banking was anything but laissez-faire. This exceptional treatment was neither an accident nor a mistake. Some industries thrive with limited ongoing regulatory oversight: The use of personal computers has flourished with little more than FCC certification of models. In other cases, extensive regulation is essential: Automobiles, for example, require continuous traffic control and regular safety inspection. In banking, regulation was crucial and its development arduous. It took nearly 150 years, during which the banking system and the economy endured many a breakdown, before a suitable regulatory structure was put in place.

Antebellum Banking

The American colonies had no banks; rather, merchants who had access to British capital through their personal connections provided whatever banking services they could. Alexander Hamilton argued in 1781 that banks had "proved to be the happiest engines that were invented for advancing trade,"[1] but, as economist Benjamin Klebaner's history of the industry notes, not a single bank had yet been started in the United States. A few banks did operate in Europe, where, as in the Middle Ages, their principal function was money changing. London goldsmiths had been taking deposits and extending loans in a rudimentary way since the early 1600s,[2] but they were not important players in the economy.

The Bank of North America, the first in the United States, opened in Philadelphia in January 1782, under a charter granted by the Congress of the Confederation. For three years, it functioned as a quasi-central bank: It issued paper currency that could be converted into "specie" (gold or silver coin) and lent over $1.25 million to the Confederation. It was rechartered in 1785 (under a different name) but under conditions that ended its central banking functions.

In 1791, Congress chartered the First Bank of the United States for a period of twenty years. Congress agreed not to grant a federal charter to any other banks during this period, although states were free to charter banks that operated within their boundaries. The First Bank also issued convertible paper currency and served as banker to the U.S. government, receiving the government's deposits and providing it with credit. Although the First Bank was privately owned, the federal government provided some of its capital, and government officials comprised a fifth of the bank's twenty-five-member governing body.[3]

The First Bank's size and power, however, evoked opposition to the renewal of its charter, forcing it to close in 1811. The closure created many problems for the federal government, especially in financing the War of 1812. Efforts to charter a successor ultimately succeeded in 1816, when the Second Bank of the United States was incorporated with a twenty-year charter. It was also privately owned and had expanded to twenty-five branches by 1830. Like the First Bank, the size and power of the Second evoked hostility, especially from Andrew Jackson, who ran on a platform opposing renewal of the bank's charter. As president, Jackson withdrew the federal government's deposits from the bank in 1833, thus putting it into financial difficulties and forcing it to call its loans. In 1836, the Second Bank's expiring charter was not renewed, and for the next twenty-five years federal chartering of banks ceased.

Meanwhile, the states chartered many banks throughout the antebellum era. By 1794, just thirteen years after the first bank had opened in Philadelphia, eighteen banks operated in the United States. By contrast, Britain had just five banks chartered, even though it had a much older banking history (the Bank of England had opened in 1694). At the time of the 1800 census, there were twenty-nine banks in the United States, with all but three towns in New England having one. From 1800 to 1820, the number of banks grew twelvefold. Numbers then grew roughly in line with the expansion of the population: A threefold increase between 1820 and 1840 and a doubling between 1840 and 1860 brought the total to more than 1,500 in operation.

Banks were early users of the corporate form. In fact, starting with Massachusetts and New Hampshire, which banned unincorporated banks altogether in 1799, many states prohibited unincorporated banks from carrying out basic banking activities, especially the issuance of banknotes. As I have mentioned, the federally chartered First and Second Banks played a quasi-central banking role, including the issue of currency notes. But they did not have a monopoly. A state-chartered bank could also issue notes, and indeed that was how banks extended credit: A bank, capitalized with specie—"hard money" gold and silver—would extend loans, typically to merchants, by giving the borrower its notes. Merchants would use the bank's notes to pay suppliers for the goods they purchased, and suppliers could use the notes for their own purchases—or they could present the note to the issuing bank for redemption into specie.

Banks were supposed to maintain enough specie reserves—from their capital or to a lesser extent from deposits—to honor demands for redemption of notes, but they couldn't always do so. Then, as now, banks extended more loans than they had capital, so they usually had many more notes in circulation than they had specie at hand. In fact, "Very soon after the first banks opened, their notes came to exceed coins," and by 1818, paper currency was used in the United States "to a greater extent than anywhere else in the world," according to the testimony of Alexander Baring, a leading British banker.[4]

The wide circulation of banknotes had advantages and disadvantages. It provided a medium of exchange that could keep up with a rapidly growing economy because banks issued more notes than their specie capital. If the medium of exchange had been restricted to specie, its growth would have been tethered to the overall balance of trade (with the supply of specie increasing when trade was in surplus and shrinking when the nation's trade fell into a net deficit) or the discovery of new sources (as happened with gold in California). Of course, the commitment to maintain convertibility meant that there had to be some long-term relationship between the volume of banknotes in circulation and the specie backing them, but it was not rigidly fixed.

This flexibility was also a drawback: Banks were tempted to overissue notes, and the fear that notes had insufficient specie backing could set off runs on banks. Banks often went to considerable lengths to discourage note holders from trying to redeem them (see box); even so, runs could not be prevented, and when these runs turned into panics, banks would either fail or suspend conversion of notes to specie.

Discouraging Redemptions

One way that banks avoided redeeming their notes was to put the onus on borrowers to ensure they weren't redeemed, according to Klebaner. Banks lent borrowers "marked" notes with a loan agreement that made the borrower responsible if the notes were redeemed before a certain period, say, a year.

Another tactic was to make the notes payable in a faraway location. Tennessee's Union Bank issued more than $1.5 million in notes redeemable in New Orleans and a larger amount in Philadelphia. Toms River, a New Jersey village with four stores and a tavern, was the official place of issue of the notes of two banks that did business mainly on Wall Street. When asked to redeem notes, the tavern keeper, who was president of one of the banks, would take advantage of a New Jersey law giving banks three days' grace to summon the necessary specie from New York City. Often the remote note redemption tactic was undertaken as a joint venture by two distant banks: Bank A would lend borrowers the notes of Bank B and vice versa.

Strangers who appeared in town to redeem notes of local banks faced the risk of physical harm. Would-be note-redeemers in Ohio, Indiana, and Missouri "were threatened with lynching or being tarred and feathered." An agent from Lexington, Kentucky, who appeared in Versailles, Kentucky, to redeem notes from a local bank "was hanged in effigy" by residents and "promised an early demise if he ever again molested their bank's specie."[5]

Episodes of widespread suspension of the conversion of banknotes to specie occurred several times during the nineteenth century. In addition, there were localized suspensions because of bank failures in particular regions. The quandary of the typical note-holder in such an episode was described by General Sherman during a bank run in San Francisco in 1855. Upon finally receiving his money at the counter, an exasperated Frenchman exclaimed: "If you got the money, I no want him; if you no got him, I want it like the devil!"[6]

The Farmers' Exchange Bank of Gloucester, Rhode Island, was the first bank to fail in the United States. When it closed in 1809, it had circulated more than half a million dollars of notes—with less than $10,000 of capital. Although the rate of failure of banks thereafter was never low—two-fifths of all banks started before the Civil War failed in less than ten years—there was considerable bunching. For instance, about a quarter of all banks closed in the six years that followed the Panic of 1837.

Bank runs, suspensions, and failures naturally hurt note holders who didn't convert to specie quickly. They also harmed the economy by reducing the circulating medium of exchange—the mirror image of the benefits realized through its rapid expansion. Bank problems may not have been the primary cause of monetary and economic contractions, but very likely they exacerbated them. As the economist Burke Parsons put it, "While the banks did not originate business fluctuations, they transmitted and magnified the impulses making for expansion or contraction."[7]

The ability of state-chartered banks to issue their own notes, whose value depended on the location and soundness of the issuing bank, also hindered trade. Thousands of notes circulated. A few were regarded as being as "good as gold"—in which case a dollar note could be used to buy a dollar's worth of goods. But most were not. Furthermore, the discount from face value was different for each note and from place to place. These problems were exacerbated when the Second Bank shut down—its notes and their market share (a fifth of all circulation in 1830) had set a standard for soundness that others could not fall too far below. Lesser banks could circulate their notes in places where the Second Bank's were not easily available, but only up to a point, thus restraining their tendency to overissue. Not surprisingly, in the five years after Second Bank's federal charter expired, the "currency situation" in the United States became "worse than that of any other country,"[8] in the view of Albert Gallatin, a former secretary of the Treasury.

For about the first forty years of the nineteenth century, states granted charters, by acts of the legislature, to individual banks for fixed periods on a discretionary basis. Some states, however, refused to charter any banks because of hostility toward the paper money they issued and "the instability banks were thought to create."[9] Thomas Jefferson referred to note-issuing banks as "more dangerous than standing armies," and John Adams declared a lifelong abhorrence of the entire U.S. banking system.[10] A University of Pennsylvania economist wrote in 1839 that the American banking system was "a compound of quackery and imposture" without a single "redeeming quality."[11] In 1845, former president Andrew Jackson, who had fought renewal of the Second Bank's charter, wrote to Sam Houston urging that the Texas constitution prohibit paper-issuing banks, "to protect your morals and to cap the climax of your prosperity."[12] The ban was duly included. Other states that refused to incorporate banks at various times before the Civil War included Arkansas, California, Iowa, and Oregon.

States that refused to charter banks could not escape the circulation of paper money, however. Banks from Illinois and Wisconsin, for instance, flooded Iowa, which did not charter banks, with "some of the worst money in the Union" in the mid-1850s.[13]

As the nineteenth century wore on, the system of discretionary legislative chartering fell into increasing disrepute. Charters were supposed to contain safeguards against failures, and these safeguards manifestly did not work. Worse, legislators bestowed charters on friends and withheld them from their adversaries—or traded charters for bribes and favors. Chartering in New York State "became so shameless and corrupt that it could be endured no longer,"[14] observed Millard Fillmore, who served as a state assemblyman and congressman before his election as the thirteenth president of the United States.

In April 1848, New York passed the Free Banking Act, which a contemporary called "equal to a second declaration of independence." The Federal Reserve's Bray Hammond later called the act "the most important event in American banking history" because it established a distinctively American system of banking. It was not the first free-banking act, however; Michigan preceded New York by thirteen months, its governor commending the Michigan law for destroying "the odious features of a bank monopoly and giving equal rights to all classes of the community."

Free banking did not mean unregulated banking. It meant that anyone who met requirements set by state legislatures was entitled to a charter. A key requirement was that banks purchase bonds to back their notes: New York, for example, required state or U.S. government bonds, or mortgages on New York real estate. A bank would send its bonds and notes of the same face value as the bonds to state authorities, who would sign and return the notes, but keep the bonds in their custody for as long as the notes remained in circulation. Free-banking laws also required banks to maintain minimum levels of capital and specie, and to convert their notes into specie, at par value, on demand. If a bank failed to redeem (after a grace period), the state authorities would close the bank and pay off note holders by selling the bonds in their custody.

In principle, the rules prevented banks from overissuing notes (because they couldn't circulate more notes than the bonds they deposited). In reality, however, the concurrent growth of a new medium of exchange—checks drawn on demand deposits—offered some leeway. Instead of paying a supplier with a note, a merchant could pay by check. Recipients could then cash the check (for notes or specie) or deposit the checks in their own bank accounts. But how did merchants have money in their accounts in the first place? One way was simply by depositing notes or specie. But banks could also "create" deposits, just as they had been previously able to create paper money, by making loans. Instead of giving borrowers notes, banks could "deposit" funds in the borrowers' checking accounts (see box).

Paying by Check

Checks had been used in payments from the early days of U.S. banking, but initially in a roundabout way. A check would be used to withdraw cash; the cash would then be used to make payments. Later, the checks themselves were used as payments. In 1809, Gallatin observed that payments were as likely to be made from bank deposits by check or draft as by banknotes. By 1840, most large payments in U.S. cities were made by check. The use of checks even for smaller transactions accelerated as the number of bank accounts grew twentyfold in the 1850s.

The funds in the accounts on which checks were drawn were, to a large degree, the result of loans, although "the general public held to the literal, erroneous view that these deposits represented mainly money brought to the bank for safekeeping." As Samuel Hooper, congressman from Massachusetts (and businessman) wrote in 1860, "The great mass of deposits in the banks of the large commercial cities originate in discounts [i.e., loans] made by banks, and is therefore the creation of the banks." The extension of credit through deposits rather than through notes was also reflected in the changing liabilities of banks, especially in the cities. In 1829 rural or "country" banks had 1.77 times more notes outstanding than their deposit liabilities, whereas banks in the seven largest cities had 1.35 times more deposits than notes and in New York City nearly twice as many notes as deposits. By 1849, New York City banks had 3./

---

times more deposits than notes, whereas their rural counterparts in the state had 2.23 times more notes than deposits. A decade later, even the country banks in New York State had more deposits than notes (1.28 times); in New York City, deposits had grown to more than ten times the number of notes.[15]

As with the creation of paper money, the creation of deposits was a double-edged sword. On one hand, it allowed the medium of exchange to grow faster than the supply of bonds used to back the banknotes. This was a good thing since a money supply comprising just notes and constrained by the issuance of bonds unrelated to the level of economic activity could dampen economic growth. On the other hand, depositors' (rather than just banknote holders') concerns about excessive or imprudent lending could trigger bank runs and cause a collapse in the medium of exchange. Furthermore, the bank notes themselves weren't always fully backed by bonds and mortgages of equivalent value. Unscrupulous bankers could also skip the bond depositing step and forge the signature of state officials authorizing the notes, or alter the face value of properly authorized notes from, say, $5 to $10.

In any event, the overall record of free banking was mixed. In Bray Hammond's history, people of states where banking was banned were better off than the people of states that had free banks.[16] Others, however, have argued that although the early years of free banking were troubled, its performance improved over time, in part because of "adjustments in the laws in response to problems that arose."[17] As the monetary scholar Anna Schwartz points out, "It was not dissatisfaction with free banking that ended the experiment."[18] Rather, it was the formation of a national banking system patterned, as we will later see, after the free-banking principle of backing banknotes with bonds.

As is apparent from the preceding account, banking was extensively regulated—especially in comparison to other businesses. From the early history of the United States through the present, the rules had three important goals: protecting the people's savings; protecting the economy from slumps caused or magnified by the destruction of the medium of exchange (a goal that went hand in hand with the protection of savings); and correcting perceived biases in lending.

Consider the safety goal. Bank charters specified what a bank could—and could not—do. Early charters contained specific exclusions forbidding dealings in real estate, merchandise, or bonds of the United States, except in liquidating loan collateral. In 1825, a landmark charter granted by the New York state legislature to the Commercial Bank of Albany contained a sweeping exclusion: It gave the bank "powers to carry on the business of banking by discounting bills, notes, and other evidences of debt; by receiving deposits; by buying gold and selling bills of exchange, and by issuing bills, notes and other evidences of debt." It also specified that the bank would have "no other powers whatever, except such as are expressly granted by this act." The definition, including the broad restriction, was later used in New York's Free Banking Act and widely adopted in state and federal banking legislation.

States required banks to provide regular reports of their financial condition, starting in the early 1800s. Banks however often "disregarded the reporting requirement or submitted inaccurate or misleading statements." States also examined banks somewhat half-heartedly (see box), and the absence of "an effective supervisory mechanism" made statutory constraints imposed on banks "largely meaningless."[19]

On-Again, Off-Again Supervision

In 1829 New York established the nation's first bank supervisory authority with banking commissioners who made on-the-spot examinations of banks four times a year. After the 1837 panic the New York model was copied by many other states, but in 1843 the New York state legislature abolished the examining commissioners, reasoning that they were unnecessary if bankers were honest and useless if they weren't. New York reestablished its banking department in 1851, but the superintendent of banking could only conduct an examination if there was suspicion of illegal or unsound activity. This condition discouraged examination: Its conduct signaled official suspicion and could trigger a run on the bank. The banking superintendent therefore asked the legislature to abolish his examining powers in 1858. Other states did not "go even to the limited extent that New York did" in supervising their banks.[20]

Many bankers and lawmakers believed that only the note-issuing function of banks required regulation. Everything else, as former Treasury secretary Gallatin wrote in 1841, "not only must be open to all, but requires no more restrictions than any other species of commerce." A similar distinction between the need to regulate note issuance, but not the deposit-taking and lending activities, was made in 1848 by Millard Fillmore when he was New York State comptroller. On the other side, a book published in 1859 by Stephen Coldwell argued that "the real banking problem of the day involved deposit regulation even more than the protection of note issues," but few others agreed.[21]

California's first constitution, for instance, prohibited banks from issuing paper money but allowed them to accept deposits. Similarly, many states established reserve requirements to control the over issue of notes[22] but not banks' deposit liabilities.

Safety was also a consideration with schemes to insure creditors against bank failures. In 1829, New York required its banks to contribute to a fund to insure creditors against bank failure; and, in 1834, Indiana instituted a somewhat different scheme with the same end in mind (see box). The Indiana scheme was more successful and served as a model for other states. In principle, the schemes were intended to protect all creditors, but, in practice, they focused on protecting note holders. For instance, in 1842, after a series of bank failures drained New York's insurance fund, its bank commissioners asserted that the 1829 legislation enabling the fund had intended only "to secure bank noteholders, and not depositors or other creditors."[23] The Ohio and Iowa programs had limited insurance coverage from the outset to circulating notes.[24]

Insuring against Bank Failure: New York versus Indiana

New York's insurance scheme was proposed at a time when a number of banks' charters were up for renewal.[25] Considerable public dissatisfaction with their operation created an opening to try something innovative. Governor Van Buren endorsed a plan designed by Joshua Forman, a businessman from Syracuse. Under the plan, the state would establish an insurance fund to which all banks would be required to contribute to qualify for renewal of their charters. Forman said the plan had been suggested by regulations governing Hong merchants in Hong Kong, each of whom had been given the right to trade with foreigners, which made all of them liable for each other's debts. The situation regarding banks, Forman argued was similar: "They enjoy[ed] in common the exclusive right of making a paper currency for the people of the state, and by the same rule should in common be answerable for that paper." Forman's plan also called for regular and full examination of banks by salaried officials, "a degree of supervision almost unthinkable at that time." The bill approved by the legislature created a so-called Safety Fund that would require banks to contribute 0.05 percent of their paid-in capital each year, until their total contribution to the Fund reached 3 percent of paid-in capital.[26]

With minor differences, the New York plan of insurance and examination was adopted by Vermont in 1831 and Michigan in 1836.

Indiana created a different kind of bank obligation scheme at the same time that it set up a banking system in 1834. A constitutional ban on private note-issuing banks led to the creation of a state-owned bank with privately owned "branches." Although each branch bank was separately owned and managed, Indiana law made all branches jointly responsible for the debts of any branch that failed, thus creating strong incentives for the kind of mutual monitoring found in classical investment-banking partnerships. No insurance fund was created, however. The scheme envisioned levies on all branches after losses were incurred.

The Michigan version of the New York model, which had been established just a year before the Panic of 1837, could not cope. Every insured bank failed, and nothing was paid to creditors. The Vermont system was "seriously weakened." The New York scheme survived 1837, but, after a series of bank failures in the early 1840s, its insurance fund "proved inadequate to meet all the claims of creditors of banks which had failed." In Indiana, however, there was only one bank failure, and its banking system "ranked with the strongest in the nation."[27]

The Indiana success was due mainly to "the relationship between its insurance plan and bank supervision," according to Carter Golembe.[28] Indiana's scheme gave supervisory powers to the board of directors of the state-owned bank, with its president acting as a kind of banking commissioner.

The board mainly comprised representatives of the branch banks. This "could have been disastrous, since one bank might have been willing to overlook the misdeeds of another, in return for the same favor to itself. But since the banks were also tied together in an insurance plan that provided for assessments to meet the obligations of a failing member, the result was that each bank could best protect its interests by seeing to it that no other bank reached a position that would endanger the rest. To put it another way, the insurance system gave each participating bank a stake in the sound operation of every other Indiana bank, while the supervisory structure gave it the power to enforce its interests." For instance, loans to directors and stockholders of the branch banks were "carefully watched" by the board and president of the state bank.[29] They also discouraged speculative real-estate lending that was the undoing of banks in other states.

Banking rules, almost from the beginning, also addressed concerns about biases in lending. Farmers were afraid that banks would channel credit away from them. When the Union Bank, the second bank to be chartered in Massachusetts, opened in Boston in 1792, it was required to make one-fifth of its loans to farmers outside the city. Similarly, thirteen of fourteen Massachusetts banks chartered during 1802 and 1803 had to allocate an eighth of their lending to farmers.

But rules to mitigate biases in lending sometimes conflicted with rules to ensure safety. Rules intended to make banks safe discouraged lending against the collateral of land, whereas Massachusetts's rules mandating agricultural loans required banks to accept the security of real estate. Such conflicts have been a problem for bank regulation ever since.

In some cases, however, rules against favoritism also promoted safety. For instance, banks were commonly believed to offer favorable loan terms to their directors, against the dubious collateral of their stock, while "refusing loans to others offering superior security." Virginia's banks reported in 1840 that they had lent nearly a fourth of their capital to their directors. Laws were therefore passed banning or limiting loans to bank stockholders against the security of their stock.[30] Some states also "tried to prevent favoritism and to diffuse the benefits of banks as widely as possible" by limiting the loans that could be made to any individual—to $50,000 in Philadelphia and Maryland.[31]

The Emergence of Dual Banking

The demise of the Second Bank, in 1836, meant that the federal government could no longer borrow—or secure other banking services from a national bank. This created an enormous roadblock to the financing for the Civil War and caused the Treasury to issue its own paper money ("greenbacks") to pay the federal government's bills; the Legal Tender Act of 1862 required creditors accept greenbacks even when they were not convertible into specie.

To raise more funds, Congress in 1863 passed the National Currency Act, which was then amended as the National Bank Act of 1864. The legislation created nationally charted banks that were capitalized by their stockholders with specie and required to purchase bonds issued by the U.S. government. Following the ideas of the free-banking acts, nationally chartered banks were given the right to issue notes against the U.S. government bonds they had to buy.

Although primarily intended to raise funds for the federal government, the acts also had a "second and more permanent purpose: to establish a more orderly, and ultimately exclusively federal banking system to replace the chaotic explosion of state banks," writes Robert Litan. Before the 1862 act authorizing the issue of greenbacks, the United States did not have a uniform national currency. By 1862, 7,000 different banknotes issued by 1,600 state banks circulated in the Union states.[32] These were joined by 5,500 kinds of fraudulent notes; in 1863 Ohio senator John

Sherman observed that only 253 banks had not had their notes altered or counterfeited.[33] The different notes, in turn, were valued at different discounts to their face value when used for payments.

The new legislation also created the Office of the Comptroller of the Currency (OCC). When a nationally chartered bank deposited U.S. government bonds with the OCC, it received notes of uniform design in return. In addition to the bond collateral, banks were also required to hold a specie reserve against the notes they issued, as well as against their deposits. Furthermore, the new laws guaranteed national banknotes. If a bank failed, the Treasury would take responsibility for redeeming its notes and canceling the bonds that had served as collateral. Under the previous state free-banking acts, note holders weren't paid immediately and were at risk if the value of the collateral posted by a failing bank turned out to be lower than the amount of its notes. The federal guarantee thus ensured that all banknotes would have the same value in making payments, namely their face value.

Jay Cooke, a leading financier of the time, said the new system combined "the unity of action and general control, and the uniformity of currency"—the best features of the previous nationally chartered First and Second Banks—with the geographic "diffusion of [note] issue and freedom in local management" of the antebellum state system.[34] But all bankers did not share Cooke's optimism that Congress would allow them to maintain "freedom in local management," and the expectations of lawmakers that all state-chartered banks would quickly convert to national charters weren't realized. Between February 1863 and June 1864, only 24 of the 456 national charters granted were to banks converting their state charters, and by mid-1864 national banknotes accounted for less than 15 percent of the currency in circulation. Only about 125 more state-chartered banks converted by the end of 1864.

Senator Sherman then introduced a bill to tax state banknotes out of existence by imposing a 10 percent annual levy. State-chartered banks soon converted after the tax was imposed in March 1865, with fewer than 300 retaining their charters. All $239 million of outstanding state banknotes were retired, and similar amounts of national notes were in circulation by 1866.

In spite of their inability to issue notes, state-chartered banks made a comeback, however, and by the turn of the century they constituted a clear majority (see box). Contrary to the intention of the 1860s laws that all banks would be nationally chartered, a dual system of state and national banks emerged.

The Comeback of State-Chartered Banks

In just two years, the tax Congress imposed on their notes forced down the number of state-chartered banks from 1,466 in 1866 to 247 by 1868.[35] In 1882, the number of state-chartered banks had climbed back to 704. The number of nationally chartered banks had also increased to 2,239 (from 1,634 in July 1866). In another ten years, however, nationally chartered banks were outnumbered, and by 1900 there were 5,000 state-chartered banks and 3,790 national banks. By 1913, there were twice as many state-chartered banks as national banks. The share of deposits of state-chartered banks likewise rose from 40 percent of the total in 1867, to 49 percent in 1882, to 55 percent in 1900, and 58 percent by 1913.[36]

Several factors accounted for the resurgence of state-chartered banks. The economic benefits of the right to issue notes declined. As checking accounts grew in popularity (and were "aggressively marketed"[37] by state-chartered banks), banks didn't need to issue notes to attract customers. And the profitability of note issuance was uneven. In the 1880s, for instance, when the U.S. government's budget was in surplus, it repurchased its bonds and raised their prices to above face values. But banks weren't allowed to issue notes worth more than 90 percent of the face value of the bonds they owned. Therefore, if a bond was trading a premium of 10 percent to its face value, a bank would have to tie up $110 for every $90 in notes it could issue.

State-chartered banks also faced lower capital requirements and fewer restrictions on their lending activities. Before 1900, the minimum capital required to start a nationally chartered bank ranged from $50,000 (in places with populations of less than 6,000) to $200,000 (in places with populations exceeding 50,000). State charters commonly required $10,000 in capital. In 1900, the minimum capital required for a national bank serving a small town (with less than 3,000 inhabitants) was cut to $25,000, but even this reduced amount was greater than that demanded by many states.[38] Similarly, nationally chartered banks could not make mortgage loans; the National Bank Act "strictly limited national banks to extending commercial credit." Many states, however, allowed their banks to make loans secured by real estate; therefore, "state chartered banks flourished in the expanding rural areas of the country, where farmers used their real estate as collateral to obtain crop loans."[39]

National charters did, however, confer more prestige and helped attract distant investors. In 1889, nonresidents owned about 33 percent of the stock of national banks in the prairie and Rocky Mountain states, whereas investors in state-chartered banks were predominantly local residents.[40]

The dual banking system that emerged was, by design, also highly fragmented. In the antebellum era, most northern states had discouraged or banned banks from operating more than one branch. Branch banking was, however, more prevalent in the southern states of Virginia,

Louisiana, and Kentucky. Small Virginian river towns that could not support a stand-alone bank benefitted from having branches. Fifteen banks chartered in Louisiana between 1818 and 1836 had their headquarters in New Orleans, but were authorized to open branches in twenty-six different towns. Branching, according to Klebaner, made the banks safer because they pooled "illiquid rural loans with the more diversified commercial loans" extended in New Orleans. Overall, however, the total number of branches in the antebellum era was small: With about 1,600 banks operating in 1861, the total number of branches was just 174.[41]

In the postbellum era, the National Bank Act did not permit branching, which was viewed as antithetical to the principles of free banking that served as a model for the act. In the words of Comptroller Charles Dawes, American banks had been "built up by protecting the rights and the opportunities of the small man, and the small bank." Banks called national because of their federal charter weren't national in scope; rather, they were single-branch or "unit" banks. In principle, an 1865 amendment to the National Bank Act of 1864 permitted banks converting from state charters to keep their existing branches. Nonetheless, the comptroller of the currency required a Maryland bank to divest its branches, citing a technicality of the 1864 law. This precedent was followed until the early 1900s, when banks converting from a state charter were finally allowed to keep their branches. Congress, however, refused the pleas of a succession of comptrollers to allow nationally chartered banks to open branches in their head-office cities or in small communities that did not have a nationally chartered bank.[42] As for state-chartered banks, most states also refused to allow them to operate branches. In 1910, only twelve (including notably California and New York) did. As a result, there were just nine national banks and 283 state-chartered banks operating a total of 542 branches in 1910, whereas the total population of banks numbered nearly 27,000.[43] Over the previous half century, the number of banks had grown five times as fast as the population.[44] According to the free-banking foundation of the 1864 National Bank Act, anyone who had the necessary capital—"however unfamiliar with banking principles"—could start a bank.[45]

No Respite

The National Bank Act failed to stabilize the banking system, although it succeeded in creating a reliable and uniform currency. Runs on banks to convert notes to specie ceased because the U.S. Treasury paid the holders of national banknotes in full, whatever might be the financial condition of the issuing bank. Banks did, however, face runs by depositors wanting to turn their balances into currency. Whereas banks had once suspended the conversion of their notes into specie when runs occurred, banks would now suspend cash withdrawals from their accounts by depositors. And the crises that followed the suspension of withdrawals occurred with "unpredictable but embarrassing frequency."[46] Between the Civil War and the U.S. entry into World War I, six deep depressions—in 1873, 1884, 1890, 1893, 1896, and 1907—followed financial panics.[47]

The inelastic supply of currency—underlying the rapidly growing amounts held in bank accounts—helped increase the frequency of panics and the severity of their consequences (see box).

The Price of an Inelastic Currency

The National Bank Act helped make the supply of currency inelastic by requiring national banks to hold U.S. government bonds in amounts at least equal to the notes they issued. The supply of these bonds was more or less fixed—increasing mainly in times of government deficits, which were not then the norm. But the demand for a medium of exchange was growing with the expansion of the economy, and was also subject seasonal and sporadic fluctuations.

The growth of checking accounts did provide an alternative, more flexible medium of exchange, but only up to a point. Thanks to the extensive use of checks by businesses, by 1881 more than 90 percent of the total money coming into banks took the form of checks and drafts. By 1910, the "check habit" had also become widely ingrained in individuals.[48] Although the supply of currency was fixed, banks could create (subject to reserve requirements) money in checking accounts by extending loans. As Harvard professor Charles Dunbar noted in 1887, deposits adapted "to the demand of moment without visible effort." As the growth of the economy increased the demand for credit and a medium of exchange, the ratio of bank deposits to currency multiplied: from $1.53 in 1870, to 2.21 in 1882, to 4.42 in 1900, and 7.19 in 1913.[49]

The use of checks and deposit accounts was not, however, uniform across the country. High capital requirements discouraged the chartering of national banks in lightly populated rural areas, and without a nearby branch to serve their needs, people shied away from check payments. Iowa farmers relied mainly on currency and coin in the mid-1880s. In the last third of the 1800s, per capita bank assets in the South were about a fifth of the national average; in the prairie and mountain states, about half the national average. Moreover, any jump in the demand for currency could not be satisfied by creating more deposits. Indeed, because bank deposits had to be backed in some proportion

The growing interconnectedness of banks—but without a robust mechanism to coordinate responses in times of stress—added to the instability (see box) caused by an inflexible supply of currency. The problem of banks running on each other helped create and prolong the panic of 1907—the "most extensive and prolonged breakdown of the country's credit mechanism since the establishment of the national banking system."[51] As one observer of the time wrote, "Two-thirds of the banks of the country entered upon an internecine struggle to obtain cash, had ceased to extend credit to their customers, had suspended cash payments and were hoarding such money as they had." Because the credit system of the country had stopped operating, "Thousands of men were thrown out of work, thousands of firms went into bankruptcy [and] the trade of the country came to a standstill."[52]

The Problems of Interconnected Banks

The expanding use of check payments led banks to maintain deposits with each other to facilitate settlements. Moreover, as the railroad and telegraph increased the integration of the real economy, more payments and interbank transactions took place across distant locations. Another reason for the growth of interbank deposits were laws that allowed nationally chartered banks located outside the main cities ("country banks") to keep 60 percent of their reserve requirements as deposits with banks located in the large cities. In good times this arrangement was mutually advantageous: The city banks paid the country banks attractive interest rates on their deposits, and then pyramided these deposits as reserves to expand their own lending activities. But it also increased the vulnerability of the city banks to withdrawals by the country banks, especially if the loans made by the city banks could not be easily liquidated without large loss.

Their interdependency did encourage banks to coordinate their responses in times of financial stress. One notable mechanism was through clearinghouses that had originally been set up in large cities to "net out" and settle checks drawn on each other. Their proximity, their ongoing interactions, and the risk that they would all go down together caused clearinghouse members to put up a united front when runs occurred: All would suspend cash withdrawals by depositors, and issue clearinghouse certificates that could be used in lieu of cash. Commercial life could go on after a fashion—employers could pay their employees with clearinghouse certificates that would be accepted by many local merchants. But certificates weren't an effective medium of exchange outside the clearinghouse area, and, while the suspension was in force, new lending would also cease.

The clearinghouse had no national counterpart, and there was no formal mechanism that allowed banks with surplus cash to safely lend it to banks that had pressing needs, although there were understandings between correspondent banks (that had frequent dealings with each other) for such loans to be made. As a rule, however, banks would fend for themselves and try to shore up their own cash reserves.

By 1907, the system had become highly vulnerable to banks running on each other. Nearly half the reserves of the national banking system had been placed as deposits with city banks, rather than held in vaults as cash. About a third of such interbank deposits were with New York City banks that often pyramided the deposits to make loans for securities speculation. The Knickerbocker Trust Company, the third largest in the city, suffered a run on October 22, 1907. The second largest was hit the following day. The legendary financier J. P. Morgan organized a pool of $25 million on the twenty-fourth and another $10 million on the twenty-fifth to advance cash to weak banks. But just as things seemed to calm down, country banks demanded the return of the reserves they had placed on deposit with banks in New York City. The banks then restricted depositor withdrawals of cash and on October 26 the New York clearinghouse started issuing certificates in lieu of cash. Shortly thereafter banks suspended cash withdrawals in two-thirds of cities with a population of more than 25,000.

The comptroller of the currency's 1907 annual report said that the panic wasn't due to "the lack of confidence of the people in the banks, but more to a lack of confidence of the banks in themselves." It demonstrated "beyond the possibility of denial," said the report, "that perfectly solvent banks—if independent, isolated units with no power of cooperation except through such voluntary association as their clearing houses—cannot protect themselves in a panic and save themselves from failure with such a suspension of payments as to produce disorder and demoralization in all the business of their customers."[53]

▆▆▆▆ Enter the Federal Reserve

Following the havoc wreaked by the panic of 1907, Congress created the bipartisan National Monetary Commission to study banking and monetary reform. The commission submitted thirty reports between 1909 and 1912 that stimulated the discussion and debate that informed the Federal Reserve Act of 1913. The preamble of the act stated two concrete intentions: "to furnish an elastic currency" and to "afford means of rediscounting commercial paper." The majority report of the Senate Banking Committee put the goals of the act in broader terms: "to give stability to the commerce and industry of the United States; prevent financial panics or financial stringencies; make available effective commercial credit for individuals engaged in manufacturing, in commerce, in finance, and in business to the extent of their just deserts; put an end to the pyramiding of the bank reserves of the country and the use of such reserves for gambling purposes on the stock exchange."[54]

To achieve the goal of a more elastic currency, the Federal Reserve System (the "Fed") was empowered to issue currency in amounts that would accommodate changes in demand, for instance, during the spikes at harvest time. But matching the overall supply of currency to its demand wasn't enough to ensure stability if banks with extra cash didn't lend it to those in need. The 1913 act therefore envisioned the Fed becoming a reliable "lender of last resort" to banks that were short; instead of liquidating their loans to raise cash, banks could borrow against these loans from the Federal Reserve. The Fed would only make cash advances against short-term loans made by banks "for agricultural, industrial or commercial purposes," and not for stock market "speculation." Therefore, predicted University of Chicago economist J. Laurence Laughlin, Federal Reserve notes and bank credit would "adjust themselves to the needs of trade."[55]

To assuage concerns about the centralization of monetary power, the Federal Reserve System was set up as twelve more-or-less independent reserve banks, each owned by its member banks. The National Monetary Commission had conceived of the Fed as a cooperative enterprise to increase the security of banks and provide them with a reservoir of emergency resources; but nationally chartered banks had to become members of this cooperative enterprise—or forfeit their charters. Member banks were required to subscribe to the stock of a reserve bank. They also had to deposit the reserves they were required to hold with the Fed; unlike the city banks, the Fed would not pay interest on these reserves. In return, member banks had the assurance of borrowing from the Fed. State-chartered banks were encouraged, but not required, to join. By the end of 1918, 930 had joined, but ten times as many state-chartered banks remained outside: Not only did banks entering the Federal Reserve System face higher reserve requirements, but also the loss of interest on reserves.

A third objective stated in the preamble to the 1913 act was "to estab-lish more effective supervision of banking." The need was urgent, according to a later Minneapolis Fed publication: "In testimony before the House that year, the comptroller of the currency said bluntly: 'The whole question of bank examination is illogical, unscientific, and simply impossible under the present laws.' National bank examiners, clearing-house examiners, and state examiners were all clamoring for the same information, sharing some with their counterparts and jealously guard-ing other bits of information."[56]

National bank examination had come into being with the Civil War legislation chartering national banks and the creation of the OCC, whose duties included examination. However, the comptrol-ler of the currency admitted to the National Monetary Commission in 1908 that the OCC's supervision of banks had been "ineffectual and disastrous."[57] OCC examiners weren't paid salaries. Rather they got a flat fee, based on the capital of the bank examined, encouraging "superficiality." Selection of examiners, moreover, was "not necessar-ily based on merit." State examination of state-chartered banks wasn't much more thorough. In 1884, the comptroller said that states subjected their banks to "very little interference and scarcely any espionage on the part of officials." At the time, just eight states conducted regular bank examinations.[58]

After the 1913 act, examiners were paid a salary, a career system was established, and the field force was placed under the control of twelve chief national bank examiners. The act made nationally charted banks subject to twice-a-year examination. The legislation did not succeed in eliminating duplication, for Fed examinations of member banks added to the OCC's examination of national banks and state examination of state-chartered banks. Until the 1930s, however, the Federal Reserve was more concerned with its role as central banker and did not regularly exercise its examination powers.[59]

■■■ Concluding Comments

In 1914, the comptroller of the currency asserted that the Federal Reserve Act had made panics "mathematically impossible," and the following year the Federal Reserve chairman predicted that "we will never have any more panics." This confidence seemed to be justified at first: In 1920, wholesale prices fell by 44 percent and industrial production by 32 percent.[60] Yet banks did not scramble for cash and contracted their loans in an orderly manner. The economy soon returned to robust growth for the rest of the 1920s.

Of course, the mission of stabilizing the banks was far from accomplished, for reasons that we will discuss in the next chapter. But first, let us pause to draw some inferences from the story of bank regulation told so far that will be useful when we discuss financial reform in the concluding chapter.

Lawmakers in the United States took the regulation of banks seriously from the very beginning, in contrast to the securities industry, where legislation came quite late. States granted charters bank by bank, for specified periods and purposes. Some states permitted only state-owned banks to issue notes, while others prohibited all note-issuing banks.

Lawmakers could not, however, anticipate the problems that would arise in a rapidly evolving economy. There could be no simple rules for regulating banks, or a silver bullet to ensure their stability. It was one thing to want regular examination, but questions of who would examine, how often, and for what purpose, were not easily answered.

The regulatory system evolved with much trial and great error. Very likely, progress was made: Free-banking rules, with notes backed by government bonds, replaced corrupt chartering and poorly backed note issuance. The principles of free banking were then used to establish a uniform national currency in the Civil War. Civil War banking legislation also incorporated rules that had evolved in some states requiring reserves against both deposits and banknotes. This legislation was successful in creating a sound currency. On the minus side, not much progress was made in stabilizing deposits. Frequent panics ultimately led to the creation of the Federal Reserve in 1913. But even this legislation proved inadequate to stabilize a banking system that, by today's standards, sought to provide rudimentary functions: take deposits, provide for payments by check, and extend short-term commercial credit.

The great difficulty in providing a suitable regulatory structure for relatively simple banking ought to give pause to those who imagine that more modern regulation will easily stabilize megabanks, now heavily engaged in complex financial engineering and derivatives trading.

The nexus between the evolution of banking rules and distinctively American political ideologies, traditions, and structures is also noteworthy. In many other countries central banks were established before commercial banks at a time when governments did not face general elections or the pressure of common opinion. Britain's central bank, the Bank of England, was established in 1694, when Parliament was far from representative of the country's population. Other U.K. banks were chartered after the Bank of England. In the United States, a more open political system and hostility to centralized governmental authority prevented the formation of a real central bank until 1913. The First and Second Banks of the United States, which performed some central banking functions, did not have their charters renewed. Therefore, when the Federal Reserve was finally established, it had to adapt to a banking system that had long been in place.

Bank regulation in the United States also had to contend with a structure that was much more highly fragmented than in other industries and banking in other countries. In general, the United States isn't especially averse to big business. Political opposition to the expansion of Wal-Mart has not stopped the company from becoming a dominant force in retailing, whereas in Japan and many countries in Europe, lobbying by small shopkeepers has checked the growth of large discount chains. According to some historians, the United States has spawned more large companies than other countries partly because of a more tolerant regulatory attitude. Granted: The United States was a pioneer in antitrust legislation and "trust-busting" politicians did attempt to curb the power of large corporations after the Second Industrial Revolution started around 1880. But as the business historian Thomas McCraw points out, U.S. antitrust legislation was not synonymous with antibigness law. The most conspicuous targets of antitrust were giant companies, but the majority of prosecutions were against groups of small firms engaging in collusive behavior.[61]

Nor can it be said that businesses in the United States have been especially backward in seeking and securing favors from government: The railroads benefited immensely from land grants. However, the American political system does tend to spread favors around. Competition between individual politicians and interest groups, a federal form of government, and institutionalized checks and balances make it difficult for any one business to enjoy large-scale monopoly power bestowed by government. Franchises created by laws or regulations may not be available to all, but they are rarely limited to one.

The tendency to spread favors and franchises relatively widely has had a profound influence on the structure of U.S. banking. As we have seen, the right to provide banking services is granted by government, not earned through unfettered competition. Distributing this right widely created a system with far more—and therefore smaller—banks than is the case in most other developed countries. Reciprocally, the fragmentation of banking may have made it harder for regulators to ensure its stability. To take an extreme case: Suppose banking, and not just currency issuance, was in the hands of a single state-owned or controlled monopoly. There would be no question of depositors running on such a system because there would be no other place for them to run. A similar stability might also be secured through a system of tightly regulated, oligopolistic, universal banks, empowered by the state to provide all possible financial functions, as has more or less been the case in Germany. But the concentration of credit in the hands of a few banks would also suppress the decentralization of judgment that, as I argued in part I, is the hallmark of an innovative economy. And it would conflict with the nature of the political system of the United States.

The distinctively national historical character of banking also has relevance for the future of regulation: However desirable harmonization of standards and global coordination might be in principle, reformers cannot simply wish away long-standing national differences in banking rules, structures, and practices.

Chapter 11

Not There Yet

Modern commercial banks, Merton Miller writes, perform a "miracle" of liquidity creation. They make illiquid loans that cannot be converted back into cash without significant costs and delays; "yet the banks' depositors, who put up most of the funds for those illiquid assets, have a perfectly liquid investment" they can turn into cash at virtually no cost or delay. Depositors, he continues, "also get the services of skilled loan officers to invest their funds in illiquid assets earning far higher returns than the depositors could hope to earn on their own."

This "marvelous mechanism for channeling into productive investments the huge flow of household savings" is, however, fragile, as Miller also points out. The maturity mismatch of long-term fixed-rate loans versus short-term, floating-rate deposits, along with the first-come, first-served aspect of deposit obligations, holds banks hostages to fickle depositors. "As long as every depositor believes the bank will honor its promises," Miller observes, "the bank will be able to do so. The withdrawals from any one account will be offset, on average, by deposits into other accounts, buffered by small amounts of till cash. But if for any reason doubts about the safety of the deposits arise on any large scale, then nobody can withdraw, except for the lucky few who get to the tellers' windows before the till cash is gone."[1]

Depositors may also, quite rationally, rush to the exits even when they are confident that the bank's loans are solid and well secured, if they are afraid that other depositors—individuals, businesses, and other banks—will, unreasonably, lose confidence. The stability of banks thus requires bankers and regulators not just to reassure depositors about the condition of their banks, but also reassure depositors about each other's confidence. This had not been accomplished by the 1920s.

Nor had the miracle of maturity transformation been realized yet. Concern about unexpected withdrawals made banks reluctant to use liquid, short-term deposits to extend long-term illiquid loans. The role of banks and "skilled loan officers" was, accordingly, circumscribed. As Justice Brandeis observed in 1914, banks and trust companies were "depositaries, in the main, not of the people's savings, but of the business man's quick capital." Likewise, the legitimate sphere of the banking business, wrote Brandeis, was "the making of temporary loans to business concerns."[2]

Yet the demand for long-term financing was increasing. Mass production and mass consumption were coming to the fore during the Roaring Twenties: a transformation that also altered the financing needs of business and consumers, away from the kinds of loans that bankers and regulators thought prudent. As we will see in this chapter, the mismatch between traditional lending and the new financing needs of businesses and consumers helped drive banking into dangerous terrain.

Pushed to the Margins

The Federal Reserve Act of 1913 sought to ensure a reliable supply of bank credit for businesses and discourage banks from financing speculation in securities or speculating on their own account. Quite the opposite actually occurred in the 1920s. In a pattern reprised in the 2008 crisis, direct lending to Main Street stalled, while banks increased their direct and indirect involvement in Wall Street. They bought bonds instead of making loans, greatly expanded their securities lending, and established investment-banking affiliates.

Commercial loans, which accounted for nearly half of banks' assets in 1922, fell to just a third by 1929. Even in absolute amounts, loans fell in the first half of the 1920s and then made only a gradual recovery. The $15.5 billion peak of commercial loans in 1920 wasn't regained until

1929—in spite of the nearly uninterrupted economic expansion that occurred during most of those years.

The 1920s did start with a sharp fall in economic activity, however, and the decline in the role of bank loans for the rest of the decade arose, in part, because of the apparent success of the banks in coping with that early fall. As I have mentioned, there was no panic in 1920 in spite of what would now be inconceivable declines (of more than 30 percent) in prices and production. Depositors' demands for cash had been met by banks collecting on their expiring loans and through stopgap advances from the Fed.

But this wasn't a happy outcome for many businesses unable to renew or repay their loans and, subsequently, taken over by banks. Businesses saw this outcome as a lesson to avoid short-term debt. But banks and their regulators considered it imprudent to make long-term loans (see box). Therefore, businesses turned to the securities markets for long-term financing, even for their short-term working capital needs: They sold bonds to the public and during 1927–29 issued significant amounts of stock.[3]

Keeping It Short

The reality of bank runs had long made bankers and regulators disbelievers in miracles of maturity transformation—using liquid "demand" deposits to make illiquid long-term loans. Rather, they embraced the classical "real bills" doctrine enunciated in Adam Smith's *Wealth of Nations:* Banks should only make "short-term, self liquidating loans to finance the conversion of raw materials into goods and their transportation to market."[4] In 1842, Louisiana passed a law requiring banks to hold short-term self-liquidating assets in accordance with the "real bills" principle. In other commercial centers, even though laws didn't require short-term lending, banks made it their practice.[5] The National Bank Act of 1864, prohibiting nationally chartered banks from making mortgage loans, also reflected the "real bills" principle. In 1875, the comptroller of the currency declared that "a bank is in good condition just in proportion as its business is conducted upon short credits, with its assets so held as to be available on brief notice."[6]

The Federal Reserve Act of 1913 reaffirmed the belief that banks should stick to making short-term, self-liquidating loans: According to the act, the Federal Reserve could only lend to member banks against short-term paper "issued or drawn for agricultural, industrial or commercial purposes."[7] Bank examiners also discouraged banks from medium and long-term lending. Until the late 1930s, federal and state supervisory authorities had three categories for "criticized loans": "estimated loss," "doubtful," and "slow." Loans that were not "strictly of a seasonal character" were classified as slow, regardless of their soundness or the certainty of their ultimate collection. This categorization "discouraged banks from lending to business concerns in any other way than through the traditional short-term note payable in entirety at maturity."[8]

The Federal Reserve's preference for short-term lending by its member banks was consistent with its role as "lender of last resort": The 1913 act did not guarantee depositors that they could turn their balances into cash, making episodes of mass withdrawals unavoidable. The Fed wanted banks to cope on their own, as far as possible, by turning their loans into cash when depositors demanded cash. This was more easily done if loans were of short duration. The Fed saw its role as merely stepping in if these short-term loans could not be immediately liquidated.[9]

The push to long-term bond and stock financing, and away from short-term borrowing from banks, was especially pronounced among very large business enterprises. These had appeared in the last half of the nineteenth century,[10] and, by the end of World War I, "dominated the core industries in the United States."[11] Corporations grew through mass production, marketing, and sales. The Ford Motor Company sold just 6,191 cars in 1908, the year it introduced the Model T.[12] It then grew from making 40,000 cars in 1911 to 1.4 million in 1925, selling them through a distribution system of 6,400 dealers. Ford's workforce exceeded 100,000 employees in 1925, 58,000 of whom worked at its highly integrated and automated River Rouge plant. Businesses such as Ford were highly capital intensive and required considerable financing for long-term plant and equipment. They also needed to steadily produce and sell in high volumes to cover their fixed costs; they couldn't rely on short-term loans that might not be renewed.

The fragmented nature of the banking system also made it difficult for banks to make loans in the amounts required by giant corporations.[13] The 1920s saw some movement toward consolidation of the banking industry, but the growth of large banks lagged far behind the growth of large businesses. Banking remained highly decentralized to a fault (see box).

Modest Consolidation and Growth

The number of banks fell in the 1920s mainly because of the failure or acquisition of small banks, and a few mergers of big banks.[14] In 1930, after merging with two other trust companies in New York, Chase National Bank became the largest bank in the world. Six months later, the Bank of Italy, which had become the largest bank in the United States west of Chicago sixteen years after it had been started by A. P. Giannini in San Francisco in 1904, merged with another Giannini-owned bank to form the Bank of America National Trust and Savings Association.

The banking industry therefore became a little more concentrated. The share of bank assets held by the 100 largest U.S. banks increased from about 25 percent of the total in 1920 to about 33 percent ten years later. The top four banks controlled half of bank assets in most metropolitan areas and an even greater proportion in smaller cities.[15] But this concentration was confined to local regions—different banks dominated banking in different cities. There were no banking behemoths to match Detroit's Big Three automobile companies, who dominated their national market as there were in the U.K. and Continental Europe.

Ninety-seven percent of banks continued to operate out of a single location in 1930, and of the few who had a branch, most had just one. Branches represented only 13 percent of commercial bank offices, although this was up from 4 percent in 1920. In 1921, the comptroller of the currency permitted nationally chartered banks to operate teller windows that could accept deposits and cash checks. Full-powered branches were permitted after 1927, but only in the banks' head-office cities. Furthermore, the 1921 and 1927 permissions only applied in states that gave state-chartered banks similar privileges; in 1930, ten states allowed banks to open branches in a single city or contiguous territory, and nine others allowed statewide branches. Everywhere else one office per bank was the rule for state as well as nationally chartered banks.[16]

At the same time, large businesses found it easier and easier to go to Wall Street to issue bonds and stocks. "Not uncommonly," Benjamin Klebaner observes, "the leading corporations in an industry had no outstanding bank loans." In cities where "the booming industries of automobiles, steel machinery, and electrical equipment were located, bankers bemoaned the disappearing large borrower."[17]

Banks continued lending to small and medium-sized borrowers who, unlike big companies, couldn't sell securities to raise funds. Loans to such borrowers grew from about 60 percent of all commercial loans in 1920 to 75 percent in 1930. But the number of good-quality industrial and commercial borrowers dwindled as they were acquired by large businesses. Similarly, borrowing by rural merchants shrank because of the growth of chain stores, mail-order houses, and shoppers driving to larger cities.[18] Overall, the share of bank loans of corporate debt fell from 32.1 percent in 1920 to 23.3 percent in 1929.[19]

Banks were also poorly positioned to participate in the consumer lending boom of the 1920s, which complemented the rise of the giant industrial enterprise. Without mass consumption, there could be no mass production: Henry Ford's engineering genius and pioneering assembly-line production technology would have been for naught without millions of venturesome consumers lining up to buy the Model T. However, they needed loans to purchase them: Even though revolutionary manufacturing methods made cars much more affordable, the price wasn't low enough for most buyers to pay with savings. By 1926, two-thirds of all cars were purchased on credit.[20] Mass purchasing of newly mass-produced consumer durables such as radios, refrigerators, and vacuum cleaners also required credit, often secured through an installment plan, which, according to historian Lendol Calder, "was to consumer credit what the moving assembly line was to the automobile industry."[21]

Banks did start establishing personal loan departments in 1918, but could not play a major role because they were supposed to lend to businesses, not consumers. (Besides, installment plans weren't short-term loans, although they were designed to be "self-liquidating." Banks examiners would therefore put them in the undesirable "slow" category.) Instead, new lenders who had emerged around the early 1900s were responsible for most of the growth in personal borrowing (see box). These lenders used more stable sources of financing, such as equity or bonds, not deposits that could be withdrawn without notice, and were therefore better placed than banks to extend longer term credit. By 1930, consumer loans accounted for just 3 percent of all commercial bank loans, and banks made about a sixth of all consumer loans.[22] Banks did, however, lend to other lenders who were more active in consumer lending.

How Consumer Finance Took Off

Notwithstanding what Calder calls "the myth of lost economic virtue," heavy personal indebtedness has long been commonplace in the United States. Thrift was widely regarded as "a core value of American citizenship, as well as a mainspring for national prosperity,"[23] writes Calder in *Financing the American Dream*. But in reality, debt "was a heavy burden for the Pilgrims, a chronic headache for colonial planters (including George Washington and Thomas Jefferson), and a common hardship for nineteenth-century farmers and workers. A river of red ink runs through American history," although it was often "concealed in the grocer's book and the pawnshop ledger, in the butcher's tab and the memory of friends." From colonial days "everyone knew that life in the United States required financing, which meant debt."[24]

The extent and nature of personal borrowing did change markedly after the 1920s. In the first two decades of the twentieth century, personal debt ranged between 4 to 6 percent of income. The ratio nearly doubled in the 1920s.

Similarly the "real debt" per household (adjusted for the prices of major durable goods) actually declined a little between 1900 and 1916, although in nominal terms it had risen at the rate of four dollars per household per year. In the 1920s, real household debt almost doubled, and, in nominal terms, households increased their borrowing by fourteen dollars a year on average. Many people apparently borrowed for the first time in the 1920s or significantly added to their indebtedness.[25]

Although consumers in the 1920s who "took to indebtedness as a way life" "followed in the tracks of seventeenth-century colonists, eighteenth-century planters, and nineteenth-century farmers,"[26] much did change. Borrowing became "a badge of middle-class respectability" rather than "a marker of improvidence and poverty."[27] In the nineteenth century, "borrowing was generally conducted on the subterranean levels of society. Credit was usually a matter between private individuals. If it was necessary to go outside the circle of family and friends for a loan, the likely options were retailers, pawnbrokers, and illegal moneylenders, or loan sharks. Because this kind of credit operated mostly in secret, it was easy for later generations to forget it existed."[28]

Starting in the early twentieth century, however, new lenders who brought legitimacy and more professional practices emerged. Examples of those started mainly for business reasons included installment sales finance companies (such as the General Motors Acceptance Corporation), retail installment lenders (particularly department stores), licensed consumer finance companies (such as the Beneficial Loan Company),[29] and Morris Plan "industrial banks." Credit unions operated as cooperatives making loans to their members. Other lenders were created by reformers. For instance, the Provident Loan Society of New York was started with seed capital raised from wealthy financiers, such as George Baker, whose First National Bank would never think of lending to individuals. But the Provident was "a charitable and uplifting organization not a profit-making one," writes James Grant. It sought to "relieve distress through enlightened and liberal lending" and "force lower margins on profit-making pawnbrokers." By 1919, it "eclipsed private pawnbroking" and became the largest provider of individual loans in New York City.[30]

Evans Clark compared the growth of personal lending that emerged from these foundations in the 1920s to "a skyscraper that rises from a hole in the ground to fifty stories of towering efficiency between spring and autumn." Lenders "made household credit one of the most heavily promoted consumer services of the 1920s," writes Calder. "By the end of the decade, phrases such as 'Buy Now, Pay Later!' and 'Take Advantage of Our Easy Payment Plan!' were standard phrases in the vocabulary of American consumership"[31]

Borrowing to purchase homes—another long-standing American tradition—grew considerably in the 1920s, along with borrowing by consumers to purchase cars and other consumer durables. Here, too, the role of commercial banks was modest. The National Bank Act of 1864 forbade nationally chartered banks from making real-estate loans. Most states, however, allowed state-chartered banks to make such loans, so national banks, "with the complicity of the Comptroller of the Currency," used indirect methods to circumvent the ban. For instance, they would organize mortgage companies that had the same premises and management as the bank. Nonetheless, the overall share of banks—state and national—was less than a tenth of total residential mortgages in 1913.[32]

In 1913, the prohibition on national banks making real-estate loans was lifted—but only for farmland. National banks were allowed to extend one-year first mortgages on nonfarm property in 1916, and after 1927, to extend five-year first mortgages. In 1929, national and state-chartered banks' share of residential mortgages was 10.7 percent, up from 8.8 percent in 1920. Likewise, the duration of mortgages extended by banks rose from two to three years in the early 1920s to about three years in 1930. (A thirty-year mortgage would have been an intolerably "slow" loan.) Banks also limited mortgages to about half the value of a property. Thus, even the relatively small proportion of homebuyers who got their first mortgage from a bank, often got second, and sometimes third mortgages from other lenders.[33] As with other kinds of consumer credit, these other sources of mortgage lending were entities that had less fickle sources of funds than bank depositors. In the case of farm mortgages, individual lenders provided nearly half the total.[34]

The Securities Scramble

Unable to lend to large businesses—or their end-consumers—to any significant degree, banks turned to precisely the activity that sponsors of the Federal Reserve Act had wanted to discourage—financing securities. Although lending for the purchase of securities fell outside the four corners of the "real bills" principle (see first box), it was short term: Banks would make call loans to brokers who would use the funds to make margin loans to their customers; and, as its name indicates, banks could demand repayment of a call loan at any time. With rising securities prices and growing speculation, demand for such loans was strong at the same time that demand for traditional commercial credit was slack. Therefore, the proportion of loans by national banks against the collateral of securities grew from 28 percent of their total loans in 1915 to 35 percent in 1929.

A second way in which banks put their money to work in securities was by buying them for their own accounts. Banks found the liquidity of corporate bonds attractive—they were actually regarded as a form of "secondary" reserve, especially by country banks. With the growing financing needs of large industrial corporations, the supply of corporate bonds was also abundant. Banks thus indirectly financed the long-term debts of companies that weren't interested in short-term bank loans. By 1930, corporate bonds accounted for 11 percent of total bank assets, up from 8 percent in 1920.[35] Banks' purchases of foreign securities also came into vogue as New York started to rival London as a center of international finance in the 1920s.[36] Many of these issues would default in the early 1930s as international trade collapsed.[37]

A third, and possibly the most significant, connection of banks to securities in the 1920s was through their role as underwriters and investment bankers. Nationally chartered banks had been formally prohibited in 1902 from underwriting corporate securities. Many states allowed state-chartered banks and trust companies (originally established to manage estates) to underwrite securities; national banks therefore created affiliates to own state-chartered banks or trust companies. Between 1922 and 1929, the number of banks or bank affiliates engaged in the securities business jumped from 205 to 356.[38]

The McFadden Act of 1927 made matters more straightforward: It allowed national banks to underwrite securities that had been approved by the comptroller of the currency. Initially, the comptroller approved the underwriting only of corporate bonds, but later also allowed stocks. The share of banks and affiliates in underwriting quickly rose: from 22 percent of all bond issues in 1927 to 45 percent by 1930.[39] In the top tier of underwriters, underwriting by commercial banks and their affiliates came to surpass underwriting by regular investment banks.[40]

The role banks played during the 1920s in financing securities purchases—buying them for their own account and underwriting securities—was by no means unprecedented, except perhaps in the amounts involved. Banks had periodically been involved in such activities for nearly a century, sometimes with unhappy results (see box).

An Old and Oft-Unwelcome Affection

Banks were involved in securities underwriting starting about the 1820s. In the nineteenth century, the securities business, writes Litan, "revolved almost exclusively around the placement of federal and state government bonds, and somewhat later of railroad bonds, with institutional investors and wealthy individuals." Pools of wealthy merchants—"investment syndicates"—bought newly issued bonds with the intention of resale. Often the syndicates borrowed from banks to finance their purchases. In the 1820s and 1830s, banks started bypassing the syndicates and underwriting new bond issues. The Second Bank became a major underwriter of government bonds until its charter expired in 1836.[41]

Banks' underwriting activities were, even then, controversial, especially after the crash of 1837, when nearly a fourth of all banks failed. One of the largest failures, the United States Bank of Pennsylvania, "was brought down primarily because of its heavy involvement in securities underwriting." The many bank failures then "prompted a number of states, including New York, to restrict incorporated banks from securities trading and investment."[42] For the next twenty years, investment banking was dominated by private banks that did not have banking charters, but nonetheless took deposits, made loans—and underwrote securities.[43]

Nationally chartered banks that were created by the National Bank Act were also barred from underwriting securities. For the next two decades, newly formed investment banks, including Goldman Sachs, Lehman Brothers and Kidder Peabody, who were "adept at marketing" to a "mass market" dominated the underwriting of government bonds and the "explosion" of railroad bonds issued to finance railroad lines across the West. Some state-chartered banks and trust banks also participated in the underwritings.[44]

At first, the participation of national banks in securities was primarily through their purchase and by making "call loans" to brokers. Securities purchases naturally included U.S. government bonds, since this was a requirement, until 1913, for a national charter. In 1900, half the interest-bearing U.S. government debt was owned by banks, and by 1913 more than three-quarters. But because the government's deficits weren't large, the supply of its bonds was limited— the total outstanding was lower in 1913 than in 1900, for instance. Banks' holdings of corporate and state and local government bonds ("municipals") "increased dramatically," however.[45] About a fourth of all railroad bonds issued between the Civil War and the outbreak of the First World War were purchased by banks.[46]

Banks bought bonds for income, capital gains, and sometimes with the hope of providing other services to issuers, but they were not considered liquid assets. For liquidity, banks purchased short-term commercial paper—"unsecured promises-to-pay of well-known, sizeable firms." The practice of placing surplus funds in commercial paper started with a few banks in the 1860s, and by 1900, most large cities had some banks purchasing the paper. Bank holdings of such paper increased "after favorable experience in the panic of 1907."[47]

Banks also used call loans as liquid assets—a practice often regarded with disfavor as promoting speculation and instability. As I mentioned in the previous chapter, New York banks used the deposits of country banks to make call loans. When the country banks asked for the return of their deposits, call loans had to be called, helping to trigger the panic of 1907. And indeed, one of the goals of the Federal Reserve Act was to discourage such "pyramiding" of interbank deposits into call loans. Nonetheless, the supposed liquidity and security of call loans (the collateral was generally about 25 percent greater than the amount of the loan)[48] continued to tempt banks.[49] In 1913 a third of all loans made by national banks in New York were call loans.[50] In 1914, however, as the war loomed and investors dumped their holdings, the NYSE closed on July 31 and did not resume for nearly five months. Call loans could not be liquidated, "creating a prejudice" against such loans, only to be shed in the bull market of the 1920s.[51]

The prohibition against underwriting by national banks in the 1864 legislation also did not endure. Many became partners in underwriting syndicates to buy "newly issued bonds at favorable prices." Buying securities for their own account led to "purchases on behalf of customers" and, in some banks, to "a full range of investment banking activities." In 1902, the comptroller of the currency formally declared investment banking to be out of bounds for nationally chartered banks. The very next year, James Forgan, who ran the First National Bank of Chicago, figured out how to circumvent the prohibition. The First National Bank created a security affiliate, the First Trust and Savings Bank, chartered as a state bank, and therefore eligible to engage in investment banking. The First National Bank and its affiliate had identical stockholders.[52]

The Chicago plan was copied by two major New York banks. George Baker's First National Bank created the First Security Corporation in 1908, and James Stillman's National City Bank established the National City Corporation in 1911. At the same time, investment banks and private banks that did not have banking charters, such as J.P. Morgan and Kuhn, Loeb and Company, started taking deposits. In 1912 J.P. Morgan's deposits were more than half of those of National City, the largest commercial bank in New York.[53]

The blurring of the lines was criticized on the grounds that it created a dangerous concentration of power. In 1911, Woodrow Wilson, then governor of New Jersey, declared that "the great monopoly in this country is the money monopoly.... Our system of credit is concentrated. The growth of the nation, therefore, and all our activities are in the hands of a few men, who necessarily, by every reason of their own limitations, chill and check and destroy genuine economic freedom."[54] The Pujo Committee, formed by Congress in May 1912, similarly reported that "all the facilities for raising money or selling large issues of bonds" had been concentrated in the hands of a "few bankers and their partners and allies." The "control of credit through the domination of these groups over our banks" was "far more dangerous than all that has happened to us in the past in the way of elimination of competition in industry."[55]

Complementing their investment-banking activities, many banks tried to create "financial department stores." Starting a trust department—an activity permitted to national banks in 1915—became common. By 1920, 1,294 national banks had secured permits from the Federal Reserve Board to operate a trust department. That number doubled by 1930, with most sizable banks offering trust services. Safe-deposit boxes were authorized by a 1927 law. An up-to-date bank, George Dowrie wrote in 1930, was "a composite of the old commercial bank, savings bank, trust company, bond house, insurance company, safe deposit company, and mortgage house" and was equipped to render any form of financial service.[56]

The same notion would reemerge more than seventy years later under the label of financial supermarket, rather than department store.

Harbingers

In spite of an economic boom from 1921 to 1929 (interrupted only by two minor recessions) and the creation of the Federal Reserve, banks failed at an average rate of 600 per year. This was ten times the rate in the prior decade.[57] The 5,400 failures from 1921 to 1929 considerably exceeded the total over the preceding fifty-six years. Failure rates were especially high in the second half of the 1920s: Nearly a quarter of banks operating in the mid-1920s closed by the end of the decade. About one bank a day failed in this period; in 1926, an average of 2.7 banks failed per day.[58]

The high failure rates helped end insurance schemes that eight states had established between 1907 and 1917 to protect depositors in banks chartered by them. By 1930, none were still operating (see box). No safety net remained for depositors of either state-chartered or nationally chartered banks.

A Second Misfire

Six states had established programs to insure against bank failures in the antebellum period. They followed an insurance fund model pioneered by New York State or Indiana's mutual responsibility and monitoring structure described in the last chapter. Plans with insurance funds were overwhelmed by claims arising from widespread bank failures. The Indiana model of monitoring held failures in check and was able to function through the onset of the Civil War. Plans based on the Indiana model, however, petered out after the National Bank Act of 1864. That act, and the follow-up tax on the notes of state-chartered banks, forced them to convert to national charters. Participation in state insurance programs accordingly shrank. Moreover, the National Bank Act offered a credible mechanism to protect holders of banknotes. By 1866, therefore, all state insurance schemes had been wound up.

The 1864 act did not, however, protect depositors—and the circulating medium of checking accounts—against bank failures. But uninsured deposits, which could be

---

created by banks' lending activities, provided a more convenient store of liquidity and form of payment than insured banknotes, whose supply was relatively inelastic. Before 1860 banknotes had constituted half the circulating medium.[59] By 1882, deposits in banks were more than twice as large as notes in circulation and by 1900 more than four times as large, as mentioned in the last chapter.[60]

Attempts to protect bank depositors started in Congress in 1866, and nearly 150 proposals for federal deposit insurance or guarantees were introduced between then and 1933, often following financial crises. More than thirty proposals were offered to the Sixtieth Congress after the panic of 1907. None were enacted. Meanwhile between 1907 and 1917 eight states, seven located west of the Mississippi "in predominantly agricultural areas" (which were often not as well covered by nationally chartered banks as urban centers), adopted deposit insurance programs.[61]

Until bank failures picked up in 1921, the state programs "were considered highly successful."[62] After the Texas program (started in 1909) had been in operation for ten years, the state's commissioner of insurance and banking reported that it had accorded its banking system a "prestige" that few other states possessed. The growth of the Texas banking system "to its present colossal proportions," said the commissioner, had been "due in a large measure to the increasing public confidence in its impregnable solidarity and strength which this guaranty against public loss engenders." According "absolute protection" had "induced the public to turn its funds freely over to the banks for use in promoting the public welfare." It had also "utterly eliminated from community life the injurious effects of a bank failure. State banks may close today; but if they do, the serenity of the people is not disturbed, for the depositors know that within a few weeks at the longest, their funds will be returned to them." All this had cost Texan banks, over ten years, just $300,000—about one-tenth of 1 percent of their deposits.[63]

None of the programs survived the 1920s, however. The decade started with a depression, and although the economy as a whole prospered thereafter, problems persisted in agriculture. Banks in agricultural areas—where most of the insurance schemes had been started—failed in large numbers, and claims by their depositors generally exceeded the amounts in the insurance funds. The Texas fund managed to meet all its claims, but in other states, depositors lost up to 70 percent of their insured deposits.[64]

Bank failures did not cause much concern at the time, however. Most of the banks that failed were small rural banks. National banks, located mainly in urban areas, weren't in distress, averaging profits of 8 percent on total capital from 1919 through 1929. "The disappearance of small, weak banks would only strengthen the banking system, it was thought," writes Klebaner. "Failures in the Federal Reserve view resulted from bad management and dislocations brought about by World War I."[65]

▨▨▨▨ Concluding Comments

By the 1920s, the banking system in the United States was badly out of sync with a transformed economy in which innovation had become a pervasive, massively multiplayer game (described in chapter 1). The second half of the nineteenth century had been a period of extraordinary invention. New products invented between 1850 and 1900 include the monorail, telephone, microphone, cash register, phonograph, incandescent lamp, electric train, steam turbine, gasoline engine, and streetcar, as well as dynamite, movies, motorcycles, linotype printing, automobiles, refrigerators, concrete and steel construction, pneumatic tires, aspirin, and X-rays. (These may well overshadow inventions credited to the entire twentieth century.)

But new products were developed in the nineteenth century by the few, and for the few. Low production volumes and small development teams made new products insufficiently reliable and affordable for widespread use. The first automobiles were so rudimentary that they could only be used by a "few buffs riding around the countryside terrifying horses."[66]

The innovation game became widely inclusive after the end of World War I. On the one side, the landscape of business was transformed from producers comprising mainly small-scale manufacturers, merchants, and inventors to the giant—and dynamic—industrial enterprises that developed and mass-produced reliable and low-cost goods. On the other side arose an "upstart consumer society" with a largely "middle class profile," according to historian Victoria de Grazia.[67] Both sides were willing and able to play a venturesome role in developing, producing, and using new products—if they could secure the financing.

Banks could not easily supply this money. Businesses and consumers needed long-term financing, not just short-term loans. Bankers, however, rightfully considered it imprudent to make long-term loans with volatile, "on demand" deposits, but there was little they could do on their own to create the broad-based confidence that would make deposits more stable. The establishment of the Fed as a lender of last resort allowed banks to satisfy the demand for cash withdrawals, up to a point, but it could not provide the reassurance necessary to prevent sudden withdrawals from occurring in the first place.

Stagnant or dwindling demand for short-term commercial loans prompted banks to look for alternatives. Their security and real-estate lending (sometimes conducted through indirect channels) grew at a rapid clip: It exceeded commercial lending by 1923 and continued to grow till the Crash of 1929.[68] Banks' affiliates also became key players in securities underwriting and other investment-banking functions. Yet even though traditional bank loans were being pushed to the margins, checking accounts continued to be the dominant medium of exchange, so the economy remained as vulnerable as ever to bank failures; and, although they were ignored at the time, bank failures were frequent during the 1920s.

The parallels between what happened to the banking system in the 1920s and the period before the 2008 crash are also noteworthy: These include, as we will see, a progressive disintermediation of bank lending, an upsurge in bank purchases of securitized debt and involvement in investment banking, and a substantial circulating medium of exchange in uninsured accounts. History does not repeat itself, as Mark Twain said, but it does rhyme.

Chapter 12

Finally on Track

The Fed's unflustered view of bank failures in the 1920s—just like Fed Chairman Bernanke's assessment of the impact of the subprime crisis in 2007[1]—wasn't borne out by subsequent events. The extent of the banking system's collapse, and its consequences for the economy, may have been of a piece with prior panics—those in 1837 and 1907, for instance—but the ramifications for the legal and regulatory system of the United States were extraordinary. The speed and scope of New Deal legislation was unprecedented, and its consequences continue to be debated more than seven decades later. The Banking Acts of 1933 and 1935, I will argue in this chapter, were among the best of an uneven menu of New Deal laws. They finally put an end to depositor runs and ensuing panics. As a bonus, the rules also helped create the "miracle" of liquidity transformation: Stabilizing deposits gave bankers the confidence to make longer-term loans to businesses and finance the American dream of consumers.

A Catastrophic Collapse

The stock market crashed in October 1929: The Dow Jones Industrial Average, which closed at 306 on October 23, the day before Black

Thursday, dropped by 35 percent by November 13. Although it climbed back to 294, regaining 96 percent of its value on the day before Black Thursday, the trouble was just beginning. Later in 1930, banks started failing in large numbers.

Although some economic historians, like Richard Sylla, argue that the 1930 bank failures had "almost nothing to do" with the 1929 crash,[2] causality in such matters is hard to determine. New York banks were heavily involved in the securities business in several ways, and their troubles did have the potential to spill over to the state banks that placed deposits with them. Banks had become highly leveraged. The proportion of banking funds supplied by the owners was around 12 percent, compared to 35 percent in 1875. "No other business," the FDIC's Homer Jones later observed, "attempted to operate with so small a portion of its funds supplied by owners."[3] In addition, the absence of deposit insurance—along with interbank deposits—made perceptions of soundness critical. Thus, even if the Dow did recover most of its losses by spring 1930, the 1929 crash may have done serious harm to banks that just took time to surface.

Whatever the catalyst, the number of bank failures doubled from 659 in 1929 to an unprecedented 1,350 in 1930. Depositor losses more than tripled as large city banks failed, not just small agricultural banks, as had been largely the case in the 1920s.[4] The casualties included one of country's largest banks, the Bank of United States, based in New York City.[5]

According to an official history of the FDIC:

[A] wave of bank failures during the last few months of 1930 triggered widespread attempts to convert deposits to cash. Many banks, seeking to accommodate cash demands or increase liquidity, contracted credit and, in some cases, liquidated assets. This reduced the quantity of cash available to the community which, in turn, placed additional cash demands on banks. Banks were forced to restrict credit and liquidate assets, further depressing asset prices and exacerbating liquidity problems. As more banks were unable to meet withdrawals and were closed, depositors became more sensitive to rumors. Confidence in the banking system began to erode and bank "runs" became more common.[6]

The Federal Reserve did little to ease the liquidity problems of banks,[7] the FDIC history notes, drawing on Milton Friedman and Anna J. Schwartz's *Monetary History*. The Fed "believed that bank failures were an outgrowth of bad management and, therefore, were not subject to corrective action by the Federal Reserve." Besides, most banks that failed in 1930 weren't members of the Federal Reserve, and so officials felt no responsibility.[8]

After a respite in the early part of 1931, bank failures picked up as the public resumed converting deposits into currency. Later in the year, there was another, more serious, scramble for liquidity, and again the Fed didn't inject enough liquidity. To complicate matters, the problem acquired an international dimension after Great Britain abandoned the gold standard in September 1931. The fear that the United States would follow prompted foreigners to start converting money in U.S. bank accounts into gold. To stem the outflow of gold, the Federal Reserve Bank of New York raised its rediscount rate, but took no steps to replenish depleted bank reserves by buying securities (which would have released more cash into the system).[9]

About 2,300 banks failed in 1931—three times the average of the 1921–29 period, and nearly twice the number that had failed in 1930. Depositors lost more than the sum of all depositor losses in 1921–28.[10]

In October 1931, a private initiative to lend to weak banks, the National Credit Corporation, was organized. It failed in a few weeks. In January 1932, the Hoover administration created the Reconstruction Finance Corporation (RFC), which, by year's end, authorized nearly $900 million in loans.[11] Many banks, however, refused to borrow from the RFC. Disclosure that a bank had received funds from the RFC was "interpreted as a sign of weakness and frequently led to runs on the bank." One month after the RFC was created, the Glass-Steagall Act of February 27, 1932, made it easier for banks that were members of the Federal Reserve System to borrow from the Fed.[12]

Nonetheless, as 1932 came to a close, banking conditions were rapidly deteriorating. Starting with Nevada, state after state declared banking moratoria. Banks in those states would then pull their deposits from banks that had not yet declared a moratorium. Depositors, anticipating that their accounts would soon be frozen, rushed to turn their balances into cash. After Franklin D. Roosevelt was elected in November 1932, rumors that the new administration would devalue triggered a further rush to convert bank deposits into foreign currencies, gold, and gold certificates.[13]

The panic peaked during the first three days of March 1933. By March 4, the day of Roosevelt's inauguration, every state in the United States had declared a bank holiday. Right after Roosevelt assumed office, he declared a four-day bank holiday, starting on March 6. On March

9, Congress passed the Emergency Banking Act to legalize the national bank holiday, "set standards for reopening banks after the holiday," expand the RFC's powers to help banks, and provide for the issuance of Federal Reserve notes that the Fed could lend to member banks "without requiring much collateral."[14]

In the first of his fireside chats delivered March 12, the president said that banks that were members of the Federal Reserve whose soundness had been "properly certified" would reopen in twelve cities the next day and, the day after that, certified banks would reopen in some 250 cities. The reopening of certified banks in other cities would soon follow. The same schedule was expected with state-chartered banks. Not every bank would open, however—and some 4,000 never did.[15] As the banks started reopening, "public confidence increased significantly and widespread hoarding" of currency and gold ceased.[16]

The Banking Acts

The banking crisis set the stage for tough, comprehensive banking legislation. Few, if any, of the provisions of the banking laws were novel in the manner of the preemptive orientation of the Securities Act passed in the same year. The ambition and scope of the Banking Act of 1933 (better known as the Glass-Steagall Act) and its 1935 namesake were, however, unprecedented.

One of the most controversial features of the acts was the creation of a federal insurance program to insure bank deposits. Two waves of state programs—one just before the Civil War and the other from 1907 to 1917—had been tried, but failed to survive, as we have seen. Nearly 150 proposals for federal insurance had been suggested by Democrats and Republicans, but none had made it into law. In 1933, however, the perseverance of the chairman of the House Committee on Banking and Currency, Henry B. Steagall, got deposit insurance included in the Banking Act.

This was no small achievement; the opposition was formidable. The president opposed deposit insurance, and the Treasury secretary was an even more vociferous critic. So was the comptroller of the currency, who testified in 1932 that he was "unequivocally and unalterably opposed" to deposit insurance legislation.[17] Senator Glass, who killed that year's House bill, was also "an adamant opponent," favoring instead legislation to separate commercial and investment banking.[18]

The banking lobby, particularly the representatives of the larger banks, also lined up against federal deposit insurance. The president of the American Bankers Association declared that deposit insurance was "unsound, unscientific and dangerous."[19] The association also "provided a detailed quantitative analysis of the state insurance scheme failures."[20] Bankers "felt that well-run institutions should not have to pay for the bad, dishonest, incompetent ones;"[21] and, rubbing it in, a Cleveland banker said that except for Prohibition, there was no other legislation "with a more sweeping record of unbroken failure."[22] Some critics regarded deposit insurance as an unjustified intrusion by the federal government into the private sector.

One of the primary objections of the administration was the potential use of taxes to pay for insurance, a source of funds it "viewed as unacceptable." Further, the comptroller, like many others, opposed deposit insurance because he believed that it would protect small country banks—which had failed by the thousands—and block a nationwide or regional system of branch banking. The "only one sound remedy for the country bank situation," the comptroller told Congress the previous year, "is a system of branch banking built up around strong city banks operating under close Government supervision." Deposit insurance legislation and the principles that the comptroller advocated stood at opposite poles: "A general guaranty of bank deposits [was] the very antithesis of branch banking."[23] On the other side, advocates such as Representative Steagall and Senator Vandenberg* of Michigan favored deposit insurance *because* it would protect small banks.[24]

Why then did legislation that was "not a part of the President's program, bitterly fought by some of the most powerful interests in the land [and] beset by enemies in high places,"[25] succeed after all earlier efforts had failed? The change in the public mood and opinion was a crucial factor. Previously, deposit insurance had been one of the hundreds of issues that came before Congress. As economic historian Charles Calomiris observes, they received scant attention from the general public; their fates "were determined by the relative weights of special interests measured on hidden scales in smoke-filled rooms." The banking crisis, however, "moved the debate from the smoke-filled room to the theater

*After the Banking Act of 1933 and another law providing for immediate, stopgap insurance were passed, Senator Vandenberg declared that Congress had taken the "first government action of this depression" to "save small banks" and "reverse the vicious trend" toward "an America whose credit would be controlled by a few men pulling the strings from New York" (Golembe 1960, 197).

of the public debate." Now public support—not just special interests—would determine congressional voting.[26]

Public opinion had turned solidly in favor of deposit insurance: An April 12, 1933, article in *Business Week* reported: "Washington does not remember any issue on which the sentiment of the country has been so undivided or so emphatically expressed as upon this."[27] The opposition of bankers counted for little: They were held in low esteem, and the popular press referred to them as "banksters." Accordingly, Senator Glass yielded to public opinion and dropped his opposition. He was intent on passing banking reform legislation and realized that a bill without deposit insurance would not be satisfactory "either to Congress or to the public."[28]

After tense negotiations, the House and Senate reached a compromise to reconcile their versions of bank reform bills. (As a concession to the Senate, the House included provisions reducing—but not removing—branching restrictions on national banks. As I have mentioned, proponents of branching believed that risks to depositors should be reduced by geographic diversification.) President Roosevelt signed the Banking Act of 1933 into law on June 13; Section 8 of the act created the Federal Deposit Insurance Corporation.

The legislation required all banks that were members of the Federal Reserve System—meaning all nationally chartered banks—to secure FDIC insurance and pay an annual assessment (tantamount to an insurance premium) equal to one-twelfth of 1 percent of their deposits. Although the rate was low compared to what would have been necessary to cover losses during 1865–1934, it was argued that reforms and improvements would lead to much fewer bank failures in the future.

State chartered banks that weren't members of the Federal Reserve System weren't required to participate,[29] but could if the FDIC accepted them after examining their soundness and prospects.

To complement its insurance functions, the FDIC was given supervisory powers over some 6,800 insured, state nonmember banks, thus becoming the third federal banking regulatory agency, following the OCC and the Fed. The politics of the 1933 legislation "did not permit taking any supervisory authority away from existing federal or state agencies."[30]

The plan limited insurance to a maximum of $5,000 for each depositor at an insured institution. But banks were required to pay an assessment to the FDIC based on their entire deposits, not just those covered by insurance. This provision was thought to be unfair to large banks, where the proportion of deposits insured would be relatively low.

An FDIC economist predicted in 1938, however, that the government would protect all deposits in large banks and questioned the policy of capping amounts covered by deposit insurance (see box).

A Case for Full Coverage

Deposit insurance, Homer Jones argued in a 1938 issue of *The Economic Journal*, was useful to the public at large as well as to depositors. By discouraging panicky withdrawals, insurance helped maintain confidence and the quantity of circulating medium. But if deposits remained partly uninsured—at the time only 43 percent of deposits in FDIC insured banks were covered—panicky withdrawals wouldn't be fully discouraged.

Full coverage, wrote Jones, would add little to the costs: The FDIC was empowered to lend to an insolvent bank so that its deposits could be taken over by a healthy bank. Therefore, 100 percent coverage was already in place from a "cost standpoint, but not from the standpoint of socially desirable effects."[31]

Often, by the time a bank actually failed, depositors had already withdrawn amounts that exceeded their coverage; therefore, "The insurer has the costs of practically 100 per cent insurance, but the social disadvantage of deposit withdrawals from the banks remains."[32]

Finally, and most presciently, Jones predicted that "in the light of past experience the Government will probably not in the future permit failure of the very large banks—the banks which hold the bulk of the uninsured deposits. If this is true, the depositors in these banks have what is in effect 100 per cent insurance at the present time. But in the absence of official recognition of the fact the Government bears the risk or cost without the maximum social benefit."[33]

True: Taxpayers would be on the hook for claims that exceeded the amounts in the insurance fund, but Jones argued that the insurance scheme wasn't based on sound actuarial principles to start with. The "bulk of the losses to depositors in the past ha[d] been concentrated in a few periods of extreme crisis"; and "the existence of such an extreme catastrophe hazard in any field [was] generally judged to preclude the possibility of insurance."[34]

In fact, the public's confidence in insurance already turned on the belief that "the Government guarantees the deposits," rather than the FDIC's insurance fund. Why not, then, "officially" remove "all doubt in the minds of the public as to the true situation" and thus secure all the "possible social benefits" rather than just a fraction?[35]

Besides, Jones argued, using taxes to pay for the insurance system—whose costs were impossible to estimate in advance anyhow—was in keeping with the widely accepted idea that the government ought to "supply a circulating medium involving as little risk as possible, without attempting to assess costs on a benefit basis."[36] Even if the U.S. government "had paid all losses to depositors in commercial banks which failed... since 1865, the cost to date would have been about $2,000,000,000. If this entire cost had been added to the national debt and never repaid, the national debt would not be sufficiently larger than is now the case to have any significant effect upon the structure and operation of the economy."[37]

Separating Commercial and Investment Banking

The Banking Acts did much more than create a system of federal deposit insurance. For Senator Glass, deposit insurance was something he had to swallow to realize his project of separating investment and commercial banking. Glass, who was respected for his financial know-how and his role in passing the Federal Reserve Act of 1913, believed that bankers should stick to the "real bills" style of banking and that "the intertwining of commercial and investment banking in the 1920s had contributed to the 1929 stock market crash and to the wave of bank failures that swept across the country in the early 1930s." Glass's view was not novel, as we have seen; yet in the early years of the Depression, Congress repeatedly rejected his proposals to divorce investment and commercial banking. The political climate became more receptive after 1932, when hearings led by the chief counsel of Glass's subcommittee "uncovered various abuses involving large banks and their securities affiliates" and "revealed that several leading bankers had evaded income taxes."[38]

In addition, leading bankers themselves had begun to question the wisdom of securities affiliates. Before President Roosevelt declared a banking holiday in March 1933, Winthrop Aldrich, the recently installed chairman of Chase Manhattan (and son of Senator Nelson Aldrich, who had chaired its Finance Committee and drawn up the Aldrich Plan, the basis for the Federal Reserve), announced that Chase would drop its securities affiliate. "The spirit of speculation should be eradicated from the management of commercial banks," Aldrich declared. The same month, the National City Bank, also under new leadership, dropped its securities affiliate. The speed with which two of the largest banks in the country were able to divest their securities affiliates encouraged Congress to set an ambitious timetable for the rest: All commercial banks had to shed their investment-banking operation within a year of the signing of the Banking Act on June 16, 1933.[39]

The 1933 act did, however, leave several loopholes in its separation of commercial and investment banking. State-chartered banks that weren't members of the Federal Reserve System were exempt. Banks could underwrite U.S. government and "general obligation" state and local government bonds. Bank affiliates could participate in prohibited underwriting activities provided they weren't "principally engaged" in these activities. Banks could execute orders for securities trades for customers if they didn't also give investment advice. And, finally, banks were allowed to underwrite corporate securities outside the United States.[40] Decades later, commercial banks vigorously exploited each of these exemptions to the point where the separation of investment and commercial banking had little bite—just as had happened in the 1920s.

As an additional measure to discourage banks' "overinvestment in securities of all kinds," as the Senate Banking Committee put it, the 1933 act reduced the maximum amount banks could invest in obligations of any one borrower. (The Banking Act of 1935 lowered the amount to 10 percent of a bank's capital and surplus.)[41] The 1933 act also sought "to prevent the undue diversion of funds into speculative operations" by asking Federal Reserve Banks to monitor whether bank credit was being used excessively for speculation.[42] This intention got real teeth when a provision of the Securities Act of 1934 empowered the Fed to set margin requirements for all lenders—including stockbrokers—and not just member banks. In 1936, the Fed adopted Regulation U, which imposed limits on commercial bank loans to purchase and carry margin stock.[43]

The Banking Act of 1933 forbade the payment of interest on every kind of demand deposit. The practice of paying interest on balances held by individuals or other banks in accounts with no restrictions on withdrawals had been long-standing—and had been criticized for just as long. The comptroller of the currency's 1873 annual report complained that the practice of paying interest on deposits had "done more than any other to demoralize the business of banking." The head of the Philadelphia National Bank told the American Bankers Association in 1884 that banks in good condition did not pay interest to depositors. Yet the practice had become ubiquitous after the Civil War. As of 1909, amounts in demand deposits paying interest were six times as large as the amounts in deposits that did not pay interest.[44]

Interest paid on deposits by other banks was considered especially problematic. The New York Clearing House had proposed a ban after the panic of 1857, arguing that otherwise a bank would be impelled to "expand its operations beyond all prudent bounds." After the panic of 1873, the comptroller of the currency had urged clearinghouse members to agree not to pay interest. After the panic of 1884, members of the New York Clearing House limited payment on interbank deposits to 2 percent.[45]

The hope that the establishment of the Federal Reserve would stop New York City banks from competing for the deposits of country banks (which they channeled to Wall Street) had been belied. In fact, competition drove up rates on bankers' balances to 3 percent in 1818, although criticism by the Fed had led to an agreement by the New York Clearing House to reduce the rate to 2.5 percent.[46]

The Banking Act of 1933 banned all such payments, in order to "forestall ruinous competition among banks."[47] It also authorized the Federal Reserve Board to set ceilings on time-deposit rates paid by its member banks. In addition, the Banking Act of 1935 required the FDIC to prohibit the nonmember banks it insured from paying interest on demand deposits and to limit the rates of interest paid on savings and time deposits. These rules reflected the belief that "unfettered competition in the past had resulted in excesses and abuses in banking."[48]

The Banking Act of 1935 also ended the century-old principle of free banking—the notion that anyone who had the necessary capital could start a bank. Senator Glass argued that the lack of "real bankers" had been an important cause of the crisis. There were, he told the Senate, too many "little corner grocerymen who run banks, who get together $10,000 or $15,000, invite the deposits of their community, and at the very first gust of disaster topple over and ruin their depositors!"[49] Under the new law, when the OCC chartered a new national bank (and the FDIC insured a state nonmember bank), regulators had to consider factors such as the applicant's future earnings prospects and the convenience and needs of the community to be served by the bank. The FDIC applauded the new law on the grounds that it would "prevent the overbanked condition of the early twenties." In the ten years after the law had passed, new banks opened at about a fifth of the pace of 1921–35.[50]

▨▨▨▨ The Return of Calm

On January 1, 1934, when the Temporary Federal Deposit Insurance Fund opened, it insured 13,201 banks: 12,987 commercial banks and 214 mutual savings banks.[51] These represented 90 percent of all commercial banks and 36 percent of all mutual savings banks. (Many mutual savings banks hadn't been hit hard by bank runs because they could legally restrict withdrawals, so they didn't see the value of deposit insurance.)[52] The permanent plan that became effective August 23, 1935, covered 14,163 commercial banks and 56 mutual savings banks.[53]

Just nine insured banks—all but one small—failed in 1934. Deposits in commercial banks increased by $7.2 billion dollars, or 22 percent. Such growth had almost never occurred in the past, and restored about half the deposits that had been withdrawn over the past three years.[54] Even the American Bankers Association was impressed: It publicly endorsed extending the temporary insurance plan in April.[55] Improvement in economic conditions also helped stabilize banks: Unemployment fell sharply after 1933, and real GDP expanded at an annual rate of 9.5 percent from 1933 to 1937. Banks faced another test in the second leg of the Depression, in 1937–38, but came through without difficulty.[56] In total, the FDIC handled 370 bank failures, mainly of small banks, from 1934 through 1941.[57] That wasn't a small number, but about twice as many, it may be recalled, had failed every year during the 1920s boom. According to the FDIC, "Without the presence of federal deposit insurance, the number of bank failures undoubtedly would have been greater."[58]

Although deposits returned, bankers remained gun-shy for the rest of the 1930s. They kept lots of cash in their vaults and accumulated U.S. government bonds.[59] Banks also increased their purchases of municipal bonds by 70 percent during the 1930s, while scaling back their holdings of corporate bonds. In 1940, banks owned more municipal bonds than private sector bonds for the first time ever.

Banks loans were cut by half in just three years after 1929 and did not regain their 1929 levels until 1948. In fact, for nearly ten years starting in 1938, banks' cash holdings exceeded their loans. The unwillingness of businesses to borrow, rather than of banks to lend, may have been the main reason. Surveys of manufacturing firms for the years 1933–38 found that less than a tenth of respondents—and mainly those from smaller firms—reported difficulties in securing loans.[60]

Although the total amounts banks lent to businesses stalled, banks did undertake new kinds of lending that deviated from the "real bills" principle of sticking to short-term commercial loans. In 1933, banks started extending term loans that had maturities of longer than one year, and like installment credit and mortgages, contained provisions for periodic amortization of the principal. In seven years, term loans outstanding grew to $2.2 billion, accounting for about 12 percent of all loans extended by banks (see box).

Slow but Steady

Banks adapted the "technology" for term loans from Federal Housing Administration (FHA) mortgages, according to a book published by the National Bureau of Economic Research in 1942. First extended in 1934, FHA mortgages substituted a "predetermined plan of amortizing a long-term loan for the former plan of making a medium-term loan without specific amortization features and with the expectation of renewal." Through their participation in FHA mortgages, "bankers became more acutely aware of the fact that terms of loans could often be safely extended beyond traditional limits if amounts of debts were systematically reduced in accordance with the income and expenditure pattern of the borrower."[61]

Term loans became popular for several reasons. One was the "belief of bankers that deposit insurance increased the stability of deposits." Bankers also knew that even if deposits were unexpectedly withdrawn, member banks could obtain cash for any sound asset they held, thanks to the 1933 legislation that broadened the "rediscount and advance powers of the Federal Reserve."[62] In addition, "revised policies and methods of bank examination" increased the willingness of banks to make term loans. Bank examiners had "habitually included" all but short-term loans in the "criticized category" of "slow." In 1934, a bank examiners' conference recommended excluding from the slow classification "loans reasonably certain of payment, whatever their maturities." In 1938, examining agencies decided to discontinue the slow classification altogether, thus clearing the way for banks to make term loans without being criticized by examiners.[63] This "technical revolution in debt financing"[64] included installment financing of commercial and industrial equipment patterned after techniques developed in the 1920s for consumer purchases. Industrial installment finance had been pioneered by finance companies, but by 1940 commercial banks had become the leaders.

Installment financing and "the spectacular growth of term-loans accelerated the trend toward longer average maturities." By 1940, only 30 percent of bank loans matured in 90 days or less, whereas, in 1913, the proportion had been nearly twice as high. About half of banks' business loans in 1940 had maturities exceeding a year.[65]

Banks also became more active in offering longer term credit to individual borrowers. Bank holdings of residential mortgages had fallen by nearly 25 percent between 1929 and 1934, but then climbed back to a record high of $3 billion in 1940—about an eighth of all mortgages outstanding. And commercial banks increasingly extended mortgage loans for home buying rather than for commercial properties. Dwellings accounted for 42 percent of bank mortgages until the mid-1920s, 56 percent in 1930, and 74 percent by 1940. By 1940, commercial banks had also surpassed mutual saving banks in lending to one- to four-family homes.[66]

Banks also increased other kinds of consumer lending. The number of personal loan departments grew nearly eightfold from 1929 to 1940. In 1940, banks extended fifteen times as much consumer installment credit as they had in 1930. Auto loans also increased fifteenfold during this period.[67]

The consolidation of banking that would be expected in a highly fragmented industry after a crisis did not, however, take place to any significant degree. After numerous small bank failures, more than 90 percent of all banks remained single-office "unit banks."[68] The Banking Act of 1933 did give national banks the same rights to open branches as their state-chartered counterparts, but capital requirements for branches remained onerous until 1952. Twelve of the twenty states that had previously banned branches started allowing them between 1931 and 1935. This was apparently to encourage larger banks to take over failed or failing unit banks and maintain banking services to their communities. For the same reason, several other states that had allowed branching on a limited scale relaxed territorial restrictions. New York, for instance, had allowed only citywide branches. In 1934, it set up nine districts where banks could be allowed to branch. For all that, however, the number of banks with at least one branch represented just 7 percent of all banks by 1940.[69]

As opponents of deposit insurance had feared—and its advocates had trumpeted—deposit insurance had been effective in preserving "Tom, Dick and Harry type of banking with its thousands of small, independent establishments."[70] As the FDIC itself put it, the effectiveness of its deposit insurance "may have limited the necessity for some banks to merge, and may have indirectly encouraged retention of restrictive state branching laws." That said, deposit insurance did not preclude creating banks capable of serving large industrial corporations. Unfortunately, meaningful progress in the direction of better aligning the size distribution of banks and their business customers did not occur for more than half a century after the Banking Acts.

During the Second World War, banks recovered from the financial damage suffered in the Great Depression. Their assets and profits doubled even though tax rates were raised in 1940 and 1941 to finance increased defense spending.[71] In 1945, the return on capital of national banks was the highest it had been in the seventy-five years for which records had been maintained. Only twenty-eight insured banks failed during the war years.[72] The ratio of assets deemed to be substandard to the total capital of banks dropped to 8 percent from 49 percent in 1939.[73]

Banks prospered because business activity was vigorous during the war and deposit outflows were negligible. Most important, banks could focus on the virtually riskless—and highly profitable—activity of financing the government's war effort. Banks purchased nearly 40 percent of U.S. government securities issued between July 1940 and December 1945—purchases that equaled the total of all their assets at the start of the period. Heavy bond purchases pushed banks' income from investments above their income from loans for the first time ever in 1943. Banks also lent to other bond buyers and handled 75 percent of war bonds sold to the public.[74]

When the war ended, bank loans amounted to barely a quarter of their holding of U.S. government bonds and just a sixth of their assets. Some observers questioned whether banks would resume their traditional lending—as opposed to buying the government's war bonds—but "these concerns proved groundless."[75] Bank lending increased by nearly two and a half-fold in the 1950s, growing at an annualized rate of over 9 percent a year, far outstripping the growth of the economy as a whole. The proportion of loans in banks' assets quickly bounced back—from 16 to 25 percent in 1947 alone, to 40 percent in the mid-1950s and 50 percent in the early 1960s.[76]

Yet there were few bank failures: Only five banks failed in 1955, the high-water mark of the 1950s. According to the FDIC, the failure rate was low because bankers were, by later standards, "very conservative" and recessions were "mild and short."[77] Some lawmakers thought that the low failure rate was also a sign that "bank regulators were overly strict."[78] In a 1963 speech, Wright Patman, the chairman of the House Banking Committee, said: "I think we should have more bank failures. The record of the last several years of almost no bank failures and, finally last year, no bank failure at all, is to me a danger signal that we have gone too far in the direction of bank safety."[79] In fact, the proportion of bad loans had increased. The ratio of loan losses to total loans grew from 0.16 percent in 1950 to 0.25 percent in 1960. But even the higher ratios did not jeopardize the solvency of the banking system.

Bank lending maintained its rapid expansion in the 1960s, growing at a 9.5 percent annualized rate, again outstripping the growth of the economy as a whole. As a result, the ratio of bank loans to the gross national product also expanded—from 11 percent in 1945 to 29 percent in 1972. Likewise, banks' share of total credit almost doubled—to about 40 percent of total funds raised in credit markets—between the late 1950s and the late 1960s.[80]

Innovative, longer term loans became the leading sources of bank growth in the 1950s and 1960s. Term loans, which started in 1933, "expanded greatly during periods of heavy business investment outlays in the mid-1950s" and accounted for 38 percent of loans made to businesses by large banks in 1972.[81]

Lending to consumers—considered verboten by bankers and regulators from the time of Adam Smith—took off as banks stepped in to finance the spending spree that occurred after the war.[82] Starting in 1953, and every year thereafter, banks' consumer loans and real-estate loans, mainly on residences, exceeded their commercial and industrial loans by widening margins (see box). By 1960, there were very few wholesale banks that lent mainly to business customers—a practice that had been the norm till the 1930s.[83]

Consumer Banking Takes Off

Consumer credit (from all sources) had fallen in the early years of the Depression, but surpassed its previous peak in 1937 and then never flagged. In 1958, consumer borrowing broke its trend line, more than doubling in just seven years.[84] Banks that had started becoming serious about this segment of the market in the 1930s—which they had previously shunned—became major players in the decades that followed. Banks accounted for 25 percent of all consumer debt in 1945, 34 percent in 1955 (by which time they had surpassed consumer lending by nonfinancial companies), and 40 percent by 1972. In auto loans, banks became dominant, securing a little under half the total market by 1960 and a 57 percent share by 1972.[85] Furthermore, nearly all banks took consumer loans seriously—in 1940, only about a tenth of all banks extended installment credit to consumers, for instance.[86]

New York's Franklin National bank had extended the first bank-sponsored credit cards in 1951, but this line of business was slow to take off. Although some large banks issued credit cards in the late 1950s, the number of banks doing so remained small till 1966. In 1967, nearly 200 banks had credit card programs and, by 1970, there were about 15 million cardholders. The amounts owed on the cards were relatively small, however: Card balances were under 20 percent of consumer installment debt by the early 1970s.[87]

Banks also became important mortgage lenders. In 1933, mortgages accounted for 5.5 percent of bank assets. After falling during the Depression years, the share of mortgages climbed back to 8.6 percent of banks' assets in 1965 and 12.2 percent in 1972. The share of mortgages made by banks also climbed from about 12.5 percent in 1940 to over 18 percent in the 1960s, in part because in 1964 national banks were finally allowed to offer mortgages on the same terms as savings and loans associations: The maximum maturity was extended to twenty-five years, and maximum loan-to-value ratios increased to 80 percent. Recall that in 1930, the average maturity of a bank mortgage was three years and the amount limited to half the value of a property.[88]

One reason that banks' consumer lending exceeded business lending was that progress toward a system with large banks capable of satisfying the credit needs of large corporations remained modest. As states continued to reduce restrictions on branching, the proportion of single-office, unit banks among all banks did fall from 92 percent at the end of World War II to about 70 percent in the early 1970s; likewise their share of banking offices declined from 72 percent to about 26 percent. Unit banks also held less than a quarter of all deposits in commercial banks by the early 1970s, compared to a little under a half at the end of the war.[89] Bank holding companies established to circumvent state rules on branching and restrictions on banking powers were legitimized by the Bank Holding Company Act of 1956.[90]

Increased branching and holding companies did increase the role of large banking organizations mainly at the city and state level; and, as I have mentioned, the concentration of banking in most large cities was already high in the early 1930s, when two or three banks had 60–80 percent market shares.* Restrictions on interstate banking remained severe, however, even as rules for branching within states were relaxed. Therefore, although big businesses operating on a national scale were

---

*Concentration was usually lower in Western Europe and Canada, where three to five large national banks and often a couple of large regional banks usually competed in each city.

ubiquitous, big banks were not. As Klebaner observed in 1974, the United States was home to twenty-one of the world's thirty largest industrial companies, but only nine of the world's thirty largest banks, mainly because of state laws that forbade out-of-state banks from establishing full-powered branches.[91]

Large U.S. banks often found it easier to expand abroad than at home: American banks had been empowered to operate abroad through Edge Act Corporations since 1919. Banks had taken quick advantage—operating 181 branches abroad by 1921—but then retrenched during the Great Depression and World War II. In 1945, just 72 overseas branches operated by seven U.S. banks remained. By 1965, the number of overseas branches returned to their 1921 level. Seven years later, the numbers increased nearly fivefold, with 627 branches in seventy-three countries operated by 107 banks.[92] In the late 1960s, about a dozen large banks used their overseas branches to raise Eurodollar deposits that they then repatriated to the United States in order to make loans to domestic customers. These deposits grew from less than $1 billion in 1964 to more than $14 billion in 1969, when they became the "largest nondeposit source of bank funds" for U.S. banks.[93]

Within the United States, banks could operate nationally mainly in roundabout and limited ways. They could establish loan production offices (LPOs) outside their home states solely to extend loans. Under Edge Act provisions, they could also accept deposits and make loans outside their home states to "aid international trading transactions."[94] In February 1961, First National City Bank of New York started issuing large-denomination negotiable certificates of deposit (CDs). Other large New York banks quickly followed. The certificates, which were issued in denominations of $100,000 and up and could be sold in the open market by investors needing cash before they matured, allowed banks to circumvent Regulation Q rules limiting the interest rates banks could pay on their time deposits. As I have mentioned, because of concerns about "ruinous competition," the Banking Acts had forbidden banks to pay interest on demand deposits and empowered the Fed to cap rates on time deposits. Certificates of deposit not only helped pull funds away from regulated time deposits, they also "became a useful vehicle for banks to attract funds from other states."[95] Commercial paper issued by bank holding companies became another such vehicle.

Although CDs, commercial paper, and Eurodollars allowed banks to raise funds from outside their home states, they were not a good substitute for traditional deposits. In fact, increasing reliance on such sources would help destabilize the financial system, as we will see in the next chapter.

Concluding Comments

The classic structure of a bank, offering liquid demand deposits on one side and making illiquid loans on the other, poses a regulatory challenge. Stapling the two functions together creates a "marvelous mechanism for channeling into productive investments the huge flow of household savings" (to recall Merton Miller's characterization), but it also makes banks prone to periodic meltdowns. The problem of retaining depositors' confidence is especially acute in an advanced economy. In small agrarian communities, depositors can personally know their bankers and assess the prudence of their lending practices and the steadfastness of other depositors; in a complex, dynamic economy, that's impossible.

It took nearly a century and a half after the first bank had opened in the United States to develop a regulatory structure to stabilize banks. The last crucial pieces of the system were put in place during the Great Depression through the Banking Acts of 1933 and 1935. These acts created a comprehensive system of deposit insurance; toughened supervision; prohibited the payment of interest on checking accounts—deposits most susceptible to panicky withdrawal—and regulated interest rates on time deposits; forced commercial bankers to focus on commercial banking by forbidding them to play investment banker; and established standards for opening new banks.

This comprehensive system may have been unnecessary merely to protect banks from runs. Perhaps that could have been accomplished, and the Great Depression avoided—as Milton Friedman and Anna Schwartz argued—by a proactive and aggressive supply of cash by the Fed whenever depositors rushed to withdraw their money. The multifaceted system, with explicit deposit guarantees, was, however, more stable—and this stability gave bankers the confidence to make medium- and long-term loans. Apparently, satisfying bank examiners rather than jittery depositors was liberating and brought banking into sync with a modern economy where both producers and consumers require longer term credit.

Subjective judgments by "bankers on the spot" who had ongoing relationships with borrowers also became more necessary and feasible. Making medium- to long-term loans requires more comprehensive and difficult evaluations of the borrower's condition and prospects than extending short-term commercial credit. Longer term lending also provides the basis and need for an ongoing relationship and dialogue between banker and borrower because, for example, terms may have to be modified before the loan is repaid. None of this would have been possible without a corresponding stability of relationships between banks and depositors sustained by tough regulation.

One problem remained, however: the extreme fragmentation of the banking system created by rules against interstate banking. Indeed, retaining fragmentation had been the goal of many advocates of deposit insurance and the reason that many opposed it. According to both sides, the choice was between unit banking with deposit insurance, on the one hand, and banks with national branches without deposit insurance, on the other. In fact, there was no reason for such a stark choice: Deposit insurance could coexist with large banks. Moreover, banking didn't have to be either utterly concentrated or totally fragmented—there was lots of room in between. As I argued in chapter 4, there are greater diseconomies of scale in finance than in the semiconductor, steel, or automobile industries. We should therefore expect to find many small banks—as we do with restaurants or accounting or law firms. This does not mean that all banks should be small. Just as national and even international restaurant chains, accountancies, and law firms have their place, so do large banks in an economy where large corporations account for about half of all business borrowing.

Although New Deal rules brought banks considerably into sync with the modern real economy by allowing them to make term loans to businesses and extend installment credit to consumers, branching restrictions continued to limit the amounts they could lend to large businesses. It is not surprising, thus, that after the Second World War banks flourished by serving small, rather than large, borrowers. Starting with virtually nothing in the 1930s, consumer loans, which could be made by small or medium-sized banks, came to exceed loans to businesses by the early 1950s. Similarly, term loans, which came to account for more than a third of banks' business lending by the end of the 1960s, were extended primarily to small and medium-sized borrowers. It wasn't that longer term loans were unsuitable for large companies.* Rather, banks with small deposits could not lend much to any one borrower.

*Although, as I argued in chapter 4, with large borrowers there is a horse race between arm's-length securitized debt and relationship-based bank loans.

Perversely, the inability of banks to secure insured deposits on a national scale would ultimately help undo the hard-won stability created through deposit insurance. As I have mentioned, starting in about the 1960s, large banks began to seek "nondeposit" sources of funding, such as large-denomination CDs, commercial paper, and Eurodollar deposits. "Earlier generations of bankers looked askance at the practice of paying interest for loanable funds," Klebaner wrote in 1974. They had good reason: With deposit insurance and no interest permitted on checking accounts, depositors had little reason to withdraw their funds unless they needed money. The new sources were both uninsured and "hot"— they would flock to the highest rate and flee at the first sign of trouble. There was no ongoing relationship between bank and depositor. Thus, banks could not prudently use deposits to make long-term loans—and they again became vulnerable to runs, this time from providers of hot funds, as we saw in 2008.

Chapter 13

Derailed by Deregulation

Bank stability, which took more than century to create, was undone rather more quickly. Starting in the early 1970s, many regulatory props and bindings were removed or loosened. Indeed, the formal repeal of Glass-Steagall's separation of commercial and investment banking, in 1999, marked a culmination of a multifaceted process—not a single knockout blow to the kind of banking that had flourished in the 1950s and 1960s. Nor was the sequence of changes that brought back the instability that prevailed before the Great Depression planned or inevitable. Rather, it was the result of the interaction several factors, including the failure to control inflation in the 1970s, followed by a deregulatory ethos and belief in arm's-length markets, developments in financial theory (discussed in chapters 5, 6, and 7), and the weakening of corporate governance brought about by securities rules (discussed in chapters 8 and 9).

The Beginnings of Deregulation

Banks had started to change in the 1960s, according to the FDIC's history.[1] A new generation of bankers who hadn't experienced the Depression abandoned the traditional conservatism that had marked the industry and "began to strive for more rapid growth in assets, deposits and income." Large banks led the trend toward aggressiveness and risk-taking and began to push the limits of allowable activities, expanding into fields involving "more than the traditional degree of risk for commercial banks." Depression-era rules to limit competition were also relaxed: States liberalized branching laws, and bank holding companies were created as vehicles for multioffice banking and entering new product markets. Banks did face some new rules, but they were intended to improve consumer protection and securities disclosure rather than to increase prudence.

Nonetheless, banks weren't "noticeably harmed" by increased risk-taking in the 1960s. Loan-loss ratios did not grow in spite of another two and a half-fold increase in lending because, according to the FDIC, good economic conditions allowed "marginal borrowers to meet their obligations. With the exception of relatively mild recessions, the economy produced high levels of production, employment and income during most of the period."

In the 1970s, however, loan losses and bank failures jumped as the result of a tougher economic climate. In 1971, the United States went off the gold standard and adopted a regime of floating exchange rates. Two years later, Arab states placed an embargo on oil exports to America and other Western countries in response to their support of Israel in the Yom Kippur War—and possibly to try to recoup losses they suffered from the reduced value of a freely floating dollar. Oil prices rose substantially, from $3 a barrel to $12, triggering first a recession and then, after significant monetary easing by central banks, high inflation.

The increased risk-taking that hadn't hurt banks in the more forgiving climate of the 1960s now resulted in more defaults as the recession made it difficult for borrowers to repay loans. Inflation also hurt because a large proportion of bank lending was now long-term. Because banks had not expected inflation to spike, they had made these loans, such as thirty-year mortgages, at low, fixed rates of interest. Since rates were now below the rate of inflation, the loans were effectively underwater even if the borrowers were sound.

Large banks, along with banks with substantial real-estate exposures, were particularly hard hit by the tougher macroeconomic climate. The ratio of loan losses to total loans had never exceeded 0.27 percent in the 1950s and 1960s. In the 1970s, however, the ratio never fell below 0.33 percent, and, in 1975 and 1976, it exceeded 0.65 percent. The frequency of bank failures likewise increased, as did the size of failing banks.

Inflation also had a profound long-term impact. It spawned alternatives to banks and eroded relationships with their depositors and borrowers. Money market funds, the first of which was launched in 1970, both attracted deposits away from banks and purchased short-term instruments that substituted for bank loans (see box).

How Money Market Mutual Funds Got Going

Unlike banks, money market funds were free to pay high rates. (Recall that to control "ruinous competition," the Banking Acts had imposed ceilings on the rates that banks could pay on time deposits and prohibited the payment of any interest on checking accounts.) With high inflation and zero interest, deposits in bank checking accounts lost real value by the day. In money market mutual funds, deposits could at least keep up with inflation.

Money market mutual funds enjoyed other advantages. As I have mentioned, they didn't incur the costs of due diligence or of maintaining loan-officer relationships. In addition, as nonbanking entities, they didn't have to pay the FDIC for deposit insurance or maintain non-interest-bearing reserves to cover losses or unexpected withdrawals. They weren't subject to regular examination by multiple regulators. And they didn't have to comply with consumer-protection rules or demonstrate their contribution to the local community. True, they couldn't offer deposit insurance; but they did carry a regulatory imprimatur: They were supervised by the SEC under the 1940 Investment Company Act. Apparently this was good enough for many depositors, either because they couldn't understand the difference between FDIC insurance and SEC regulation, or because they astutely realized that whatever the legal differences, the government would make them whole if disaster struck.

The banking lobby could have squelched money market mutual funds, when they were still small and not influential, with the kind of campaign they had mounted against deposit insurance in 1933. But they underestimated the threat in the early 1970s. Nor did regulators and lawmakers take action.

Initially, money market mutual funds invested almost exclusively in T-bills because rates were high enough to draw money away from bank accounts. Later, competition between money market funds—based to a large degree on the yields the funds offered to investors—led to purchases of commercial paper that paid higher interest rates than T-bills. Commercial paper wasn't a new instrument—borrowers had used it as a substitute for bank loans since the 1860s—but with a new set of buyers on the scene, the substitution of bank debt could occur on a larger scale.

Faced with the loss of depositors to money market funds, and borrowers to commercial paper bought by these funds, banks lobbied for and eventually secured the right to offer their own money market funds. Banks also would learn to use the money market channel as a substitute for deposits in an indirect way: They issued commercial paper that was bought by money market funds either in their own names or on behalf of entities they created to make loans. For instance, a bank could make consumer loans funded by commercial paper issued in its own name—or it could roll these consumer loans into a bank-sponsored vehicle that issued commercial paper.

The new style of intermediation—raising money from savers in two stages (by selling shares in money market funds and then selling commercial paper issued by vehicles that would make loans)—was profoundly different from the traditional process of taking deposits and making loans. In addition to being more transactional and arm's length, it was also more mechanistic because it required operating on a larger scale. Huge sums had to be raised through mass marketing—and lent out either by making big loans to big borrowers or by making a large number of small loans to small borrowers. The big borrowers didn't need banks—they had long learned to issue securities directly to investors—so if banks wanted to stay in the game of lending to small borrowers, they had to automate and scale up the process. Out went the loan officer who made laborious case-by-case judgments. In came computerized credit-scoring models that could process huge numbers of loan applications in a jiffy and at a very low variable cost. High tech displaced high touch.

But mass-producing consumer loans isn't like mass-producing hamburgers: In the latter case there are virtually no bad customers,[2] whereas a few deadbeat borrowers can be disastrous. The losses from making bad loans are therefore usually much greater than the opportunity costs of not making good loans. Moreover, as was mentioned in chapter 4, the performance of quantitative models to extend credit tends to deteriorate as other lenders start using similar models and borrowers learn to game them. Thus, what might have initially have been a good thing from the point of view of public policy—broadening the availability of credit—would eventually become a problem when large amounts were lent to reckless borrowers.

The growth of money market funds would create yet another public headache. Like uninsured deposits before the Banking Acts, money market funds were an uninsured, hot medium of exchange because people could write checks against their fund balances. Just as uninsured bank deposits quickly became the dominant medium of exchange, balances in money market funds amounted to several times the balances in traditional bank deposits by 1985—just fifteen years after the launch of the first money market fund.[3]

The common wisdom was that money market funds were "unrunnable," because all withdrawals (redemptions) could be met by selling the assets of the fund. The illusion was shattered in September 2008. The pioneering Reserve Fund had large holdings of commercial paper issued by Lehman Brothers; the failure of Lehman triggered redemption requests for more than $20 billion on September 15, but less than half could be honored by selling assets since the markets were frozen. By the end of the next day, more than $40 billion of redemption requests were received. On the seventeenth, redemption requests were surging at all money market funds, but the funds were unable to sell any but their safest and shortest term securities. The commercial paper market froze and with it the capacity of issuers—both financial institutions and industrial companies—to raise the funds needed for day-to-day functioning.

All this—the growth of mechanistic consumer credit to pathological proportions, the run on money market funds—would take decades to play out, and although the foundations were laid in the early 1970s, there were many regulatory developments in the interim, mainly in the direction of a progressive loosening of constraints on banks, as we will now see.

Picking Up Steam

The rise in bank failures in 1970s, as in the 1920s, was followed by an even sharper spike. According to a *History of the Eighties* published by the FDIC, the distinguishing feature of the decade was an "extraordinary upsurge in the numbers," with more banks failing than in any other period since the advent of deposit insurance in the 1930s.[4] The *History* noted that in the 1970s, the "banking industry's share of the market for loans to large business borrowers declined, partly because of technological innovations and innovations in financial products. Between 1980 and 1990, commercial paper outstanding increased from 7 percent of bank commercial and industrial loans (C&I) to 19 percent. As a result, many banks shifted funds to commercial real estate lending—an area involving greater risk. Some large banks also shifted funds to less-developed countries and leveraged buyouts, and increased their off-balance-sheet activities."

The peak in bank failures came well after the deep recession of the early 1980s, during which both inflation and unemployment crossed

10 percent. The FDIC report also pointed out that bank failures were concentrated in regions that hadn't been the worst hit during recession. Rather, they followed regional booms and busts, such as occurred in Texas because of a spike followed by a collapse in oil prices. Banks failures in the Rust Belt, which had not boomed, were relatively low, presumably because banks had not been drawn into making imprudent loans.[5]

The banking problems of the 1980s, like those of the early 1930s, elicited a vigorous legislative and regulatory response. Congress passed five laws between 1980 and 1991 and considered significant bills in nearly every session.[6] Regulatory change was equally extensive. Federal banking agencies implemented new changes under the new laws as well as under the authority of old statutes.[7] But there was a basic philosophical difference between the New Deal rules and those adopted during and after the 1970s. The 1933 and 1935 acts sought to limit competition and other stimulants and opportunities for imprudent lending. But the reformers of the Carter administration—and their allies in Congress—believed in the curative and prophylactic benefits of deregulation and market mechanisms in several industries, including trucking, commercial aviation, and finance. The same approach was even more vigorously pursued during the Reagan administration and continued during the Bush I, Clinton, and Bush II presidencies.

In the new orthodoxy, banks weren't the victims of predation by free-riding money market funds. Rather, banks had "earned monopsony profits by being able to acquire deposit funds at below-market rates," while money market funds were innovations that helped undercut these excess profits and paid depositors attractive rates.[8] What was needed was even more competition for depositor funds. Similarly, commercial paper and other such securitized forms of debt, such as the "junk bonds" pioneered by Drexel Burnham Lambert's Michael Milken in the late 1970s, were thought to offer better risk-bearing than the loans they replaced. While a bank would bear the entire risk of a loan, the risks of commercial paper issued by the company could be widely distributed across many purchasers. Moreover, by facilitating the diversification of credit risks, securitization reduced borrowing costs. The policy implication was that rather than shield banks from securitization, the rules should be changed to allow banks to participate in the revolution by scrapping provisions of the Banking Act of 1933 that separated commercial and investment banking.

To the degree that banks couldn't securitize and sell off all their assets, fans of new finance advocated more diversification of their activities and better use of innovative risk-management technologies and markets. For instance, it was argued that banks could have mitigated the 1970s problem of holding fixed-rate mortgages when interest rates were rising, if they had been more diversified and had used interest-rate futures (which had then just started trading in Chicago) to hedge their risks. Again, the solution was to allow banks to enter new lines of business more freely, and ease regulatory constraints on the development of new risk-management tools and markets.

The first major legislation of the 1980s, the Depository Institutions Deregulation and Monetary Control Act (DIDMCA), was signed into law by President Jimmy Carter on March 31, 1980. This legislation allowed banks to start offering competitive rates on checking accounts and mandated that all other interest-rate limits (administered through Regulation Q ceilings) be eliminated by March 1986. The Depository Institutions Act (known as the Garn–St. Germain Act), enacted in 1982, allowed banks to offer accounts that, like money market funds, had no reserve requirements or restrictions on rates. Garn–St. Germain also eliminated statutory restrictions on real-estate lending by national banks that had imposed maximum loan-to-value ratios and required repayment of the principal within thirty years for many kinds of loans.

A controversial proposal to grant commercial banks new powers to underwrite securities and deal in mutual funds, and thus repeal important provisions of the Glass-Steagall Act's separation of commercial and investment banking, didn't make it into the final version of Garn–St. Germain. The Reagan administration was strongly in favor, as was Senator Jake Garn, who had just become chairman of Senate Banking Committee. In fact, Garn made the expansion of banks' powers a priority of his chairmanship. But the securities and insurance industries lobbied against legislation that would allow banks to enter their businesses. And some influential voices in Congress, notably Senators John Heinz and William Proxmire, and Representatives St. Germain and John Dingell, argued that expanded banking powers would inject too much risk into the system.

No effort was made to dilute the deposit-insurance provisions of Glass-Steagall. The 1933 legislation had limited insurance coverage to $2,500 for each depositor, raised to $5,000 in the next year. Subsequent increases—$10,000 in 1950, $15,000 in 1966, $20,000 in 1969, and $40,000 in 1974—usually reflected changes in inflation. As a practical matter, though, there was no limit, as Homer Jones had pointed out in 1938, because of the way the FDIC often handled bank failures. Rather than close down a failed bank and pay off depositors up to the limit of their insurance, the FDIC facilitated its merger with a healthy bank that would take on all of the failed bank's deposits.

This de facto unlimited coverage—especially in large banks—concerned the FDIC, which believed it discouraged large depositors from scrutinizing the lending practices of their banks, and thus deprived regulators and small depositors (who were presumed to be entitled to a free ride) of an additional level of monitoring. Thus, one of the goals of deregulators in the early 1980s was to increase the level of monitoring by depositors and reduce the role of regulators. Yet, in spite of concerns about depositor complacency, the 1982 Garn–St. Germain Act more than doubled the insurance limit, from $40,000 to $100,000. The chairman of the FDIC had testified that an inflation adjustment could justify an increase to $60,000, but this figure was increased to $100,000 at a late-night House-Senate conference. The beleaguered savings and loan industry lobbied for the increase in the hope that it would attract and keep large deposits that would otherwise go into money market funds.[9]

The assurance provided by high de jure and de facto deposit insurance limits also had the unintended consequence of facilitating the banks' use of new markets and instruments. This development had both good and bad consequences. With more stringent depositor discipline, it is unlikely that banks could have used the futures markets that emerged in the 1970s to hedge the risks of making long-term loans with short-term deposits. Without generous insurance limits, most depositors—even sophisticated ones—would likely have shunned banks that traded futures. Paltry passbook rates simply wouldn't compensate for the risks. Later, depositors' complacency also allowed banks to take their chances with racier and more opaque derivatives.

After 1982, the main objective of proponents of deregulation was to repeal Glass-Steagall and expand the powers of banks. But a thrift and banking crisis intervened, and none of the subsequent bills enacted in the 1980s had significant deregulatory provisions. "Deregulation remained an undercurrent" in Congress, however, and some skeptics were converted to the cause. In 1988, for instance, Senator Proxmire promoted legislation to undo some of the limitations on banking powers.[10] Federal regulatory agencies—the OCC, the FDIC, and the Federal Reserve Board—increasingly interpreted existing statutes to grant banks under their jurisdiction entry into new areas. During the early 1980s, national banks were authorized to offer discount-brokerage and investment-management services, operate futures brokerages, and underwrite credit life insurance. A 1990 article in the *Banking Law Journal* argued that, for all practical purposes, most Glass-Steagall restrictions on bank powers had been repealed by "regulatory and judicial reinterpretation."[11]

State legislators and banking authorities also contributed to the deregulation movement. State-chartered, nonmember banks (those not belonging to the Federal Reserve System) had always been exempt from Glass-Steagall. In the 1980s, states increasingly allowed state-chartered banks to enter securities, insurance, and real-estate activities that were not permitted by federal statutes. By the end of the decade, twenty-nine states gave state-chartered banks at least some power to underwrite securities, and all but seven allowed banks to engage in securities brokerage. Half the states permitted some form of real-estate development, and six allowed insurance underwriting beyond credit life insurance.

Starting in 1981, new regulations required all banks to hold a minimum amount of capital in fixed proportions of the assets on their balance sheet. Previously, "Capital regulation was relatively ad hoc and depended largely on the judgment and discretion of a bank's supervisors."[12] The standardization of capital requirements reflected a growing mechanistic, top-down, Markowitz-style approach to risk management by banks and their regulators, in place of the traditional bottom-up, case-by-case, loan-by-loan approach. Standardization also triggered a cat-and-mouse game to circumvent the rules. The 1981 capital requirements applied only to assets on balance sheets and did not discriminate between more or less risky assets. Banks therefore moved assets off their balance sheets and favored more risky assets on their balance sheets.

Regulators then instituted more complex top-down rules. Starting in 1990, banks were subject to the internationally agreed on Basel Accords for risk-based capital standards. The Basel rules covered both on- and off-balance sheet assets, categorized assets according to their risks, and required banks to hold more capital for more risky categories. For instance, capital requirements for commercial loans were about twice those for most residential mortgages and five times greater than for mortgage-backed securities that had AA or AAA ratings.[13] Furthermore, Basel rules exempted bank-sponsored Structured Investment Vehicles (SIVs) and other off-balance-sheet entities (OBSEs) from capital requirements.[14] Predictably, banks, especially the larger and more sophisticated ones, proliferated SIVs—Citibank had sponsored six when the 2008 crisis broke. They also bought the highest yielding—and thus riskiest—AA or AAA mortgage-backed securities they could find. In 2008, 30 percent of the world's AAA-rated mortgages and other asset-backed securities—including a large chunk of subprime mortgage-backed securities—were held by banks and another 20 percent were owned by bank-sponsored SIVs and OBSEs.[15]

Off to the Races

A 1995 Brookings Institution paper described the transformation of U.S. banking over the previous fifteen years—which the authors attributed mainly to regulatory changes such as the deregulation of deposit accounts and the expansion of bank powers. The transformation saw a "tremendous explosion" in the number of products, such as derivatives, that commercial banks could hold and offer. Banks, however, also lost about a third of their share of total credit market debt from 1979 to 1984; apparently, in spite of the deregulation of interest rates, the process of disintermediation by nonbank competitors and the replacement of bank loans by securitized debt did not abate.[16]

The declining share (and profitability) of traditional lending reduced the number of banks by nearly a third, but it did not diminish the size and profits of the banks that took advantage of broader banking powers to expand into new activities. The new financial technologies—Markowitz-style risk management and BSM-based pricing models—made selling and trading of derivatives especially attractive. And megabanks were at the forefront: In 1983, the notional value of their derivatives positions amounted to 82 percent of the value of their assets, whereas in 1994 derivatives amounted to more than eleven times the value of their assets. Correspondingly, "other noninterest income,"[17] such as fees earned from issuing counterparty guarantees and derivative instruments earned by megabanks, increased from 7 percent of operating income in 1979 to 21 percent in 1994.[18]

The second half of the 1990s and the first half of the next decade, which spanned the Democratic and Republican administrations of Bill Clinton and George W. Bush, saw much more of the same.

New forms of multilayered debt securitization took off. As I have mentioned, debt securities had previously been issued by large businesses as a substitute for bank credit. For instance, General Motors issued commercial paper directly to investors instead of securing a short-term loan from its bank. Later, securitized debt was issued by intermediaries who used the proceeds to extend credit (see box).

Layering It On

The origins of intermediated asset-backed securities (ABSs) go back to the 1970s, when federally sponsored agencies such as Fannie Mae and Freddie Mac pooled residential mortgages and sold off interests in these pools to investors (using the proceeds to make more mortgage loans). Eventually, other kinds of financial assets were pooled into ABSs. By the late 1980s, ABSs had become a viable means for commercial banks and other private lenders to package and sell off other kinds of debts such as car loans, credit-card balances, mortgages on commercial properties, and lease receivables.

Later, securitized assets came to include computer leases, nonconforming mortgages, franchise loans, health care receivables, health club receivables, intellectual property cash flows, insurance receivables, motorcycle loans, mutual fund receivables, manufactured housing loans, stranded utility costs, student loans, trade receivables, time share loans, tax liens, taxi medallion loans, viatical settlements (the sale of a life insurance policy by the policy holder before the policy matures),[19] and David Bowie's music royalties.

The economic benefit expected of ABSs issued by financial intermediaries was fundamentally different from that of traditional securities issued by large business corporations. In the latter case, securities helped raise capital for large projects, such as refineries, railroads, or wireless networks that any one financial institution might not be able to fund; without securitized debt, users of funds would have to forgo economies of scale or so-called network effects in their projects. In addition, traditional securitization, while arm's length, did involve case-by-case judgments by underwriters and rating agencies, and these judgments often involved a dialogue with the borrower. With ABSs, economies of scale were expected from mechanization of the financing activity (e.g., using computers to issue credit cards) rather than in the use of funds, as discussed in chapter 4. This new form of securitization did away with case-by-case judgment and dialogue, and not just ongoing relationships.

By 2002, privately issued asset-backed securities accounted for about a quarter of the entire corporate bond market, and, by 2007, privately issued ABSs exceeded corporate bond issuance. Issuers of ABSs also became dominant issuers of short-term paper: In 2002, securitized pools of loans represented nearly half of commercial paper outstanding. Other kinds of short-term paper issued by financial institutions had also grown, so that, in 2002, the share of commercial paper accounted for by industrial companies (and other nonfinancial entities) had fallen to a fifth of the total.

The widening range of ABSs progressively increased the riskiness of the assets that backed the securities and the number of layers between the ultimate users and investors. In the 1980s, ABSs mainly comprised packages of low-risk loans issued by brand-name intermediaries with high credit ratings. The creditworthiness of an ABS was also typically enhanced by guarantees, provided by banks or insurance companies, to pay for some or all of the losses arising from the default of the loans. Later, new techniques involving complex structures were used to securitize increasingly higher-risk loans. For instance, the loans might be placed in a special purpose vehicle that would then issue multiple classes of securities with different levels of risk and return. The top level would have the first claim on the cash flows generated by the loans, enabling that security to get a high credit rating from the rating agencies. Interest rates paid to investors in this secure, "senior" or "super-senior," tier were accordingly low. The cash flows left over for the lower levels were, of course, riskier, had lower credit ratings, and paid higher interest rates. Famously, this sort of slicing and dicing enabled supposedly rock-solid AAA securities to be extracted from highly risky subprime mortgages.

The new kinds of securities, which were then often packaged and repackaged, also spawned new derivative contracts that could be used to hedge them—and, to an even greater degree, to take speculative side-bets on the prices of the securities. The now-notorious credit default swaps (CDSs), for instance, were sold as insurance (by companies like AIG) against events such as missed payments or credit downgrades, as described in the introduction. Often the insurance purchased amounted to ten or more times the value of the underlying security, suggesting that most of the purchasers were buying CDS contracts just to bet on bad things happening to the security.

Thanks to lobbying by their promoters, CDSs and other such derivative products escaped regulation by the Commodities Futures Trading Commission,[20] and instead were traded in the unregulated over-the-counter (OTC) market. On the positive side, the OTC market provided a home for a much larger number of contracts than could traditional commodities exchanges. The large number meant that speculators and hedgers could find instruments that more precisely fit their preferences. With exchange-traded contracts, participants have to adapt to whatever contract best suits their needs from a fixed and relatively small menu (see box).

But the capacity of the OTC market to support a wide range of derivatives also had disadvantages. One was the absence of the daily settling up of gains and losses through an exchange. In OTC markets, buyers and sellers settle up with each other according to the terms of their bilateral agreements. This can create counterparty risks: If the bilateral agreements are not well drafted, or diligently adhered to, one or the other party may not be able to collect what it is owed by a trading partner who goes bust.

In addition, the dispersion of the potential interest of day-traders across many OTC derivatives meant that the liquidity in any one was low.

Direct transactions between buyers and sellers, rather than through an exchange, also contributed to illiquidity and settling-up problems in the following way: In exchange-traded contracts, anyone who can post the necessary margin can buy or sell. Direct trading in CDSs limited players to a relatively small number of professionals; within this circle, anyone who could pay the premiums could buy insurance on the default of a security—but not everyone had the credibility to sell insurance. This asymmetry further limited active trading. The absence of a deep secondary (or "resale") market did not seem to hold back buying derivatives in huge volumes, however. The worldwide notional value of derivatives outstanding increased more than sixfold, from $95 trillion to $684 trillion, between 2000 and mid-2008.[21]

Large commercial banks and bank holding companies had played an important role in the growth of the ABS and derivative markets ever since they first packaged and sold off their auto and consumer loans. Regulatory reinterpretations and new laws continued to expand the role banks could play in such nontraditional activities thereafter. In 1996, for instance, the OCC reinterpreted its "incidental" powers, granted under the National Banking Act of 1864, to permit operating subsidiaries of national banks to underwrite municipal revenue bonds, corporate bonds, and even equity securities. The OCC also decided that some products, like annuities, were banking rather than insurance products and could thus be sold by banks.

The November 1999 enactment of the Gramm-Leach-Bliley Act (GLBA) formally repealed the long-eroded Glass-Steagall prohibitions on mixing banking with securities or insurance businesses. It permitted, for instance, the creation of a new kind of holding company: one that could own, as subsidiaries, banks and other entities that could engage in a variety of financial activities (including underwriting and dealing in securities; sponsoring and distributing mutual funds; insurance underwriting and agency activities; and merchant banking) that banks or their subsidiaries might be otherwise forbidden from performing.

Megabanks and their holding companies, like Citigroup and J.P. Morgan, again were at the forefront in taking advantage of deregulation. In fact, a J.P. Morgan team, not a traditional investment-banking firm, invented CDSs. The ratio of noninterest income to banks' total operating income continued to rise at the same rapid rate in the ten years after 1994 as it had in the previous decade, thanks to the continued rapid growth of activities such as securitization and trading. As before, the largest banks took the lion's share: The top five banks accounted for more than 80 percent of total trading revenues earned by all commercial banks in 2001 and nearly two-thirds of all securitization income.

The profits of the commercial banking sector as a whole rebounded strongly in the second half of the 1990s as it recovered from problems it had faced in the early 1990s. Commercial banks' share of finance and insurance-industry profits, however, fell as investment banks' share rose. As a 2004 FDIC research paper observed, in the 1990s, while banks were "returning to record-setting earnings," investment banks and other financial-service providers were regaining their even higher prior earnings levels. But early in the next decade, as banks continued their expansion into nontraditional domains such as securitization and the trading of derivatives, the growth in their profits "outpaced that of other financial sectors."[22]

The profits from securitization and derivatives, however, came with much higher risks, although the subtle nature of these risks may have caused banks and their regulators to ignore them. For instance, banks were more willing to offer subprime mortgages to borrowers who would not qualify for regular mortgages because these mortgages could be packaged and sold instead of being held to maturity. Although banks wouldn't receive interest payments, they would earn underwriting fees for originating subprime mortgages, and possibly ongoing fees for servicing them— all without taking the risk that borrowers would default. Involvement in securitization posed other risks, however. Banks would sometimes provide credit enhancements to ABSs that did create some exposure to defaults. There was also the risk of financing warehouses of loans awaiting securitization. Loans that went into ABSs could not be securitized as soon as they were made, and, besides carrying their own loans, banks sometimes extended credit against the inventory of other originators. In principle, these were well-secured short-term credits. But as banks were to discover in the 2008 financial crisis, when the ABS market seized up, they could find themselves locked into warehouses full of unsalable loans.

In complex, sliced-and-diced ABSs, banks would often have to keep the thinner, most risky slices, in other to encourage others to buy the thicker, less risky ones.[23] And even as banks sold off to investors low-risk slices of packages of loans they had originated, they would often turn around and buy slices of someone else's packages. Thus, banks were simply swapping the credit risks of the loans they had originated for the credit risks embedded in an ABS.

Moreover, new derivatives, such as CDSs, created opportunities to speculate with virtually unlimited leverage and could thus generate huge profits or losses. Yet as we have seen, with a large number of derivatives traded over the counter (instead of a few that survive the Darwinian selection of trading on an exchange), liquidity was low. Low liquidity made highly leveraged trading especially risky. For instance, speculators could—and often did—purchase default insurance amounting to many times the total issuance of a security. But, in the absence of a liquid market, they could not easily reverse the trade. Risk management was also challenging. In a liquid market, positions can be accurately "marked to market" by the minute. With illiquid derivatives, however, traders could hide losses by asserting, like the Red Queen, that the value of their positions was whatever they said it was. Unreliable prices also made end-of-the-day settling up of gains and losses more difficult and exacerbated the counterparty risks that are an unavoidable feature of OTC trading. Banks were therefore exposed not only to their own trading mistakes, but also the missteps of their trading partners: If a hedge fund (such as Long-Term Capital Management) or an investment bank (such as Bear Stearns) couldn't honor its trading obligations, commercial banks would often be left holding the bag.

The Interaction of Securities and Banking Deregulation

The story of increasingly tight regulation of equities markets, leading to diffuse, hands-off monitoring of management, as told in chapter 8, ties in with the story of banking deregulation. Banks' CEOs weren't concerned about the escalation of risks as they led their banks further and further away from traditional lending. Freed of stockholder restraints (thanks to the Securities Acts) and depositor restraints (thanks to the FDIC), banks became sprawling, too-complex-to-manage enterprises whose balance sheets and trading books were but wishful guesses. Furthermore, turning a blind eye to reckless bets wasn't a bad policy for executives with limited personal downside.

American industry   businesses in the real U.S. economy—had long ago learned hard lessons in the virtues of focus. In the 1960s, the prevailing wisdom favored growth through diversification. Many benefits were cited. Besides synergistic cost reductions offered by sharing resources in functions such as manufacturing and marketing, executives of large diversified corporations allegedly could allocate capital more wisely than external markets. In fact, the synergies often turned out to be illusory and corporate executives out of touch. The weaknesses of diversification were sharply exposed by the recession of the early 1980s and by Japanese competition. Later in the decade, raiders used junk bonds to acquire conglomerates at deservedly depressed prices and sold off their components at a handsome profit.

Banks had missed the 1960s conglomeration party because the separation between investment and commercial banking severely limited diversification. But as the rules were dismantled, financial institutions plunged right in. The traffic went in both directions: Just as commercial banks accelerated their efforts into what had traditionally been investment-banking activities, investment banks—now freed from worries about bankrupting their partners—went the other way. They took deposits from the public through cash management accounts that had been pioneered by Merrill Lynch. By 1984, Merrill had more than a million such accounts, containing over $70 billion in customer assets, which combined traditional brokerage with check writing, a credit card, and a money market fund. A Merrill vice president said at the time that if the accounts "were a bank, it would be number four in the U.S. by asset size, right behind Chase Manhattan."[24] Later, investment banks would join commercial banks in raising about $10 trillion in short-term funds from "repos" and "reverse repos." Investment banks also extended credit not just as margin loans to brokerage customers, but also to provide bridge financing for company acquisitions and warehouses of assets awaiting securitization.

The early results of the intermingling weren't promising. Efforts to sell stocks and socks at Sears went nowhere, as did the Prudential Insurance Company's foray into the brokerage business and Morgan Stanley's venture into credit cards. But the forces that had curbed diversification in the industrial sector did not restrain financial institutions. Low-cost Japanese competitors did not show up inefficiencies; and, in many financial businesses, the driver of long-run profits lies in the prudent management of risks and returns, not in cost control. Raiders couldn't use junk bonds to dismantle conglomerates: Financial institutions are too highly leveraged for regulators to allow them to be taken over with borrowed money.

Moreover, compensation arrangements made conglomeration irresistible. Many financial firms pay out nearly half their gross profits as bonuses—even if these profits are secured by loading up on risk. Bonuses paid are paid forever, even if the bets ultimately go bad. Conglomeration offered CEOs the opportunity to take ever larger bets—and to earn staggering personal returns—without much personal risk. Sandy Weil laughed all the way to the bank from Citibank, which he had turned into a hodgepodge of investment banking, trading, retail brokerage, commercial banking, and insurance, with 2,400 wholly owned subsidiaries. Robert Rubin received $101 million[25] for providing direction and counsel at Citigroup while its stock lost 70 percent of its value.

Even after the current crisis broke, battered CEOs seemed bent on doubling up to recoup their bad diversification bets instead of cleaning house. In 2007, Bank of America CEO Ken Lewis declared that he had had "all the fun I can stand in investment banking." Yet in September 2008, Lewis engineered the acquisition of Merrill Lynch—albeit with much prodding by the Treasury Department and the Fed.

Securities regulators also inadvertently helped centralized, judgment-free securitized finance displace bank lending in other ways. In the 1930s, when banks had large holdings of corporate bonds because demand for loans was low, bank regulators prohibited banks from purchasing bonds that were below "investment grade" according to "recognized ratings manuals." In the decades that followed, insurance regulators and pension fund regulators imposed similar rules. "Recognized rating manuals" weren't explicitly specified, although by convention they were ones published by Moody's, Standard and Poor's, and Fitch. In 1975, the SEC created a designation of nationally recognized statistical rating organization that it awarded to the three leading ratings agencies. Other regulators followed, "so that these three firms' judgments of bonds' safety came to be *official* determinants of the bond portfolios of most major American financial institutions." Four additional firms were recognized by the SEC in the next twenty years, but by the end of 2000, mergers had caused the number to shrink back to three.[26]

Bond investing, which had always been more arm's length than bank lending, thus also became highly centralized as bond buyers relied, often because they had to, on the judgments of three rating agencies. Furthermore, as the nature of securities changed, the ratings process itself became more arm's length and mechanistic. With old-fashioned corporate or municipal bonds, analysts of rating agencies usually had extensive face-to-face discussions—and sometimes negotiations—with borrowers. For instance, a rating agency might tell the borrower that adding a covenant to a bond would secure a higher rating. With multi-level asset-backed securities, however, contact with the final borrower was impossible; rating agencies, and issuers, had to rely on statistical models rather than case-by-case judgments.

As I have mentioned, the SEC also provided its imprimatur to money market funds that competed with insured bank deposits; and, deviating from its usual practice, the SEC regulated the holdings of the funds. The SEC normally regards itself primarily as a disclosure agency. It did not object to the floatation of worthless dot-com stocks in 1999–2000 because prospectuses disclosed the risks. The SEC's rule 2a-7, however, required at least 95 percent of a money market mutual fund's assets to comprise securities rated AAA or AA by a "recognized"—by the SEC—ratings agency.[27]

Although the SEC does not guarantee money market funds, or stand behind the ratings published by the agencies it recognizes, its influence is not trivial. Other regulators take their cue from the SEC, and the SEC's endorsement provides a convenient safe harbor for trustees and other fiduciaries.

Individuals investing their own funds also trust the SEC. For instance, the investigation of Bernard Madoff's Ponzi scheme by the agency's inspector general "found that investors who may have been uncertain about whether to invest with Madoff were reassured by the fact that the SEC had investigated and/or examined Madoff, or entities that did business with Madoff, and found no evidence of fraud. Moreover, we found that Madoff proactively informed potential investors that the SEC had examined his operations. When potential investors expressed hesitation about investing with Madoff, he cited the prior SEC examinations to establish credibility and allay suspicions or investor doubts that may have arisen while due diligence was being conducted."[28]

Concluding Comments

By the first couple of years of the twenty-first century, most of the now old New Deal rules for banking had been jettisoned. Deregulation made the credit system excessively centralized, mechanistic, and arm's length. This new concentration and mechanization misallocated capital in the regular course of events, and it made the system unstable. As in the Roaring Twenties, large commercial banks plunged deep into securities activities, with traditional lending becoming a vestigial appendage. Except now, use of the new derivatives technologies made the risks much greater. The rules also helped create a parallel system for taking deposits that weren't insured, but represented a large proportion of the circulating medium of exchange.

Bank regulators were more concerned than bank executives about the growing risks. But they apparently succumbed to the idea, peddled by financiers and modern finance theorists, that if a little financial innovation was good, a lot must be great. Instead of curbing the issuance of ABSs, or the growth of derivatives that were far outside regulators' capacity to monitor, they tried to adapt: They trusted Basel rules requiring banks to hold more capital for riskier assets and disclose what proportion of their trading positions could not be marked-to-market. Meanwhile, the Federal Reserve pressed dealers to improve the processing of trades in over-the-counter derivatives. Unsurprisingly, given the asymmetry of resources and incentives, these measures proved inadequate: The regulators could not keep up.

Not all the deregulation was undesirable. Barriers to interstate banking, which were removed in the 1990s, prevented banks from creating the large, stable deposit base necessary to make long-term loans to big companies. But by then, large companies had found securitized alternatives and banks had also lost interest in traditional lending, thanks in part to Basel rules that required them to set aside more capital for loans than for securities.

I do not mean at all to imply that by 2001–2 it was obvious that a housing bubble would form and burst, or that the specific missteps that caused these events were unimportant. Tax policy toward housing and the role of government-sponsored housing finance agencies in the United States have been perverse for about as long as financial regulation has been on the wrong track. The missteps and perversities, which have been extensively analyzed elsewhere, are, however, outside my scope (beyond the brief sketch provided in the introduction). Nonetheless, my analysis does suggest that the financial system was an accident waiting to happen and that it made what came after 2002 much worse.

Consider the argument made by John Taylor, Richard Posner, and many others that the Fed inflated the housing bubble by keeping monetary policy too loose and recklessly ignoring the rise in mortgage debt. At the time, the Fed said it was keeping rates low because of a savings glut emanating in China and that it had no capacity, in any case, to recognize bubbles. Perhaps there is something to the Fed's claim, and, given the unprecedented circumstances,* the Fed did the best it could. But a jump in China's savings had to be matched by a jump in consumption or investment somewhere else. In the United States, consumers have always been eager and willing to increase spending; and the financial system seemed to have the capacity to channel funds to borrowers who would later repay. This capacity was shown to be illusory.

Now try the following thought experiment: Given the same Federal Reserve monetary policy and the same spendthrift attitudes of consumers, would housing prices and debts have skyrocketed if lending decisions had been made by many Hayekian bankers who knew their communities and borrowers instead of by a few wizards, rating agencies, and megabanks? Should we seek to restore Hayekian banking supervised by dispersed examiners, or tighten the centralized control of the wizards, rating agencies, and megabanks? This is the central question for regulatory reform that we will examine in the next and final chapter.

---

*After China reformed its economy, its production of items such as Nike shoes jumped ahead of its capacity or willingness to increase its consumption of such goods. Edmund Phelps and I argued in a 2005 paper that the imbalance, which created a new source of savings for the world's economy, was an inevitable consequence of rapid development and would likely persist until China's consumption caught up with its surging production.

Chapter 14

Restoring Real Finance

Before I discuss my reform proposals, I would like to summarize my arguments about the dysfunctions of the financial system and how they arose.

In Part I, I explained why a good financial system ought to reflect features of the real economy that make capitalism an attractive way of organizing economic life. Well-functioning capitalism creates widespread prosperity through a widely inclusive system of innovation in which many contribute to—and benefit from—the development and use of new products and technologies. Inclusiveness is achieved through decentralized judgment tied to responsibility: individuals and businesses exercise their imagination and wit to undertake uncertain initiatives, but also bear the responsibility for outcomes—good or bad.

Decentralized judgments and initiatives are coordinated by prices, dialogue, ongoing relationships, and organizations that regulate, but do not eliminate, the autonomy of their members. Well-designed laws and regulations are also crucial. The concern here, though, is that new technologies often demand new rules that also increase opportunities for rent seeking.

A financial system that supports the real economy, I argued, will have identical features: decentralized judgment tied to responsibility, with prices, dialogue, relationships, and organizations that strike the right balance between control and autonomy—all sustained by good laws and regulations.

Yet for more than two decades, finance has become highly centralized, mechanistic, and arm's length, and a relatively small number of financiers have been able to secure great rewards with little personal downside. These features hinder dynamism in the real economy, undermine the legitimacy of capitalism, and make the financial system prone to crisis.

Part II showed how this sorry circumstance came to pass.

First we saw that economic theories based on unrealistic assumptions provided the intellectual underpinnings. Until about the 1940s, at least some economists—most notably John Maynard Keynes and Frank Knight—emphasized the importance of uncertainties that could not be reduced to quantifiable probabilities. But then the growing popularity of mathematical economics favored theories in which all uncertainties could be quantified, like bets on a roulette wheel. Deciding whether to place a bet simply required calculating the probability-weighted return.

This alone didn't eliminate the need for subjective judgment: Individuals still had to think about the right probability distribution. But the pursuit of mathematical elegance took the theory further: Risks became like coin tosses, or spins of a roulette wheel, where everyone naturally knows the right odds. The theories assumed not just rationality in the ordinary sense of the word, but also universal omniscience.

In this scheme, liquid financial markets seemed to be perfect for mobilizing and allocating capital. Competition between traders—who all "know" the right odds—ensures that the price is always right, making case-by-case assessments unnecessary. Market liquidity makes it easy to diversify away the risks of individual securities without reducing the overall return. Initially, financiers were skeptical that blind diversification could substitute for due diligence and ongoing oversight. But over time, academic theory permeated common practice.

Theories of efficient portfolio construction and option-pricing based on known, quantifiable probabilities, created opportunities for financial engineers to create derivative securities that could be used to manage risks in ways that went well beyond simple diversification. In principle, starting with the debt or equity of real companies and individuals, financial engineers could synthesize packages of risks and returns precisely tailored to an investor's needs. Contacting the actual borrower or issuer of equity was unnecessary.

We then saw how regulators and lawmakers, during and after the New Deal, helped put the academic theories into practice. The Crash of 1929 led Congress to pass the Securities Acts of 1933 and 1934. These acts and the expansion of investor protection rules in the decades that followed played an important role in maintaining the liquidity of U.S. stock markets by certifying their integrity. Casinos with reputations for rigged games eventually drive away patrons. But the rules also severely impaired corporate governance. For instance, although penalties for insider trading undergird a liquid market in which many buyers bid for stocks without much regard for the identity or motivations of the seller, they also place special burdens on insiders that discourage stockholders from accumulating controlling positions or even serving on the boards of directors. Inevitably, boards come to consist of individuals who don't have a significant economic stake in the company.

The weak or casual oversight of banks and other financial institutions allowed top executives to diversify into activities that generated large—and, as far as the executives were concerned, largely risk-free—bonuses. Once financial conglomerates had been patched together, their boards of directors had neither the incentive nor the capacity to stay on top of what was going on. When Joe Cassano's little unit at AIG was insuring trillions of dollars of CDSs that later brought down the insurer, the company's board was peopled by luminaries: distinguished economists, senior banking executives, partners of law firms, cabinet members, and even a former chief accountant of the SEC.[1] What the board apparently lacked was a clue—or the incentive to investigate—how Cassano's unit was earning high returns. And calculated carelessness of top executives and directors was the norm in virtually all large financial institutions.

SEC rules also facilitated the securitization of debt and helped centralize investment choices in such securities. The securities laws apply broadly to a wide range of financial instruments and intermediaries. For example, after money market funds were invented, the SEC introduced rules to protect investors; thus, even though money market funds weren't guaranteed, the SEC rules provided valuable reassurance to their users. The SEC also provided its imprimatur to a very few rating agencies to certify the creditworthiness of money market funds and debt securities: In 1975 the SEC designated Moody's, S&P, and Fitch as the only three "nationally recognized statistical rating organizations."

The problem with the regulation of commercial banking arose in a different way. Whereas the progressive tightening of securities rules and the broadening of their application promoted centralization and arm's-length financing, *loosened* banking rules had the same effect.

The Banking Acts of 1933 and 1935 ended disastrous bank runs and ushered in a golden age of banking that lasted several decades. Tough rules freed bankers from having to worry about jittery depositors and helped them significantly expand the credit they provided to business and individual customers. But the weakening of these rules after the 1970s helped securitized, arm's-length alternatives displace traditional, relationship lending. The purchase of commercial paper by money market funds, for example, provided tough competition for banks making business loans.

The substitution of traditional lending by securitized instruments—cheered on by theories that favored anonymous markets over relationships and supported by certifications provided by the SEC—forced banks to look for alternative sources of profit. In this, the banks were aided by a changing regulatory ethos that not only promoted securitization, but also allowed banks to diversify into new lines of business and did not regard the consolidation of finance into a few giant enterprises as a problem. As the banks that were the most willing and able to roll the dice created highly profitable—and risky—products such as CDSs, their less enterprising brethren fell by the wayside or were acquired. Decentralized, relationship-based finance thus took a double hit. It was assaulted both by securitization and financial engineering and by the gathering of these activities into a few large institutions.

▨ Insider Diagnoses and Remedies

Many insiders of finance—practitioners, academic researchers, regulators, and politicians who specialize in writing banking and securities laws—offer a starkly different interpretation. They start with the premise that advances in modern financial technology, like those in, say, semiconductor technology, have been a great plus for society. Credit default swaps aren't simply a vehicle that facilitated reckless mortgage lending and enabled Wall Street traders to place highly leveraged bets. They are supposedly good for Main Street, as well. In this view, the 2008 crisis was the result of a regulatory apparatus that had fallen behind the development of modern financial theory and practice. There were too many gaps in the regulation. By filling them, the financial status quo can be saved from its excesses. Yale's Robert Shiller goes further, arguing for regulations that will promote the development of even more complex financial products (see box).

More

In an op-ed published in the *Financial Times* on September 27, 2009, Robert Shiller defends financial innovation. He argues that there is nothing the matter with complex financial products as long they "have an interface with consumers that is simple enough to make them comprehensible, so that they will want these products and use them correctly." In fact, financial products, according to Shiller, have remained too rudimentary. "The advance of civilization has brought immense new complexity to the devices we use every day," Shiller writes. "A century ago, homes were little more than roofs, walls and floors. Now they have a variety of complex electronic devices, including automatic on-off lighting, communications and data processing devices. People do not need to understand the complexity of these devices, which have been engineered to be simple to operate."

Financial products, however, have not kept up. Rather, Shiller observes, "We are still mostly investing in plain vanilla products such as shares in corporations or ordinary nominal bonds, products that have not changed fundamentally in centuries." Option-adjustable rate mortgages and other such innovations in mortgage finance "are not products of sophisticated financial theory." Instead, Shiller proposes "continuous workout mortgages, motivated by basic principles of risk management" that would "protect against exigencies such as recessions or drops in home prices. Had such mortgages been offered before this crisis, we would not have the rash of foreclosures." He also argues for "liquid international markets for real estate price indices, owner-occupied and commercial, for aggregate macroeconomic risks such as gross domestic product and unemployment, for human longevity risks, as well as broader and more effective long-term markets for energy risks."

New products, in turn, require "an increasingly complex financial infrastructure" and regulatory agencies with "a stronger mission of encouraging innovation. They must hire enough qualified staff to understand the complexity of the innovative process and talk to innovators with less of a disapprove-by-the-rules stance and more that of a contributor to a complex creative process." It is "critical," in Shiller's view, "that we take the opportunity of the crisis to promote innovation-enhancing financial regulation and not let this be eclipsed by superficially popular issues."

The article's byline identifies Shiller as a professor of economics and finance at Yale University and chief economist at MacroMarkets LLC. As a professor, Shiller has pioneered the study of behavioral finance that highlights the herdlike behavior of stock markets and their propensity to form bubbles. MacroMarkets, which Shiller cofounded, develops innovative financial products traded on these very markets.

Outsiders, as well, perhaps daunted by the complexity of the system, often buy into the insider view that all we need is better regulation of modern financial innovations. When Barack Obama was on the campaign trail, in 2008, he declared that the regulatory system needed to be updated because "old institutions cannot adequately oversee new practices." Updating means more rules that cover more institutions and markets. The Obama administration's plan released on June 17, 2009, reflected the insider consensus. It proposed a "new foundation for financial regulation...that rewards innovation and that is able to adapt and evolve with changes."[2] Financial firms and markets would face more robust and comprehensive supervision and regulation (see box). Introducing the blueprint, the president reaffirmed his view that the financial system had failed because "a regulatory regime basically crafted in the wake of a 20th-century economic crisis—the Great Depression—was overwhelmed by the speed, scope, and sophistication of a 21st-century global economy."

The New Foundation

The Obama administration's reforms laid out five key objectives:

1. Promote robust supervision and regulation of financial firms.
2. Establish comprehensive supervision of financial markets.
3. Protect consumers and investors from financial abuse.
4. Provide the government with the tools it needs to manage financial crises.
5. Raise international regulatory standards and improve international cooperation.

The specific measures proposed to achieve these objectives included

- A new Financial Services Oversight Council of financial regulators to identify emerging systemic risks and improve interagency cooperation.
- New authority for the Federal Reserve to supervise all firms that could pose a threat to financial stability, even those that do not own banks.

- Stronger capital and other prudential standards for all financial firms, and even higher standards for large, interconnected firms.
- Enhanced regulation of securitization markets, including new requirements for market transparency, stronger regulation of credit-rating agencies, and a requirement that issuers and originators retain a financial interest in securitized loans.
- Comprehensive regulation of all over-the-counter derivatives.
- International reforms to strengthen the capital framework; improve oversight of global financial markets; coordinate supervision of internationally active firms; and enhance crisis management tools.

U.S. Treasury, *Financial Regulatory Reform: A New Foundation*, pp. 2–3.[3]

President Obama's new foundation provided a template for the Dodd-Frank Wall Street Reform and Consumer Protection Act of 2010. Although most Republicans voted against it, at its core, the legislation isn't very different from the proposals offered by the Bush administration in 2008. Bush's treasury secretary, Hank Paulson, in fact supported the Dodd-Frank act. The Bush, Obama, and Dodd-Frank initiatives reflect the long-held view of insiders favoring top-down, preferably global, regulation. Efforts to standardize risk-based capital requirements, for instance, go back decades to the Basel Accords.

These top-down measures failed for a reason. Risk can be quantified only to a degree, as I argued in chapter 5. Risk also depends on specific circumstances; to assume that risks within broad categories (for instance, commercial loans or mortgage-backed securities) are even roughly similar is dangerous. Regulations based on such an assumption encourage financial institutions to load up on the supposedly low-risk category with the riskiest assets they can find in that category. Moreover, the top-down approach assumes that executives running complex financial firms have a good handle on their assets and risk exposures. This remains a far-fetched assumption for banks with hundreds—and, in some cases, thousands—of subsidiaries and hundreds of thousands of complex derivative contracts whose terms bankers almost never read.[4]

Effective, ongoing coordination of international regulators is a persistent pipe-dream. Long experience shows that even in matters of life and death, coordination among different organizations dealing with law and order, and security, within national borders is hard. The problems multiply when national borders are crossed. If coordinated international action cannot control brazen piracy off the Somali coast, how effective is it likely to be in dealing with the covertly risky behavior of financiers? Ben Bernanke and Alan Greenspan, the current and past chairmen of a Federal Reserve that employs hundreds of economists, continue to assert that a nationwide housing bubble was unrecognizable before it collapsed. Will an interagency council formed to "identify emerging systemic risks" be more prescient?

The idea of defusing hundreds of trillions of dollars of OTC derivatives by putting them on an exchange is relatively new, but also a fantasy. Exchange trading certainly has advantages, such as transparent pricing and daily settlement. Interest-rate futures contracts have been used for speculation and hedging for more than three decades without causing any harm, and if CDSs on subprime mortgages had also been actively traded on exchanges, AIG might not have unraveled. Unfortunately, the number of instruments that can be actively traded on an exchange is limited (see box), and simply listing the myriad OTC derivatives sloshing around is no great improvement. Enthusiasts for the listing solution ignore or forget that commodities exchanges, which compete with OTC markets, are always on the lookout for new products to trade. If exchanges weren't able to create liquid markets in CDSs before, is it likely to happen now, just because regulators say it should?

Few Hits, Many Misses

Commodities exchanges are always trying to develop new derivative products. They have new product groups comprising members of the exchanges and full-time staff who try to gauge demand and design contracts that will have the broadest possible appeal. Nevertheless, most new products fail to attract and sustain the level of interest necessary to maintain an active market. As mentioned in the previous chapter, derivative products that were introduced with much fanfare, but failed to survive, include futures on the CPI, a municipal bond index, and a corporate bond index.

It isn't just committees of futures exchanges that have a hard time. Robert Shiller has been trying to promote trading in contracts on housing prices for more than a decade. Many versions have been tried. None has been traded actively.

Apparently exchange trading involves what are known as "network externalities." Successful contracts that are liquid attract more traders, making them even more liquid. Illiquid contracts wither away.

Furthermore, although there is considerable luck in whether a contract succeeds, success also requires, according to the CME's Leo Melamed,

---

> "planning, calculation, arm-twisting, and tenacity to get a market up and going. Even when it's chugging along, it has to be cranked and pushed."[5] To make the CME's S&P 500 contract a success, Melamed called in all his chits: Every trader for whom Melamed had done favors was asked to trade the future; every member of the CME was asked to spend at least fifteen minutes in the trading pit; and Melamed himself spent as much time trading the S&P contract as he could.[6]
>
> Such efforts can only be devoted to a few contracts. Doing this for tens of thousands of OTC derivatives is out of the question.

Another practical problem with proposals to modernize and expand the scope of financial regulation is that no agency seems to have the capacity necessary to undertake new responsibilities. Bank examiners continue to struggle with traditional lending, just as the SEC does with garden variety fraud. The Fed hasn't yet mastered the problem of central banking in a globalized economy or even properly supervised bank holding companies that have long been under its purview. Furthermore, hiring capable regulatory staff to oversee fiendishly complex innovations and institutions—and then keeping them from going over to Wall Street to make the big bucks—isn't like recruiting baggage screeners at airports. Regulators have found it difficult to hire enough staff to keep up with the expansion of the institutions they regulate. The number of FDIC employees declined by more than half between 2006 and 1996, falling from 9,151 to fewer than 4,476.[7] Total assets in FDIC commercial banks during this period, however, more than doubled, from about 4.6 trillion to over $10 trillion.[8]

Getting beyond these practical problems: Suppose, somehow, with a substantial increase in effort and hiring, the top-down approaches could be made to work and OTC derivatives could be repotted into exchanges. Is it worth making the effort to preserve and protect the financial innovations of the last two decades?

Why Bother?

As a general rule, we should not question the value of commercially successful innovations. If a new product attracts buyers, we have to assume that it creates value even if sophisticates consider it tasteless. *De gustibus non est disputandum*. In a decentralized economy, we don't tell innovators what to develop and consumers what to purchase.

But there are exceptions, when transactions between willing sellers and willing buyers *aren't* adequate proof of value. One example is subsidized products such as biofuels and biotechnologies where taxpayers, not just the buyers, pay for the development or manufacture. The overall costs and benefits are then a matter of public concern. Such concerns also arise if the use of innovation has "negative externalities"—it hurts innocent bystanders, as it were. For instance, we would look askance at a farmer's use of a potent pesticide if it poisoned the water table.[9]

This does not mean that any innovation that harms bystanders should automatically be banned. Thousands of pedestrians are killed every year, yet it would be unthinkable to ban automobiles. Nonetheless, the potential or actual harm to bystanders does create a legitimate societal interest in discouraging, limiting, regulating, supervising, or, in extreme cases, banning the use of an innovation. In figuring out which of these options is best, the overall costs and benefits must be estimated. For instance, a consensus that automobiles provide a huge benefit to society encouraged the institution of limits on who can drive (minors aren't allowed) and how (drivers must stop at red lights) that minimized, but did not eliminate, the deaths of pedestrians. Indeed, the value we attribute to automobiles has justified expenditures on a regulatory system that goes beyond protecting pedestrians to also keeping traffic flowing smoothly.

The recent financial meltdown has demonstrated, beyond most reasonable people's doubt, that innovations like CDSs can cause grave harm to bystanders. They have also been, like biofuels and biotechnology, covertly subsidized by virtue of the government's explicitly guaranteeing the deposits and implicitly all the other liabilities of many financial institutions that sell or use these innovations. It is unlikely that the products could flourish in self-regulating markets: They need the equivalent of traffic cops, and traffic cops need to be paid. Therefore, we cannot simply accept the use of such innovations as proof of their utility.

Empirical evidence of the value of modern financial innovations for society at large—to the extent it is offered at all—is flimsy at best. For instance, advocates cite data showing that countries with good systems for basic banking services do better than countries that don't. But to use such data to argue that sophisticated innovations have more benefits than costs is like asserting that because the judicious use of mild pesticides constitutes good agricultural practice, so must the indiscriminate use of highly potent pesticides. Given flimsy direct evidence, a priori beliefs and arguments inevitably come into play.

Most insiders believe that the basic changes that have occurred in the last two decades, principally the securitization of credit previously extended by banks and the development of risk management products, are highly desirable.

In 1987, Lowell Bryan, a McKinsey & Company director, wrote that "a new technology for lending—securitized credit—has suddenly appeared on the scene. This new technology has the capacity to transform the fundamentals of banking, which have been essentially unchanged since their origins in medieval Europe."[10] Bryan predicted that traditional lending might soon become obsolete: "About half of all debt in the national economy is raised through securities; that number might increase to 80 percent in the next decade."[11] Moreover, he argued that the new technology offered more checks and balances than traditional banking: "Under a securitized credit system, in which an outside agency assigns a rating to the issue, credit risk will likely be properly underwritten before investors will buy an issue. In many cases, another third-party credit underwriter (a bank, a finance company, or an insurance company) must guarantee a portion of the credit risk in the issue. So at least one and often two skeptical outside parties review the credit underwriting before the issue can be placed with investors."[12] Bryan also asserted that the rates on securities were set by an objective market, not by the subjective judgments of bankers.

In a now celebrated paper given at the annual Jackson Hole conclave of central bankers in 2005, Raghuram Rajan warned that in reality, financial innovation had made the economy riskier. But his critique was aimed mainly at the perverse incentives of financiers and did not question the value of the new financial technology that Bryan had celebrated. In fact, according to Rajan, financial innovations had produced "beneficial, real effects, increasing lending, entrepreneurship, and growth rates of GDP, while reducing costs of financial transactions."[13]

At the same conclave, Donald Kohn, vice chairman of the Fed, endorsed what he called the Greenspan doctrine (named after the Fed chairman), applauding the development of derivatives and other such financial technologies. These instruments enabled "risk and return to be divided and priced to better meet the needs of borrowers and lenders" and allowed institutions "to choose their risk profiles more precisely, and to improve the management of the risks they do take on."[14]

In 2006, Ben Bernanke, Greenspan's successor as chairman of the Fed, claimed that "banking organizations of all sizes have made substantial strides over the past two decades in their ability to measure and manage risks." The use of "concepts such as duration, convexity, and option-adjusted spreads" provided better risk returns to stockholders and "greater resilience of the banking system."[15] After the 2008 collapse, Greenspan admitted to shock, but his successor remained steadfast in his positive assessment. In April 2009, Bernanke observed that the "perception" that financial innovation was a problem went "too far." Innovation was and would continue to be "a tool for making our financial system more efficient" as long as it was properly implemented and regulators were "more alert to its risks."[16]

Illusory Benefits

A small but growing number of what I will call informed outsiders take the opposite view. The most prominent of these is Paul Volcker, Alan Greenspan's predecessor as Fed chairman, who argues that most financial innovations are worse than worthless—they are dangerous. Credit default swaps and collateralized debt obligations (CDOs) "took us right to the brink of disaster," Volcker said in an interview. "I wish," he continued, "that somebody would give me some shred of neutral evidence about the relationship between financial innovation recently and the growth of the economy, just one shred of information." He recalled asking a Nobel Prize winner, "one of the inventors of financial engineering," what it did for the economy. To Volcker's surprise, "this leader in the world of financial engineering" responded that it did "nothing" for the economy except "move around the rents in the financial system." It was also a "lot of intellectual fun."

In Volcker's view, financial engineering increased the rents of the financial system, not just moved them around. That was why the financial sector generated 40 percent of the profits in the country and its share of value added had risen from 2.5 percent of GDP to 6.5 percent.[17] In fact, Volker observed, the most important financial innovation he had seen in the past twenty years was the automatic teller machine, and even that was more of a mechanical innovation than a financial one.[18]

The arguments presented in this book line up with Paul Volcker's skeptical perspective. I question, for instance, Rajan's assertion that growth of securitization has been good for the economy as well as his analysis of why it occurred.

Rajan argues that securitization resulted from new technologies that made "hard" information on firms and individuals from centralized sources, such as Dun and Bradstreet, widely available, allowing loan officers to cut down on regular visits to borrowers. Some "soft information that is hard to collect and communicate," such as judgments of character, was certainly lost when regular visits were ended.[19] But, he claims, the increased availability of hard information more than compensates for the loss of soft information. Moreover, unlike soft information, hard information (for instance, credit histories and accounting data) can be automatically processed, further reducing costs and raising the productivity of lending.

Productivity-enhancing technologies also changed the nature of borrower-creditor relationships, Rajan argues, so that many transactions moved from being "embedded in a long-term relationship between a client and a financial institution to being conducted at arm's length in a market."[20] To be sure, there was a trade-off: Long-term relationships produced "greater trust and understanding." But they also constrained each party's choices. Thanks to technological changes (and their knock-on effects on regulatory and institutional arrangements), the trade-off favored long-term relationships mainly for "the most complicated, innovative or risky financial transactions."[21]

My analysis puts securitization in quite a different light.

The claim that the automated processing of hard information provided by a centralized source is usually a superior substitute for the subjective judgments of a banker—Hayek's "man on the spot"—ignores the unquantifiable uncertainty that is an important feature even of seemingly routine lending decisions. Using a credit score produced by feeding a few items of hard data into a mathematical model to assess the likelihood of default assumes that all risks are quantifiable. And that's just one of the many assumptions at work. For instance, credit-scoring formulas also assume that the probability that all loans of a certain kind will default derives from exactly the same risk factors; that these risk factors are all combined or "weighted" in exactly the same way; and that somehow an omniscient modeler knows the right weighting scheme.*

Like criminal trials and faculty hiring decisions, the traditional lending process implicitly took into account unquantifiable uncertainties and

---

*Such assumptions would be risible in other walks of life: replacing "routine" felony trials with a scoring model is inconceivable, whatever the cost savings might be. Nor do economics departments economize on the costs of hiring even entry-level faculty or Ph.D. students by using predictive quantitative models (save perhaps in countries such as France where junior faculty in many public universities are hired on the basis of scores in a competitive national exam).

the uniqueness of individual circumstances. Visits produce information that is wider in its range (and can cover private information not available to Dun and Bradstreet) and better tuned to the specific circumstances of the borrower.[22] For instance, a commercial loan officer may take note of changes in the number of cars in the visitors' lot of an industrial distributor, but ignore such changes for an Internet retailer. Similarly, loan officers and committees traditionally used a wide range of information (including both quantitative data on past and projected financial performance and qualitative observations about competitors and customers) to construct a coherent case or "narrative."

Analyzing so much hard and soft data may amount to overkill in certain kinds of lending: extending mortgages with high down payments to tenured professors of finance and economics, for instance. But it is hard to imagine that in a dynamic, ever-changing economy, mechanistic lending is an appropriate rule for most credit decisions, and that case-by-case ought to be reserved for unusual situations. The Soviet economy couldn't match the supply and demand of the most basic goods because, as Hayek pointed out, central planners cannot cope with the minute but constant changes that occur in seemingly unvarying everyday activities. Planners must therefore rely on highly abstracted statistics that ignore the unique circumstances of time and place. Automated lending to buy homes or cars suffers from this very problem.

Likewise, embedding financial transactions in long-term relationships, instead of conducting them at arm's length in an "objective" marketplace, has merit in many seemingly mundane contexts (see box), and not just for "the most complicated, innovative or risky financial transactions."

Banking On Relationships

Banks whose lending far exceeded their base of long-term depositors have discovered that it is dangerous to rely on funding by yield chasing strangers in wholesale money markets. That holds true for the extension of credit: A financial institution that underwrites securitized credit for resale becomes, to a significant degree, a sales agent for the borrower. Of course, sensible sales agents, who value their relationships with customers, will exercise some care in what they sell; nonetheless, the degree of care is diluted by the expectation that customers will do their own analysis and by the absence of any direct financial risk to the sales agent. A bond underwriter cannot be expected to exercise the prudence of a banker making a loan that will remain on the bank's balance sheet.

> Long-term relationships between lenders and borrowers have great value even after credit has been extended, akin to the benefits of shareholder-manager relationships. Borrowers can share private information with lenders just as managers could (if not barred by law), and thus have a greater opportunity to send early warnings of danger. In addition to self-interested restraints on opportunistic behavior, the parties know they are stuck with each other, for a banker cannot dump a loan as easily as a mutual fund can sell a bond. As a result, there may develop an additional sense of mutual solidarity. A banker may thus renew a line of credit in hard times while an arm's-length purchaser would not roll over the same issuer's maturing commercial paper. Renegotiating the terms of a loan with one banker is easier than corralling many dispersed bondholders to discuss the modification of bond covenants. One of the consequences of the slicing and dicing of mortgage loans is that it is now often practically impossible for homeowners in default to work out problems with their lenders, as they might if their mortgage had a single owner, especially one located at the nearby branch of their bank.[23]

There is a vast difference between the age-old securitization of debt issued by railroads and electric utilities and the newer securitization of mortgage and consumer loans. The issuance of railroad or utility bonds entails holistic, case-by-case due diligence and extensive dialogue with issuers. Ongoing relationships between issuers and buyers of bonds certainly are limited, but the economies of scale in the railroad or power plant that is financed compensate for the absence of close relationships. When housing and auto loans are securitized, there is no detailed analysis of the borrowers' circumstances, no relationship, and no economy of scale in the activity financed. The supposed benefits are mainly due to the low costs of automated, large-scale lending. But low-cost lending to borrowers who can't repay isn't a bargain for anyone. The mass production of consumer loans isn't like the mass production of consumer goods. The customer isn't always right, and the long-run consequences of excessive lending can be disastrous for borrowers, creditors, and society at large.

Why was there such a mass displacement of long-term, relationship- and judgment-based lending by arm's-length securitization? In the narrative offered by Rajan and several other economists, exogenous technologies played a deterministic role, inexorably forcing changes in regulation and financing arrangements. But technology might, instead, have facilitated relationship banking. For instance, collaborative software (such as Lotus Notes) could have improved the capacity of large lending teams serving far-flung borrowers to share a wide range of data, observations, and judgments. The outcome was not predetermined. In fact, in the story that I have told, the increased share of securitized financial assets was driven mainly by the beliefs of financial economists and regulators rather than by the efficiencies of automation, although in the short run, automation did reduce costs and increase the volume of lending and stock trading.

The value of many derivative instruments created in the last two decades is also dubious, as Volcker argues. In opposing legislation that would ban CDSs—essentially bets on bonds or loans going bust—Treasury secretary Geithner claimed that they "perform a useful function" in the real economy. Similarly, the chief strategist at Credit Derivatives Research warned that prohibitions would "inevitably lead to higher costs of funding across all U.S. corporations."[24] But there is no data whatsoever showing that CDSs reduced funding costs for real-world businesses, even when the market was in full swing. And its subsequent collapse helped raise borrowing costs to record levels above Treasury rates. As Volcker points out, the world did very well before CDSs were invented in 1998. Furthermore, even the logic behind arguments that CDSs serve the common good is weak (see box).

Do CDSs Help Real-World Businesses?

According their proponents, CDSs are more liquid than the bonds they insure: This gives bondholders a cheaper and quicker "out" (they can buy a CDS to close out positions instead of selling bonds), which, in turn, encourages them to accept lower interest rates. Put aside how many bondholders can practically or legally do this: Why might CDSs be more liquid? CDSs supposedly attract more liquidity supplying speculators because they don't have to put up as much capital to trade and can go short more easily. Unfortunately, markets that depend on thinly capitalized players tend to seize up when liquidity is most needed. Unsurprisingly in the recent crisis, the huge spike in prices and the absence of creditworthy sellers made CDSs no bargain for bondholders wanting to exit.

CDSs also supposedly give bondholders a valuable tool for insuring risks. But bondholders aren't like individuals, property owners, or purchasers of TVs who need insurance against death, fire, or manufacturing defects—they can just hold a diversified portfolio of bonds instead. (And aren't bondholders supposed to bear credit risks?) Nor can suppliers to a business use CDSs in the manner that farmers sell futures to hedge crops. Most suppliers can't buy CDS contracts to protect their receivables through a broker. They can, however, follow the long-standing practice of selling receivables to a factor. Or, if really overcome by cleverness, they can short their customers' stock (although most sensible real-world suppliers avoid such games).

The argument that CDS prices provide a better signal of creditworthiness than bond yields also turns on the incorporation of the opinions and information of more traders: Allegedly, pessimistic votes can go uncast in the bond market because of the difficulty of short-selling. But more cheap voting by traders whose knowledge of creditworthiness is usually second- or thirdhand doesn't add up to more sensible results; it is hard to imagine that the wild swings in CDS rates in 2008 had much to do with real changes in solvency. Moreover, which sensible creditor would put much weight on CDS prices instead of firsthand due diligence? Physicians use thermometers to measure the temperature of their patients, not some betting pool outside their window.

Against these largely fictitious benefits, we have experienced the real and catastrophic costs triggered by a collapse of the CDS market. Apologists assert the panic was unwarranted. Perhaps. But possibly imaginary fears that CDSs had compromised the solvency of institutions supposed to be systemically important have had unquestionably harsh consequences.

The enormous leverage offered by CDSs and other derivatives has also generated huge rents for bankers. In 1983, when the top bonus at Lehman was $1.5 million and the total bonus pool amounted to $27 million, senior partners (who included Richard Fuld and Robert Rubin) argued over who should get $25,000 more or less. In 2009, when Goldman Sachs was pressured to show restraint, its bonus pool amounted to $16.2 billion.[25] CEO Blankfein (awarded a $9 million bonus in 2009) told the *London Times* that Goldman "does God's work," a remark he later said was a joke; but it did not amuse at a time when unemployment was crossing 10 percent. In the same interview, Blankfein asserted that Goldman Sachs served a "social purpose" by "help[ing] companies to grow by helping them to raise capital. Companies that grow create wealth. This, in turn, allows people to have jobs that create more growth and more wealth. It's a virtuous cycle."[26]

Blankfein's claim, which was presumably not intentionally jocular, is hard to take seriously as an explanation for the tripling of the Goldman's revenues from $13 billion in 1999 to $46 billion in 2007, and of employee compensation from $6 billion to over $20 billion. Equity underwriting—issuing stock for real companies–accounted for about

3 percent of Goldman's 2007 revenues, and debt underwriting (which includes mortgage and other asset-backed securities, not just corporate debt) accounted for another 4 percent of revenues. Meanwhile, trading and principal investments amounted to 68 percent of revenues, and asset management and securities services (which also have little to do with raising money for real companies) 16 percent. It is also difficult to imagine that trading and principal investment revenues were more than five times as great in 2007 as they had been in 1999[27] because Goldman's traders had become five times better. Rather, Goldman multiplied its trading profits by multiplying its risk taking and leverage,[28] borrowing vast sums from banks and shadow banks.

Goldman wasn't the only player racking up huge trading profits—only the most successful. In fact, one of the sorriest consequences of our financial system is the toll exacted on the legitimacy of providing great rewards for great contributions. Finance certainly contributes to prosperity, but the vast wealth secured in recent years by a small number of financiers does not map into a commensurate increase in their economic productivity: They haven't created or financed new industries or turned around failing companies. Rather, they have used subsidized borrowing to leverage the returns of questionable schemes, secure in the knowledge that if things go wrong the authorities will step in, trying to shore up asset prices or prop up failing counterparties. The sharp rise in income inequality at the top of the scale[29] in the twenty-first century owes much more to reverse Robin Hood regulation than to a small decline in personal income tax rates.

The palpable toxicity—and the low likelihood of offsetting benefits from many financial innovations—poses a dilemma. Banning them, or trying to confiscate the rents they generate, would be unwise. Blanket prohibitions rarely work, and their unintended consequences can be worse than the condition they are supposed to cure. It would be almost impossible to pass legislation to cover all dangerous derivatives, and attempts to do so would just create more work for regulators, lobbyists, and lawyers. Prohibitions could also impede more useful instruments, such as bond and currency futures; like CDSs, these instruments are vehicles for speculation, but they also really do help real-world businesses hedge their risks; and they haven't been known to cause harm except to speculators on the losing side of trades.

Similar arguments apply against proscribing the securitization of debt. I have argued that the securitization was excessive in amount and kind. This does not mean that the right amount of securitized credit is zero, or that we can even know what the right amount is. In its early days, the high-yield bond market may well have been structured to add value (see box), especially given the fragmented banking system's inability to extend large unsecured loans. Who is to say how much dialing back to the 1980s would be appropriate?

How High Yield Got Junked

Don Gogel, currently CEO of the private equity firm Clayton, Dubilier & Rice and former partner at Kidder Peabody, recalls:

> When the Commitment Committee of Kidder, Peabody evaluated the firm's underwriting exposure for relatively risky assets like high yield bonds in the late 1980s, the firm's partners had their own exposure clearly in mind. For a firm owned wholly by its partners, it was clear that poor risk judgments would have a measureable and often immediate impact on the firm's—and individual partners'—financial well-being. In parallel, early investors in highly-leveraged private placements like the Prudential and Equitable insurance companies were very demanding in their credit and business analysis since they knew they would be holding those securities for a very long time. Even when Drexel Burnham created more liquidity in public high yield issues, investors like Trust Company of the West put an enormous amount of energy and resources behind individual company credit analysis. However, as investment bank partnerships became public companies and as securities were bundled and purchased in ever-larger portfolios, ownership and discipline became victims of scale. For issuers and investors alike.[30]

Likewise, regulating compensation and bankers' bonuses to bring them in line with their true value added is an impossible task and sets a dangerous precedent.

At the same time, the questionable benefits from innovations such as CDSs and CDOs argue against the insider prescription of devoting more effort to regulating their use: Why go to the trouble and expense of establishing the equivalent of a financial highway patrol to shore up an activity that doesn't contribute materially to the public good? If it's not necessary to regulate, as Chief Justice Roberts might say, it's necessary not to regulate.

Yet doing nothing is not an attractive option. The status quo is intolerable.

A Modest Proposal

The proposals of skeptical outsiders offer a way out.

Insiders, such as Daniel K. Tarullo, a member of the Fed's board of governors, take it for granted that "systemically important institutions are likely to be with us into the indefinite future." Accordingly, their proposals are "oriented toward forcing those institutions to internalize more of the risks they create and thus making it less likely they will create problems for the system as a whole."[31] But outsiders, many who once occupied important positions in the financial system, reject such containment policies as inadequate and favor a radical restructuring. The heart of the restructuring proposals, offered by the likes of Paul Volcker, Joseph Stiglitz (2001 Nobel laureate in economics), Simon Johnson (former chief economist of the IMF), Mervyn King (governor of the Bank of England), and John Kay (professor at the London School of Economics and *Financial Times* columnist) lies in a reinstatement of Glass-Steagall's wall between investment and commercial banking. As King puts it colorfully, we need to separate utility banking from casino banking.

There are differences among the restructuring proposals in the extent of the restrictions they would impose on the utility banks. Some "narrow banking" proposals would limit deposit-taking institutions to holding virtually riskless government securities, whereas the Volker proposals would give commercial banks considerably more leeway. The reform I favor falls somewhere in between.

My proposal comprises broad goals and principles rather than unambiguous bright-line rules. Bright-line rules have their advantages: It is usually better to specify a speed limit than to enjoin drivers from speeding. Yet in many situations broad rules are unavoidable. Regulating finance is one of those situations that require considerable reliance on broad rules. One set of capital requirements doesn't fit all, as we have seen. If bankers are given a precise definition of activities that fall under the rubric of casino banking, they will surely find other ways to gamble.

The effective and fair implementation of broad rules requires decentralized, case-by-case judgments. The judicial system provides a good model: Legislatures and precedents enshrined in the common law provide general rules, but the disposition of specific cases is left to courts dispersed around the land. Similarly, responsibility for regulatory oversight in banking and finance should also be decentralized to the extent possible. In other words, we need to bolster examination in the field rather than place our bets on new "super" or "systemic" regulatory bodies.

Reciprocally, decentralized oversight has implications for the nature and scope of the broad rules. The responsibilities of regulators, and the rules they enforce, should lie within the capacities of an average person in the same way that laws ought to be written for the typical lawyer and judge rather than a brilliant legal scholar. We can't have regulators enforcing financial rules that are accessible only to exceptionally talented and well-trained individuals. Furthermore, case-by-case judgment is labor intensive, and hiring large armies of regulators is neither practical nor desirable. Therefore, although the rules have to be broad, their purpose needs to be focused.

In my view, the primary goal of banking regulation should be to maintain a sound and confidence-inspiring system for depositing the "ready cash" of individuals and businesses and for making payments with the deposited cash. Achieving this goal, our experience from the 1950s and 1960s suggests, would also provide credit to businesses and consumers within prudent bounds and contain the frequency and scope of the fallout from speculative manias.

Specifically, I propose we reinstate old-fashioned banking, where bankers know their borrowers, by *tightly limiting what banks can do: nothing besides making loans to individuals and nonfinancial businesses—after old-fashioned due diligence—and simple hedging transactions.* The standard would simply be whether the loan (or hedge) can be monitored by bankers and examiners who don't have PhDs in finance, and whether the risk is one that bankers would take if it was their own money—a "prudent lender" rule, as it were.

These rules would apply to any institution or entity taking short-term deposits from the public, whether or not it was called a bank. In addition, institutions whose prudence is already subject to regulatory oversight, such as insurance companies, pension funds, and endowments, would be allowed to place their short-term funds only with intermediaries licensed to accept deposits from the public. Public companies would not be so required, but would have to secure the approval of their boards of directors to place their deposits elsewhere.

Anyone else—investment banks, hedge funds, trusts, and the like— could innovate and speculate to the utmost, free of any additional oversight. But they would not be allowed to trade with, or secure credit from, regulated banks, except perhaps through well-secured loans against liquid securities (such as Treasuries and NYSE stocks) under terms that can be monitored by run-of-the-mill bankers and examiners. No lending against, or purchasing of, Collateralized Debt Obligations or financing warehouses of securities awaiting securitization, for instance. Unregulated financial institutions would be free to raise debt or equity—but not on a short-term basis from the public or from regulated fiduciaries. A finance company that securitized mortgages could issue equity or high-yield bonds without any additional restraints; it could even issue short-term commercial paper, as long as it wasn't sold to the public or to pension funds and other such regulated fiduciaries.

No effort to further regulate the derivatives market is envisioned. Detoxifying specific products lies outside the scope of what we can realistically expect regulators to accomplish; and, even if it could be done, it would be a temporary fix. Rather, my solution seeks to exclude those players who gamble with taxpayers' funds and guarantees. Similarly, I can think of no sensible way to regulate bankers' compensation; but, again, reducing the subsidized leverage that has generated excessive rents would naturally shrink oversized bonuses.

These rules would drastically reduce the assets in money market mutual funds, and many would go out of business altogether. As we have seen under the current system, money market funds rely on certifications—provided at zero cost—by rating agencies. The howls of protest emanating from these free riders at rules that would make them take some responsibility for their investment choices are telling—and best ignored.[32] There is no reason to let them continue to enjoy the free ride they have enjoyed for decades.

Money market mutual funds could attempt to circumvent rules requiring them to take more responsibility for credit analysis by turning themselves into short-term bond funds, blurring the difference between safe stores of liquidity and longer term investments whose prices are expected to fluctuate. Therefore, it may be worth placing limits on how frequently all mutual funds can be redeemed. This is not a radical restraint on vehicles that are supposed to be repositories of long-term savings. After all, people do cope with the illiquidity of their homes, which account for a significant portion of the net worth of many individuals. Money in IRA funds cannot be withdrawn until retirement age, and reallocation of assets in many company-sponsored retirement plans is limited to one change per year. Investors in hedge funds can usually withdraw funds only at the end of each quarter, with ninety-day notice. Why not restrict mutual fund redemptions to, say, once a month?

Commercial banks would face more stringent limits under my proposal than they would if we simply reinstated Glass-Steagall prohibitions on investment banking. But we should note that it wasn't the kinds of activities that the old prohibitions targeted—principally securities underwriting—that caused a banking crisis. As it happens, the securities business now encompasses very different kinds of activities than it did in the 1930s, and who can tell what it will include in the future? My proposal therefore follows the principle of bank chartering pioneered by New York State in 1825: Specify a limited number of activities and attach a broad exclusion—"no other powers whatever, except such as are expressly granted" was the language used by the legislature.

For megabanks, this exclusion would require unwinding, or spinning out, derivatives activities that even after the 2008 crisis continue to loom extraordinarily large. (At the end of 2009, according to the OCC, the five biggest bank derivative dealers in the United States held 97 percent of the more than 200 trillion in notional derivatives value held by U.S. banks. J.P. Morgan held about $79 trillion, Bank of America $44 trillion, Goldman Sachs $42 trillion, Citibank $38 trillion, and Wells Fargo $4 trillion.) For these banks, according to hedge-fund titan Kenneth Griffin, domination of the derivatives market "translates into billions of dollars in trading revenue each year—revenue that is generated from the dealers' privileged position as credit intermediaries with implied government guarantees."[33]

Requiring banks to shed these activities does not at all constitute unwarranted meddling. Without deposit guarantees, who would keep a deposit earning 1 to 2 percent in annual interest in banks that had trillions of dollars of derivatives exposure? And because the government guarantees the deposits of megabanks, it has a responsibility to ensure that the megabanks don't put trading profits ahead of prudence. Sensible bankers at J.P. Morgan wouldn't allow its borrowers to build up huge derivatives books. Why should taxpayers let J.P. Morgan do so?*

Unlike some narrow banking proposals, my approach does not require banks—or anyone else in the financial system, for that matter—to stop taking risks. I am not even suggesting breaking up the core

---

*A brilliant coup executed in the spring of 2009 by Amherst, a small, Texas-based brokerage, suggests that controls at megabanks remain lax. Amherst got the likes of J.P. Morgan and Bank of America to place about $130 million of bets that around $27 million of dicey loans would default—and then arranged to have the loans paid off in full. Amusing but not surprising: Crisis or no crisis, why should the traders and their bosses at too-big-to-fail banks forsake calculated carelessness?

deposit-taking and lending activities of large banks. In fact, one of the few good things that came out of the deregulation of the 1990s was the creation of banks that have the deposits necessary to make loans to large companies. Relationship lending can finally compete with arm's-length securitized credit in areas where size does matter. No need to give that up. Too big to fail wouldn't be an issue if banks were restricted to activities in which proper supervision was feasible.

Speculation and bubbles would not be eliminated, but walling off the banking system would limit the extent of collateral damage. When the Internet bubble burst, for instance, stock market losses were comparable to—or possibly greater than—the fall in the value of houses when the housing bubble burst. But because banks remained solvent and liquid, the impact on the economy as a whole was modest.

This proposal isn't an untried gamble. In fact, it takes us back to the kind of regulation that sustained a sound banking system that supported robust growth in the real economy for several decades. Tough comprehensive regulation of all institutions that hold the nation's ready cash would complete the process of securing and standardizing the medium of exchange that was started with Civil War and New Deal banking acts. Recall that Civil War rules replaced a multitude of privately issued banknotes with a uniform and secure national currency and ended the dislocations caused by panicky redemptions of notes for gold and silver. The shoring up of currency proved inadequate, however, as payments by checks drawn on bank accounts became the dominant medium of exchange and runs to redeem deposits for currency continued to trigger depressions. This problem was largely but not fully solved by New Deal deposit insurance: as Homer Jones pointed out in 1938, insurance did not explicitly cover all deposits. Worse, new uninsured instruments that resembled cash and deposits were created and grew to many times the amount of money held in insured deposits and as currency.

In fact, a good case may be made for asserting the government's monopoly over all forms of money (see box).

Modernizing the Money Monopoly

There isn't much difference, for most people, between the paper notes in their wallets and the balances in their bank accounts, apart from the fiction that the balances are the liabilities of banks. Why not confront reality and make all short-term deposits explicitly the liability of the government? Already, a few (and mainly wealthy) individuals use "TreasuryDirect" accounts to buy treasury bills. If similar accounts became universal and all payments were made either by government-issued currency or through transfers between accounts held with the government, we wouldn't have the kind of financial contagion that swept through the economy after the Lehman collapse when banks stopped trusting each other and people fled from money market funds.[34]

Making all deposits of ready cash explicit liabilities of the government need not require the government make case-by-case credit decisions or create any additional politicization or concentration of lending. The government's monopoly over the issuance of currency after the Civil War did not lead to the nationalization of credit. Similarly, a government that assumed liability for deposits could pass them on to the banks that brought in the deposits under a formula that replicates current reserve and capital requirements.

Prohibiting banks from activities that cannot be easily regulated would allow the government to ensure the safety of the entire stock of the nation's ready cash without having to impose new insurance levies on banks or burden taxpayers with more bailouts. Bank regulators wouldn't have to monitor "emerging systemic risks," and the Fed could focus on its "macro," monetary responsibilities. No new agencies and no more regulators would be required. Less, would in fact, be more.

Depriving financial engineers of subsidized credit (and implicit counterparty guarantees) would alarm those who claim that its sophisticated financial system is a prime cause of U.S. prosperity. Although a modern economy does need the effective provision of financial basics, such as risk capital, credit, and insurance, claims that all the bells and whistles developed over the last couple of decades are a net plus are implausible. More likely, the real economy prospered in spite of the resources consumed by the expansion of finance. Highly profitable wizardry caused bankers to neglect traditional borrowers, especially small businesses. When the magic stopped working in 2008, banks couldn't lend to anyone, however creditworthy. If banking now shrinks back to the basics, so much the better for our long-run prosperity.

The scope for reorienting the academic study of finance is vast. The subject could be treated as a practical discipline, such as engineering or medicine, that produces useful, albeit often ad hoc, know-how, instead of an imposter science that "retreat[s] into purely formal or tautological analysis," as Milton Friedman might put it, producing no testable hypotheses and making outlandish assumptions. Financial economists might then begin to appreciate the difference between complex physical innovations, such as computers, and complex financial products: Computers are based on unchanging laws of nature, subjected to extensive testing and physically shielded from variations in the environment. Complex financial products, however, have to cope with an ever changing economy, can't be tested, and can't be put in a protective case.

Likewise, there is much to be said for rethinking securities laws that promote the breadth and liquidity of arm's-length markets but impair governance. Unfortunately, this rethinking is unlikely because in most businesses, the absence of insider oversight represents a hidden tax and a drag on performance that cannot be easily tied to wholesale failure. The misgovernance of financial firms is an exception, however; we could thus imagine support for tweaking the rules to address these problems without any basic reform of the securities laws. A simple fix might be to limit the leverage of firms not already subject to banking, insurance, or utilities rules for their borrowing. The major exchanges already delist companies whose shares fall below $1; why not delist companies who borrow (on or off their balance sheets) more than five times their equity capital?

Finally and Hopefully

On the surface, prospects for meaningful structural reform of banking do not appear promising. When the crisis struck in 2008, the establishment panicked. Just as the Nixon administration abandoned its conservative principles to impose wage and price controls to fight inflation, the specter of debt deflation stampeded the Bush administration into helter-skelter bailouts that reeked, whatever the reality, of cronyism. When small businesses get into trouble, lenders routinely ask the owners to invest every cent they have back into the enterprise—and sign personal guarantees. Putting bankers to such trouble wasn't part of the Troubled Assets Recovery Program. (The citizens of the Republic, according to the Fed, weren't even entitled to know to whom it lent $2 trillion. The Fed fought—and lost—a case demanding disclosure filed by Bloomberg News. As of this writing, the Fed's appeals against the decision continue.)

Instead of unraveling the tangle in banking that would help separate the good from the bad, and creating institutions whose books CEOs could honestly certify, politicians and regulators encouraged commercial banks to acquire failing investment banks. They subsidized J.P. Morgan's acquisition of Bear Stearns instead of allowing it to go bankrupt. They sought to bury Merrill Lynch's unknown liabilities into Bank of America's impenetrable balance sheets. And—in spite of their past failures with the likes of Citicorp—they midwifed the creation of more megabanks by turning Morgan Stanley and Goldman Sachs into bank holding companies.

The president hails the 2,300-page Dodd-Frank act as sweeping and historic. In fact, the enactment seems more like refurbishing regulators' deck chairs salvaged from the *Titanic*. Nearly four out of five Americans surveyed in a Bloomberg National Poll in July 2010 said they had little or no confidence that the legislation would prevent or significantly soften a future crisis.

Below the surface, however, prospects for meaningful structural reform are more promising. The multi-trillion-dollar bailouts engineered by the Treasury Department and the Federal Reserve were hailed by insiders as heroic measures that saved us from economic catastrophe.[35] The public, however, did not seem to regard handing over its money to bail out bankers as courageous. Fifty-nine percent of respondents in a February 2009 poll opposed the $700 billion bank bailout plan that had been proposed by the Bush administration and passed by Congress in the previous fall. Only 9 percent thought it had helped the economy. In the same poll, only 20 percent supported the Obama administration's $2.5 trillion plan to provide more assistance to banks.[36]

Ben Bernanke secured a second term as Federal Reserve chairman, but the Fed appears to have lost the public's confidence. In a July 2009 Gallup Poll, the Fed came in dead last in the public's approval of federal agencies. Just 30 percent of respondents thought it was doing a good or excellent job, whereas the usually much-maligned IRS got a 40 percent approval rating.

Under the circumstances, discrediting the establishment and its consensus is a good thing. Elected officials need not know much about finance, but they can't ignore voters. Recall that Congress enacted deposit insurance in 1933, in spite of opposition from the administration, influential lawmakers, and the banking establishment because the public was strongly in favor. Insiders and special interests may have excessive influence, but they don't have a permanent lock on government. The Standard Oil Company and Ma Bell were ultimately broken up, and the power of once fearsome railroad companies was destroyed.

The number of influential skeptics pressing for true structural reform may yet be small, but it is growing. John Reed, who as CEO of Citicorp lobbied to repeal Glass-Steagall, has become a convert to the cause of its reinstatement. "I would compartmentalize the industry for the same reason you compartmentalize ships," says Reed. "If you have a leak, the leak doesn't spread and sink the whole vessel.... We learn from our mistakes. When you're running a company you do what you think is right for the stockholders. Right now I'm looking at this as a citizen."[37] Senator Blanche Lincoln's amendment in the Senate's version of the 2010 financial reform bill could have forced banks to spin out their derivatives-trading businesses. Volcker has been relentless in making his case to bankers and policymakers. Mervyn King's proposals were rejected by the government of Britain, but the views of a sitting governor of the Bank of England cannot be ignored on either side of the Atlantic. Simon Johnson, John Kay, and Joseph Stiglitz have reached wide audiences through the popular press. Perhaps they are having some effect: In January 2010, the Obama administration changed course and embraced some of the Volcker proposals, although they were then watered down in the Dodd-Frank act. The act also diluted the Lincoln amendment restricting banks' derivatives activities.

We should not be discouraged by the lack of bold action so far. After the panic of 1907, it took six years, during which the Monetary Commission submitted thirty reports, before Congress passed the Federal Reserve Act. The Crash of 1929 led to new securities laws four years later. Deposit insurance was passed during the 1933 banking crisis, but the issue had been debated for more than half a century. Volcker engineered a tough monetary policy that quelled inflation when he was appointed chairman of the Fed in 1979—eight years after Nixon's ineffectual 1971 price controls. And Congress has been known to relegislate quickly, passing multiple banking acts in the 1860s, 1930s, and 1980s and two securities acts in 1933 and 1934. A weak first bill doesn't have to be the last word.

Reform deferred isn't reform denied. In fact, radical, ill-considered action is worse than cosmetic legislation. We need change. The public demands it. But first we need a serious, open debate about what kind of financial system will sustain real, inclusive dynamism that enriches the lives of all.

ACKNOWLEDGMENTS

Many of my intellectual debts are almost as long-standing as the financial problems I analyze in this book. Discussions with Carliss Baldwin, the late Peter Bernstein, Michael Jensen, Steve Kaplan, Andrei Shleifer, and Howard Stevenson that go back to the 1980s have influenced significantly my views of finance. Hundreds of lunches with Ned Phelps helped shape a Hayekian view of the economy, and Ned's creation, the Center on Capitalism and Society, provided a valuable forum for trying out many of the arguments made in this book. My ideas about innovation and about the epistemology of social studies have been derived from Dick Nelson to a degree that the notes in the manuscript do no justice to. An extended conversation with John Kay radically altered my understanding of Knightian uncertainty.

Coming to the here and now: Über-editor and economic historian Susan Lee transformed the manuscript through arthroscopic, painless cuts and deft rearrangements. Wish I could really write the way the book now reads. Richard Isomaki's copyediting added even more clarity and smoothness.

David Warsh provided first-rate writer's lodgings and an excellent sounding-board. Srikant Datar somehow made time—as he has always done—to provide feedback on chapters as I was writing them, practically every other week. Other scholars—from a variety of disciplines—who provided feedback included Bob Aliber, Ashish Arora, Ray Ball, Ben Esty, Jeffrey Friedman, Walter Friedman, Mark Granovetter, Glenn Hubbard, Arnold Kling, Colin Mayer, Enrico Perotti, Richard Posner, Walter Kuemmerle, Richard Robb, Michael Roberts, Michael Romero, R. D. Simek, Erik Sirri, Charles Stowe, Gus Stuart, Steven Teles, and Larry Weiss. Friends from business and government who provided data, real-world insights, and editorial help included Stephen Adams, Anders Barsk, Matthew Bishop, Yves De Balmann, Paul DeRosa, David Chaffetz, Don Chew, Gerardo Espinoza, Dick Floor, Don Gogel, Brad Golding, Jasmina Hasanhodzic, Ajit Jain, Jeff Kehoe, Walter Kirkland, Vikram Kuriyan, Mike Lawler, Raymond McConaghy, Lars Östling, Kenneth Pierce, Ylva Sovik, and Susan Webber.

Some of the ideas in this book crystallized through op-eds and essays written in 2008 and 2009 that were edited (or commissioned) by Howard Dickman, Elizabeth Eaves, Aaron Edlin, Jeffrey Friedman, Robert Pollock, Deborah Stead, Ciro Scotti, Joseph Stiglitz, and Tunku Varadarajan.

David Musson of Oxford University Press saw this book project through the approval process and then handed it over to Terry Vaughn, who became an enthusiastic supporter, as did Joe Jackson. My agent Andrew Stuart provided sensible counsel. Keith Faivre has been more patient and responsive in producing this book than an author has any right to expect.

The Kauffman Foundation provided a timely grant, and the Foundation's Robert Litan, Carl Schramm, and Robert Strom gave moral support—as they have for nearly ten years.

Bill Strong, one of the least known of the investment geniuses of our time, demonstrated to my great satisfaction and relief that exceptional talent shines brightest in difficult times. Whew!

Richard Zeckhauser invited me to visit the Mossavar-Rahmani Center at Harvard's Kennedy School to write this book, and the Center's Dan Crane, Scott Leland, Miranda Daniloff Mancusi, and Roger Porter made me feel right at home.

The always warm hospitality of my sister Gauri and her husband Michael Romero and of Iain and Johanna Cockburn provided much needed breaks. Lila, a plainspoken Cordelia who has long urged that I get a life, took me to a movie.

My heartfelt thanks to all of you.

Preface

1. This was at a conference organized by the Center on Capitalism and Society held at the Council on Foreign Relations in November 2007. See http://www.cfr.org/content/meetings/bhide_presentation.ppt

Introduction

1. Seib 2008.

2. The economist Bradford DeLong (2000) reports a ten-and-a-half-fold increase in real per capita GDP in the twentieth century.

3. See Robb (2009) for an insightful discussion of the bearing of Nietzsche's theories of "becoming" on economic choices.

4. In the preface of George Stigler's (1985) essay written on the occasion of the one hundredth anniversary of the birth of Knight.

5. Granovetter 1985.

6. Ibid., 484.

7. The landmark Copyright Act passed by the British Parliament in 1709 only covered printed books.

8. The saying is usually attributed to Balzac, but his actual words in *Le Père Goriot* were "Le secret des grandes fortunes sans cause apparente est un crime oublié, parce qu'il a été proprement fait" ("The secret of great wealth with no obvious source is some forgotten crime, forgotten because it was done neatly").

9. Baumol 2002.

10. Nordhaus 2005. Other studies reporting (or implying) large consumer surpluses include Mansfield et al. 1977, Bresnahan 1986, Trajtenberg 1989, Hausman 1997, and Baumol 2002.

11. Gjerstad and Smith 2009, 271.

12. Ibid., 277.

13. Ibid., 272.

14. Extensive bank holdings of subprime-based securities are documented by Acharya and Richardson (2009).

15. Gjerstad and Smith 2009, 287.

16. Ibid., 285.

17. Ibid., 280.

18. An SEC complaint filed in April 2010 alleged (among other things) that Goldman fraudulently concealed bets against a security that it sold to investors in 2007.

19. Gjerstad and Smith 2009, 280.

20. Ibid.

21. Lewis 2009.

22. Ibid.

23. Ibid.

24. Wikipedia entry on mortgage brokers (downloaded on August 1, 2009) and verified by email correspondence (August 3, 2009) with Wholesale Access. According to these emails, the numbers in 2006 were "roughly the same." The study has not been updated "due to lack of interest on the part of lenders," but Wholesale Access believes that "the number of brokerage firms is down to 20,000 and heading lower."

25. http://www.bloomberg.com/apps/news?pid=20601087&sid=aVuWc7w4pjhY&refer=home.

26. Duhigg 2008.

27. According to a report filed in 2006 by Fannie Mae's regulator, the Office of Federal Housing Enterprise Oversight, which accused Raines and some of his subordinates of manipulating earnings to collect performance bonuses (http://www.webcpa.com/news/22660-1.html). Earlier, in December 2006, Raines had accepted "early retirement" as the SEC was investigating accounting irregularities at Fannie Mae.

28. http://online.wsj.com/public/resources/documents/st_ceos_20081111.html.

29. There is some dispute about whether the fall on December 12, 1914, was larger. Larger declines may also have been recorded following periods of market closure.

30. Cited in a *New York Times* editorial, "Group of 7, Meet the Group of 33," December 26, 1987, sec. 1, p. 22, and posted at http://www.nytimes.com/1987/12/26/opinion/group-of-7-meet-the-group-of-33.html.

31. http://www.pbs.org/now/politics/wallstreet.html.

32. http://www.sec.gov/news/press/2003-56.htm.

33. Blogpost at http://www.insurereinsure.com/BlogHome.aspx?entry=804. The full SEC report on rating agencies is posted at http://www.insurereinsure.com/files/upload/sec_report.pdf. The three rating

agencies have also been investigated by the Connecticut's attorney general and sued by CalPERS, the biggest U.S. pension fund. CalPERS says it might lose more than $1 billion on securities that had been given top ratings (see http://www.creditwritedowns.com/2009/07/calpers-sues-ratings-agencies-over-sivs.html).

34. See Richard Robb's presentation at the fourth Annual Conference of the Center on Capitalism and Society (2007).

35. Adler 2009.

Chapter 1

1. Jensen and Meckling (1990) argue that "alienability"—the right to sell or transfer rights and to capture the proceeds—is "the institutional device through which markets co-locate knowledge with decision rights and control decision makers." I use "property rights" as a colloquial representation for this argument.

2. The advantages of competing decentralized innovations have been extensively discussed by Rosenberg and Birdzell (1986) and Nelson (1987) and summarized by Mokyr (1990).

3. Although this is how Israel Kirzner has characterized the entrepreneurial function.

4. According to Simon (1992): "In everyday speech we use the word intuition to describe a problem-solving or question-answering performance that is speedy and for which the expert is unable to describe in detail the reasoning or other process that has produced the answer. The situation has produced a cue; this cue has given the expert access to information stored in memory, and the information provides the answer. Intuition is nothing more and nothing less than recognition" (p. 155).

5. Downloaded from http://www.danbricklin.com/history/saiidea.htm on August 20, 2009, and reproduced by permission. For more about the early development of the spreadsheet, see chapter 12 of Bricklin's book *Bricklin on Technology* (2009).

6. Although the innovator's expertise and track record do provide advantages.

7. See Bhidé 2008b, chap. 11.

8. Khurana 2008, 271.

9. Datar, Garvin, and Cullen 2010.

10. Ibid.

11. Moreover, it is not enough to identify the occupations whose wages are more sensitive to years of work experience. To make a legitimate claim to "statistical significance at the 95 percent level" for an estimate, the researcher must have precisely the right equation for how wages vary with work experience for every occupation.

12. See Bhidé 2008b, chap. 6, for a complete discussion of the material in this box.

13. See for example, Richard Nelson 2003 and 2008

14. Jana 2009, 44.

15. Kindleberger 1996, 10.

Chapter 2

1. Chandler 1977.
2. Ibid.
3. Chandler and Salsbury 1971.
4. According to the economist Oliver Williamson (1975), vertical integration mitigates problems of opportunistic behavior by placing specialized upstream and downstream units under common ownership.
5. Chandler 1962.
6. Ibid.
7. Ibid.
8. Baumol 1993, 117. Baumol (282) goes on to cite the example of Eastman Kodak, which used computers to generate "pseudo photographs" with variation in contrasts, brightness, balance of colors, and so on. Kodak then polled panels of consumers and professional photographers to decide "which of the computer generated pseudo photographs promise to be the most saleable, and the company laboratories are assigned the task of inventing a film that will yield the desired results" (Baumol 1993, 282).
9. Moore 1996, 169.
10. Rodgers, Taylor, and Foreman 1993, 105.
11. Rodgers 1990, 88–89.
12. Kelley (with Jonathan Littman) 2005.
13. Kalberg 1980.
14. Weber 1947.
15. See Bhidé 2000, 2006, 2008b.

Chapter 3

1. Friedman and Friedman 1980, 14–15.
2. Ibid., 13.
3. See Bhidé 2008b, chap. 2, for a detailed discussion of the interactive nature of innovation.
4. Bhidé 2000.
5. See Friedman's 2004 book, *Birth of the American Salesman*.
6. Tedlow 2001, 232.
7. As discussed in Bhidé 2008b, chap. 4, "Offshoring."
8. McCraw and Tedlow 1997, 288.
9. Sloan 1963.
10. A reader comments: "The mission statement, in its entirety, of my local Toyota dealer, which delivers awesome service: 'Building relationships.'"
11. Friedman and Friedman 1980, 13.
12. This last quote is from the *Free to Choose* TV series that preceded the book of the same name. The transcript was downloaded on August 23, 2009, from http://economics.about.com/b/2007/11/22/milton-friedman-on-trade-the-story-of-the-pencil.htm; emphasis added.
13. In 2004 Motorola had spun out its microprocessor business into a new company, Freescale.

14. There is an obvious connection between the propositions in the two chapters: Bosses cannot make good judgments about what to delegate to their subordinates without extensive dialogue.

Chapter 4

1. For a sample loan application, see MacPhee 1984, 43–54.
2. For the contents of a typical term sheet, see Deloitte, Haskins & Sells 1988, 47–50.

Part II

1. Fama and Jensen 1983, 301.

Chapter 5

1. Krugman 2009.
2. Cochrane 2009.
3. Though I happen to be as skeptical as Cochrane about Krugman's prescriptions for fiscal policy.
4. Bernstein 1996, 1.
5. Ibid., 225–27.
6. Keynes 1936, 149–50
7. Knight 1921, 224–25 ff.
8. Ibid., part III, chap. 7, para. 37.
9. Ibid., para. 39.
10. Ibid., para. 42.
11. Ibid., para. 42.
12. Ibid., para. 47.
13. Friedman 1976, 282. Implicitly, the modern view seems to deny the existence of any true one-offs—every situation is drawn from a pot of many other similar situations. The main difference between subjective and objective probabilities lies in whether a decision maker has complete information about the parameters of the distribution of the items in the pot or whether some guesswork is necessary. Or as Bewley (2002) put it, from the point of view of modern "Bayesian" theory, "Knight's distinction has no interesting consequences" because "decision makers act so as to maximize the expected value of their gain, no matter whether the fluctuations faced are risky or uncertain."
14. LeRoy and Singell 1987.
15. Assuming the individual is risk-neutral.
16. http://blog.bookies.com/specials/230/51-that-osama-bin-laden-is-captured-and-other-2009-specials.html.
17. Kay 2009.
18. Samuelson 1962, 18.
19. Morgan 2003, 277, cited in MacKenzie 2006, 7.
20. Morgan 2003, 279, cited in MacKenzie 2006, 7.
21. Grubel and Boland 1986, 425, cited in MacKenzie 2006, 7.
22. Perforce, tractable equations are also parsimonious—even the most brilliant mathematicians cannot solve equations with a large number

of variables. But I'm not convinced that parsimony is as highly valued for its own sake as it is claimed to be.

23. But not impossible. See, for example, Brandenburger and Stuart 2007, Stuart 2007, Bewley 2002 and 1987, and Gilboa and Schmeidler 1995. According to Stuart (personal communication), "There are decision theorists and economists who work with Knightian uncertainty, but they tend not to be widely read, especially by financial economists and macroeconomists. The real issue with economics is not that the ideas are not there, it is that the wrong ideas often get picked up."

24. Because after-the-fact outcomes constitute a sample that may be different from the true population.

25. Citing prior work by John Neville Keynes.

26. If anything, the experimental economic evidence contradicts the hypothesis.

27. It is hard to imagine how in any concrete situation, the Nash equilibrium precondition that everyone knows everyone else's strategy could be even approximately satisfied.

28. A reader suggested that I'm being a little unfair to Akerlof: The value of the lemons model, he writes, is "to impel a search for what has been left out," namely reputational capital, even though the model "obviously does not conform to the facts." Quite apart from the fact that this justification does not fit Milton Friedman's argument for unrealistic assumptions, I disagree. The world was well aware of the problem of information asymmetry and the importance of reputation before Akerlof's model. An elegant proof that gravity should cause birds to fall from the sky provides no useful insight about the mechanism through which they do take wing. People did study birds to figure out how they overcame the force that pulls other creatures back to earth long before Newton figured out the laws of gravity. The value of Newton's laws in designing airplanes lies in helping us calculate the size of the gravitational forces that have to be overcome, not in proving that without a counteracting force, planes couldn't fly. Akerlof's model does nothing of the sort.

29. Knight 1921, part III, chap. 8, para. 8.

Chapter 6

1. Summers 1985, 633–34.
2. MacKenzie 2006, 38.
3. Ibid., 39.
4. Simon 1996, 144, cited in MacKenzie 2006, 39.
5. Merton H. Miller, from his testimony in Glendale Federal Bank's lawsuit against the U.S. government, December 1997, downloaded on October 6, 2009, from http://pages.stern.nyu.edu/~adamodar/New_Home_Page/articles/MM40yearslater.htm. The usual reaction to the story, according to Miller, was, "And you mean to say they gave you a [Nobel] prize for that?"
6. MacKenzie 2006, 42.
7. Modigliani and Miller 1958, 296.

8. MacKenzie 2006, 245, writes that the extent to which the work of Modigliani and Miller "informed market practice is unclear."

9. Durand 1952, 230–31, cited in MacKenzie 2006, 43.

10. The result, incidentally, evokes personal memories of a close brush with bankruptcy from trying to short an obviously overheated lumber market in 1993.

11. Keynes 1936, 156.

12. Akst 2000.

13. Making the judgment that Internet stocks were overvalued wasn't entirely unrewarding, however. In 1996 I had, also by chance, invested in a VC fund. By 1999 and through most of 2000, the start-ups the fund had invested in started going public and the fund made numerous distributions of newly issued stocks. The prospectuses sent with the distributions made for eye-opening reading: How could these companies, I wondered, possibly be going public? My wonderment caused me to sell the stocks as quickly as I could. For a while this seemed like a bad move as prices of the newly issued stocks shot up. But within a couple of years they fell to virtually nothing.

14. Lowenstein 1995, 312.

15. The thought experiment was offered by Warren Buffett in response to Michael Jensen's observation: "If I survey a field of untalented analysts all of whom are doing nothing but flipping coins, I expect to see some who have tossed two heads in a row and even some who have tossed ten heads in a row" (Lowenstein 1995, 317).

16. See Grossman and Stiglitz 1980.

17. Fox 2009, 134.

18. Cootner 1964, 337, cited in Fox 2009, 134.

19. MacKenzie 2006, 49.

20. Bernstein 1996, 252–53.

21. Ibid., 257.

22. Ibid.

23. Welles 1971, 25, cited in MacKenzie 2006, 51.

24. Fox 2009, 58.

25. Bernstein 1996, 260.

26. Ibid.

27. On March 13, 2009, the S&P closed at price of 756.55. On September 12, 2008, the day before the Lehman bankruptcy, it had closed at 1251.7, and on March 14, 2008, at 1288.14.

28. The standard deviation of daily price changes over the prior sixty days was 54 percent between mid-September 2008 and mid-March 2009, compared to 21 percent from mid-March 2008 to mid-September 2008.

29. The standard deviation of daily price changes for 118 trading days after mid-March (i.e., through the end of August 2009) was 26.31 percent, whereas in the prior 118 days it was 57.87 percent.

30. Fans of modern portfolio theory will claim that investors should form subjective estimates rather than use historical data. But the empirical evidence suggests that subjective estimates are nonetheless "anchored" by

or pulled toward historical data. For instance, we can infer the market's subjective estimate of S&P volatility from the prices of S&P 500 options. This "implied volatility" shows pretty much the same pattern as "historic" volatility. On March 13, 2009, the implied volatility of S&P 500 options was 38.4 percent, compared to 22.4 percent on September 12, 2008. This 70 percent hike is indeed better than the doubling of historic volatility but nonetheless is a terrible predictor of what actually happened after March 2009, when actual volatility *fell* by half.

31. I am not claiming that investors shouldn't make thoughtful choices, rather that mechanistic asset allocation is a bad idea. See Bhidé 1994b.

32. Paul DeRosa, personal email communication.

33. Baumol 1966, 98–99, cited in MacKenzie 2006, 52.

34. Bashe et al. 1986, 446–48, cited in MacKenzie 2006, 52.

35. MacKenzie 2006, chap. 2, and Fox 2009, 55.

36. Markowitz 1959, 100.

37. Fox 2009, 86.

38. Sharpe 1995, 217–18, cited in MacKenzie 2006, 53.

39. Lindbeck 1990.

40. Sharpe 1964, 435.

41. Fox 2009, 86.

42. Black, Jensen, and Scholes 1972.

43. Fama and French 1992, 440.

44. MacKenzie 2006, 92.

45. Ibid., 93.

46. Friedman 1953, 11.

47. MacKenzie 2006, 66.

48. Mehrling 2005, 108.

49. Samuelson 1974, 17–18.

Chapter 7

1. Bernstein 1996, 304.

2. MacKenzie 2005, 40–41.

3. Ibid., 36.

4. Ibid., 37.

5. Fox 2009, 148.

6. MacKenzie 2005, 5.

7. MacKenzie 2006, 139.

8. Ibid., 141.

9. Ibid., 142.

10. To calculate the "market" price of the option, I used the implied volatility numbers downloaded from Bloomberg and plugged them into the Black Scholes Merton formula.

11. Fox 2009, 146.

12. Rubinstein 1994, 772.

13. Ross 1987, 332.

14. MacKenzie 2005, 27.

15. Ibid., 26.
16. MacKenzie 2006, 163.
17. Ibid.
18. Black 1975, 5, cited in MacKenzie 2006, 160.
19. Black 1975, cited in MacKenzie 2006, 160.
20. MacKenzie 2006, 158.
21. Fox 2009, 147.
22. Miller 1999, cited in Fox 2009, 138.
23. Mason et al. 1995, 786, cited in MacKenzie 2006, 182.
24. Voorhees 1988, 57.
25. Melamed and Tamarkin 1996, 362–63, cited in MacKenzie 2006, 3.
26. This paragraph summarizes a more extensive discussion in MacKenzie 2006, chap. 3.
27. Cootner 1977, 553–54, cited in MacKenzie 2006, 73.
28. See Arrow 1964.
29. Colander et al. 2009, 251.
30. Ross 1976, 76.
31. MacKenzie 2006, 147.
32. Ibid., 148.
33. Ibid., 149.
34. Ibid., 158.

Chapter 8

1. SEC 1984, 1.
2. *Economist*, March 30, 1991, 79.
3. See Jensen's (1989) discussion of "active" investing.
4. Seligman 1982, 1.
5. SEC 1984, 7.
6. Meyer 1934, 11.
7. Phillips and Zecher 1981.
8. SEC 1984, 7.
9. Hearings before the Committee on Interstate and Foreign Commerce 1944, 4.
10. Meyer 1934, 11.
11. As described in Section 2 of the 1934 act.
12. Meyer 1934, 19–20.
13. Phillips and Zecher 1981.
14. Hearings before the Committee on Interstate and Foreign Commerce 1944, 12–13.
15. Ibid., 14–15.
16. Ibid., 13, 149–59.
17. Purcell, Foster, and Hill 1946.
18. Ibid., 11–12.
19. SEC 1984, 46.
20. Phillips and Zecher 1981, 12.
21. Ibid., 11.
22. See Reilly 1985.

23. Demsetz 1968, 50.

24. See Demsetz 1968 on the relationship between liquidity and the number of stockholders. Garbade (1982) and Stoll (1985) provide evidence that bid-asked spreads for stocks are inversely related to the number of stockholders.

25. Berle and Means 1932.

26. Clark 1985, 57.

27. Roe 1990, 8.

28. Ibid., 24.

29. Ibid., 26.

30. Pecora Report 1934, 393, cited in Roe 1990, 12.

31. Roe 1990, 13.

32. Some sections of the 1940 act do, however, discourage trading by taxing excessive short-term gains.

33. Schwimmer and Malca 1976, 3.

34. Blume, Siegel, and Rottenberg 1993, 107.

35. Mahar 1991, 13–14.

36. Blume, Siegel, and Rottenberg 1993, 107.

37. *Wall Street Journal,* June 28, 1990, C1.

38. Blume, Siegel, and Rottenberg 1993, 107.

39. Ibid.

40. Seligman 1982, 351–52.

41. Securities Industry Association 1990, 21–23.

42. Roe 1990, 15.

43. Vawater, in Tuttle and Maginn 1983.

44. Blume, Siegel, and Rottenberg 1993, 133.

45. Ibid., 134.

46. Ibid., 135–36.

47. Ibid., 136.

48. Ibid., 139.

49. Report of the United States Presidential Task Force on Market Mechanisms 1988, II-15.

50. Blume, Siegel, and Rottenberg 1993, 141.

51. Baskin 1988, 222.

52. Ibid., 216.

53. Vinzant 1999.

54. Bertoneche 1984.

55. Grundfest 1990, 105.

56. Breeden 1993, 77.

57. Chandler and Salisbury 1971, 573, 580.

58. Gorman and Sahlman 1989.

59. Buffett 1987, 83.

60. Ibid., 52.

61. As Blau (1964) points out, we expect our approval to be valued by those with whom we have built and sustained a relationship.

62. Baskin 1988, 213.

63. Chandler 1990a

64. Jensen 1993.

65. Rappaport 1990.
66. Bhidé 1989.

Chapter 9

1. See Fama and Jensen 1983.
2. Grant 1992, 50.
3. Ibid., 65.
4. Klebaner 1974, 11.
5. Jones 1938b, 337. The legislation eliminating double liability was enacted two years earlier, in 1935. Double liability for state-chartered banks continued in some states for a little longer. See Esty 1998.
6. Jones 1938b, 337.
7. Fama and French 2001, 2.
8. Weinberg 2009.
9. Robards 1969, 70.
10. *International Directory of Company Histories* 1990, 445.
11. Robards 1969, 1.
12. Blume, Siegel, and Rottenberg 1993, 110–11.
13. Robards 1969.
14. Ibid.
15. Bloomberg and Winkler 1997, 3.
16. Hoffman 1984, 40–41.
17. Bloomberg and Winkler 1997.
18. Auletta 1985.
19. Hoffman 1984, 36.
20. Ibid., 37.
21. Chernow 1990, 695.
22. Downloaded on November 10, 2009, from http://investing.businessweek.com/research/stocks/ownership/ownership.asp?ric=MS.
23. Judge Medina's judgment, cited in Hoffman 1984.
24. Sherman 1988.
25. McLean and Serwer 1998.
26. Spiro 1999.
27. Bebchuk, Cohen, and Spamann 2010.
28. Weinberg 2009.
29. Gapper 2009.
30. Byrne 1998.
31. Nasr and Frantz 1994, D1.
32. Hansell 1997.
33. "A Monoline Meltdown?" *Economist,* July 26, 2007.
34. Boyd 2008.
35. Hoffman 1984, 48.
36. Email communication, November 10, 2009.
37. Loomis 2009.
38. Reuters report, downloaded on November 9, 2009, from http://www.reuters.com/article/ousiv/idUSN1712706420090317.

Chapter 10

1. Klebaner 1974, 2.
2. They would, for instance, issue "notes" backed by their gold inventory. The borrower who received the notes could use them as payment for goods and services.
3. Vietor and Davidon 1985.
4. Klebaner 1974, 17.
5. Ibid., 21–22.
6. Ibid., 23.
7. Parsons 1958, 340, cited in Klebaner 1974, 48.
8. Klebaner 1974, 20.
9. Ibid., 12.
10. Ibid., 49.
11. Ibid., 48.
12. Ibid., 49.
13. Merritt 1900, 137, cited in Klebaner 1974, 20.
14. Klebaner 1974, 9.
15. Ibid., 26.
16. Hammond 1957, 626, cited in Dwyer 1996, 2.
17. Dwyer 1996, 16.
18. Schwartz 1993, 362.
19. Klebaner 1974, 42.
20. Ibid., 41–42.
21. Ibid., 42.
22. Virginia was the first, in 1837, to require banks to hold specie reserves in proportion to their note liabilities, and by 1861 a dozen states had established similar rules.
23. Golembe 1960, 190.
24. FDIC 1984, 14.
25. The material in the text box summarizes the accounts of Carter Golembe, a financial economist at Federal Deposit Insurance Corporation, published in 1955 and 1960.
26. Golembe 1960, 183.
27. Golembe 1955, 115.
28. Ibid.
29. Ibid., 116.
30. Klebaner 1974, 36.
31. Ibid., 37.
32. Litan 1987, 21.
33. Klebaner 1974, 20.
34. Ibid., 54.
35. Litan 1987, 21.
36. Klebaner 1974, 57. Bank deposits exclude those placed by other banks and by the federal government.
37. Litan 1987, 21.
38. Klebaner 1974, 57.
39. Litan 1987, 21.

40. Klebaner 1974, 58.

41. Ibid., 13–14.

42. Ibid., 59.

43. Ibid., 60.

44. Ibid., 98.

45. As the 1898 report of the Monetary Commission of the Indianapolis Convention of Boards of Trade observed (ibid., 97).

46. Klebaner 1974, 88.

47. Gorton 2009, 16.

48. Klebaner 1974, 66.

49. Ibid., 68.

50. Ibid., 89.

51. Andrew 1908, 497, cited in Klebaner 1974, 91.

52. Federal Reserve Bank of Minneapolis, "Born of a Panic: Forming the Fed System," published August 1988, downloaded on January 7, 2010, from http://www.minneapolisfed.org/publications_papers/pub_display.cfm?id=3816.

53. Comptroller of the Currency, Annual Report 1907, 79, cited in Klebaner 1974, 91–92.

54. Klebaner 1974, 104.

55. Ibid., 105.

56. Federal Reserve Bank of Minneapolis 1998.

57. Klebaner 1974, 96–97.

58. Ibid., 95.

59. FDIC 1984, 112.

60. Klebaner 1974, 104.

61. McCraw 1997, 330.

Chapter 11

1. Miller 1998, 9.

2. Brandeis 1914, 26.

3. Klebaner 1974, 110. Klebaner also reports that after 1921, as their profits rebounded with the economy, businesses relied on retained earnings. They were also able reduce their needs for working capital by taking advantage of improved transportation and inventory control.

4. Litan 1987, 14.

5. Klebaner 1974, 35.

6. Ibid., 75.

7. Ibid., 105.

8. Jacoby and Saulnier 1942, 26.

9. If a loan had, say, fifteen days to run until it was due for repayment, the Fed would as a stopgap measure lend the bank cash for fifteen days till the loan was repaid. But if a bank's loans weren't due for repayment for, say, another three years, the Fed's role in making sure that it satisfied depositors' demands for cash would require it to provide long–term, rather than emergency, stopgap, assistance.

10. Chandler 1990b, 1.

11. Ibid., 2.

12. Chandler 1962, 118.

13. Banks had small, not merely flighty, deposit bases; they were also prevented by law from allowing loans to a single borrower to exceed 10 percent of their total loan portfolio.

14. Although more than 6,000 new banks were started in the 1920s, the total number of banks fell by 6,600. The decline was partly due to bank failures and mergers—sometimes in order to avoid failures. The pace of acquisitions had picked up: In the first decade of the twentieth century about sixty to seventy-five banks were acquired each year. The annual rate doubled from 1910 to 1918, and steadily increased thereafter: 180 per year for 1919–20; 330 per year for 1921–25, and 550 per year for 1926–1930 (Klebaner 1974, 125).

15. Ibid.

16. In the late 1920s holding companies, or "group banking," emerged as a device to link banks, especially in states that did not allow or limited branching. The stock market boom helped assemble the holding companies, and most of the holding companies that would be important for the next four decades were organized at this time. But "linking" through a holding company did not create organizations that could provide unified credit or other banking services to large industrial companies.

17. Klebaner 1974, 112.

18. Ibid.

19. Ibid.

20. Calder 1999, 19.

21. Ibid., 17.

22. Klebaner 1974, 115.

23. Calder 1999, 24.

24. Ibid., 26.

25. Ibid., 19.

26. Ibid., 27.

27. Ibid., 20.

28. Ibid., 19.

29. Ibid.

30. Grant 1992, 85.

31. Calder 1999, 20.

32. Klebaner 1974, 79.

33. Ibid., 115.

34. Ibid., 113.

35. Ibid., 119.

36. More than $1 billion of foreign securities were issued on Wall Street each year from 1924 through 1928. By 1929 foreign securities accounted for 7.7 percent of the investments of national banks, up from 2.3 percent in 1913 (ibid., 120).

37. Ibid.

38. Litan 1987, 23.

39. Ibid.

40. Klebaner 1974, 121.

41. Litan 1987, 17.

42. Ibid.

43. Ibid., 18.

44. Ibid., 22.

45. Such securities, which accounted for just 1 percent of national bank assets in the 1860s, grew to 4 percent by 1890, 8 percent by 1903, and 9 percent by 1913 (Klebaner 1974, 81).

46. Ibid.

47. Ibid., 80.

48. Ibid.

49. Ibid.

50. Although that proportion was down from the 1880s and 1990s, when almost half of the loans of New York City banks were call loans (ibid., 79).

51. Ibid., 117.

52. Ibid., 82.

53. Ibid.

54. Quoted by Brandeis 1914, 1.

55. Quoted by Brandeis 1914, 2.

56. Dowrie 1930, 24, cited in Klebaner 1974, 120.

57. FDIC 1984, 33.

58. Klebaner 1974, 129.

59. FDIC 1984, 15.

60. Klebaner 1974, 68.

61. FDIC 1984, 24.

62. Warburton 1959, 47.

63. Ibid., 48.

64. FDIC 1984, 28.

65. Klebaner 1974, 129.

66. Rosenberg 1976, 72–73.

67. de Grazia 2006, 10.

68. Klebaner 1974, 112.

Chapter 12

1. In 2007 Bernanke testified that "the impact…of the problems in the subprime market seems likely to be contained." Testimony before the Joint Economic Committee, U.S. Congress, March 28, 2007, downloaded on September 25, 2009, from http://www.federalreserve.gov/newsevents/testimony/bernanke20070328a.htm.

2. Downloaded on October 29, 2009 from http://blogs.wsj.com/marketbeat/2009/10/28/financial-historian-on-29-great-crash-or-break-in-the-market/.

3. Jones 1938b, 336.

4. FDIC 1984, 36.

5. Ibid., 35.

6. Ibid., 33.

7. Ibid.

8. Ibid.

9. Ibid., 35.

10. Ibid., 36.

11. Ibid.

12. Ibid., 37.

13. Ibid.

14. Ibid., 38–39.

15. Ibid., 39.

16. Ibid., 40.

17. Golembe 1960, 197.

18. Calomiris 2000, 188.

19. FDIC 1984, 41.

20. Calomiris 2000, 193.

21. Klebaner 1974, 137.

22. Ibid.

23. Golembe 1960, 197.

24. Calomiris (2000, chap. 3) provides a detailed account.

25. Golembe 1960, 181.

26. Calomiris 2000, 194.

27. "Deposit Insurance," *Business Week*, April 12, 1933, 3, quoted in FDIC 1984, 41.

28. FDIC 1984, 41.

29. The 1933 act had required that all FDIC-insured banks become members of the Fed, but this requirement was later removed (ibid., 51).

30. Ibid., 112–13.

31. Jones 1938a, 700.

32. Ibid.

33. Ibid., 701.

34. Ibid.

35. Ibid., 701–2.

36. Ibid., 703.

37. Ibid., 704–705.

38. Litan 1987, 27.

39. Klebaner 1974, 140.

40. Litan 1987, 28.

41. Klebaner 1974, 143.

42. Ibid., 152.

43. Regulation T of 1934 had set limits just for margin loans made by broker dealers, which could potentially be circumvented by borrowing from banks.

44. Klebaner 1974, 65.

45. Ibid., 138.

46. Ibid., 138–39.

47. FDIC 1984, 5.

48. Ibid., 53.

49. Klebaner 1974, 141.

50. Ibid., 157–58.

51. Of the 214, 169 withdrew after six months.

52. Some state laws also prevented mutual banks from signing up with the FDIC.

53. FDIC 1984, 51–52.

54. Ibid., 49.

55. Ibid., 50.

56. Ibid., 49.

57. Ibid., 5.

58. Ibid.

59. U.S. government bonds had reached a World War I peak in mid-1919, accounting for 18.5 percent of all bank assets. In 1936, they accounted for 27.6 percent of bank assets before falling a bit to 25.6 percent by the end of the decade (Klebaner 1974, 153).

60. Ibid., 146.

61. Jacoby and Saulnier 1942, 25.

62. Ibid., 23.

63. Ibid., 26.

64. Ibid., 139.

65. Klebaner 1974, 148.

66. Ibid., 151.

67. Ibid. In the midst of the Great Depression, the Bank of America started blanketing San Francisco with billboards and newspaper and radio ads offering auto loans.

68. By the eve of World War II the unit banks' share of total banking deposits did fall to slightly less than half, however.

69. Klebaner 1974, 158–59.

70. Cited in ibid., 159.

71. U.S. Department of Treasury, "History of the U.S. Tax System," downloaded on December 2, 2009, from http://www.treas.gov/education/fact-sheets/taxes/ustax.shtml.

72. FDIC 1984, 6.

73. Klebaner 1974, 163.

74. Ibid.

75. FDIC 1984, 6.

76. Ibid.

77. Ibid.

78. Ibid., 7.

79. Ibid.

80. Klebaner 1974, 188.

81. Ibid., 169. Klebaner also reports that term loans became the largest asset category on the books of New York City banks in the mid-1960s and by the end of that decade accounted for 68 percent of their business loans.

82. FDIC 1984, 6.

83. Klebaner 1974, 188.

84. Calder 1999, 9.

85. Klebaner 1974, 171.

86. Ibid., 151.

87. Ibid., 172.

88. Ibid., 170–71.

89. Ibid., 181.

90. The initial impact of the 1956 law was limited: In about ten years following its enactment, only about 3 percent of all banks, containing about 8 percent of total deposits, were controlled by bank holding companies. After the holding company law was amended, they did become more prominent. By the end of 1972, 10.5 percent of banks and 31.4 percent of all deposits were in holding companies (ibid., 182).

91. Ibid., 184.

92. Ibid., 185.

93. Ibid., 178.

94. Litan 1987, 35.

95. Ibid., 32.

Chapter 13

1. FDIC 1984, 7.

2. From the point of view of the hamburger maker at least.

3. Litan 1987, fig. 2.3, p. 36.

4. FDIC 1997, 3.

5. Ibid., 19.

6. These were the Depository Institutions Deregulation and Monetary Control Act of 1980 (DIDMCA); the Garn–St. Germain Depository Institutions Act of 1982 (Garn–St. Germain); the Competitive Equality Banking Act of 1987 (CEBA); the Financial Institutions Reform, Recovery, and Enforcement Act of 1989 (FIRREA); and the Federal Deposit Insurance Corporation Improvement Act of 1991 (FDICIA). Source: FDIC 1997.

7. Ibid., 87.

8. Berger, Kashyap, and Scalise 1995, 61.

9. FDIC 1997, 93.

10. Ibid., 88.

11. Kaufman and Mote 1990, 60.

12. Berger, Kashyap, and Scalise 1995, 60.

13. The accord also distinguished between different kinds of capital: for instance, Tier 1 capital included common equity and some preferred stock, and Tier 2 capital included subordinated debt and some loan loss reserves. Capital requirements were set in terms of both tiers.

14. As long as the credit lines provided by the sponsoring banks to sustain their SIVs and OBSEs were limited to a year (Friedman 2009, 145).

15. Acharya and Schnabl 2009, table 2. See also Friedman 2009 and Jablecki and Machaj 2009.

16. Berger, Kashyap, and Scalise 1995.

17. Stock analysts covering banks also placed "a premium on noninterest income," as one of them told me. "The higher the proportion of noninterest income, the higher the value assigned to the institution."

18. Berger, Kashyap, and Scalise 1995, 68.

19. Gorton 2009, 9.

20. Importantly, passage of the Commodity Futures Modernization Act of 2000 specifically barred the CFTC from regulating credit-default swaps.

21. Loomis 2009.

22. Samolyk 2004, 54.

23. As Rajan 2006 emphasized.

24. Talk given by Mary J. Rudie at the New York Chapter/AMA Sixteenth Annual New Products Conference at the Grand Hyatt Hotel, June 13, 1984.

25. Equilar, James F. Reda & Associates estimates for the *New York Times* downloaded on April 18, 2010, from http://www.nytimes.com/2010/04/18/weekinreview/18dash.html.

26. White 2009, 391–92.

27. Technically the requirement was securities in the top two categories used by the rating agency. The unusual "safety" requirement arose from the desire of money market mutual funds to offer investors steady (one "buck") valuations rather than a value that would fluctuate with market prices.

28. SEC Office of Inspector General Report of Investigation, Case No. OIG-509, Executive Summary, p. 6.

Chapter 14

1. The directors listed in AIG's 2005 annual report include Frank Zarb, former chairman of National Securities Dealers, Pei-yuan Chia, retired vice chairman of Citicorp, William Cohen, former U.S. senator and secretary of defense, Martin Feldstein, Harvard economics professor and former chairman of the President's Council of Economic Advisors, Carla Hills, former U.S. trade representative, Richard Holbrooke, former U.S. ambassador to the UN, Michael Sutton, former chief accountant of the SEC, and Robert Willumstad, former president of Citigroup.

2. U.S. Treasury 2009, 2. Downloaded from http://www.financialstability.gov/docs/regs/FinalReport_web.pdf.

3. Downloaded on April 21, 2010 from http://www.financialstability.gov/docs/regs/FinalReport_web.pdf.

4. "How could our CEO possibly certify Citicorp's accounts?" complained one of his lieutenants, shortly after the Sarbanes-Oxley Act requiring such certification had been passed. "They are just too complicated." Perhaps, I suggested, Citicorp should be split up into simpler units. Of course not! A flat world needed global financial institutions. If U.S. regulators didn't back off, they'd all flee to London. Outsiders like me just didn't get it (Bhidé 2008a).

5. Melamed and Tamarkin 1996, 295, cited in MacKenzie 2006, 173.

6. MacKenzie 2006, 173.

7. Downloaded on December 20, 2009, from http://www.fdic.gov/bank/statistical/stats/2009mar/fdic.html.

8. Downloaded on December 20, 2009, from http://www2.fdic.gov/hsob/hsobRpt.asp.

9. As of this writing a dispute has arisen about a popular weed killer, atrazine, that for has been used for decades to protect crops, golf courses, and lawns. But atrazine often washes into water supplies, and new research suggests it may be dangerous at lower concentrations than had been previously believed. See http://www.nytimes.com/2009/08/23/us/23water.html?_r=1&hp.

10. Bryan 1987, 45.

11. Ibid., 49.

12. Ibid., 50.

13. Rajan 2006, 321.

14. Remarks by Donald Kohn posted at http://www.federalreserve.gov/boarddocs/speeches/2005/20050827/default.htm.

15. Downloaded on December 23, 2009, from http://www.federalreserve.gov/newsevents/speech/Bernanke20060612a.htm.

16. Downloaded on December 20, 2009, from http://www.federalreserve.gov/newsevents/speech/bernanke20090417a.htm.

17. According to NYU finance professor Thomas Philippon, the "value added" of finance was 2.3 percent of the economy just after World War II. By 1997 it was 4.4 percent, and by 2006 it had hit 8.1 percent. From an article posted at http://online.wsj.com/article/SB125322372695620969.html.

18. Paul Volcker, interview by Alan Murray published in the *Wall Street Journal* on December 14, 2009. Downloaded from http://online.wsj.com/article/SB10001424052748704825504574586330960597134.html.

19. Rajan 2006, 319–20.

20. Ibid., 321.

21. Ibid.

22. Visits also produce more accurate information. In my last research project (on VC-backed businesses) I found huge differences between the numbers published by Dun and Bradstreet and those provided by my interviewees.

23. Servicing companies usually are responsible for dealing with delinquent mortgages that have been securitized. Tomasz, Seru, and Vig (2009) find that loans that continue to be held by banks are foreclosed at significantly lower rates than are securitized loans, possibly because servicing companies are under greater pressure to foreclose.

24. http://www.bloomberg.com/apps/news?pid=20602007&sid=a0W1VTiv9q2A#.

25. Downloaded on May 18, 2010, from http://www.americanbankingnews.com/2010/04/19/goldman-sachs-nyse-gs-finds-5-billion-for-bonuses-amidst-investigation/.

26. Downloaded on December 21, 2009, from http://www.timesonline.co.uk/tol/news/world/us_and_americas/article6907681.ece.

27. According to Goldman's annual reports, trading and principal investment revenues amounted to $5.773 billion in 1999 and $31.226 billion in 2007.

28. The average daily "Value at Risk" (VaR) measure, including the so-called diversification effect reduction, increased from in $39 million 1999 to $138 million in 2007. Excluding the diversification effect, VaR increased from in $64 million 1999 to $234 million in 2007.

29. Kaplan and Rauh (2009) show that much of the recent increase in the skewness at the top end of income distribution originates in the financial sector.

30. Don Gogel email to author.

31. Downloaded on September 15, 2009, from http://www.bloomberg.com/apps/news?pid=20601039&sid=acB6gG_pifUY.

32. Maxey 2008.

33. Griffin 2009.

34. We would still be exposed to erosion in the value of cash because of inflation. But that's a problem regardless of the proportion of the medium of exchange that is guaranteed by the government.

35. See interview Roger Altman's comments posted at http://www.cnbc.com/id/15840232?video=1226252925.

36. Rasmussen Poll results downloaded on December 23, 2009, from http://www.rasmussenreports.com/public_content/business/federal_bailout/february_2009/56_oppose_any_more_government_help_for_banks.

37. Interview with Bloomberg's Bob Ivry downloaded on November 6, 2009, from http://www.bloomberg.com/apps/news?pid=20601087&sid=a.z4KpD77s80&pos=6#.

REFERENCES

Acharya, Viral V., and Matthew Richardson. 2009. "Causes of the Financial Crisis." *Critical Review* 21(2): 195–210.

Acharya, Viral V., and Philipp Schnabl. 2009. "How Banks Played the Leverage 'Game.'" In *Restoring Financial Stability: How to Repair a Failed System*. Ed. Viral V. Acharya and Matthew Richardson. New York: Wiley.

Adler, David. 2009. "A Flat Dow for 10 Years? Why It Could Happen." *Barrons*. December 28.

Akerlof, George. 1970. "The Market for 'Lemons': Qualitative Uncertainty and Market Mechanism." *Quarterly Journal of Economics* 84: 488–500.

Akst, Daniel. 2000. "Survival of the Richest." *Industry Standard*. March 6.

Andrew, A. Piatt. 1908. "Substitutes for Cash in the Panic of 1907." *Quarterly Journal of Economics* 22: 497–516.

Arrow, Kenneth. 1964. "The Role of Securities in the Optimal Allocation of Risk-Bearing." *Review of Economic Studies* 31: 91–96.

Auletta, Ken. 1985. "The Men, the Money, the Merger." *New York Times Magazine*. February 24.

Barra, Allen. 2009. "Baseball's Costliest Walk." *Wall Street Journal*. October 28. http://online.wsj.com/article/SB10001424052748704335904574497433535880354.html.

Bashe, Charles J., Lyle R. Johnson, John H. Palmer, and Emerson W. Pugh. 1986. *IBM's Early Computers*. Cambridge, Mass.: MIT Press.

Baskin, Jonathan B. 1988. "The Development of Corporate Financial Markets in Britain and the United States, 1600–1914: Overcoming Asymmetric Information." *Business History Review* 62(2): 199–237.

Baskin, Jonathan B., and Paul J. Miranti Jr. 1997. *A History of Corporate Finance*. Cambridge: Cambridge University Press.

Baumol, William J. 1966. "Mathematical Analysis of Portfolio Selection: Principles and Application." *Financial Analysts Journal* 22(5): 95–99.

Baumol, William J. 1993. *Entrepreneurship, Management, and the Structure of Payoffs*. Cambridge, Mass.: MIT Press.

Baumol, William J. 2002. *The Free-Market Innovation Machine: Analyzing the Growth Miracle of Capitalism*. Princeton, N.J.: Princeton University Press.

Bebchuk, Lucian A., Alma Cohen, and Holger Spamann. 2010. "The Wages of Failure: Executive Compensation at Bear Stearns and Lehman 2000–2008." *Yale Journal on Regulation* 27(2) forthcoming.

Berenson, Alex. 2009. "In Fraud Case, a Deal That Lost Millions." *New York Times*. October 21.

Berger, Allen N., Anil K. Kashyap, and Joseph M. Scalise. 1995. "The Transformation of the U.S. Banking Industry: What a Long, Strange Trip It's Been." *Brookings Papers on Economic Activity* 26(2): 55–218.

Berle, Adolf A., Jr., and Gardiner C. Means. 1932. *The Corporation and Private Property*. New York: Macmillan.

Bernstein, Peter L. 1996. *Against the Gods: The Remarkable Story of Risk*. New York: John Wiley and Sons.

Bertoneche, Marc. 1984. "Institutional Aspects of European Equity Markets." In *European Equity Markets*. Ed. Gabriel Hawawini and Michael Pierre. New York: Garland.

Bewley, Truman F. 1987. "Knightian Decision Theory: Part II. Intertemporal Problems." *Cowles Foundation Discussion Papers* 835. Cowles Foundation, Yale University.

Bewley, Truman F. 2002. "Knightian Decision Theory: Part I." *Decisions in Economics and Finance* 25(2): 79–110.

Bhidé, Amar. 1989. "The Causes and Consequences of Hostile Takeovers." *Continental Bank Journal of Applied Corporate Finance* 2(2): 36–59.

Bhidé, Amar. 1992. "Bootstrap Finance: The Art of Start-ups." *Harvard Business Review* 70(6): 109–17.

Bhidé, Amar. 1993. "The Hidden Costs of Stock Market Liquidity." *Journal of Financial Economics* 34: 31–51.

Bhidé, Amar. 1994a. "Efficient Markets, Deficient Governance." *Harvard Business Review* 72(6): 129–39.

Bhidé, Amar. 1994b. "Return to Judgment." *Journal of Portfolio Management* 20(1): 19–25.

Bhidé, Amar. 1996. "Building the Professional Firm: McKinsey & Co. : 1939–1968." Working Paper 95–010, Harvard Business School.

Bhidé, Amar. 2000. *The Origin and Evolution of New Businesses*. New York: Oxford University Press.

Bhidé, Amar. 2006. "How Novelty Aversion Affects Financing Options." *Capitalism and Society* Vol. 1 : Iss. 1, Article 1.DOI: 10.2202/1932–0213.1002

Bhidé, Amar. 2008a. "Insiders and Outsiders." Forbes.com. September 25.

Bhidé, Amar. 2008b. *The Venturesome Economy: How Innovation Sustains Prosperity in a More Connected World*. Princeton, N.J.: Princeton University Press.

Bhidé, Amar, and Edmund Phelps. 2005. "A Dynamic Theory of China-U.S. Trade: Making Sense of the Imbalances." *World Economics* 8(3): 7–25.

Bhidé, Amar, Howard H. Stevenson, and Philip Bilden. 1990. Note on Acquiring Bank Credit. Harvard Business School Note 391–010.

Black, Fischer. 1975. "The Option Service: An Introduction." Private paper in the possession of Mark Rubenstein, University of California at Berkeley.

Black, Fischer. 1989. "How to Use the Holes in Black-Scholes." *Journal of Applied Corporate Finance* 1(4), 67–73.

Black, Fischer, Michael C. Jensen, and Myron Scholes. 1972. "The Capital Asset Pricing Model: Some Empirical Tests." In *Studies in the Theory of Capital Markets*. Ed. Michael C. Jensen. New York: Praeger.

Blau, Peter M. 1964. *Exchange and Power in Social Life*. New York: John Wiley and Sons.

Bloomberg, Michael, and Matthew Winkler. 1997. *Bloomberg on Bloomberg*. New York: John Wiley & Sons.

Blume, Marshall E., Jeremy J. Siegel, and Dan Rottenberg. 1993. *Revolution on Wall Street: The Rise and Decline of the New York Stock Exchange*. New York: W. W. Norton.

Boyd, Roddy. 2008. "Has Wilbur Ross Lost His Mind?" *Fortune*. January 25.

Brandeis, Louis D. 1914. *Other People's Money: And How the Bankers Use It*. New York: Frederick A. Stokes.

Brandenburger, Adam, and Harborne Stuart. 2007. "Biform Games." *Management Science* 53(4): 537–49.

Breeden, Richard C. 1993. "Leave It to the Markets." *Harvard Business Review* 71(1): 76–77.

Bresnahan, Timothy F. 1986. "Measuring the Spillovers from Technical Advance: Mainframe Computers in Financial Services." *American Economic Review* 76: 742–55.

Bricklin, Daniel. 2009. *Bricklin on Technology*. New York: Wiley.

Bryan, Lowell L. 1987. "The Credit Bomb in Our Financial System." *Harvard Business Review* 65(1): 45–51.

Buffett, Warren E., 1987. *Berkshire Hathaway Inc.: Letters to Shareholders, 1979–1985*.

Burck, Charles G. 1972. "Dan Lufkin Goes Public." *Fortune*. January.

Byrne, John, 1998. "How Jack Welch Runs GE." *BusinessWeek*. June 8.

Calder, Lendol. 1999. *Financing the American Dream: A Cultural History of Consumer Credit*. Princeton, N.J.: Princeton University Press.

Calomiris, Charles W. 2000. *U.S. Bank Deregulation in Historical Perspective*. Cambridge: Cambridge University Press.

Chandler, Alfred D., Jr. 1962. *Strategy and Structure*. Cambridge, Mass.: MIT Press.

Chandler, Alfred D., Jr. 1977. *The Visible Hand: The Managerial Revolution in American Business*. Cambridge: Harvard University Press.

Chandler, Alfred D., Jr. 1990a. "The Enduring Logic of Industrial Success." *Harvard Business Review* 68(2): 130–40.

Chandler, Alfred D., Jr. 1990b. *Scale and Scope: The Dynamics of Industrial Capitalism*. Cambridge. Mass.: Belknap Press of Harvard University Press.

Chandler, Alfred D., Jr., and Stephen Salsbury. 1971. *Pierre S. DuPont and the Making of the Modern Corporation*. New York: Harper and Row.

Chernow, Ron. 1990. *The House of Morgan: An American Banking Dynasty and the Rise of Modern Finance*. New York: Atlantic Monthly Press.

Clark, Robert C. 1985. "Agency Costs versus Fiduciary Duties." In *Principals and Agents*. Ed. John W. Pratt and Richard Zeckhauser. Boston: Harvard Business School Press.

Cochrane, John H. 2009. "How Did Paul Krugman Get It So Wrong?" September 16. Downloaded on January 19, 2010, from http://faculty. chicagobooth.edu/john.cochrane/research/Papers/krugman_ response.htm.

Colander, David, Michael Goldberg, Armin Haas, Katarina Juselius, Alan Kirman, Thomas Lux, and Brigitte Sloth. 2009. "The Financial Crisis and the Systemic Failure of the Economics Profession." *Critical Review* 21(2): 249–67.

Cootner, Paul. 1964. *The Random Character of Stock Prices*. Cambridge, Mass.: MIT Press.

Cootner, Paul L. 1977. "The Theorems of Modern Finance in a General Equilibrium Setting: Paradoxes Resolved." *Journal of Financial and Quantitative Analysis* 12: 553–62.

Datar, Srikant, David Garvin, and Patrick Cullen. 2010. *Rethinking the MBA: Business Education at a Crossroads*. Boston: Harvard Business School Press.

de Grazia, Victoria. 2006. *Irresistible Empire: America's Advance through Twentieth-Century Europe*. Cambridge, Mass.: Harvard University Press.

Deloitte, Haskins & Sells. 1988. *Financing Business Growth*. New York: Deloitte, Haskins & Sells.

DeLong, J. Bradford. 2000. "The Shape of Twentieth Century Economic History." NBER Working Paper No. 7569, February.

Demsetz, Harold. 1968. "The Cost of Transactions." *Quarterly Journal of Economics* 82: 33–53.

Dowrie, George W. 1930. *American Monetary and Banking Policies*. New York: Longmans.

Duhigg, Charles. 2008. "Loan-Agency Woes Swell from a Trickle to a Torrent." *New York Times*. July 11. http://www.nytimes. com/2008/07/11/business/11ripple.html?ex=1373515200&en=8ad220 403fcfdf6e&ei=5124&partner=permalink&exprod=permalink.

Durand, David. 1952. "Costs of Debt and Equity Funds for Business: Trends and Problems of Measurement." In *Conference on Research in Business Finance*. New York: National Bureau of Economic Research.

Dwyer, Gerald P., Jr. 1996. "Wildcat Banking, Banking Panics, and Free Banking in the United States." *Economic Review* (Federal Reserve Bank of Atlanta), December 1996, 1–16.

Elster, Jon. 2007. *Explaining Social Behavior*. Cambridge: Cambridge University Press.

Elster, Jon. 2009. "Excessive Ambitions." *Capitalism and Society* Vol. 4 : Iss. 2, Article 1. DOI: 10.2202/1932–0213.1055 4(2), article 1.

Esty, Benjamin. 1998. "The Impact of Contingent Liability on Commercial Bank Risk Taking." *Journal of Financial Economics* 47(2): 189–218.

Fama, Eugene F., and Kenneth R. French. 1992. "The Cross-Section of Expected Stock Returns." *Journal of Finance* 47: 427–65.

Fama, Eugene F., and Kenneth R. French. 2001. "Disappearing Dividends: Changing Firm Characteristics or Lower Propensity to Pay." *Journal of Financial Economics* 60: 3–43.

Fama, Eugene F., and Michael C. Jensen. 1983. "Separation of Ownership and Control." *Journal of Law and Economics* 26: 301–25.

Federal Deposit Insurance Corporation (FDIC). 1984. *The First Fifty Years: A History of the FDIC 1933–1983*. Washington, D.C.: FDIC.

Federal Deposit Insurance Corporation (FDIC). 1997. *History of the Eighties—Lessons for the Future*. Washington, D.C.: FDIC.

Federal Reserve Bank of Minneapolis. 1998. "Answering the Call for Banking Supervision." Downloaded on January 19, 2010, from http://www.minneapolisfed.org/publications_papers/pub_display.cfm?id=3824.

Ferris, Paul. 1984. *The Master Bankers*. New York: William Morrow.

Fox, Justin. 2009. *The Myth of the Rational Market: A History of Risk, Reward and Delusion on Wall Street*. New York: HarperCollins.

Friedman, Jeffrey. 2009. "A Crisis of Politics, Not Economics: Complexity, Ignorance, and Policy Failure. *Critical Review* 21(2): 127–84.

Friedman, Milton. 1953. *Essays in Positive Economics*. Chicago: University of Chicago Press.

Friedman, Milton. 1976. *Price Theory: A Provisional Text*. Rev. ed. Chicago: Aldine.

Friedman, Walter A. 2004. *Birth of a Salesman: The Transformation of Selling in America*. Cambridge, Mass.: Harvard University Press.

Friedman, Milton, and Rose Friedman. 1980. *Free to Choose: A Personal Statement*. New York: Harcourt Brace Jovanovich.

Galbraith, John Kenneth. 1954. *The Great Crash*. Boston: Houghton Mifflin.

Galbraith, John Kenneth. 1967. *The New Industrial State*. Boston: Houghton Mifflin.

Gapper, John. 2009. "Goldman's Risky Business." *Financial Times*. October 26.

Garbade, Kenneth. 1982. *Securities Markets*. New York: McGraw Hill.

Gilboa, Itzhak, and David Schmeidler. 1995. "Case-Based Decision Theory." *Quarterly Journal of Economics* 110(3): 605–39.

Gjerstad, Steven, and Vernon L. Smith. 2009. "Monetary Policy, Credit Extension, and Housing Bubbles: 2008 and 1929." *Critical Review* 21(2): 269–300.

Golembe, Carter H. 1955. "Origins of Deposit Insurance in the Middle West, 1834–1866." *Indiana Magazine of History*. June.

Golembe, Carter H. 1960. "The Deposit Insurance Legislation of 1933: An Examination of Its Antecedents and Its Purposes." *Political Science Quarterly* 75(2): 181–200.

Gorman, Michael, and William Sahlman. 1989. "What Do Venture Capitalists Do?" *Journal of Business Venturing* 4(4): 231–48.

Gorton, Gary. 2009. "Slapped in the Face by the Invisible Hand: Banking and the Panic of 2007." Prepared for the Federal Reserve Bank of Atlanta's "Financial Markets Conference: Financial Innovation and Crisis," May 11–13.

Granovetter, Mark. 1985. "Economic Action and Social Structure." *American Journal of Sociology* 91: 53–81.

Grant, James. 1992. *Money of the Mind: Borrowing and Lending in America from the Civil War to Michael Milken*. New York: Farrar, Straus and Giroux.

Griffin, Kenneth. 2009. "We must overturn the status quo in derivatives." *Financial Times*. October 27.

Grossman, Sanford J., and Joseph E. Stiglitz. 1980. "On the Impossibility of Informationally Efficient Markets." *American Economic Review* 70: 393–408.

Grubel, Herbert G., and Lawrence A. Boland. 1986. "On the Efficient Use of Mathematics in Economics: Some Theory, Facts and Results of an Opinion Survey." *Kyklos* 39: 419–42.

Grundfest, Joseph A. 1990. "Subordination of American Capital." *Journal of Financial Economics* 27(1): 89–114.

Hammond, Bray. 1957. *Banks and Politics in America from the Revolution to the Civil War*. Princeton, N.J.: Princeton University Press.

Hansell, Saul. 1997. "A Scoundrel or a Scapegoat?" *New York Times*. April 6.

Hausman, J. A. 1997. "Valuation of New Goods under Perfect and Imperfect Competition." In *The Economics of New Goods*, ed. Timothy F. Bresnahan and Robert J. Gordon, 209–48. Chicago: University of Chicago Press.

Hayek, Friedrich A. 1945. "The Use of Knowledge in Society." *American Economic Review* 35: 519–30.

Hearings before the Committee on Interstate and Foreign Commerce. 1944. *Security and Exchange Commission Proxy Rules, Part 1*. Washington, D.C.: United States Government Printing Office.

Hoffman, Paul. 1984. *The Dealmakers: Inside the World of Investment Banking*. Garden City, N.Y.: Doubleday.

International Directory of Company Histories. 1990. Vol. 2. Chicago: St James Press.

Jabłecki, Juliusz, and Mateusz Machaj. 2009. "The Regulated Meltdown of 2008." *Critical Review* 21(2): 301–28.

Jacoby, Neil H., and Raymond J. Saulnier. 1942. *Term Lending to Business*. New York: National Bureau of Economic Research. http://www.nber.org/books/jac042–1.

Jacoby, Neil H., and Raymond J. Saulnier. 1947. *Business Finance and Banking*. New York: National Bureau of Economic Research. http://www.nber.org/books/jac047–1.

Jana, Reena. 2009. "Dusting Off a Big Idea in Hard Times." *BusinessWeek*. June 22.

Jensen, Michael C. 1989. "Eclipse of the Public Corporation." *Harvard Business Review* 67(5): 61–74.

Jensen, Michael. 1993. "The Modern Industrial Revolution, Exit, and the Failure of Internal Control Systems." *Journal of Finance* 48(3): 831–80.

Jensen, Michael C., and William H. Meckling. 1990. "Specific and General Knowledge, and Organizational Structure." Paper presented at "Contracts: Determinants Properties and Implications." Nobel Symposium No. 77. Saltsjobaden/Stockholm, August 18–20.

Jones, Homer. 1938a. "Insurance of Bank Deposits in the United States of America." *Economic Journal* 48: 695–706.

Jones, Homer. 1938b. "Some Problems of Bank Supervision." *Journal of the American Statistical Association* 33(202): 334–40.

Kalberg, S. 1980. "Max Weber's Types of Rationality: Cornerstones for the Analysis of Rationalization Processes in History." *American Journal of Sociology* 85: 1145–79.

Kaplan, Steven N. and Joshua Rauh. 2009. "Wall Street and Main Street: What Contributes to the Rise in the Highest Incomes?" *Review of Financial Studies*, 23(2): 1004–50.

Kaufman, George, and Larry Mote. 1990. "Glass-Steagall: Repeal by Regulatory and Judicial Reinterpretation." *Banking Law Journal* 107: 388–421.

Kay, John. 2009. *The Long and the Short of It—Finance and Investment for Normally Intelligent People Who Are Not in the Industry*. London: Erasmus Press.

Kelley, Thomas, with Jonathan Littman. 2005. *The Ten Faces of Innovation: IDEO's Strategies for Beating the Devil's Advocate & Driving Creativity Throughout Your Organization* New York: Currency/Doubleday;

Keynes, John Maynard. 1936. *The General Theory of Employment, Interest and Money*. New York: Harcourt Brace & World.

Keynes, John Maynard. 1948. *A Treatise on Probability*. London: Macmillan, 1921. Reprint. London: Macmillan.

Khurana, Rakesh. 2008. *From Higher Aims to Hired Hands: The Social Transformation of American Business Schools and the Unfulfilled Promise of Management as a Profession*. Princeton, N.J.: Princeton University Press.

Kindleberger, Charles P. 1996. *Centralization versus Pluralism*. Copenhagen: Copenhagen Business School Press.

Klebaner, Benjamin J. 1974. *Commercial Banking in the United States: A History*. Hinsdale, Ill.: Dryden Press.

Knight, Frank H. 1921. *Risk, Uncertainty, and Profit*. Boston: Hart, Schaffner & Marx; Houghton Mifflin. http://www.econlib.org/library/Knight/knRUP6.html.

Krugman, Paul. 2009. "How Did Economists Get It So Wrong?" *New York Times Magazine*. September 2.

LeRoy, Stephen F., and Larry D. Singell Jr. 1987. "Knight on Risk and Uncertainty." *Journal of Political Economy* 95(2): 394–406.

Lewis, Michael. 2009. "The Man Who Crashed the World." *Vanity Fair*. August. http://www.vanityfair.com/politics/features/2009/08/aig200908.

Lindbeck, A. 1990. "Presentation Speech by Professor Assar Lindbeck of the Royal Swedish Academy of Sciences, December 10, 1990." http://nobelprize.org/nobel_prizes/economics/laureates/1990/presentation-speech.html.

Litan, Robert E. 1987. *What Should Banks Do?* Washington, D.C.: Brookings Institution.

Loomis, Carol. 2009. "Derivatives: The Risk That Still Won't Go Away." *Fortune*. June 24.

Lowenstein, Roger. 1995. *Buffett: The Making of an American Capitalist*. New York: Doubleday.

Luce, Edward. 2010. "Reality Dawns for Republicans over Wall Street. *Financial Times*. April 22.

MacKenzie, Donald. 2005. "Is Economics Performative? Option Theory and the Construction of Derivatives Markets." Paper presented to the Annual Meeting of the History of Economics Society, Tacoma, Wash., June 25.

MacKenzie, Donald. 2006. *An Engine, Not a Camera: How Financial Models Shape Markets*. Cambridge, Mass.: MIT Press.

MacPhee, William A. 1984. *Short-Term Business Borrowing: Sources, Terms and Techniques*. Homewood, Ill.: Dow Jones–Irwin.

Maddy, Penelope. 2008. "How Applied Mathematics Became Pure." *Review of Symbolic Logic* 1: 16–41. doi:10.1017/S1755020308080027.

Mahar, Maggie. 1991. "The Great Pension Fund Raid. *Barrons* 12(2): 8.

Mansfield, E., J. Rapoport, A. Romeo, S. Wagner, and G. Beardsley. 1977. "Social and Private Rates of Return from Industrial Innovations." *Quarterly Journal of Economics* 91(2): 221–40.

Markowitz, Harry M. 1959. *Portfolio Selection: Efficient Diversification of Investments*. New Haven: Yale University Press.

Mason, Scott P., Robert C. Merton, André F. Perold, and Peter Tufano. 1995. *Cases in Financial Engineering: Applied Studies of Financial Innovation*. Englewood Cliffs, NJ: Prentice-Hall.

Maxey, Daisy. 2008. "Money-Fund Chorus: We're Not Raters." *Wall Street Journal*. August 29.

McCraw, Thomas K. 1997. "American Capitalism." In *Creating Modern Capitalism: How Entrepreneurs, Companies, and Countries Triumphed in Three Industrial Revolutions*. Ed. Thomas K. McCraw. Cambridge, Mass.: Harvard University Press.

McCraw, Thomas K., and Richard S. Tedlow. 1997. "Henry Ford, Alfred Sloan, and the Three Phases of Marketing." In *Creating Modern Capitalism: How Entrepreneurs, Companies, and Countries Triumphed in Three Industrial Revolutions.* Ed. Thomas K. McCraw. Cambridge, Mass.: Harvard University Press.

McLean, Bethany, and Andrew Serwer. 1998. "Goldman Sachs: After the Fall." *Fortune.* November 9.

Mehrling, Perry. 2005. *Fischer Black and the Revolutionary Idea of Finance.* New York: Wiley.

Melamed, Leo, and Bob Tamarkin. 1996. *Leo Melamed: Escape to the Futures.* New York: Wiley.

Merritt, Fred. 1900. *Early History of Banking in Iowa.* Iowa City: University of Iowa Press.

Meyer, Charles H. 1934. *The Securities Exchange Act of 1934.* New York: Francis Emory Fitch.

Miller, Merton H. 1998. "Financial Markets and Economic Growth," *Journal of Applied Corporate Finance* 11(3): 8–15

Miller, Merton H. 1999. "The History of Finance." *Journal of Portfolio Management* 25(4): 95–101.

Modigliani, Franco, and Merton H. Miller. 1958. "The Cost of Capital, Corporation Finance and the Theory of Investment." *American Economic Review* 48: 261–97.

Mokyr, Joel. 1990. *The Lever of Riches: Technological Creativity and Economic Progress.* New York: Oxford University Press.

Moore, Gordon E. 1996. "Some Personal Perspectives on Research in the Semiconductor Industry." In *Engines of Innovation: U.S. Industrial Research at the End of an Era.* Ed. Richard S. Rosenbloom and William J. Spencer. Boston: Harvard Business School Press.

Morgan, Mary S. 2003. "Economics." In *The Cambridge History of Science,* vol. 7: *The Modern Social Sciences.* Ed. T. Porter and D. Ross. Cambridge: Cambridge University Press.

Nasr, Sylvia, with Douglas Frantz. 1994. "Dramatic Rise and a Nasty Fall." *New York Times.* April 22.

Nelson, Richard R. 1987. *Understanding Technical Change As an Evolutionary Process.* Amsterdam: North-Holland.

Nelson, Richard, R. 2003. "On the Uneven Evolution of Human Know-How." *Research Policy* 32: 909–22.

Nelson, Richard R. 2006. "What Makes an Economy Productive and Progressive? What Are the Needed Institutions?" LEM Working Paper Series 2006/24, September. http://ideas.repec.org/p/ssa/lemwps/2006–24.html.

Nelson, Richard, R. 2008. "Factors Affecting the Power of Technological Paradigms." *Industrial and Corporate Change* 17(3): 485–97; doi:10.1093/icc/dtn010.

Nelson, Richard R., and Sidney G. Winter. 1982. *An Evolutionary Theory of Economic Change.* Cambridge, Mass.: Belknap Press of Harvard University Press.

Nordhaus, W. D. 1997. "Do Real-Output and Real-Wage Measures Capture Reality? The History of Lighting Suggests Not." In *The Economics of New Goods*. Ed. Timothy F. Bresnahan and Robert J. Gordon. Chicago: University of Chicago Press.

Parsons, Burke A. 1958. "British Trade Cycles and American Bank Credit: Some Aspects of Economic Fluctuations in the United States 1815–1840." Ph.D. diss., University of Texas.

Petroski, Henry. 1990. *The Pencil: A History of Design and Circumstance*. New York: Alfred A. Knopf.

Phillips, Susan M., and J. Richard Zecher. 1981. *The SEC and the Public Interest*. Cambridge, Mass.: MIT Press.

Piskorski, Tomasz, Amit Seru, and Vikrant Vig. 2009. "Securitization and Distressed Loan Renegotiation: Evidence from the Subprime Mortgage Crisis." Chicago Booth School of Business Research Paper No. 09–02. September 30.

Purcell, Ganson, Roger S. Foster, and Alfred Hill. 1946. *Corporations: Enforcing the Accountability of Corporate Management and Related Activities of the S.E.C.* New York: Practicing Law Institute.

Rae, John. 1895. *Life of Adam Smith*. London: Macmillan.

Rajan, Raghuram. 2006. "Has Financial Development Made the World Riskier?" *European Financial Management* 12: 313–64.

Rappaport, Alfred. 1990. "The Staying Power of the Public Corporation." *Harvard Business Review* 68(1): 96–104.

Reilly, Frank K. 1985. *Investment Analysis and Portfolio Management* New York: Dryden Press.

Robards, Terry. 1969. "Big Board Defied by Member Firm." *New York Times*. May 23.

Robb, Richard. 2007. "Presentation on Regulation and Financial Innovation." Paper presented at the Fourth Annual Conference of the Center on Capitalism and Society, November.

Robb, Richard. 2009. "Nietzsche and the Economics of Becoming." *Capitalism and Society* Vol. 4 : Iss. 1, Article 3. DOI: 10.2202/1932–0213.1051 4(1): article 3.

Rodgers, T. J. 1990. "No Excuses Management." *Harvard Business Review* 68(4): 84–98.

Rodgers, T. J., William Taylor, and Rick Foreman. 1993. *No-Excuses Management: Proven Systems for Starting Fast, Growing Quickly, and Surviving Hard Times*. New York: Currency/Doubleday.

Roe, Mark J. 1990. "Political and Legal Restraints on Ownership and Control of Public Companies." *Journal of Financial Economics* 27(1): 7–41.

Rosenberg, Nathan. 1976. *Perspectives on Technology*. New York: Cambridge University Press.

Rosenberg, Nathan. 1982. *Inside the Black Box: Technology and Economics*. New York: Cambridge University Press.

Rosenberg Nathan, and L. E. Birdzell Jr. 1986. *How the West Grew Rich: The Economic Transformation of the Industrial World*. New York: Basic Books.

Ross, Stephen A. 1976. "Options and Efficiency." *Quarterly Journal of Economics* 90(1): 75–89.

Ross, Stephen A. 1987. "Finance." In *The New Palgrave Dictionary of Economics*. Vol. 2. Ed. John Eatwell, Murray Milgate, and Peter Newman. London: Macmillan.

Rubinstein, Mark. 1994. "Implied Binomial Trees." *Journal of Finance* 49: 771–818.

Sahlman, William A. 1990. "The Structure and Governance of Venture-Capital Organizations." *Journal of Financial Economics* 27(2): 473–521.

Samolyk, Katherine. 2004. "The Evolving Role of Commercial Banks in U.S. Credit Markets." *FDIC Banking Review* 16(2): 31–65.

Samuelson, Paul A. 1962. "Economists and the History of Ideas." *American Economic Review* 52: 1–18.

Samuelson, Paul A. 1974. "Challenge to Judgment." *Journal of Portfolio Management* 1(1): 17–19.

Schwartz, Anna J. 1993. "Are Central Banks Necessary?" *Critical Review* 7(2): 355–70.

Schwimmer, Martin J., and Edward Malca. 1976. *Pension and Institutional Portfolio Management*. New York: Praeger.

Securities and Exchange Commission (SEC). 1984. "...good people, important problems and workable laws." New York.

Securities Industry Association. 1990. *The Securities Industry of the Eighties*. New York: Securities Industry Association.

Seib, Gerald F. 2008. "In Crisis, Opportunity for Obama." *Wall Street Journal*. November 21.

Seligman, Joel. 1982. *The Transformation of Wall Street*, Boston: Houghton Mifflin.

Sharpe, William F. 1964. "Capital Asset Prices: A Theory of Market Equilibrium under Conditions of Risk." *Journal of Finance* 19: 425–42.

Sharpe, William F. 1995. "William F. Sharpe." In *Lives of the Laureates: Thirteen Nobel Laureates*. Ed. William Breit and Roger W. Spencer. Cambridge, Mass.: MIT Press.

Sherman, Stratford P. 1988. "GE's Costly Lesson on Wall Street." *Fortune*. May 9.

Shleifer, Andrei, and Robert W. Vishny. 1997. "The Limits of Arbitrage." *Journal of Finance* 52(1): 35–55.

Simon, Herbert A. 1992. "What Is an "Explanation" of Behavior?" *Psychological Science* 3(3): 150–61.

Simon, Herbert A. 1996. *Models of My Life*. Cambridge, Mass.: MIT Press.

Skidelsky, Robert. 2009. *Keynes: The Return of the Master*. London: Allen Lane.

Sloan, Alfred P. 1963. *My Years with General Motors*. New York: Doubleday.

Sloan, Allan. 2009. "What's Still Wrong with Wall Street." *Time*. October 29.

Smith, Adam. 1808. *The Theory of Moral Sentiments*. 11th ed. Edinburgh: Bell and Bradfute.

Spiro, Leah Nathans. 1999. "Goldman Sachs: How Public Is This IPO?" *BusinessWeek*. May 17.

Stigler, George J. 1985. "Frank Hyneman Knight." Working Paper No. 37, Center for the Study of the Economy and the State, University of Chicago.

Stoll, Hans. 1985. "Alternative Views of Market Making." In *Market Making and the Changing Structure of the Securities Industry*. Ed. Yakov Amihud, Thomas S. Y. Ho, and Robert A. Schartz. Lexington, Mass.: Lexington Heath.

Stuart, Harbourne W., Jr. 2007. "Creating Monopoly Power." *International Journal of Industrial Organization* 25(5): 1011–25.

Summers, Lawrence H. 1985. "On Economics and Finance." *Journal of Finance* 40(3): 633–35.

Tedlow, Richard S. 2001. *Giants of Enterprise: Seven Business Innovators and the Empires They Built*. New York: HarperBusiness.

Trajtenberg, M. 1989. "The Welfare Analysis of Product Innovations, with an Application to Computed Tomography Scanners." *Journal of Political Economy* 97: 444–79.

Tuttle, Donald L. and John L. Maginn. 1983. *Managing Investment Portfolios*. Boston: Warren, Gorham and Lamont.

Vawter, Jay. 1983. "Determination of Portfolio Policies: Institutional Investors." In *Managing Investment Portfolios*. Ed. John L. Maginn and Donald L. Tuttle. Boston: Warren, Gorham and Lamont.

Vietor, Richard H. K., and Dekkers L. Davidson. 1985. "Regulation and Competition in Commercial Banking." Harvard Business School Case 9–385–247. Rev. 10/87.

Vinzant, Carol. 1999. "The Pavers of Wall Street." *Fortune*. July 5.

Voorhees, Mark. 1988. "Can Portfolio Insurance Make a Comeback?" *Institutional Investor*. January.

Wallace, J. and J. Erickson. 1992. *Hard Drive, Bill Gates and the Making of the Microsoft Empire*. New York: HarperBusiness.

Warburton, Clark. 1959. *Deposit Insurance in Eight States during the Period 1908–1930*. Washington, D.C.: Federal Deposit Insurance Corporation.

Weber, Max. 1947. *The Theory of Social and Economic Organization*. Trans. A. M. Henderson and Talcott Parsons. New York: Free Press.

Weinberg, Peter. 2009. "Wall Street Needs More Skin in the Game." *Wall Street Journal*. September 30.

Welles, Chris. 1971. "The Beta Revolution: Learning to Live with Risk." *Institutional Investor*. September.

White, Lawrence J. 2009. "The Credit-Rating Agencies and the Subprime Debacle." *Critical Review* 21(2): 389–99.

Williamson, Oliver E. 1975. *Markets and Hierarchies*. New York: Free Press.

arm's-length markets, 7
arm's-length securities, 81–82, 284
arm's-length stockholding/
    stockholders, 161–63, 169,
    177, 178
  diffusion of, 179–80
  and executives, 173
  growth of, 178–79
Arrow, Kenneth, 95, 150
asset allocation models, 124
asset-backed securities (ABSs), 260,
    261, 262
  complex, 264
  credit enhancements to, 264
  multilevel, 267
  privately issued, 260
assumptions, 97–98
  in BSM models, 135–36
  far-fetched, 99–100
  historic data, 101–2
  importance of, 98–102
  and risk management, 126
  of universal omniscience, 96, 97,
    98, 103, 105, 108, 110
  unrealistic assumptions, 99, 101–2
attention and interest practices,
    deprivation of, 149
auto-innovation, 43
automated lending, 77, 282–83, 284
automated feedback and
    adjustments, 42, 282, 285

bad loans, 69, 244, 253
bailout plan, 296
Baker, George, 178, 221, 225, 296
Baldwin, Robert, 183
Bankers Trust, 152
bank holding companies, 245, 262
Bank Holding Company Act of
    1956, 245
Banking Act (Glass-Steagall Act)
    (1933), 163, 183, 232, 233, 234,
    235, 237–39, 242, 252, 255–58,
    289, 297
  deposit-insurance provision, 256
Banking Act (1935), 230, 247, 252
banknotes, 194–96, 204, 227, 293

Bank of America, 292, 296
Bank of America National Trust and
    Savings Association, 219
Bank of England, 213
Bank of Italy, 218
Bank of North America, 193
banks (*see also* central banks;
    commercial banks; consumer
    banks; federal reserve
    system; investment banks;
    nationally chartered banks;
    state-chartered bank)
  affiliates of, 229
  in agricultural areas, 227
  antebellum banking, 193–203
  bankers, 184–86
  bank examiner, 241, 278
  branching, 202, 205–6, 219, 242,
    245, 248, 251
  checks, 198–99, 207, 208
  clearinghouse certificates, 209
  corporate charters, 178
  corporate form, 194
  credit (*see* credit; loans/lending)
  in customer lending boom,
    219–20
  declining share in credit market
    debt, 259
  deposits, 198–99, 207, 215–16, 232
  dual banking, 203–6
  elastic currency, 210
  expansion of powers, 256, 257
  failure rates, 196, 218–19, 224,
    226–27, 230, 231–32, 240, 243,
    254–55
  and Federal Reserve, 210–11,
    231–32
  financial department stores, 225
  financing securities, 222–26
  fragmented nature, 218, 248, 288
  free banking, 197–98, 199, 212
  growth and stability, 243–47, 250
  holdings of residential mortgage,
    241
  indirect long-term lending, 223
  inelastic supply of currency,
    207–8

Gorton, Gary, 25
government
    intervention in economy, 8
    money monopoly, 293–94
    securities, 243
Graham, Benjamin, 149
Gramm-Leach-Bliley Act (GLBA),
    263
Granovetter, Mark, 8, 9, 63
Grant, James, 221
Great Crash, 24, 157
Great Depression, 237, 240, 243
Great Moderation of inflation and
    fluctuations, 23
greenbacks, 203
Greenspan, Alan, 277, 281
Greenspan doctrine, 280
Greenspan Federal Reserve
    easy money policy, 22
Griffin, Kenneth, 292
Grundfest, Joseph, 169
guesses, 97, 102–3, 136

Haack, Robert, 181
Hamilton, Alexander, 193
Hammond, Bray, 197, 199
hard and soft data, 39, 282, 283
Hathaway, Berkshire, 170, 171
Hayek, Friedrich, 4, 7, 30, 31, 32,
    37–38, 41, 46, 80
    on prices, 44
hedge funds, 3, 189, 291
Heinz, John, 256
Hewlett-Packard, 43
hidden costs, 171–75
high-tech industry, control over
    innovation, 48–49
Hilaly, Aaref, 57
hiring decisions, 90, 91
Hirschman, Albert, 149, 162
historic (backward looking)
    volatility, 123, 124, 154
    as predictor of future, 137
historic data, 307–8n30
    and assumptions, 101–2
    in decision making, 92–93
    and future prediction, 123

for predicting future, 145–46,
    148–49
History of the Eighties, 254–55
Hobbes, Thomas, 8
holding companies, 263, 314n16
holding period, 170–71
holdup problem, 62
Homestead Act, 11
honest mistakes, 69
Hooper, Samuel, 198
Hoover administration, 232
housing bubble, 1, 14, 269
    deconstruction of, 15–25
    and Fed, 269
housing loans, 221
Houston, Sam, 197

IBM, 38, 58, 118, 175
idealism, 151
illiquid loans, 247
imagination, 35
immigrants, and thrift, 19
impersonal operation of price
    system, 60–61
income inequality, 287
Indiana banking model, 201,
    202, 226
individual investors, 165, 169
inelastic supply of currency, 207–8,
    227
inflation, 251, 252, 269
informal social associations, 9
informed outsiders, 281
insiders, 81, 111, 170, 280, 289, 296
    diagnosis and remedies, 273–78
    rejection of radical measures, 2
insider trading, 156, 168, 169
    rules, 160, 161
installment plans, 220, 241, 242, 248
institutional investors, 161, 165
institutional trading, 166–67
insurance, 261, 293 (*see also* life
    insurance)
    against bank failure, 201–2
    on mortgage-backed securities, 17
    price of, 17
insured banks, 240

outcomes prediction. *See* predictive
models
out-of-the-blue explanations, 23–24
out-of-the-money call options, 137,
138
outsiders, 2, 33, 275
informed outsiders, 281
skeptical outsiders, 289
over the counter (OTC) derivatives,
133–34, 148, 261, 262, 268, 277
(*see also* derivatives)
overtrading, 113

Page, Larry, 33
Paine, William Alfred, 182
Paine Webber, 182
Pangloss, 81, 82
panic of 1837, 96, 202
panic of 1857, 238
panic of 1873, 239
panic of 1884, 239
panic of 1907, 208, 227
paper currency, 194, 197, 199
Parsons, Burke, 196
partnerships, 178, 185, 188
active partners, 178
Patman, Wright, 243
Paulson, Hank, 19
Pecora report, 163
pension funds
legislation for, 165–66
pension plans, 164
persuasive dialogue, 59
Peters, Tom, 50
Peterson, Pete, 183
Pfizer, 43
Phelan, John, 167
Phelps, Edmund, 269
Phibro Corporation, 182
Philadelphia National Bank, 238
planning, 30
Ponzi scheme, 267–68
Populists, 151
portfolio insurance, 23, 147–48
portfolios, 106, 120, 130
low beta subsets, 128
replicating portfolio, 135

stock returns, 120, 121
volatility, 120, 122
Markowitz approach (*see under*
Harry Markowitz)
position limits, 143, 146, 147
positive component, of economics,
97–98
positive science, 98
positive theories
abstract model, 100, 101
real world rules, 100
Posner, Richard, 269
power sharing, 49–51
practical discipline, 295–96
practice-research interaction, 105
predicting future
issue of, 86–87
mechanized predictions, 41–43
pitfalls, 39–41
preponderance of evidence, 92
Priceline, 7
prices/price system, 6–7, 47, 112
anomalous pricing, 138
anonymity, 60
commodity prices, 125
and decentralized innovation, 7
EMH, 116–19
free to choose, 29
Hayek on, 32
impersonal operation of, 60–61
and information transmission, 56
marvel of, 32
normal (bell-shaped) probability
distribution, 117, 118–19
price fluctuation, 111
pricing error, 139
and property rights, 32
randomness of, 116–17
rise in, and consumption, 32
unpredictability, 110–12, 114–15,
116–19
value of flexible system, 56–57
pricing financial future, 134
pricing options, 134–35
Principles of Economics (Marshall), 5
private banks, 225
private organizations, 47

probability distributions, 96–97
probability estimates
    in VC investing, 93
probability theory, 86, 89 (*see also*
        statistical models)
producers
    communication with, 59
    subjective judgments by, 37–38
productivity-enhancing
        technologies, 282
professional investment, 111
professional management, 48
profit, 88
property rights, 32
Provident, 221
Proxmire, William, 256, 257
proxy solicitations, 158
prudence, 14, 20, 75, 114, 166, 177,
        178, 189, 216, 239, 247, 249,
        251, 266, 283, 290, 292, 294
prudent man rule, 165, 166
Prudential Insurance Company,
        266, 288
public listing, 180
publicly traded companies, 176
public ownership, diffused, 188
public pension funds, 165
public policies, 154, 170
Pujo Committee, 225
Purcell, Ganson, 158
purchasers, subjective judgments
        by, 37–38
puts, 115, 138, 147

quantitative approach, 126

raiders, 174, 189, 265
    constraints on, 174
railroad bonds, 76, 208, 224, 284
Raines, Franklin, 21, 299n27
Rajan, Raghuram, 280, 281–82, 284
ranking likelihoods, 92
rapid adaptation, to change, 31,
        32–33
rating agencies, 2, 267
    and housing bubbles, 15
rational expectations, 96

Reagan administration, 256
"real bills" principle, 217, 222, 237
real debt, 221
real economy, 79
real estate loans, 222, 228–29, 244
realignment, of real economy and
        financial sector, 25
recession of 2001, 15
Reconstruction Finance Corporation
        (RFC), 232, 233
recontracting, 14
Red Queen, 116, 264
Reed, John, 297
Regulation U, 238
Regulation Q, 246
relationships, 60–63, 149, 150, 248
    banking on, 282–84
    in bank lending, 72–73
    gaps in agreements, 61
    holdup problems, 62
    knowledge accumulated through,
        61
    learning through repeated
        transactions, 61
    lending, 293
    long-term, 162, 171
    ongoing relationships, 61–62
    in VC investing, 68
renegotiation, 284
rent-seeking, 8
repeated events and
        unpredictability, 91
replicating portfolio, 135, 136
repressive political structures, 9
research-practice interaction, 105
reserve banks, 210–11
Reserve Fund, 254
responsibility, 32
    avoidance, 278
    dilution of, 51–52
    profit as reward for, 88
returns on stock options
    replication, 135
Ricardo, David, 103
Riegle-Neal Interstate Banking and
        Branch Efficiency Act (1994),
        179

Texas banking system, 227
Texas Gulf Sulfur case (1966), 159
theory, 99
theory, good, 99
Theory of Economic Development (Schumpeter), 5
third-party credit underwriter, 280
top-down approaches, 120, , 129, 142, 152, 153, 258, 276, 278
top management, 174 (*see also* CEOs)
tradable instruments (*see also* specific instruments), 13
trade-off, 75–77, 282
trading commissions, 166–67
trading in stock options, 132, 133, 146
  public interest, 151
transactions
    costs, 156, 164
    embedded in relationships, 8
Treasury Department, 296
"TreasuryDirect" accounts, 294
Treatise on Probability, A (Keynes), 86
Treynor, Jack, 127
trial and error methods, 97
Troubled Assets Recovery Program, 295
trust, 72
trust banks, 224
Trust Company of the West, 288
trustees, 164

uncertainty, 84, 111, 153
  one-offs (*see* one-offs)
uniform national currency, 203–4
unit banks, 242, 245
United Kingdom
  Bank of England, 213
United States Bank of Pennsylvania, 224
universal omniscience. *See* omniscience
unknown outcomes. *See* a priori probabilities; one-offs; statistical probabilities
unpredictability of prices, 110–12, 116–19

EMH and, 116–19
unrealistic assumptions, 99, 101–2, 128
  and risk management, 126
unregulated financial institutions, 291
unsolicited tender offers, 174
"Use of Knowledge in Society, The" (Hayek), 30, 46
users
  of innovations, 37
  subjective judgments by, 36–37

value investors, 116
Value Line index, 133
value of modern financial innovations, 279, 280
Vandenberg, Arthur H., 234
venture capital (VC) investing/ investors, 12, 64–69
  autonomy in, 67
  and banking, 73–75
  challenge for, 65
  dialogue, 68
  and entrepreneur, 67
  funding requests, 65
  funds growth, 53
  historic data, in decision making, 92–93
  information asymmetries, 66
  information-gathering, 68
  misaligned incentives, 66
  narratives, construction and evaluation, 92
  on-the-spot judgments, 65, 66–67
  partners, 67, 170
  probability estimates, 91, 93
  relationships, 68
  structured and routine judgments, 67
  subjective knowledge, 66
  winner's curse, 65
Venture Economics, 69
venturesome consumption, 19
venturesomeness, 58
Vermont program, 201, 202
vertical integration, firm growth, 48
Vishny, Robert, 109

Vinzant, Carol, 168
volatility, 120, 145
  of asset price, 123
  historic volatility, 123, 123,
    124, 154
  and mispricing of options, 139
  as predictor of future, 137
  of returns, 123
Volcker, Paul, 281, 285, 289, 297

Wachovia, 17
Wall Street firms/traders, 18, 19, 23,
    114, 156, 169, 175, 181, 216,
    219, 273, 278
Wall Street laws, 163, 169
Wal-Mart, 33
Walton, Sam, 33
Warren Buffett, 113–14, 115, 170,
    174–75
  investment strategies, 170

Washington Mutual, 17
Waterman, Robert H., 50
wealth, unjust accumulation of, 1
Wealth of Nations (Smith), 3–4,
    217
Webber, Wallace G., 182
Weber, Max, 50
Weil, Sandy, 266
Weinberg, Peter, 185
Welch, Jack, 186
Wells Fargo, 292
wheat market example, for
    assumptions, 98–99
Whitehead, John, 184
Wilson, Woodrow, 225
working capital loan, 70
writing options. *See* selling
    options

ZZZZ Best, 114